BASEBALL AMERICA'S 1992 DIRECTORY

*Major And Minor League
Names, Addresses, Schedules,
Phone and FAX Numbers:
Plus Detailed Information
On International, College and
Amateur Baseball*

PUBLISHED BY
BASEBALL AMERICA

EDITOR
Allan Simpson

ASSISTANT EDITOR
Julie Lanzillo

PRODUCTION MANAGER
Shannon Cain

PRODUCTION ASSISTANT
Susan Merrell

PUBLISHER
Miles Wolff

ASSOCIATE PUBLISHER
Dave Chase

EDITORIAL ASSISTANT
Jim Callis

©1992 Baseabll America, Inc.
All Rights Reserved

Distributed by Simon & Schuster

No portion of this book may be reprinted or reproduced without the written
consent of the publishers. For additional copies, send $8.95
to Baseball America, P.O. Box 2089, Durham NC 27702.

B A S E B A L L
G L O V E S

We don't claim that using a Louisville Slugger glove makes Wade Boggs a better third baseman. But he does. The finest baseball gloves in the world are now made by Louisville Slugger.

Louisville Slugger®
The finest baseball gloves in the world.

H&B Hillerich & Bradsby Co., Louisville, Kentucky

1992 DIRECTORY CONTENTS

MAJOR LEAGUES

Commissioner's Office...9
American League..11

Baltimore	12	Milwaukee	26
Boston	14	Minnesota	28
California	16	New York	30
Chicago	18	Oakland	32
Cleveland	20	Seattle	34
Detroit	22	Texas	36
Kansas City	24	Toronto	38

National League..41

Atlanta	42	Philadelphia	56
Chicago	44	Pittsburgh	58
Cincinnati	46	St. Louis	60
Houston	48	San Diego	62
Los Angeles	50	San Francisco	64
Montreal	52	Colorado	66
New York	54	Florida	67

MINOR LEAGUES

National Association..73

American Assoc.	74	Midwest	115
International	78	South Atlantic	121
Pacific Coast	82	New York-Penn	127
Eastern	87	Northwest	133
Southern	91	Appalachian	137
Texas	96	Pioneer	141
California	100	Arizona	145
Carolina	105	Gulf Coast	145
Florida State	109		

Minor League Schedules...147

MISCELLANEOUS

Mexican League...168
Japanese Baseball...170
Winter Baseball..172
College Baseball..175

    NCAA Division I Conferences...176
    NCAA Division I Schools...179

High School Baseball...175
Amateur Baseball...191
Youth Baseball...194
Index With FAX Numbers...196
Service Directory...202

Major League Schedules,
Spring Training Information
Located With Individual Club Listings

HNTB

The Birthplace of Innovative Sports Architecture

More than 20 years ago, HNTB set a new standard for baseball stadiums with the design of Royals Stadium. A tradition we proudly continue today.

Royals Stadium*
Kansas City, Missouri

New Texas Rangers Stadium**
Arlington, Texas

Fenway Park Renovation
Boston, Massachusetts

Maverick Stadium
Adelanto, California

Drillers Stadium Renovation
Tulsa, Oklahoma

SkySox Stadium
Colorado Springs, Colorado

Milwaukee Brewers Spring Training Facility
Chandler, Arizona

Texas Rangers Spring Training Facility
Port Charlotte, Florida

HNTB

Sports Architecture

Tom Tingle, AIA
1201 Walnut, Suite 700
Kansas City, Missouri 64106
(816) 472-1201

*With Charles Deaton
**With David M. Schwartz

BASEBALL AMERICA

ESTABLISHED 1981

PUBLISHER: Miles Wolff

EDITOR: Allan Simpson
SENIOR ASSOCIATE EDITOR: John Royster
ASSOCIATE EDITOR: Jim Callis
ASSISTANT EDITOR: Dean Gyorgy
STAFF WRITER: Alan Schwarz
EDITORIAL ASSISTANT: Julie Lanzillo

PRODUCTION MANAGER: Shannon Cain
PRODUCTION ASSISTANT: Susan Merrell

ASSOCIATE PUBLISHER: Dave Chase
CIRCULATION MANAGER: Eric Miller
FULFILLMENT MANAGER: Ronnie McCabe
CUSTOMER SERVICE: Randy Edwards, Shirley Carter
OFFICE MANAGER: Toni Small
RECEPTIONIST: Felicia McKie

ADVERTISING SALES
Kris Grubbs, Advertising Manager
P.O. Box 2089, Durham, NC 27702
Phone (800) 845-2726

Advertising Assistant: Bobbi Rosell

Tom Llewellyn
P.O. Box 13703, Tallahassee, FL 32312
Phone (904) 386-6668

Bob Kremer, New York Representative
P.O. Box 87, Bronxville, NY 10708
(914) 793-5026

MEDIA RELATIONS
Wirz and Associates, Norwalk, CT; Phone (203) 866-9245.

NATIONAL NEWSSTAND CONSULTANT
John Blassingame, P.O. Box 292, Linden, NJ 07036
Phone (201) 862-4651

BASEBALL AMERICA OPERATED BY
BASEBALL AMERICA, Inc.
P.O. Box 2089, Durham, NC 27702
Street Address: 600 S. Duke St., Durham, NC 27701
Phone: (919) 682-9635
Toll-Free: (800) 845-2726
FAX: (919) 682-2880

BASEBALL AMERICA, the nation's most complete all-baseball newspaper, publishes 24 issues a year. Subscription rates are $35.95 for one year, payable in U.S. funds.

BASEBALL AMERICA PUBLICATIONS
1992 Almanac
A comprehensive look at the 1991 season, featuring major and minor league statistics and commentary. **$9.95**
1992 Directory
Names, addresses, phone numbers, major and minor league schedules—vital to baseball insiders and fans. **$8.95**
1992 Great Minor League Ballparks Calendar
$7.95

1992-93 CALENDAR

March, 1992

Sun	Mon	Tues	Wed	Thur	Fri	Sat
1	2	3	4	5	6	7
8	9	10	11	12	13	14
15	16	17	18	19	20	21
22	23	24	25	26	27	28
29	30	31				

April, 1992

Sun	Mon	Tues	Wed	Thur	Fri	Sat
			1	2	3	4
5	6	7	8	9	10	11
12	13	14	15	16	17	18
19	20	21	22	23	24	25
26	27	28	29	30		

May, 1992

Sun	Mon	Tues	Wed	Thur	Fri	Sat
					1	2
3	4	5	6	7	8	9
10	11	12	13	14	15	16
17	18	19	20	21	22	23
24	25	26	27	28	29	30
31						

June, 1992

Sun	Mon	Tues	Wed	Thur	Fri	Sat
	1	2	3	4	5	6
7	8	9	10	11	12	13
14	15	16	17	18	19	20
21	22	23	24	25	26	27
28	29	30				

July, 1992

Sun	Mon	Tues	Wed	Thur	Fri	Sat
			1	2	3	4
5	6	7	8	9	10	11
12	13	14	15	16	17	18
19	20	21	22	23	24	25
26	27	28	29	30	31	

August, 1992

Sun	Mon	Tues	Wed	Thur	Fri	Sat
						1
2	3	4	5	6	7	8
9	10	11	12	13	14	15
16	17	18	19	20	21	22
23	24	25	26	27	28	29
30	31					

September, 1992

Sun	Mon	Tues	Wed	Thur	Fri	Sat
		1	2	3	4	5
6	7	8	9	10	11	12
13	14	15	16	17	18	19
20	21	22	23	24	25	26
27	28	29	30			

October, 1992

Sun	Mon	Tues	Wed	Thur	Fri	Sat
				1	2	3
4	5	6	7	8	9	10
11	12	13	14	15	16	17
18	19	20	21	22	23	24
25	26	27	28	29	30	31

November, 1992

Sun	Mon	Tues	Wed	Thur	Fri	Sat
1	2	3	4	5	6	7
8	9	10	11	12	13	14
15	16	17	18	19	20	21
22	23	24	25	26	27	28
29	30					

December, 1992

Sun	Mon	Tues	Wed	Thur	Fri	Sat
		1	2	3	4	5
6	7	8	9	10	11	12
13	14	15	16	17	18	19
20	21	22	23	24	25	26
27	28	29	30	31		

January, 1993

Sun	Mon	Tues	Wed	Thur	Fri	Sat
					1	2
3	4	5	6	7	8	9
10	11	12	13	14	15	16
17	18	19	20	21	22	23
24	25	26	27	28	29	30
31						

February, 1993

Sun	Mon	Tues	Wed	Thur	Fri	Sat
	1	2	3	4	5	6
7	8	9	10	11	12	13
14	15	16	17	18	19	20
21	22	23	24	25	26	27
28						

March, 1993

Sun	Mon	Tues	Wed	Thur	Fri	Sat
	1	2	3	4	5	6
7	8	9	10	11	12	13
14	15	16	17	18	19	20
21	22	23	24	25	26	27
28	29	30	31			

April, 1993

Sun	Mon	Tues	Wed	Thur	Fri	Sat
				1	2	3
4	5	6	7	8	9	10
11	12	13	14	15	16	17
18	19	20	21	22	23	24
25	26	27	28	29	30	

EVENTS CALENDAR

March 1992-February 1993

March 18—Opening Day: Mexican League.

April 6—Opening Day: American League, National League.

April 9—Opening Day: American Association, International League, Pacific Coast League, Eastern League, Southern League, California League, Carolina League, Midwest League, South Atlantic League.

April 10—Opening Day: Texas League, Florida State League.

May 1—Major league clubs may resume negotiations with their former players who refused salary arbitration and were unsigned as of Jan. 8.

May 21-26—NCAA Division III World Series at Battle Creek, Mich.

May 22-28—NAIA World Series at Des Moines, Ia.

May 23-30—Junior College World Series at Grand Junction, Colo.

May 23-30—NCAA Division II World Series at Montgomery, Ala.

May 29-June 6—College World Series at Omaha, Neb.

June 1-3—Amateur free agent draft.

June 11—Mexican League All-Star Game at Merida, Mexico.

June 15—Opening Day: New York-Penn League.

June 17—Opening Day: Northwest League, Pioneer League.

June 18—Opening Day: Gulf Coast League. California League All-Star Game at Modesto, Calif.

June 19—Opening Day: Appalachian League.

June 21—Opening Day: Arizona League.

June 22—Midwest League All-Star Game at Peoria, Ill. South Atlantic League All-Star Game at Columbia, S.C.

June 27—Florida State League All-Star Game at West Palm Beach, Fla.

July 13—Double-A All-Star Game at Charlotte, N.C.

July 14—63rd Major League All-Star Game at Jack Murphy Stadium, San Diego.

July 15—Triple-A All-Star Game at Richmond, Va.

July 20—Texas League All-Star Game at Jackson, Miss.

July 25-Aug. 9—Summer Olympiad at Barcelona, Spain.

July 22—Carolina League All-Star Game at Salem. Va.

Aug. 1—End of major league trading period without waivers.

Aug. 2—Hall of Fame induction ceremonies at Cooperstown, N.Y.

Aug. 3—Hall of Fame Game, Chicago (AL) vs. New York (NL) at Cooperstown, N.Y.

Aug. 5-16—National Baseball Congress World Series at Wichita, Kan.

Aug. 20-Sept. 1—AAA World Youth Championships at Monterrey, Mexico.

Aug. 24-29—Little League World Series at Williamsport, Pa.

Aug. 26-30—American Legion World Series at Fargo, N.D.

Aug. 31—Postseason major league roster eligibility frozen.

Sept. 1—Major league roster limits expanded from 25 to 40.

Oct. 4—Major league season ends.

Oct. 5—Beginning of major league trading period without waivers.

Oct. 6—Major league playoffs begin, cities of NL West and AL East division winners.

Oct. 17—World Series begins, city of NL champion.

Oct. TBD—Re-entry free agent declaration period begins 15 days after World Series ends.

Nov. 20—Forty-man major league winter rosters must be filed.

Dec. 5-10—90th annual Winter Meetings at Louisville, Ky.

Jan. 8-11—American Baseball Coaches Association convention at Atlanta.

Feb. 2-7—Caribbean World Series at Mazatlan, Mexico.

Here's The Pitch.

Pencil Yourself Into The Lineup.
Don't Get Caught Looking.

We take the mound 24 times a year. And as a 10-year veteran, we've developed quite a repertoire. We paint the corners with our special reports and insightful examinations of trends in the game.

Our colorful features, both major and minor league, will entice you like a lollipop curve. Our draft coverage and prospect lists are nothing but heat, right down the middle. And we may surprise you with an occasional knuckleball, just a tinge of humor and irreverence that helps weave the fabric of baseball.

We blaze the trail for you to follow your favorite prospects up the ladder to stardom, with complete minor league statistics and reports. And even before they sign their first professional contract, we've got our eye on them with college and amateur news.

From Pulaski to Pittsburgh, Tokyo to Omaha, Baseball America keeps you in touch with the game.

So come on, you're up.

Baseball America • P.O. Box 2089 • Durham, N.C. 27702

Please Send Me: ☐ **2 Year Subscription at $58.95**
☐ **1 Year Subscription at $35.95**
☐ **½ Year Subscription at $19.95**

☐ My check or money order is enclosed (in U.S. funds only)

☐ Charge to my: ☐ Visa ☐ MC ☐ AmEx

Exp. Date _____

Card No. _____

Name _____

Address _____

City _____

State _____ Zip _____

Phone (_____) _____

For Faster Service On Credit Card Orders Call Toll Free
1-800-845-2726
9-5 EST

DIR92 *Please Have Your Credit Card Ready*

OFFICE OF THE COMMISSIONER

Mailing Address: 350 Park Ave., 17th Floor, New York, NY 10022. **Telephone:** (212) 339-7800. **FAX:** (212) 355-0007.
Commissioner: Francis T. Vincent Jr.
Deputy Commissioner: Steven Greenberg.

OFFICERS AND DIRECTORS
Director, Broadcasting: David Alworth.
Controller: Thomas Duffy.
Director, Special Events: David Dziedzic.
Director, Security/Facility Management: Kevin Hallinan.
Director, Public Relations: Richard Levin. **Manager, Public Relations:** Jim Small.
Director, Baseball Operations: William Murray.
General Counsel: Thomas Ostertag.
Director, Broadcast Administration: Leslie Sullivan.
Executive Director, Licensing Operations and President, Major League Baseball Properties: Richard White.
1992 Major League All-Star Game: July 7 at Jack Murphy Stadium, San Diego.

Francis Vincent

Major League Baseball Player Relations Committee

Mailing Address: 350 Park Ave., New York, NY 10022. **Telephone:** (212) 339-7400. **FAX:** (212) 371-2242.
President: Richard Ravitch.
General Counsel: Charles O'Connor.
Associate Counsel: John Westhoff, Louis Melendez.
Contract Administrator: Barbara Ernst.
Office Manager: Eleanor Mieszerski.

Major League Baseball Properties

Mailing Address: 350 Park Ave., New York, NY 10022. **Telephone:** (212) 339-7900. **FAX:** (212) 339-7628.
President: Richard White.
Vice President, Design Services: Anne Occi. **Vice President, Licensing Services:** Frank Simio. **Vice President, Business Development:** Stu Upson. **Manager, Licensing Information Systems:** Christopher Jones. **Manager, Corporate Sponsorship:** Rick Dudley.

Major League Baseball International Partners

Mailing Address: 1633 Broadway, New York, NY 10019. **Telephone:** (212) 841-1414. **FAX:** (212) 841-1439.
President and Chief Executive Officer: Frank Heffron.
Vice President, Business Affairs: Tim Brosnan. **Vice President, Game Development:** Steve Baker. **Vice President, European Operations:** Mike Carlson. **Vice President, Licensing and Marketing:** Kathie Pellowski.
Executive Producer: Gary Abrams. **Director, Game Development:** Mark Cohon. **Controller:** Bob Clark.

AMERICAN LEAGUE

AMERICAN LEAGUE

Mailing Address: 350 Park Ave., New York, NY 10022.
Telephone: (212) 339-7600. **FAX:** (212) 593-7138.
President: Robert W. Brown, M.D.
Board of Directors: Baltimore, Boston, California, Chicago, Cleveland, Kansas City.
Vice Presidents: Gene Autry, Jean Yawkey.
Executive Director of Umpiring: Martin Springstead. **Coordinator of Umpire Operations:** Philip Janssen.
Special Assistant to Baseball: Dick Wagner.
Director of Public Relations: Phyllis Merhige.
Special Assistant to the President: Dick Butler.
Administrators: Tess Basta, Carolyn Coen.

Dr. Bobby Brown

Director of Waivers and Player Records: Timothy McCleary.
Years League Active: 1900-1992.
1992 Opening Date: April 6. **Closing Date:** Oct. 4.
No. of Games: 162.
Division Structure: East—Baltimore, Boston, Cleveland, Detroit, Milwaukee, New York, Toronto. **West**—California, Chicago, Kansas City, Minnesota, Oakland, Seattle, Texas.
Roster Limit: 25.
Umpires: Larry Barnett (Prospect, OH), Joe Brinkman (Cocoa, FL), Al Clark (Newtown, PA), Drew Coble (Graham, NC), Terry Cooney (Clovis, CA), Derryl Cousins (Hermosa Beach, CA), Don Denkinger (Waterloo, IA), Jim Evans (Austin, TX), Dale Ford (Jonesboro, TN), Rich Garcia (Clearwater, FL), Ted Hendry (Phoenix, AZ), John Hirschbeck (Poland, OH), Mark Johnson (Honolulu, HI), Jim Joyce (Beaverton, OR), Ken Kaiser (Rochester, NY), Greg Kosc (Medina, OH), Tim McClelland (West Des Moines, IA), Larry McCoy (Greenway, AR), Jim McKean (St. Petersburg, FL), Durwood Merrill (Hooks, TX), Dan Morrison (Largo, FL), Steve Palermo (Overland Park, KS), Dave Phillips (Lake St. Louis, MO), Rick Reed (Rochester Hills, MI), Mike Reilly (Battle Creek, MI), John Roe (Milford, MI), Dale Scott (Portland, OR), John Shulock (Vero Beach, FL), Tim Tschida (St. Paul, MN), Vito Voltaggio (Vineland, NJ), Tim Welke (Kalamazoo, MI), Larry Young (Roscoe, IL).

1991 Standings

East	W	L	Pct.	GB	West	W	L	Pct.	GB
Toronto	91	71	.562	—	*Minnesota	95	67	.586	—
Boston	84	78	.519	7	Chicago	87	75	.537	8
Detroit	84	78	.519	7	Texas	85	77	.525	10
Milwaukee	83	79	.512	8	Oakland	84	78	.519	11
New York	71	91	.438	20	Seattle	83	79	.512	12
Baltimore	67	95	.414	24	Kansas City	82	80	.506	13
Cleveland	57	105	.352	34	California	81	81	.500	14

*Won League Championship Series

Stadium Information

City	Stadium	LF	CF	RF	Capacity	'91 Att.
Baltimore	Camden Yards	335	400	318	48,000	2,552,261
Boston	Fenway Park	315	390	302	34,182	2,562,435
California	Anaheim	333	404	333	64,593	2,416,236
Chicago	Comiskey Park	347	400	347	44,702	2,934,154
Cleveland	Municipal	320	415	320	74,483	1,051,863
Detroit	Tiger	340	440	325	52,416	1,641,661
Kansas City	Royals	330	410	330	40,625	2,161,537
Milwaukee	County	315	402	315	53,192	1,478,814
Minnesota	HHH Metrodome	343	408	327	55,883	2,293,842
New York	Yankee	318	408	314	57,545	1,863,731
Oakland	Alameda County	330	400	330	48,219	2,713,493
Seattle	Kingdome	324	410	314	58,150	2,147,905
Texas	Arlington	330	400	330	43,508	2,297,718
Toronto	SkyDome	330	400	330	50,516	4,001,526

BALTIMORE

Office Address: Oriole Park at Camden Yards, 333 W. Camden St., Baltimore, MD 21201. **Mailing Address:** same. **Telephone:** (410) 685-9800. **FAX:** Unavailable.
Operated by: The Orioles, Inc.

Ownership, Management
Chairman of the Board: Eli S. Jacobs
President and Chief Executive Officer: Lawrence Lucchino.
Senior Vice President: Tom Daffron.
Vice President/Business Affairs: Bob Aylward.
Vice President/Administrative Personnel: Calvin Hill.
Vice President/Sales: Lou Michaelson.
Vice President/Planning and Development: Janet Marie Smith.
Vice President/Marketing: Marty Conway.
Vice President: Sven Erik Holmes.

Roland Hemond

General Administration
Public Relations Director: Rick Vaughn. **Assistant Public Relations Director:** Bob Miller. **Director of Publications:** Bob Brown.
Publications Coordinator: Stephanie Kelly.
Community Relations Director: Julie Wagner. **Assistant Community Relations Directors:** Stacey Beckwith, Jackie Patrick.
Director of Special Projects: Ken Nigro.
Chief Financial Officer: Aric Holsinger.
Traveling Secretary: Phil Itzoe.
Director of Stadium Services: Roy Sommerhof. **Assistant Director of Stadium Services:** Scott Indorf.
Head Groundskeeper: Paul Zwaska.
Club Physicians: Dr. Sheldon Goldgeier, Dr. Charles Silberstein.
Trainers: Richie Bancells, Jamie Reed.

Radio, TV
Radio Announcers: Joe Angel, Jon Miller, Chuck Thompson. **Flagship Station:** WBAL 1090 AM.
TV Announcers: WMAR—Jon Miller, Scott Garceau, Brooks Robinson; Home Team Sports—Mel Proctor, John Lowenstein, Rex Barney, Tom Davis (Home Team Sports). **Flagship Stations:** WMAR Channel 2, Home Team Sports Cable.

1992 Schedule

APRIL
6-8-9 .... Cleveland
10-11-12 .... at Toronto
13-15-16 .... at Boston
17-18-19-20 .... Detroit
21-22-23 ... at Kansas City
24-25-26 .... at New York
27-28-29 ... at Minnesota

MAY
1-2-3 .... Seattle
4-5 .... Texas
6-7 .... Minnesota
8-9-10 .... Chicago
12-13 .... at Texas
15-16-17 ...... at Chicago
18-19-20 .... Oakland
22-23-24 .... California
25-26-27 .... at Seattle
29-30-31 ...... at Oakland

JUNE
1-2-3 .... at California

5-6-7 .... Toronto
8-9-10 .... Boston
11-12-13-14 ..... at Detroit
15-16-17 ..... at Cleveland
19-20-21-22 .... New York
23-24-25 .... at Milwaukee
26-27-28 ..... Kansas City
29-30 .... Milwaukee

JULY
1 .... Milwaukee
3-4-5 .... at Minnesota
6-7-8 .... Chicago
9-10-11-12 ..... Minnesota
16-17-18-19 ..... at Texas
20-21-22 ...... at Chicago
23-24-25-26 .... Texas
28-29-30 ..... at New York
31 .... at Boston

AUGUST
1-2 .... at Boston
3-4-5 .... Detroit
7-8-9 .... Cleveland

10-11-12-13 ... at Toronto
14-15-16 .. at Kansas City
18-19-20 .... Seattle
21-22-23 .... Oakland
24-25-26 .... California
28-29-30 .... at Seattle
31 .... at Oakland

SEPTEMBER
1-2 .... at Oakland
4-5-6 .... at California
7-8-9 .... New York
11-12-13 ...... Milwaukee
14-15-16 ..... Kansas City
18-19-20-21 . at Milwaukee
22-23-24 .... Toronto
25-26-27-28 ...... Boston
29-30 .... at Detroit

OCTOBER
1-2-3-4 ..... at Cleveland

12 • 1992 DIRECTORY

ORIOLES

Major League Staff
Manager: Johnny Oates.
Coaches: Greg Biagini, Dick Bosman, Elrod Hendricks, Davey Lopes, Cal Ripken Sr.

Baseball Operations
Executive Vice President/General Manager: Roland Hemond.
Assistant General Manager: Frank Robinson.
Assistant General Manager and Director of Player Personnel: Doug Melvin. **Administrative Assistant:** Debbie Dickman.
Special Assistants to the General Manager: Gordon Goldsberry, Fred B. Uhlman.
Minor League Camp Coordinator: Lenny Johnston.
Roving Instructors: Tim Bishop (strength and conditioning), Tom Brown (pitching), Rich Dauer (infield), Wally Moon (hitting), Reid Nichols (baserunning, outfield).

John Oates

Minor League Affiliates:

Class	Farm Team	Manager	Coach(es)
AAA	Rochester	Jerry Narron	Steve Luebber, Mike Young
AA	Hagerstown	Don Buford	Moe Drabowsky, Joe Durham
A	Frederick	Bob Miscik	John O'Donoghue, Oneri Fleita
A	Kane County	Joel Youngblood	Larry McCall, Rich Dauer
Rookie	Bluefield	Mike O'Berry	Unavailable
Rookie	Sarasota	Phil Wellman	Gus Gil, Chris Lein

Scouting
Scouting Director: Gary Nickels (Naperville, IL).
Assistant Scouting Director: Fred Uhlman Jr.
Scouting Supervisors: John Cox (Redlands, CA), Mike Ledna (Buffalo Grove, IL), John Stokoe (Slingerlands, NY).
Latin American Supervisor: Manny Estrada (Mesa, AZ).
Special Assignment Scouts: Deacon Jones (Sugarland, TX), Curt Motton (Webster, NY), Ed Liberatore (Abington, PA), Birdie Tebbetts (Anna Maria, FL).
Scouts: Rick Arnold (Lakewood, CA), Ray Crone (Waxahachie, TX), Lane Decker (Oklahoma City, OK), Paul Fryer (Calabassas, CA), Jim Gilbert (Hagerstown, MD), Jim Howard (Clifton Park, NY), Leo Labossiere (Lincoln, RI), Tim Luginbuhl (Batavia, OH), Miguel Machado (Miami, FL), Lamar North (Rossville, GA), Fred Petersen (Lisle, IL), Harry Shelton (Orlando, FL), Ed Sprague (Lodi, CA), Mike Tullier (New Orleans, LA), Logan White (Mesa, AZ), Jerry Zimmerman (Milwaukie, OR).

Doug Melvin

Spring Training Information

Major League Club
Hotel Address: Harley Sandcastle, 1540 Ben Franklin Dr., Sarasota, FL 33577. Telephone: (813) 388-2181. Hilton and Towers, 333 First St. S., St. Petersburg, FL 33701. Telephone: (813) 894-5000. **Stadium Address:** Twin Lakes Park, 6700 Clark Rd., Sarasota, 34241. Telephone: (813) 923-1996.

Minor League Clubs
Hotel Address: Park Inn-Bradenton, 668 67th St., Circle East, Bradenton, FL 34208. Telephone: (813) 745-1876. Day Stop, 644 67th St., Circle East, Bradenton, FL 34208. Telephone: (813) 746-2505. **Complex Address:** same as major league club.

BOSTON

Office Address: Fenway Park, 4 Yawkey Way, Boston, MA 02215. **Mailing Address:** same. **Telephone:** (617) 267-9440. **FAX:** (617) 236-6797. **Operated by:** Boston Red Sox.

Ownership, Management

General Partners: JRY Corporation (Jean Yawkey, majority owner and chairwoman of the board; John Harrington, president; William Gutfarb, vice president and treasurer; Haywood Sullivan. **Limited Partners:** H.M. Stevens Inc. (Joseph Stevens, principal); Dexter Group (Harold Alfond, principal); Jean R. Yawkey Trust; Dr. Arthur M. Pappas; Samuel Tamposi; Thomas DiBenedetto.

Lou Gorman

Executive Vice President and Counsel: John Donovan Jr.

Vice President, Stadium Operations: Joseph McDermott.
Vice President, Broadcasting and Special Events: James Healey.
Vice President and Chief Financial Officer: Robert Furbush. **Treasurer:** John Reilly. **Controller:** Stanley Tran.
Vice President, Transportation: Jack Rogers. **Traveling Secretary:** Steven August.
Vice President, Public Relations: Dick Bresciani. **Director of Publicity:** Josh Spofford. **Director of Statistics:** Jim Samia.
Vice President, Marketing: Larry Cancro.

General Administration

Director of Community Relations and Personnel Administration: Linda Ezell.
Director, Ticket Operations: Joe Helyar.
Director of Parking Facilities: Michael Silva.
Director of Facilities Management: Thomas Queenan Jr.
Superintendent, Grounds and Maintenance: Joseph Mooney.
Manager, Advertising: Karla O'Hara.
Manager, Corporate Sales: Robert Capilli.
Manager, Promotions: Lori Torbin.
Manager, Publications: Debbie Matson.
Medical Director: Dr. Arthur Pappas.
Trainer: Charles Moss.
Physical Therapist: Richard Zawacki.
Equipment Manager: Donald Fitzpatrick. **Visiting Clubhouse Manager:** Joe Cochran.

Radio, TV

Radio Announcers: Joe Castiglione, Bob Starr. **Flagship Station:** WRKO AM.
TV Announcers: Ned Martin, Jerry Remy (NESN); Bob Montgomery, Sean McDonough (WSBK). **Flagship Stations:** WSBK Channel 38, New England Sports Network Cable TV.

1992 Schedule

APRIL		
7-9	at New York	
11-12-12	at Cleveland	
13-15-16	Baltimore	
17-18-19-20	Toronto	
21-22-23	at Milwaukee	
24-25-26	Texas	
28-29	Chicago	

MAY	
1-2-3	Kansas City
4-5	Minnesota
6-7	at Chicago
8-9-10	at Kansas City
12-13	at Minnesota
15-16-17	California
18-19-20	Seattle
22-23-24	Oakland
26-27-28	at California
29-30-31	at Seattle

JUNE	
1-2-3	at Oakland
5-6-7	Cleveland
8-9-10	at Baltimore
11-12-13-14	at Toronto
15-16-17-18	New York
19-20-21	at Texas
22-23-24	at Detroit
26-27-28	Milwaukee
29-30	Detroit

JULY	
1	Detroit
2-3-4-5	at Chicago
6-7-8	Kansas City
9-10-11-12	Chicago
16-17-18-19	at Minnesota
20-21-22	at Kansas City
23-24-25-26	Minnesota
27-28-29	Texas
31	Baltimore

AUGUST	
1-2	Baltimore
3-4-5	Toronto
6-7-8-9	at New York
10-11-12-13	at Cleveland
14-15-16	at Milwaukee
18-19-20	California
21-22-23	Seattle
24-25-26	Oakland
28-29-30	at California
31	at Seattle

SEPTEMBER	
1-2	at Seattle
4-5-6	at Oakland
7-8-9	at Texas
11-12-13	Detroit
14-15-16-17	Milwaukee
18-19-20-21	at Detroit
22-23-24	Cleveland
25-26-27-28	at Baltimore
29-30	at Toronto

OCTOBER	
2-3-4	New York

14 • 1992 DIRECTORY

RED SOX

Major League Staff
Manager: Butch Hobson.
Coaches: Gary Allenson, Al Bumbry, Rick Burleson, Rich Gale, Don Zimmer.

Baseball Operations
Senior Vice President and General Manager: Lou Gorman. **Assistant General Manager:** Elaine Weddington. **Special Assistant to the General Manager:** John Pesky.
Vice President of Baseball Development: Eddie Kasko.
Director of Minor League Operations: Edward P. Kenney. **Assistant, Player Development and Scouting:** Erwin Bryant.
Roving Instructors: Steve Braun (hitting), Doug Camilli (catching), Eddie Popowski (infield), Jim Rice (hitting), Gary Roggenburk (pitching), Rac Slider (infield), Lee Stange (pitching).

Butch Hobson

Minor League Affiliates:
Class	Farm Team	Manager	Coach(es)
AAA	Pawtucket	Rico Petrocellii	Dick Pole, Mark Meleski
AA	New Britain	Jim Pankovits	Rick Wise, DeMarlo Hale
A	Lynchburg	Buddy Bailey	Jim Bibby
A	Winter Haven	Felix Maldonado	Joe Marchese
A	Elmira	Dave Holt	Unavailable
Rookie	Winter Haven	Frank White	Unavailable

Scouting
Scouting Director: Eddie Kasko.
Advance Scouts: Frank Malzone (Needham, MA), Wayne Britton (Staunton, VA).
Special Assignment Scouts: Sam Mele (Quincy, MA), Charles Wagner (Reading, PA).
Latin American Supervisor: Willie Patten (Caracas, Venez.).
Scouts: Rafael Batista (San Pedro de Macoris, Dom. Rep.), Milt Bolling (Mobile, AL), Ray Boone (El Cajon, CA), Ray Crone Jr. (Cedar Hill, TX), Luis Delgado (Hatillo, PR), George Digby (Winter Haven, FL), Danny Doyle (Stillwater, OK), Bill Enos (Cohasset, MA), Chuck Koney (Calumet City, IL), Jack Lee (Klamath Falls, OR), Lefty Lefebvre (Largo, FL), Don Lenhardt (St. Louis, MO), Howard McCullough (Greenville, NC), Phil Rossi, (Archbald, PA), Alex Scott (Mobile, AL), Ed Scott (Mobile, AL), Matt Sczesny (Dear Park, NY), Joe Stephenson (Anaheim, CA), Larry Thomas (Grove City, OH), Fay Thompson (Vallejo, CA), Luke Wrenn (Lakeland, FL), Jeff Zona (Richmond, VA).

Ed Kenney

Spring Training Information
Major League Club
Hotel Address: Holiday Inn, U.S. Route 17 South, Winter Haven, FL 33880. Telephone: (813) 294-4451. **Stadium Address:** Chain O'Lakes Park, Winter Haven, FL 33880. Telephone: (813) 293-3900.
Minor League Clubs
Hotel Address: same as major league club. **Complex Address:** same as major league stadium.

CALIFORNIA

Office Address: Anaheim Stadium, 2000 Gene Autry Way, Anaheim, CA 92806. **Mailing Address:** P.O. Box 2000, Anaheim, CA 92803. **Telephone:** (714) 937-7200 or (213) 625-1123. **FAX:** (714) 634-3410.

Operated by: Golden West Baseball Company.

Ownership, Management

Chairman of the Board: Gene Autry. **Board of Directors:** Gene Autry, Jackie Autry, Richard Brown, Stanley Schneider, John Singleton, Peter Ueberroth.

President and Chief Executive Officer: Richard Brown.

Executive Vice President: Jackie Autry.

Vice President, Treasurer and Chief Financial Officer: Ron Shirley.

Vice President, Public Relations and Broadcasting: Tom Seeberg.

Whitey Herzog

General Administration

Assistant Vice President, Media Relations: Tim Mead. **Manager of Publications:** Doug Ward. **Manager of Baseball Information:** Larry Babcock. **Director of Community Relations:** Darrell Miller. **Special Consultant, Media Relations:** Red Patterson.

Director of Marketing: Bob Wagner. **Director, Special Projects:** Corky Lippert. **Director of Creative Services:** John Sevano.

Director of Ticket Department: Carl Gordon.

Director of Group Sales and Promotions: Lynn Biggs. **Manager, Group Sales and Promotions:** Marianne Zambrano.

Controller: Catherine Sullivan.

Traveling Secretary: Frank Sims.

Assistant Vice President, Stadium Operations: Kevin Uhlich.

Director, Data Operations: Ron Moore.

Equipment Manager: Leonard Garcia.

Medical Director: Dr. Robert Kerlan. **Team Physicians:** Dr. Jules Rasinski, Dr. Lewis Yocum. **Physical Therapist:** Roger Williams.

Trainers: Rick Smith, Ned Bergert.

Sportspsych: Ken Ravizza.

Radio, TV

Radio Announcers: Al Conin, Bob Jamison. **Flagship Station:** KMPC 710 AM.

TV Announcers: Ken Wilson, Ken Brett. **Flagship Station:** KTLA Channel 5.

1992 Schedule

APRIL
7-8-9 .... Chicago
10-11-12 .... Milwaukee
13-14-15-16 ..... at Texas
17-18-19 ... at Kansas City
20-21-22 .... at Oakland
24-25-26 .... Seattle
28-29 .... at Toronto
30- .... at Cleveland

MAY
1-2-3 .... at Cleveland
4-5 .... at Detroit
6-7 .... New York
8-9-10 .... Toronto
12-13 .... Detroit
15-16-17 .... at Boston
18-19-20 .... at New York
22-23-24 ..... at Baltimore
26-27-28 .... Boston
29-30-31 .... Cleveland

JUNE
1-2-3 .... Baltimore

5-6-7 .... at Milwaukee
8-9-10-11 ..... at Chicago
12-13-14 .... Kansas City
15-16-17 .... Texas
19-20-21 .... Oakland
22-23-24 .... at Minnesota
25-26-27-28 .... at Seattle
29-30 .... Minnesota

JULY
1 .... Minnesota
3-4-5-6 .... at Toronto
7-8 .... at Cleveland
9-10-11-12 ..... at Detroit
16-17-18-19 .... New York
20-21-22 .... Toronto
23-24-25-26 ...... Detroit
27-28-29-30 ...... Seattle
31 .... at Texas

AUGUST
1-2 .... at Texas
4-5-6 ..... at Kansas City
7-8-9 .... Chicago

10-11-12 ...... Milwaukee
13-14-15-16 ... at Oakland
18-19-20 .... at Boston
21-22-23 .... at New York
24-25-26 .... at Baltimore
28-29-30 .... Boston
31 .... Cleveland

SEPTEMBER
1-2 .... Cleveland
4-5-6 .... Baltimore
7-8-9 .... Oakland
11-12-13 ... at Minnesota
15-16 .... at Seattle
17-18-19-20 ... Minnesota
22-23-24 ... at Milwaukee
25-26-27 .... at Chicago
28-29-30 .... Kansas City

OCTOBER
1 .... Kansas City
2-3-4 .... Texas

ANGELS

Major League Staff
Manager: Bob Rodgers.
Coaches: Rod Carew, Deron Johnson, Bobby Knoop, Marcel Lachemann, Ken Macha, Jimmie Reese, Rick Turner.

Baseball Operations
Senior Vice President, Director Player Personnel: Whitey Herzog.
Senior Vice President, Baseball Operations: Dan O'Brien. **Assistant to the General Manager:** Preston Gomez.
Director of Minor League Operations: Bill Bavasi. **Administrative Assistant, Clerical and National Association Matters:** Cathy Carey. **Administrative Assistant, Business Operations:** Jeff Parker.
Coordinator of Instruction: Joe Maddon.
Roving Instructors: Bob Clear (special assignments), Chuck Hernandez (pitching), Tom Lawless (baserunning), Eddie Rodriguez (defense), Sam Suplizio (defense).

Bob Rodgers

Minor League Affiliates:

Class	Farm Team	Manager	Coach(es)
AAA	Edmonton	Max Oliveras	Gary Ruby, Lenn Sakata
AA	Midland	Don Long	Nate Oliver, Kernan Ronan
A	Palm Springs	Mario Mendoza	Stu Cliburn, Gene Richards
A	Quad City	Mitch Seoane	Joe Georger, Matt Hyde
A	Boise	Tom Kotchman	Howie Gershberg, Orv Franchuk
Rookie	Mesa	Bill Lachemann	Mike Couchee, Charlie Romero

Scouting
Director of Scouting: Bob Fontaine Jr. **Coordinator of Scouting Operations:** Tim Kelly. **Administrative Assistant:** Karen Thomas.
Director of International Scouting: Ray Poitevint. **Supervisor, International Scouting:** Lee Sigman. **International Crosschecker:** Harry Smith.
Special Assignments and Scouting Coordinators: Tom Davis (Livermore, CA), Dave Garcia (El Cajon, CA), Rosey Gilhousen (Rancho Mirage, CA), Steve Gruwell (West Covina, CA), Bob Harrison (Long Beach, CA), Rick Ingalls (Anaheim, CA), Nick Kamzic (Evergreen Park, IL), Hal Keller (Issaquah, WA), Bobby Myrick (Colonial Heights, VA), Jon Neiderer (Pittsburgh, PA), Pedro Ramos (Miami, FL), Paul Robinson (Ft. Worth, TX), Rich Schlenker (Walnut Creek, CA), .

Bob Fontaine, Jr.

Scouting Supervisors: Ted Brzenk (Waukesha, WI), Roger Ferguson (Fresno, CA), Red Gaskill (La Marque, TX), Kris Kline (Mesa, AZ), Tom Kotchman (Seminole, FL), Tony LaCava (Oakmont, PA), Steve McAllister (Peoria, IL), Jim McLaughlin (Yonkers, NY), Tom Osowski (Milwaukee, WI), Vic Power (Guaynabo, PR), Eddie Rodriguez (Miami, FL), Dale Sutherland (La Crescenta, CA), Jack Uhey (Moreno Valley, CA).

Area Scouts: Joe Caro (Tampa, FL), Joe Carpenter (Burbank, CA), Angelo Cerroni (Tooele, UT), Orv Franchuk (Edmonton, Alta.), Bob Gardner (Youngstown, OH), Dick Greene (Bellingham, WA), Tom Gross (Las Vegas, NV), Fred Hatfield (Tallahassee, FL), Bill Lachemann Jr. (Great Falls, MT), Joe Lewis (Somerset, MA), Don Long Sr. (Edmonds, WA), David Martin (Chicago, IL) Chris Royer (Douglas, GA), Dick Probola (Pittsburgh, PA), Rip Tutor (Lenoir, NC).

Spring Training Information
Major League Club
Hotel Address: Hilton Inn, 1011 W. Holmes, Mesa, AZ 85210. Telephone: (602) 833-5555. Gene Autry Hotel, 4200 E. Palm Canyon Dr., Palm Springs, CA 92264. Telephone: (619) 328-1171. **Stadium Address:** Angels Stadium, Sunrise Way and Barristo Rd., P.O. Box 609, Palm Springs, CA 92262. Telephone: (619) 323-3325.
Minor League Clubs
Hotel Address: Hilton Inn, 1011 W. Holmes, Mesa, AZ 85210. Telephone: (602) 833-5555. **Complex Address:** Gene Autry Park, 4125 E. McKellip S., P.O. Box 6188, Mesa, AZ 85205. Telephone: (602) 830-4137.

CHICAGO

Office Address: 333 West 35th St., Chicago, IL 60616. **Mailing Address:** same. **Telephone:** (312) 924-1000. **FAX:** (312) 451-5116.
Operated by: Chicago White Sox, Ltd.

Ownership, Management
Chairman: Jerry Reinsdorf.
Vice Chairman: Eddie Einhorn.
Executive Vice President: Howard Pizer.
Senior Vice President/Marketing and Broadcasting: Rob Gallas.
Vice President/Finance: Tim Buzard.
Vice President/Stadium Operations: Terry Savarise.
General Counsel: Allan Muchin.

Ron Schueler

General Administration
Director of Public Relations and Community Affairs: Doug Abel. **Assistant Director of Public Relations:** Scott Reifert. **Manager of Publicity:** Dana Noel. **Manager of Community Relations:** Dan Fabian. **Manager of Fund Raising and Publications:** Barb Kozuh. **Coordinator of Publications:** John Ralph.

Director of Marketing and Broadcasting: Mike Bucek. **Director of Advertising and Promotions:** Bob Grim. **Manager of Merchandising and Special Events:** Sharon Sreniawski.

Director of Ticket Administration: Millie Johnson. **Director of Ticket Sales:** Bob Voight. **Ticket Manager:** Bob Devoy. **Assistant Ticket Manager:** Ed Cassin.

Director of Purchasing: Don Esposito. **Manager of Purchasing:** Mike Spidale.

Controller: Bill Waters.
Manager of Human Resources: Moira Foy.
Director of Park Operations: David Schaffer. **Assistant Director of Park Operations:** Dan Polvere. **Director of Diamond Suite Operations:** Joseph Cummings. **Manager of Guest Relations:** Julie Taylor.
Manager of Scoreboard Operations and Productions: Jeff Szynal.
Traveling Secretary: Glen Rosenbaum.
Trainer: Herm Schneider. **Assistant Trainer:** Mark Anderson.
Team Physicians: Dr. James Boscardin, Dr. Hugo Cuadros, Dr. Robert Daley, Dr. Bernard Feldman, Dr. David Orth, Dr. Scott Price.
Groundskeeper: Roger Bossard.

Radio, TV
Radio Announcers: John Rooney, Ed Farmer. **Flagship Station:** WMAQ 670 AM.

TV Announcers: Ken Harrelson, Tom Paciorek. **Flagship Stations:** WGN TV-9, SportsChannel.

1992 Schedule

APRIL		
7-8-9	at California
10-11-12	at Oakland
13-15-16	Seattle
17-18-19	Minnesota
21-22	New York
24-25-26	at Detroit
28-29	at Boston
30	Texas

MAY	
1-2-3	Texas
4-5	Milwaukee
6-7	Boston
8-9-10	at Baltimore
12-13	at Milwaukee
15-16-17	Baltimore
18-19-20	Kansas City
22-23-24	Toronto
26-27-28	at Texas
29-30-31	at Toronto

JUNE	
1-2-3	at Kansas City
5-6-7	Oakland
8-9-10-11	California
12-13-14	at Minnesota
15-16-17-18	at Seattle
19-20-21	Detroit
22-23-24	Cleveland
26-27-28	at New York
29-30	at Cleveland

JULY	
1	at Cleveland
2-3-4-5	Boston
6-7-8	at Baltimore
9-10-11-12	at Boston
16-17-18-19	Milwaukee
20-21-22	Baltimore
23-24-25-26	at Milwaukee
28-29-30	at Detroit
31	Seattle

AUGUST	
1-2	Seattle
4-5-6	Minnesota
7-8-9	at California
10-11-12	at Oakland
14-15-16-17	New York
18-19-20	Texas
21-22-23	Kansas City
24-25-26	Toronto
28-29-30	at Texas
31	at Toronto

SEPTEMBER	
1-2	at Toronto
3-4-5-6	at Kansas City
8-9-10	Detroit
11-12-13	Cleveland
14-15-16	at New York
18-19-20	at Cleveland
21-22-23-24	Oakland
25-26-27	California
28-29-30	at Minnesota

OCTOBER	
1	at Minnesota
2-3-4	at Seattle

WHITE SOX

Major League Staff
Manager: Gene Lamont.
Coaches: Terry Bevington, Jackie Brown, Walt Hriniak, Doug Mansolino, Joe Nossek, Mike Squires.

Baseball Operations
Senior Vice President, Major League Operations: Ron Schueler.
Senior Vice President, Baseball: Jack Gould.
Director of Baseball Operations: Daniel Evans.
Assistant to Director of Baseball Operations: Jeff Chaney.
Vice President, Scouting and Minor League Operations: Larry Monroe.
Director of Minor League Operations: Steve Noworyta. **Assistant to the Director:** Tim Ciombor.
Minor League Administrator: Judi Essex Miller.
Director of Minor League Instruction/Camp Coordinator: Buddy Bell.
Assistant to Director of Instruction: Ken Silvestri.
Roving Instructors: Vern Gambetta (conditioning), Mike Gellinger (defense), Tim Lang (conditioning), Mike Lum (hitting), Dewey Robinson (pitching), Tommy Thompson (catching), Dallas Williams (baserunning).

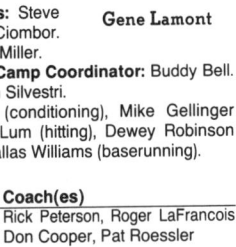

Gene Lamont

Minor League Affiliates:

Class	Farm Team	Manager	Coach(es)
AAA	Vancouver	Rick Renick	Rick Peterson, Roger LaFrancois
AA	Birmingham	Tony Franklin	Don Cooper, Pat Roessler, Sam Hairston
A	Sarasota	Rick Patterson	Mike Barnett, Kirk Champion
A	South Bend	Terry Francona	Jaime Garcia, Mark Haley, Jim Reinebold
A	Utica	Fred Kendall	Bill Ballou, Charles Culberson
Rookie	Sarasota	Mike Rojas	Curt Hasler, Chet DiEmidio

Scouting
Director of Scouting: Duane Shaffer. **Assistant to Director of Scouting:** Grace Zwit.
Major League Scouts: Ed Brinkman (Cincinnati, OH), Bart Johnson (Chicago), Dave Yoakum (Orlando, FL).
National Crosschecker: George Bradley (Tampa, FL).
Scouting Supervisors: Mark Bernstein (Great Neck, NY), Ed Pebley (Galt, CA), Marti Wolever (Papillion, NE).
Scouts: Jose Bernhardt (San Pedro de Macoris, Dom. Rep.), Juan Bernhardt (San Pedro Macoris, Dom. Rep.), Chuck Bizzell (Evanston, IL), Kevin Burrell (Fayetteville, GA), Joseph Butler (East Rancho Dominguez, CA), Scott Cerny (Davis, CA), Alex Cosmidis (Winston-Salem, NC), Warren Hughes (Mobile, AL), Miguel Ibarra (Panama), Doug Laumann (Edgewood, KY), Reggie Lewis (Elkton, MD), Guy Mader (Winter Park, FL), Dave Owen (Arlington, TX), Gary Pellant (Bellevue, WA), Victor Puig (Bayamon, PR), Mike Rizzo (Chicago, IL), Alberto Rondon (Valencia, Venez.), Mike Sgobba (Yorba Linda, CA), Ken Stauffer (Katy, TX), John Tummino (Newburgh, NY).

Larry Monroe

Spring Training Information
Major League Club
Hotel Address: Days Inn, 4900 N. Tamiami Trail, Sarasota, FL 33580. **Telephone:** (813) 355-9721. **Stadium Address:** Ed Smith Stadium, 12th and Tuttle, Sarasota, FL 34237. **Telephone:** (813) 366-8451.
Minor League Clubs
Hotel Address: Sarasota Motor Inn, 8150 N. Tamiami Trail, Sarasota, FL 34243. **Telephone:** (813) 355-7747. **Complex Address:** Ed Smith Stadium, 12th and Tuttle, Sarasota, FL 34237. **Telephone:** (813) 954-7699.

CLEVELAND

Office Address: Cleveland Stadium, Cleveland, OH 44114. **Mailing Address:** same. **Telephone:** (216) 861-1200. **FAX:** (216) 566-1287.
Operated by: Cleveland Indians.

Ownership, Management
Chairman of the Board and Chief Executive Officer: Richard Jacobs. **Vice Chairman of the Board:** David Jacobs. **Directors:** Richard Jacobs, David Jacobs, Martin Gleary, Gary Bryenton.
President and Chief Operating Officer: Rick Bay.
Senior Vice President, Business: Dennis Lehman.

John Hart

Vice President, Finance: Gregg Olson.
Vice President: Martin Cleary.
Vice President, Public Relations: Bob DiBiasio.
Vice President, Stadium Operations: Carl Hoerig.
Vice President, Marketing: Jeff Overton.

General Administration
Director of Media Relations: John Maroon. **Assistant Director of Media Relations:** Susie Gharrity.
Director of Community Relations: Glen Shumate.
Director of Advertising: Valerie Arcuri.
Manager of Operations: Kerry Wimsatt.
Director of Merchandising/Licensing: Jayne Churchmark.
Director of Ticket Services: Connie Minadeo.
Director of Team Travel: Mike Seghi.
Director of Ticket Sales: Victor Gregovits.
Director of Promotions/Sales: Jon Starrett.
Controller: Ken Stefanov.
Manager of Box Office: Gail Liebenguth.
Speakers Bureau: Bob Feller.
Indians Equipment and Clubhouse Manager: Cy Buynak.
Head Trainer: Jim Warfield. **Assistant Trainer:** Paul Spicuzza.
Medical Director: Dr. William Wilder. **Team Physicians:** Dr. Godfredo Domingo, Dr. K. V. Gopal, Dr. Zenos Vangelos.

Radio, TV
Radio Announcers: Tom Hamilton, Herb Score. **Flagship Station:** WKNR 1220 AM.
TV Announcers: Jack Corrigan, Mike Hegan. **Flagship Station:** WUAB Channel 43. **Cable:** Rick Manning, John Sanders; SportsChannel Ohio.

1992 Schedule

APRIL		
6-8-9	at Baltimore
11-12-12	Boston
13-14-15-16	Detroit
17-18-19-20	at New York
21-22-23	at Toronto
24-25-26	Milwaukee
28-29	Oakland
30	California

MAY	
1-2-3	California
4-5	Kansas City
6-7	at Texas
8-9-10	at Minnesota
12-13	at Kansas City
15-16-17	Minnesota
18-19-20	Texas
22-23-24	at Seattle
25-26-27	at Oakland
29-30-31	at California

JUNE	
2-3-4	Seattle
5-6-7	at Boston
8-9-10	at Detroit
12-13-14	New York
15-16-17	Baltimore
18-19-20-21	at Milwaukee
22-23-24	at Chicago
26-27-28	Toronto
29-30	Chicago

JULY	
1	Chicago
3-4-5-6	Oakland
7-8	California
9-10-11-12	at Texas
16-17-18-19	at K.C.
20-21-22	at Minnesota
23-24-25-26	Kansas City
27-28-29	Milwaukee
31	Detroit

AUGUST	
1-2	Detroit
3-4-5	at New York
7-8-9	at Baltimore
10-11-12-13	Boston
14-15-16	Toronto
18-19-20	Minnesota
21-22-23	Texas
25-26-27	at Seattle
28-29-30	at Oakland
31	at California

SEPTEMBER	
1-2	at California
4-5-6	Seattle
7-8-9	at Milwaukee
11-12-13	at Chicago
14-15-16-17	at Toronto
18-19-20	Chicago
22-23-24	at Boston
25-26-27	at Detroit
28-29-30	New York

OCTOBER	
1-2-3-4	Baltimore

INDIANS

Major League Staff
Manager: Mike Hargrove.
Coaches: Rick Adair, Ken Bolek, Dom Chiti, Ron Clark, Jose Morales, Dave Nelson, Jeff Newman.

Baseball Operations
Vice President of Baseball Operations: John Hart.
Director of Player Development: Dan O'Dowd.
Administrator, Player Personnel: Wendy Hoppel.
Assistant, Player Development: Mark Shapiro.
Director of Minor League Field Operations: Johnny Goryl. **Assistant Director:** Boyd Coffie.
Roving Instructors: Pat Ciccantelli (strength and conditioning), Buzzy Keller (baserunning), Harry Spilman (hitting), Billy Williams (outfield), Rick Wolff (consultant).
Dominican Program Coordinator: Minnie Mendoza.

Mike Hargrove

Minor League Affiliates:

Class	Farm Team	Manager	Coach(es)
AAA	Colorado Springs	Charlie Manuel	Dyar Miller, Luis Isaac
AA	Canton	Brian Graham	Ken Rowe, Jim Gabella
A	Kinston	Dave Keller	Ricky Horton, Rob Swain
A	Columbus	Mike Brown	Fred Gladding, Dan Norman
A	Watertown	Shawn Pender	Greg Ferlenda, Dan Williams
Rookie	Burlington	Minnie Mendoza	Greg Booker, Billy Williams

Scouting
Director of Scouting: Mickey White. **Assistant Director:** Jay Green. **Administrator:** Murray Brunton.
National Crosschecker: Tony DeMacio (Chamblee, GA).
Scouting Supervisors: Buzzy Keller (Seguin, TX), Winston Llenas (Santiago, Dom. Rep.), Shawn Pender (Winter Park, FL), Jay Robertson (Citrus Heights, CA).
Advance Scouts: Dan Carnevale (Buffalo, NY), Tom Giordano (Amityville, NY), Gordie MacKenzie (Fruitland Park, FL), Bill Werle (San Mateo, CA), Mark Wiley (Miami Springs, FL).
Scouts: Luis Aponte (Barquisimeto, Venezuela), Steve Avila (Olympia, WA), Mark Baca (Mesa, AZ), Tom Chandler (Bryan, TX), Ramon Conde (Juana Diaz, PR), Tom Couston (Chicago, IL), Jeff Datz (Sacramento, CA), Joe Delucca (Babylon, NY), Mark Germann (Lancaster, PA), Jerry LaPenta (Harwinton, CT), Bill Lawlor (Dunwoody, GA), Allan Lewis (David-Chiriqui, Panama), Rick Magnante (Studio City, CA), Buddy Mercado (Maumelle, AR), Mark McKnight (Matthews, NC), Jim Richardson (Marlow, OK), Doug Takaragawa (Fountain Valley, CA), Mark Weidemaier (Palm Harbor, FL).

Dan O'Dowd

Spring Training Information
Major League Club
Hotel Address: Viscount Suites, 4855 East Broadway, Tucson, AZ 85711. Telephone: (602) 745-6500. **Stadium Address:** Hi Corbett Field, Randolph Park, Tucson, AZ 85726. Telephone: (602) 881-5710.
Minor League Clubs
Hotel Address: Aztec Inn, 102 N. Alvernon Way, Tucson, AZ 85711. Telephone: (602) 795-0330. **Complex Address:** same as major league stadium.

DETROIT

Office Address: Tiger Stadium, Detroit, MI 48216.
Telephone: (313) 962-4000. **FAX:** (313) 962-5591.
Operated by: Detroit Baseball Club.

Ownership, Management
Owner: Thomas Monaghan.
Directors: Jim Campbell, Thomas Monaghan, Douglas Dawson, George Griffith, George Kell, Bo Schembechler.
Chairman and Chief Executive Officer: Jim Campbell.
President and Chief Operating Officer: Bo Schembechler. **Vice President, Assistant to President:** Alice Sloane.
Senior Vice President, Finance: Alexander Callam.
Senior Vice President, Future Planning and Administration: William Haase.
Senior Vice President, Marketing, Radio and TV: Jeff Odenwald.
Vice President, Media and Public Relations: Dan Ewald.
Vice President, Stadium Operations: Ralph Snyder.
Vice President, Controller: Michael Wilson.

Bo Schembechler

General Administration
Director of Media and Public Relations: Greg Shea.
Director of Radio and TV: Neal Fenkell.
Director of Ticket Operations: Ken Marchetti.
Director of Marketing Services: Scott Nickle.
Executive Consultant: Rick Ferrell.
Manager of Data Processing: Dick Roy.
Sales Manager: Chris Hill.
Director, Equipment and Clubhouse: Jim Schmakel.

Radio, TV
Radio Announcers: Rick Rizzs, Bob Rathbun. **Flagship Station:** WJR 760 AM.
TV Announcers: George Kell, Al Kaline. **Flagship Station:** WDIV Channel 4.

1992 Schedule

APRIL
6-8-9 .... Toronto
10-11-12 .... New York
13-14-15-16 ..at Cleveland
17-18-19-20 .. at Baltimore
21-22-23 .... at Texas
24-25-26 .... Chicago
28-29 .... Seattle
30 .... Oakland

MAY
1-2-3 .... Oakland
4-5 .... California
6-7 .... at Oakland
8-9-10 .... at Seattle
12-13 .... at California
15-16-17 .. at Kansas City
18-19-20-21 ... Milwaukee
22-23-24 ...... Minnesota
26-27-28 .... Kansas City
29-30-31 .... at Minnesota

JUNE
1-2-3 .... at Milwaukee
4-5-6-7 ...... at New York
8-9-10 .... Cleveland
11-12-13-14 .... Baltimore
16-17-18 ...... at Toronto
19-20-21 ..... at Chicago
22-23-24 .... Boston
25-26-27-28 ..... Texas
29-30 .... at Boston

JULY
1 .... at Boston
3-4-5-6 .... Seattle
7-8 .... Oakland
9-10-11-12 ..... California
16-17-18-19 ... at Oakland
20-21-22 ...... at Seattle
23-24-25-26 ..at California
28-29-30 .... Chicago
31 .... at Cleveland

AUGUST
1-2 .... at Cleveland
3-4-5 .... at Baltimore
6-7-8-9 .... Toronto
10-11-12 ..... New York
14-15-16 .... at Texas
17-18-19 ... at Kansas City
21-22-23 .... at Milwaukee
24-25-26 .... at Minnesota
28-29-30 .... Kansas City
31 .... Minnesota

SEPTEMBER
1-2 .... Minnesota
4-5-6 .... Milwaukee
8-9-10 ...... at Chicago
11-12-13 ...... at Boston
15-16 .... Texas
18-19-20-21 ..... Boston
22-23-24 ..... at New York
25-26-27 .... Cleveland
29-30 .... Baltimore

OCTOBER
2-3-4 .... at Toronto

22 • 1992 DIRECTORY

TIGERS

Major League Staff
Manager: Sparky Anderson.
Coaches: Billy Consolo, Larry Herndon, Billy Muffett, Gene Roof, Dick Tracewski, Dan Whitmer.

Baseball Operations
Senior Vice President, Player Procurement and Development: Joe McDonald.
Senior Vice President, Major League Personnel: Jerry Walker.
Director of Minor League Administration: Dave Miller. **Assistant Director, Baseball Operations:** Kevin Qualls. **Minor League Secretary:** Audrey Zielinski. **Administrative Assistant:** Susie Staub.
Director of Field Operations: Tom Petroff.

Sparky Anderson

Minor League Affiliates:

Class	Farm Team	Manager	Coach(es)
AAA	Toledo	Joe Sparks	Ralph Treuel, Kevin Bradshaw
AA	London	Mark DeJohn	Jeff Jones, Bruce Fields
A	Lakeland	John Lipon	Rich Bombard, Dan Raley
A	Fayetteville	Gerry Groninger	Sid Monge, Dwight Lowry
A	Niagara Falls	Larry Parrish	Ray Korn, Stan Luketich
Rookie	Bristol	Mark Wagner	Jim Van Scoyoc, Juan Lopez

Scouting
Vice President, Scouting: Joe Klein.
Scouting Supervisors: Jeff Malinoff (Kirkland, WA), Don Rowland (Oviedo, FL), Bill Schudlich (Dearborn, MI).
Major League/Advance Scouts: Gary Blaylock (Malden, MO), Jim Davenport (San Carlos, CA).
Scouts: Ruben Amaro (Miami, FL), Arnie Beyeler (Lakeland, FL), Wayne Blackburn (Portsmouth, OH), Mark Giegler (Howell, MI), Jack Hays (Tualatin, OR), Rich Henning (Sacramento, CA), Harry Koepf (Moss Beach, CA), Joe Lewis (Somerset, MA), Dennis Lieberthal (Westlake, CA), Juan Lopez (Carolina, PR), Stan Meek (Norman, OK), John Mirabelli (Cary, NC), Mark Monahan (Ypsilanti, MI), Matt Nowak (Chicago, IL), Ramon Pena (Bronx, NY), Dee Phillips (Henderson, TX), Joe Robinson (Burlington, IA), Steve Souchock (Plantation, FL), Mike Wallace (Escondido, CA), Clyde Weir (Mt. Pleasant, MI), Dick Wiencek (Rancho Mirage, CA), Rob Wilfong (West Covina, CA), Dick Wilson (Sun Valley, NV), Gary York (Rome, GA).

Joe McDonald

Spring Training Information
Major League Club
Hotel Address: Hoilday Inn-North, 4645 Socrum Loop Rd., Lakeland, FL 33809. Telephone: (813) 858-1411. **Stadium Address:** Joker Marchant Stadium, Lakeland Hills Blvd., Lakeland, FL 33801. Telephone: (813) 682-1401.

Minor League Clubs
Hotel Address: John Fetzer Hall, Tigertown, Lakeland, FL 33804. Telephone: (813) 682-3742. **Complex Address:** Tigertown, P.O. Box 90187, Lakeland, FL 33804. Telephone: (813) 686-8075.

KANSAS CITY

Office Address: One Royal Way, Kansas City, MO 64129. **Mailing Address:** P.O. Box 419969, Kansas City, MO 64141. **Telephone:** (816) 921-2200. **FAX:** (816) 921-5775.

Operated by: Kansas City Royals Baseball Corporation.

Ownership, Management
Chairman of the Board: Ewing Kauffman.
Board of Directors: Joe Burke, Charles Hughes, Ewing Kauffman, Mrs. Ewing Kauffman.
President: Joe Burke.
Vice President, Finance: Dale Rohr.
Vice President, Administration: Dennis Cryder.
Vice President, Public Relations: Dean Vogelaar.

Herk Robinson

General Administration
Assistant Directors of Public Relations: Steve Fink, Kevin Henderson.
Director of Stadium Operations: Tom Folk.
Director of Season Ticket Sales: Joe Grigoli. **Director of Ticket Operations:** Ken Willeke.
Director of Group Sales and Lancer Coordinator: Chris Muehlbach.
Traveling Secretary: Dave Witty.
Equipment Manager: Mike Burkhalter.
Groundskeeper: George Toma.
Team Physician: Dr. Steve Joyce.
Trainer: Nick Swartz. **Assistant Trainer:** Steve Morrow.

Radio, TV
Radio Announcers: Denny Matthews, Fred White. **Flagship Station:** WIBW 580-AM.
TV Announcers: Denny Trease, Paul Splittorff. **Flagship Station:** WDAF Channel 4.

1992 Schedule

APRIL		
6-8-9	at Oakland
10-11-12	at Seattle
13-14-15-16	Oakland
17-18-19	California
21-22-23	Baltimore
24-25-26	at Toronto
28-29	at Milwaukee

MAY	
1-2-3	at Boston
4-5	at Cleveland
6-7	Milwaukee
8-9-10	Boston
12-13	Cleveland
15-16-17	Detroit
18-19-20	at Chicago
21-22-23-24	at Texas
26-27-28	at Detroit
29-30-31	Texas

JUNE	
1-2-3	Chicago
5-6-7	Seattle
8-9-10	Minnesota
12-13-14	at California
15-16-17-18	at Minnesota
19-20-21	Toronto
23-24-25	New York
26-27-28	at Baltimore
29-30	at New York

JULY	
1	at New York
2-3-4-5	Milwaukee
6-7-8	at Boston
9-10-11-12	at Milwaukee
16-17-18-19	Cleveland
20-21-22	Boston
23-24-25-26	at Cleveland
28-29-30	at Toronto
31	Oakland

AUGUST	
1-2	Oakland
4-5-6	California
7-8-9	at Oakland
10-11-12	at Seattle
14-15-16	Baltimore
17-18-19	Detroit
21-22-23	at Chicago
25-26-27	at Texas
28-29-30	at Detroit
31	Texas

SEPTEMBER	
1-2	Texas
3-4-5-6	Chicago
7-8-9	Toronto
11-12-13	at New York
14-15-16	at Baltimore
18-19-20	New York
21-22-23-24	Seattle
25-26-27	at Minnesota
28-29-30	at California

OCTOBER	
1	at California
2-3-4	Minnesota

ROYALS

Major League Staff
Manager: Hal McRae.
Coaches: Glenn Ezell, Adrian Garrett, Guy Hansen, Lynn Jones, Bruce Kison.

Baseball Operations
Executive Vice President and General Manager: Spencer "Herk" Robinson.
Assistant General Manager: Jay Hinrichs.
Special Assistant to General Manager: Brian Murphy.
Director of Minor League Operations: Steve Schryver. **Assistant Minor League Director:** Bob Hegman. **Secretary, Player Development:** Bonnie Morgan.
Coordinator of Instruction: Joe Jones.
Roving Instructors: Jerry Cram (pitching), Tommy Burgess (hitting).

Hal McRae

Minor League Affiliates:

Class	Farm Team	Manager	Coach(es)
AAA	Omaha	Jeff Cox	Joe Horlen, Bob Herold
AA	Memphis	Brian Poldberg	Mike Alvarez, U.L. Washington
A	Baseball City	Ron Johnson	Pete Filson, Rafael Santana
A	Appleton	Tom Poquette	Mike Mason
A	Eugene	Bob Meacham	Tom Burgmeier, John Mizerock
Rookie	Baseball City	Mike Jirschele	Theo Shaw, Jose Tartabull

Scouting
Director of Scouting: Art Stewart.
National Crosschecker: Chuck McMichael (Phoenix, AZ).
Field Scout Training Coordinator: Carl Blando.
Special Assignment Scouts: Al Kubski (Carlsbad, CA), Steve Flores (La Habra, CA).
Major League Scouts: Boots Day (St. Louis, MO), Bob Schaefer (Norwich, CT), Buck O'Neil (Kansas City, MO).
Scouts: Allard Baird (Davie, FL), Bob Carter (Chambersburg, PA), Floyd Chandler (Fullerton, CA), Balos Davis (Charlotte, NC), Doug Deutsch (Costa Mesa, CA), Ken Gonzales (Kansas City, KS), Dave Herrera (Danville, CA), Ray Jackson (Detroit, MI), Gary Johnson (Costa Mesa, CA), Tony Levato (Peotone, IL), Ed Mathes (Westbury, NY), Jeff McKay (Eugene, OR), Wil Rutenschroer (Cincinnati, OH), Luis Silverio (Santiago, Dom. Rep.), Jerry Stephens (West Bloomfield, MI), Terry Wetzel (Sugarland, TX).

Steve Schryver

Spring Training Information
Major League Club
Hotel Address: Sonesta Villa Resort, 10000 Turkey Lake Road, Orlando, FL 32819. Telephone: (407) 352-8051. **Stadium Address:** Baseball City Stadium, 300 Stadium Way, Davenport, FL 33837. Telephone: (813) 424-7211.

Minor League Clubs
Hotel Address: Kansas City Royals Dormitory, 300 Stadium Way, Davenport, FL 33837. Telephone: (813) 424-7227. **Complex Address:** same as major league stadium. Telephone: (813) 424-7272.

MILWAUKEE

Office Address: Milwaukee County Stadium, 201 S. 46th St., Milwaukee, WI 53214. **Mailing Address:** same. **Telephone:** (414) 933-4114. **FAX:** (414) 933-7323.
Operated by: Milwaukee Brewers Baseball Club.

Ownership, Management
President, Chief Executive Officer: Allan "Bud" Selig. **Board of Directors:** Charles Krause, Bernard Kubale, Allan "Bud" Selig, Everett Smith.
  Senior Vice President: Harry Dalton.
  Vice President, Government Affairs: Dick Hackett.
  Vice President, Finance: Dick Hoffmann.
  Vice President, Broadcast Operations: Bill Haig.
  Vice President, Stadium Operations: Gabe Paul Jr.

Sal Bando

General Administration
  Director of Communications: Laurel Prieb.
  Director of Media Relations: Tom Skibosh. **Director of Publications:** Mario Ziino.
  General Counsel: Wendy Selig. **Assistant General Counsel:** Eugene Randolph.
  Director of Corporate Marketing: John Cordova.
  Director of Community Relations: Michael Downs.
  Assistant Director of Stadium Operations and Advertising: Jack Hutchinson.
  Director of Executive Club: Dean Rennicke.
  Traveling Secretary: Jimmy Bank.
  Director of Ticket Operations: John Barnes. **Assistant Ticket Manager:** Nancy Dressel.
  Director of Season Ticket Sales: Rich Fromstein.
  Director of Ticket Sales: Jeff Eisenberg.
  Director of Grounds: Gary Vandenberg.
  Director of Electronic Systems: Terry Ann Peterson.
  Trainers: John Adam, Al Price.
  Team Physicians: Dr. Paul Jacobs, Dr. Dennis Sullivan.
  Strength and Conditioning Coach: Toby Oldham.

Radio, TV
  Radio Announcers: Pat Hughes, Bob Uecker. **Flagship Station:** WTMJ 620 AM.
  Television Announcers: Unavailable. **Flagship Station:** WCGV-TV 24.

1992 Schedule

APRIL
6-8-9 .... Minnesota
10-11-12 ..... at California
14-15 .... at Minnesota
17-18-19 .... Seattle
21-22-23 .... Boston
24-25-26 ..... at Cleveland
28-29 .... Kansas City
30 .... Toronto

MAY
1-2-3 .... Toronto
4-5 .... at Chicago
6-7 .... at Kansas City
8-9-10 .... at Texas
12-13 .... Chicago
15-16-17 .... Texas
18-19-20-21 .... at Detroit
22-23-24-25 .. at New York
26-27 .... at Toronto
29-30-31 .... New York

JUNE
1-2-3 .... Detroit

5-6-7 .... California
8-9-10 .... Oakland
12-13-14 ..... at Seattle
15-16-17 ..... at Oakland
18-19-20-21 ... Cleveland
23-24-25 ...... Baltimore
26-27-28 ...... at Boston
29-30 .... at Baltimore

JULY
1 .... at Baltimore
2-3-4-5 ... at Kansas City
6-7-8 .... at Texas
9-10-11-12 .. Kansas City
16-17-18-19 .. at Chicago
20-21-22 .... Texas
23-24-25-26 ..... Chicago
27-28-29 ..... at Cleveland
30-31 .... at Minnesota

AUGUST
1-2 .... at Minnesota
4-5-6 .... Seattle
7-8-9 .... Minnesota

10-11-12 ..... at California
14-15-16 .... Boston
18-19-20 .... Toronto
21-22-23 .... Detroit
24-25-26 ..... at New York
27-28-29-30 .... at Toronto
31 .... New York

SEPTEMBER
1-2 .... New York
4-5-6 .... at Detroit
7-8-9 .... Cleveland
11-12-13 ..... at Baltimore
14-15-16-17 ... at Boston
18-19-20-21 ... Baltimore
22-23-24 ...... California
25-26-27 .... Oakland
29-30 .... at Seattle

OCTOBER
1 .... at Seattle
2-3-4 .... at Oakland

BREWERS

Major League Staff
Manager: Phil Garner.
Coaches: Bill Castro, Duffy Dyer, Mike Easler, Tim Foli, Don Rowe.

Baseball Operations
Senior Vice President, Baseball Operations: Sal Bando. **Assistant Vice President, Baseball Operations:** Bruce Manno.
Senior Consultant, Baseball Operations: Dee Fondy.
Special Assistants, Baseball Operations: Larry Haney, Denny Sommers, Chuck Tanner.
Director of Baseball Administration: Brian Small.
Director of Player Negotiations: Tom Gausden.
Director of Player Development: Fred Stanley.
Coordinator of Player Development: Bob Humphreys.
Roving Instructors: Del Crandall (catching), John Cumberland (pitching), Ron Jackson (hitting), Fred Patek (infield and baserunning), Ed Sedar (outfield), Paul Tretiak (instructor).

Phil Garner

Minor League Affiliates:
Class	Farm Team	Manager	Coach(es)
AAA	Denver	Tony Muser	Lamar Johnson, Bill Campbell
AA	El Paso	Chris Bando	Rob Derksen
A	Stockton	Tim Ireland	Mark Littell
A	Beloit	Wayne Krenchicki	Steve Foucault
Rookie	Helena	Harry Dunlop	Mike Caldwell
Rookie	Chandler	Tommy Jones	Jim Merrick, Ben Oglivie

Scouting
Vice President, Scouting and Planning: Al Goldis (Sarasota, FL).
Administrative Assistant, Scouting: Scott Martens.
Director of National Scouting: Lou Snipp (Galveston, TX).
Director of International Scouting: Dan Monzon (Odessa, FL).
Scouting Supervisors/Crosscheckers: Fred Beene (Oakhurst, TX), Ken Califano (Towson, MD), Ed Ford (Jersey City, NJ), Dick Foster (Otis, OR), Jess Flores (Ontario, CA), Rod Fridley (Tampa, FL), Roland LeBlanc (LaHabra, CA).

Al Goldis

Full-Time Scouts: Julio Blanco-Herrera (Miami, FL), Tom Calvano (Cincinnati, OH), Kevin Christman (Morgan Hill, CA), Preston Douglas (St. Augustine, FL), Ed Durkin (Palm Harbor, FL), Felix Delgado (Rio Piedras, PR), Dean Gruwell (Decatur, GA), Tommy Jones (Tempe, AZ), Harvey Kuenn Jr. (Milwaukee, WI), Demie Mainieri (Miami, FL), Mike Powers (Galveston, TX), Ron Rizzi (Joppa, MD), Phil Rizzo (Chicago, IL), Fermin Ubri (Dominican Republic), Tom Walsh (Dedham, MA), Red Whitsett (Villa Rica, GA), David Young (Kountze, TX), Walter Youse (Sykesville, MD).

Spring Training Information
Major League Club
Hotel Address: The Dobson Ranch Inn, 1666 S. Dobson Road, Mesa, AZ 85202. Telephone: (602) 831-7000. **Stadium Address:** Compadre Stadium, 1425 W. Ocotillo Rd., Chandler, AZ 85248. Telephone: (602) 895-1200.

Minor League Clubs
Hotel Address: Quality Inn, 5121 E. La Puenta Ave., Phoenix, AZ 85044. Telephone: (602) 893-3900. **Complex Address:** Chandler Complex, 4500 S. Alma School Rd., Chandler, AZ 85248. Telephone: Unavailable.

MINNESOTA

Office Address: 501 Chicago Ave. South, Minneapolis, MN 55415. **Mailing Address:** same. **Telephone:** (612) 375-1366. **FAX:** (612) 375-7417.
Operated by: The Minnesota Twins.

Ownership, Management
Owner: Carl Pohlad.
Board of Directors: Carl Pohlad, James Pohlad, Robert Pohlad, William Pohlad, Howard Fox Jr., Donald Benson, Paul Christen, Robert Woolley.
President: Jerry Bell. **Administrative Assistant to President:** Marlene Peters.
Vice President, Marketing: Dave Moore.

Andy MacPhail

General Administration
Director of Media Relations: Rob Antony. **Assistant Director of Media Relations:** Steve Rausch.
Promotions Manager: Laura Claessens. **Director of Community Relations:** Betty Piper.
Corporate Sales Manager: Conrad Smith. **Sales Administration Manager:** Phil Huebner. **Sales:** Jack Blesi, Scott O'Connell, Scott Erickson.
Communications Manager: Dave St. Peter.
Ticket Manager: Paul Froehle. **Assistant Ticket Manager:** Joe Mee.
Traveling Secretary: Remzi Kiratli.
Equipment Manager: Jim Wiesner. **Visitors Clubhouse:** Jim Dunn.
Trainer: Dick Martin. **Assistant Trainer:** Doug Nelson.
Club Physicians: Dr. L.J. Michienzi, Dr. John Steubs.

Radio, TV
Radio Announcers: Herb Carneal, John Gordon. **Flagship Station:** WCCO 830 AM.
TV Announcers: Jim Kaat, Ted Robinson, Dick Bremer. **Flagship Station:** WCCO-TV Channel 4.

1992 Schedule

APRIL		
6-8-9	at Milwaukee
10-11-12	Texas
14-15	Milwaukee
17-18-19	at Chicago
20-21-22-23	at Seattle
24-25-26	Oakland
27-28-29	Baltimore

MAY	
1-2-3	at New York
4-5	at Boston
6-7	at Baltimore
8-9-10	Cleveland
12-13	Boston
15-16-17	at Cleveland
18-19-20	at Toronto
22-23-24	at Detroit
26-27	New York
29-30-31	Detroit

JUNE	
1-2-3	Toronto
4-5-6-7	at Texas
8-9-10	at Kansas City
12-13-14	Chicago
15-16-17-18	Kansas City
19-20-21	Seattle
22-23-24	California
25-26-27-28	at Oakland
29-30	at California

JULY	
1	at California
3-4-5	Baltimore
6-7-8	at New York
9-10-11-12	at Baltimore
16-17-18-19	Boston
20-21-22	Cleveland
23-24-25-26	at Boston
27-28-29	Oakland
30-31	Milwaukee

AUGUST	
1-2	Milwaukee
4-5-6	at Chicago
7-8-9	at Milwaukee
10-11-12-13	Texas
14-15-16	at Seattle
18-19-20	at Cleveland
21-22-23	Toronto
24-25-26	Detroit
27-28-29-30	New York
31	at Detroit

SEPTEMBER	
1-2	at Detroit
4-5-6	at Toronto
7-8-9	Seattle
11-12-13	California
14-15-16	at Oakland
17-18-19-20	at California
22-23	at Texas
25-26-27	Kansas City
28-29-30	Chicago

OCTOBER	
1	Chicago
2-3-4	at Kansas City

TWINS

Major League Staff
Manager: Tom Kelly.
Coaches: Terry Crowley, Ron Gardenhire, Rick Stelmaszek, Dick Such, Wayne Terwilliger.

Baseball Operations
Executive Vice President/General Manager: Andy MacPhail.
Vice President, Player Personnel: Terry Ryan.
Assistant General Manager: Bill Smith.
Administrative Assistant, Major League Operations: Jan Evans.
Director of Minor Leagues: Jim Rantz. **Minor League Secretary:** Colleen Schroeder.
Field Coordinator, Minor League System: Don Leppert.
Roving Instructors: Glenn Adams (batting), Dwight Bernard (pitching), Jerry White (outfield, baserunning).

Tom Kelly

Minor League Affiliates:
Class	Farm Team	Manager	Coach(es)
AAA	Portland	Scott Ullger	Gorman Heimueller, Paul Kirsch
AA	Orlando	Phil Roof	Jim Shellenback, Mark Funderburk
A	Visalia	Steve Liddle	Brian Allard
A	Kenosha	Jim Dwyer	Rick Anderson
Rookie	Elizabethton	Jim Lemon	Rick Tomlin, Ray Smith
Rookie	Ft. Myers	Dan Rohn	Eric Rasmussen

Scouting
Director of Scouting: Larry Corrigan. **Administrative Assistant:** Alison Walk.
Scouting Supervisors: Vern Followell (Lakewood, CA), Mike Radcliff (Overland Park, KS), Jeff Schugel (Winter Haven, FL).
Major League Scout: Jerry Terrell (Blue Springs, MO).
Special Assignment Scouts: Floyd Baker (Youngstown, OH), Don Cassidy (Robbinsdale, MN).
Scouts: Vern Borning (Ontario, CA), Enrique Brito (Val. Carabobo, Venez.), Ellsworth Brown (Beason, IL), Gene DeBoer (Brandon, WI), Dan Durst (Sycamore, IL), Cal Ermer (Chattanooga, TN), Marty Esposito (Hewitt, TX), Earl Frishman (Hermosa Beach, CA),

Jim Rantz

Angelo Giuliani (St. Paul, MN), Scott Groot (Costa Mesa, CA), Joel Lepel (Plato, MN), Bill Lohr (Centralia, WA), Kevin Murphy (Sunnyvale, CA), Howard Norsetter (Australia), Clair Rierson (Tempe, AZ), Eddie Robinson (Ft. Worth, TX), Edwin Rodriguez (Ponce, PR), Mike Ruth (Lee's Summit, MO), Johnny Sierra (Santo Domingo, Dom. Rep.), Herb Stein (Riverdale, NY), Ricky Taylor (Lexington, KY), Brad Weitzel (Jacksonville, FL), Steven Williams (Greenville, SC), John Wilson (Haledon, NJ).

Spring Training Information
Major League Club
Hotel Address: Courtyard Marriott, 4455 Metro Parkway, Ft. Myers, FL 33901. Telephone: (813) 275-8600. **Stadium Address:** Lee County Sports Complex, 14100 Six Mile Cypress Pkwy., Ft. Myers, FL 33912. Telephone: (813) 768-4200.

Minor League Clubs
Hotel Address: Ramada Inn, 12635 Cleveland Ave. (Highway 41), Ft. Myers, FL 33907. Telephone: (813) 936-4300. **Complex Address:** same as major league club.

NEW YORK

Office Address: Yankee Stadium, Bronx, NY 10451. Mailing Address: same. Telephone: (212) 293-4300. FAX: (212) 293-8431.
Operated by: New York Yankees.

Ownership, Management
Principal Owner: George Steinbrenner. **Managing General Partner:** Daniel McCarthy.

Limited Partners: Harold Bowman, Daniel Crown, James Crown, Lester Crown, Michael Friedman, Marvin Goldklang, Barry Halper, Harvey Leighton, Daniel McCarthy, Harry Nederlander, James Nederlander, Robert Nederlander, William Rose Sr., Edward Rosenthal, Jack Satter, Joan Steinbrenner, Charlotte Witkind, Richard Witkind.

Gene Michael

Executive Vice President and Chief Operating Officer: Leonard Kleinman. **Vice President:** Joseph Molloy. **Senior Vice President:** Arthur Richman. **Vice President, Chief of Operations:** John Lawn.

Vice President, Marketing: John Fugazy. **Vice President, Community Relations:** Richard Kraft. **Vice President:** Ed Weaver. **Vice President, General Counsel and Secretary:** David Sussman.

Vice President of Finance, Chief Financial Officer: Barry Pincus. **Controller:** Steven Dauria.

Director of Administration: Hal Steinbrenner.

General Administration
Director of Media Relations and Publicity: Jeff Idelson. **Assistant Director of Media Relations and Publicity:** Brian Walker. **Assistant Directors of Public Relations:** Ed Angelino, Keith Wiarda.

Director, Special Events: Bob Pelegrino. **Director of Video Operations:** John Franzone. **Assistant Director of Video Operations:** Tim Beach. **Director of Entertainment:** Stanley Kay.

Director of Publications: Tom Bannon. **Assistant Director of Publications:** Gregg Mazzola. **Director of Television and Video Production:** Joe Violone.

Director of Stadium Operations: Tim Hassett. **Director of Customer Services:** Joel White. **Assistant Director of Stadium Operations:** Patrick McGrew. **Assistant Director of Customer Services:** David Bernstein.

Vice President, Ticket Operations: Frank Swaine. **Executive Director of Ticket Operations:** Jeff Kline. **Ticket Director:** Ken Skrypek. **Director of Group and Season Sales:** Debbie Tymon.

Team Physician: Dr. Stuart Hershon. **Head Trainer:** Gene Monahan. **Assistant Trainer:** Steve Donohue.

Radio, TV
Radio Announcers: Michael Kay, John Sterling. **Flagship Station:** WABC 770 AM.

TV Announcers: Tom Seaver, Phil Rizzuto, Bobby Murcer. **Flagship Stations:** WPIX Channel 11, MSG Network.

1992 Schedule

APRIL
7-9	Boston
10-11-12	at Detroit
13-14-15-16	at Toronto
17-18-19-20	Cleveland
21-22	at Chicago
24-25-26	Baltimore
27-28-29	Texas

MAY
1-2-3	Minnesota
4-5	at Seattle
6-7	at California
8-9-10	at Oakland
12-13	Seattle
15-16-17	Oakland
18-19-20	California
22-23-24-25	Milwaukee
26-27	at Minnesota
29-30-31	at Milwaukee

JUNE
1-2-3	at Texas
4-5-6-7	Detroit
8-9-10	Toronto
12-13-14	at Cleveland
15-16-17-18	at Boston
19-20-21-22	at Baltimore
23-24-25	at Kansas City
26-27-28	Chicago
29-30	Kansas City

JULY
1	Kansas City
3-4-5	at Texas
6-7-8	Minnesota
9-10-11-12	Seattle
16-17-18-19	at California
20-21-22	at Oakland
23-24-25-26	at Seattle
28-29-30	Baltimore
31	at Toronto

AUGUST
1-2	at Toronto
3-4-5	Cleveland
6-7-8-9	Boston
10-11-12	at Detroit
14-15-16-17	at Chicago
18-19-20	Oakland
21-22-23	California
24-25-26	Milwaukee
27-28-29-30	at Minnesota
31	at Milwaukee

SEPTEMBER
1-2	at Milwaukee
4-5-6	Texas
7-8-9	at Baltimore
11-12-13	Kansas City
14-15-16	Chicago
18-19-20	at Kansas City
22-23-24	Detroit
25-26-27	Toronto
28-29-30	at Cleveland

OCTOBER
2-3-4	at Boston

YANKEES

Major League Staff
Manager: Buck Showalter.
Coaches: Clete Boyer, Tony Cloninger, Mark Connor, Frank Howard, Monk Meyer, Ed Napoleon.

Baseball Operations
Vice President and General Manager: Gene Michael. **Assistant General Manager:** Bill Bergesch. **Assistant to General Manager:** Peter Jameson.
Vice President, Player Development and Scouting: Brian Sabean.
Director of Minor League Operations: Mitch Lukevics. **Assistant, Minor League Operations:** Jeff Mercer. **Controller, Minor Leagues:** Mike Macaluso.
Minor League Coordinator: Mark Newman.
Roving Instructors: Joe Lefebvre (hitting), Shawn Powell (strength and conditioning). **Head Trainer and Rehabilitation Supervisor:** Kevin Rand.

Buck Showalter

Minor League Affiliates:

Class	Farm Team	Manager	Coach(es)
AAA	Columbus	Rick Down	Mike Brown, Ted Uhlaender, Hop Cassady
AA	Albany	Dan Radison	Dave Jorn, Rob Thomson
A	Prince William	Mike Hart	Dave Schuler, Ken Dominguez
A	Fort Lauderdale	Brian Butterfield	Mark Shiflett, Bob Mariano
A	Greensboro	Trey Hillman	Mark Rose, Brian Milner
A	Oneonta	Jack Gillis	Fernando Arango, Joel Grampietro, Bill Schmidt
Rookie	Tampa	Gary Denbo	Hoyt Wilhelm, Rich Arena

Scouting
Office Address: Yankee Complex, 3102 N. Himes Ave., Tampa, FL 33607. Telephone: (813) 875-7753. FAX: (813) 873-2302.
Scouting Director: Bill Livesey. **Assistant Scouting Director:** Kevin Elfering.
Major League/Advance Scouts: Brandy Davis (Newark, DE), Ron Hansen (Baldwin, MD), Ron Hassey (Tucson, AZ), Clyde King (Goldsboro, NC), Bob Lemon (Long Beach, CA), Dick Tidrow (Lees Summit, MO).
Scouting Supervisors: Jack Gillis (Sarasota, FL), Don Lindeberg (Anaheim, CA), Stan Saleski (Dayton, OH).
Special Assignment Scouts: Walt Dixon (Florence, SC), Jack Llewellyn (Englewood, FL), Jim Naples (Buffalo, NY).
Scouts: Fernando Arango (Oklahoma City, OK), Mark Batchko (Arlington, TX), Joe DiCarlo (Ringwood, NJ), Lee Elder (Evans, GA), Bill Geivett (Long Beach, CA), Joel Grampietro (Shrewsbury, MA), Dick Groch (Marysville, MI), Tim Kelly (New Lenox, IL), Carl Moesche (Portland, OR), Greg Orr (Sacramento, CA), Herb Raybourn (Bradenton, FL), Joe Robison (Dayton, TX), Rudy Santin (Miami, FL), Bill Schmidt (Garden Grove, CA), Jeff Taylor (Newark, DE), Paul Turco (Sarasota, FL), Leon Wurth (Franklin, TN).

Spring Training Information
Major League Club
Hotel Address: Palm Aire Spa Resort, 2501 Palm Aire Drive North, Pompano Beach, FL 33069. Telephone: (305) 972-3300. **Stadium Address:** Fort Lauderdale Stadium, 5301 NW 12th Ave., Fort Lauderdale, FL 33309. Telephone: (305) 776-1921.

Minor League Clubs
Hotel Address: Unavailable. **Complex Address:** Yankee Complex, 3102 N. Himes Ave., Tampa, FL 33607. Telephone: (813) 875-7753.

OAKLAND

Office Address: Oakland-Alameda County Coliseum, Oakland, CA 94621. **Mailing Address:** same. **Telephone:** (510) 638-4900. **FAX:** (510) 568-3770.

Operated by: The Oakland Athletics Baseball Company.

Ownership, Management

Owner/Managing General Partner: Walter A. Haas.
President and Chief Operating Officer: Walter J. Haas.
Vice President, Business Operations: Andy Dolich.
Vice President, Finance: Kathleen McCracken.
Vice President, Administration, Personnel: Raymond Krise.

Sandy Alderson

General Administration

Director of Baseball Information: Jay Alves.
Director of Media Relations: Kathy Jacobson.
Director of Team Travel: Mickey Morabito.
Director of Season Ticket Sales: Barbara Reilly. **Director of Group Sales:** Bettina Flores.
Director of Stadium Operations: Kevin Kahn.
Director of Publications: Rob Kelly.
Director of Sales: John Kamperschroer.
Director of Broadcasting: Tom Cordova.
Director of Business Administration: Alan Ledford.
Director of Promotions: Sharon Kelly.
Assistant to the President, Community Affairs: Reggie Jackson.
Director of Community Affairs: Dave Perron.
Team Physician: Dr. Allan Pont.
Team Orthopedist: Dr. Rick Bost.
Equipment Manager: Frank Ciensczyk. **Visiting Clubhouse Manager:** Steve Vucinich.
Trainer: Barry Weinberg. **Assistant Trainer:** Larry Davis.

Radio, TV

Radio Announcers: Bill King, Lon Simmons, Ray Fosse. **Flagship Station:** KSFO 560 AM.
TV Announcers: Ray Fosse, Monte Moore. **Flagship Station:** KPIX Channel 5.

1992 Schedule

APRIL
6-8-9 .... Kansas City
10-11-12 .... Chicago
13-14-15-16 .... at K.C.
17-18-19 .... at Texas
20-21-22 .... California
24-25-26 .... at Minnesota
28-29 .... at Cleveland
30 .... at Detroit

MAY
1-2-3 .... at Detroit
4-5 .... Toronto
6-7 .... Detroit
8-9-10 .... New York
12-13 .... at Toronto
15-16-17 .... at New York
18-19-20 .... at Baltimore
22-23-24 .... at Boston
25-26-27 .... Cleveland
29-30-31 .... Baltimore

JUNE
1-2-3 .... Boston
5-6-7 .... at Chicago
8-9-10 .... at Milwaukee
12-13-14 .... Texas
15-16-17 .... Milwaukee
19-20-21 .... at California
22-23-24 .... Seattle
25-26-27-28 .... Minnesota
29-30 .... at Seattle

JULY
1 .... at Seattle
3-4-5-6 .... at Cleveland
7-8 .... at Detroit
9-10-11-12 .... at Toronto
16-17-18-19 .... Detroit
20-21-22 .... New York
23-24-25-26 .... Toronto
27-28-29 .... at Minnesota
31 .... at Kansas City

AUGUST
1-2 .... at Kansas City
3-4-5-6 .... at Texas
7-8-9 .... Kansas City

10-11-12 .... Chicago
13-14-15-16 .... California
18-19-20 .... at New York
21-22-23 .... at Baltimore
24-25-26 .... at Boston
28-29-30 .... Cleveland
31 .... Baltimore

SEPTEMBER
1-2 .... Baltimore
4-5-6 .... Boston
7-8-9 .... at California
10-11-12-13 .... Seattle
14-15-16 .... Minnesota
18-19-20 .... at Seattle
21-22-23-24 .... at Chicago
25-26-27 .... at Milwaukee
29-30 .... Texas

OCTOBER
1 .... Texas
2-3-4 .... Milwaukee

ATHLETICS

Major League Staff
Manager: Tony LaRussa.
Coaches: Dave Duncan, Art Kusnyer, Rene Lachemann, Dave McKay, Doug Rader, Tommie Reynolds.

Baseball Operations
Vice President, Baseball Operations: Sandy Alderson. **Assistant, Baseball Matters:** Bill Rigney. **Special Assistant for Baseball Operations:** Karl Kuehl.
Director of Baseball Administration: Walt Jocketty. **Assistant Director of Baseball Administration:** Pamela Pitts. **Administrative Assistants:** Ted Polakowski, Jennella Roark.
Director of Player Development: Keith Lieppman.
Instructors: Harvey Dorfman, Brad Fischer, Ron Plaza, Wes Stock.

Tony LaRussa

Minor League Affiliates:

Class	Farm Team	Manager	Coach(es)
AAA	Tacoma	Bob Boone	Glenn Abbott, Mitchell Page
AA	Huntsville	Casey Parsons	Bert Bradley
A	Modesto	Ted Kubiak	Pete Richert
A	Reno	Gary Jones	Scott Budner
A	Madison	Dick Scott	Gil Patterson
A	So. Oregon	Unavailable	Jim Slaton
Rookie	Scottsdale	Bruce Hines	Rick Rodriguez

Scouting
Director of Scouting: Dick Bogard. **Assistant Scouting Director:** Eric Kubota.
National Crosscheckers: Grady Fuson (Stockton, CA), Dave Roberts (Portland, OR), Jeff Scott (Bourbonnais, IL).
Scouting Supervisors: J.P. Ricciardi (West Boylston, MA), Ron Vaughn (Walnut, CA).
Advance Scouts: Billy Beane (San Diego, CA), Mike Paul (Tucson, AZ).
Scouts: Tony Arias (Miami, FL), Billy Bowman (Castro Valley, CA), Mark Conkin (Kingsport, TN), Tim Corcoran (La Verne, CA), Ed Crosby (Cypress, CA), Bill Gayton (Katy, TX), Michael Jones (Scottsville, VA), John Kazanas (Phoenix, AZ), Billy Merkel (Columbia, TN), Bill Meyer (Tampa, FL), Marty Miller (Chicago, IL), Steve Nichols (Tulsa, OK), Chris Pittaro (Trenton, NJ), Mike Stafford (Waterloo, IN), Craig Wallenbrock (Arcadia, CA).

Walt Jocketty

Spring Training Information

Major League Club
Hotel Address: Doubletree Suites, 320 North 44th St., Phoenix, AZ 85008. Telephone: (602) 225-0500. **Stadium Address:** Phoenix Municipal Stadium, 5999 East Van Buren, Phoenix, AZ 85258. Telephone: (602) 225-9400.

Minor League Clubs
Hotel Address: Days Inn Scottsdale Resort, 4710 North Scottsdale Rd., Scottsdale, AZ 85251. Telephone: (602) 947-5411. **Complex Address:** Scottsdale Community College, 9000 E. Chaparral Rd., Scottsdale, AZ 85251. Telephone: (602) 949-5951.

SEATTLE

Office Address: 411 1st Ave. S., Suite 480, Seattle, WA 98104. **Mailing Address:** P.O. Box 4100, Seattle, WA 98104. **Telephone:** (206) 628-3555. **FAX:** (206) 628-3340.
Operated by: Seattle Mariners, L.P.

Ownership, Management
Principal Owner and Chairman: Jeff Smulyan.
President: Gary Kaseff.
Vice President, Finance and Administration: Brian Beggs.
Vice President, Marketing: Stuart Layne.
Vice President, Communications: Randy Adamack.

Woody Woodward

General Administration
Director of Public Relations: Dave Aust. **Assistant Director of Public Relations:** Pete Vanderwarker.
Director of Community Relations: Joe Chard.
Director of Corporate Marketing: Greg Elliott.
Director of Promotions: Carl Weinstein.
Director of Team Travel: Craig Detwiler.
Director of Ticket Services: J.C. Crouch. **Director of Ticket Sales:** Chris McCartney.
Director of Stadium Operations: Tony Pereira.
Controller: Denise Podosek. **Accounting Assistant:** Shirley Shreve.
Senior Account Executive: Al "Moose" Clausen.
Club Physicians: Dr. Larry Pedegana, Dr. Mitchel Storey.
Trainer: Rick Griffin.

Radio, TV
Radio-TV Announcer: Dave Niehaus. **Flagship Stations:** KIRO-AM 710, KSTW-TV 11.

1992 Schedule

APRIL		
6-7-8-9	....	Texas
10-11-12	......	Kansas City
13-15-16	......	at Chicago
17-18-19	....	at Milwaukee
20-21-22-23	...	Minnesota
24-25-26	.....	at California
28-29	....	at Detroit

MAY		
1-2-3	....	at Baltimore
4-5	....	New York
6-7	....	Toronto
8-9-10	....	Detroit
12-13	....	at New York
14-15-16-17	...	at Toronto
18-19-20	......	at Boston
22-23-24	....	Cleveland
25-26-27	....	Baltimore
29-30-31	....	Boston

JUNE		
2-3-4	....	at Cleveland
5-6-7	......	at Kansas City
8-9-10	....	at Texas
12-13-14	......	Milwaukee
15-16-17-18	.....	Chicago
19-20-21	....	at Minnesota
22-23-24	....	at Oakland
25-26-27-28	....	California
29-30	....	Oakland

JULY		
1	....	Oakland
3-4-5-6	....	at Detroit
7-8	....	at Toronto
9-10-11-12	....	at New York
16-17-18-19	......	Toronto
20-21-22	....	Detroit
23-24-25-26	....	New York
27-28-29-30	..	at California
31	....	at Chicago

AUGUST		
1-2	....	at Chicago
4-5-6	....	at Milwaukee
7-8-9	....	Texas
10-11-12	.....	Kansas City
14-15-16	....	Minnesota
18-19-20	.....	at Baltimore
21-22-23	....	at Boston
25-26-27	....	Cleveland
28-29-30	....	Baltimore
31	....	Boston

SEPTEMBER		
1-2	....	Boston
4-5-6	....	at Cleveland
7-8-9	....	at Minnesota
10-11-12-13	...	at Oakland
15-16	....	California
18-19-20	....	Oakland
21-22-23-24	....	at K.C.
25-26-27	....	at Texas
29-30	....	Milwaukee

OCTOBER		
1	....	Milwaukee
2-3-4	....	Chicago

MARINERS

Major League Staff
Manager: Bill Plummer.
Coaches: Gene Clines, Roger Hansen, Rusty Kuntz, Marty Martinez, Russ Nixon, Dan Warthen.

Baseball Operations
Vice President, Baseball Operations: Woody Woodward. **Assistant to Vice President, Baseball Operations:** George Zuraw.
Director of Baseball Administration: Lee Pelekoudas.
Director of Player Development: Jim Beattie. **Player Development and Scouting Assistant:** Larry Beinfest. **Administrative Assistants:** Nancy Droppelman, Debbie Larson.
Field Coordinator: Jim Skaalen.
Roving Instructors: Bobby Cuellar (pitching), Ralph Dickenson (hitting), Ken Griffey Sr., Cal McLish (special assignments), Steve Smith (infield).

Bill Plummer

Minor League Affiliates:

Class	Farm Team	Manager	Coach(es)
AAA	Calgary	Keith Bodie	Ross Grimsley
AA	Jacksonville	Bob Hartsfield	Mike Goff, Jeff Andrews
A	San Bernardino	Ivan De Jesus	Gary Wheelock, Tommy Cruz
A	Peninsula	Marc Hill	Paul Lindblad
A	Bellingham	Dave Myers	Bryan Price
Rookie	Tempe	Carlos Lezcano	Steve Murray, Bill Sizemore

Scouting
Vice President, Scouting and Player Development: Roger Jongewaard. **Administrative Assistant, Scouting:** Hallie Larson.
Major League and Special Assignment Scout: Bill Kearns (Milton, MA).
National Crosschecker: Bob Wadsworth (Westminster, CA). **National Supervisor and Crosschecker:** Benny Looper.
Scouting Supervisors: Gordon Blakeley (Valrico, FL), Ron Hopkins (Seattle, WA), Ken Madeja (Novi, MI).
Full-Time Scouts: Fernando Arguells (Miami, FL), John Burden (Fairfield, OH), Kendall Carter (Tempe, AZ), Ken Compton (Cypress, CA), Ramon de los Santos (Santo Domingo, Dom. Rep.), Dan Jennings (Mobile, AL), Dave Karaff (Raytown, MO), Jerry Marik (Chicago, IL), Joe Nigro (Staten Island, NY), Cliff Pastornicky (Benicia, CA), Steve Pope (Asheville, NC), John Ramey (Lakeland, FL), Chris Smith (The Woodlands, TX).

Roger Jongewaard

Spring Training Information
Major League Club
Hotel Address: Fiesta Inn, 2100 S. Priest Dr., Tempe, AZ 85282. Telephone: (602) 967-1441. **Stadium Address:** Tempe Diablo Stadium, 2200 W. Alameda, P.O. Box 28353, Tempe, AZ 85285. Telephone: (602) 438-8803.

Minor League Clubs
Hotel Address: Comfort Inn, 5300 S. 56th St., Tempe, AZ 85283. Telephone: (602) 820-7500. **Complex Address:** Same as major league stadium.

TEXAS

Office Address: 1250 Copeland Rd., Suite 1100, Arlington, TX 76011. **Mailing Address:** P.O. Box 90111, Arlington, TX 76004. **Telephone:** (817) 273-5222. **FAX:** (817) 273-5206.

Operated by: The Texas Rangers, Ltd.

Tom Grieve

Ownership, Management
General Partners: George W. Bush, Edward "Rusty" Rose.
President: J. Thomas Schieffer.
Vice President, Business Operations: John McMichael.
Vice President, Administration: Charles Wangner.
Vice President, Public Relations: John Blake.
Vice President, Ballpark Development: Jack Hill.
General Counsel: Gerald Haddock.

General Administration
Director, Publications: Larry Kelly.
Director, In-Park Entertainment and Broadcasting: Chuck Morgan.
Director of Promotions: Dave Fendrick.
Director of Sales and Customer Service: Jay Miller.
Director of Stadium Operations: Mat Stolley.
Director, Ticket Operations: John Schriever. **Assistant Director, Ticket Operations:** Ben Marthaler.
Director, Community Relations: Taunee Paur.
Director, Group Sales: Rich Billings.
Traveling Secretary: Dan Schimek.
Controller: Steve McNeill.
General Manager of Charlotte County Operations: Ted Guthrie.
Field Superintendent: Jim Anglea. **Assistant Field Superintendent:** Brad Richards.
Medical Director: Dr. Mike Mycoskie.
Spring Training Director: John Welaj.
Equipment and Home Clubhouse Manager: Joe Macko. **Visiting Clubhouse Manager:** Zack Minasian.

Radio, TV
Radio Announcers: Mark Holtz, Eric Nadel. **Flagship Station:** WBAP-AM 820.
TV Announcers: Steve Busby, Jim Sundberg, Norm Hitzges, Greg Lucas.
Flagship Stations: KTVT-TV 11, Home Sports Entertainment.

1992 Schedule

APRIL
6-7-8-9 ....at Seattle
10-11-12 ....at Minnesota
13-14-15-16 ....California
17-18-19 ....Oakland
21-22-23...........Detroit
24-25-26 ....at Boston
27-28-29 .....at New York
30 ....at Chicago

MAY
1-2-3 ....at Chicago
4-5 ....at Baltimore
6-7 ....Cleveland
8-9-10 ....Milwaukee
12-13 ....Baltimore
15-16-17 ....at Milwaukee
18-19-20....at Cleveland
21-22-23-24 ..Kansas City
26-27-28 ....Chicago
29-30-31 ...at Kansas City

JUNE
1-2-3 ....New York
4-5-6-7 ....Minnesota
8-9-10............Seattle
12-13-14 ......at Oakland
15-16-17 ....at California
19-20-21 ....Boston
22-23-24 ....Toronto
25-26-27-28 .....at Detroit
29-30 ....at Toronto

JULY
1 ....at Toronto
3-4-5 ....New York
6-7-8 ....Milwaukee
9-10-11-12 .....Cleveland
16-17-18-19 ....Baltimore
20-21-22 ...at Milwaukee
23-24-25-26 ..at Baltimore
27-28-29 ....at Boston
31 ....California

AUGUST
1-2 ....California
3-4-5-6 ....Oakland
7-8-9 ....at Seattle
10-11-12-13 .at Minnesota
14-15-16...........Detroit
18-19-20 ......at Chicago
21-22-23.....at Cleveland
25-26-27 .....Kansas City
28-29-30 ....Chicago
31 ....at Kansas City

SEPTEMBER
1-2 ....at Kansas City
4-5-6.........at New York
7-8-9..............Boston
11-12-13 ....Toronto
15-16 ....at Detroit
18-19-20 ....at Toronto
22-23 ....Minnesota
25-26-27 ....Seattle
29-30..........at Oakland

OCTOBER
1 ....at Oakland
2-3-4 ....at California

RANGERS

Major League Staff
Manager: Bobby Valentine.
Coaches: Ray Burris, Orlando Gomez, Toby Harrah, Tom House, Dave Oliver, Tom Robson.

Baseball Operations
Vice President/General Manager: Tom Grieve.
Assistant General Manager, Player Personnel and Scouting: Sandy Johnson.
Assistant General Manager: Wayne Krivsky.
Director, Player Development: Marty Scott.
Administrative Assistant, Minor Leagues: Monty Clegg.
Roving Instructors: Perry Hill (infield), Jim Lentine (hitting).

Bobby Valentine

Minor League Affiliates:

Class	Farm Team	Manager	Coach(es)
AAA	Oklahoma City	Tommy Thompson	Oscar Acosta, Mike Berger
AA	Tulsa	Bobby Jones	Jackson Todd, Randy Whisler
A	Charlotte	Bump Wills	Marvin White
A	Gastonia	Walt Williams	Gary Mielke, Stan Cliburn
Rookie	Butte	Victor Ramirez	Travis Walden, Doug Sisson
Rookie	Charlotte	Chino Cadahia	Rick Knapp, Darrin Garner

Scouting
Scouting Supervisors: Bill Earnhart (Pensacola, FL), Doug Gassaway (Blum, TX), Bryan Lambe (North Massapequa, NY), Omar Minaya (West New York, NJ), Len Strelitz (Temple City, CA).
Special Assignment Scout: Paddy Cottrell (Santa Clara, CA).
Scouts: Hector Acevedo (Santo Domingo, Dom. Rep.), Manuel Batista (Vega Alta, PR), Jim Benedict (Long Beach, CA), Ray Blanco (Miami, FL), Joe Branzell (Sarasota, FL), Agustin Castro (San Perdro de Macoris, Dom. Rep.), Marco Cobos (Panama), Dick Coury (Wheeling, WV), Mike Daughtry (Elgin, IL), Amado Dinzey (San Pedro de Macoris, Dom. Rep.),

Sandy Johnson

Jim Dreyer (Euless, TX), Kip Fagg (Vacaville, CA), Jim Fairey (Clemson, SC), Mike Grouse (Raytown, MO), Tim Hallgren (Clarkston, WA), Wayne Krivsky (Arlington, TX), Robert Lavallee (Plaistow, NH), John Littlefield (Bull Head City, AZ), Mike Piatnik (Winter Haven, FL), Antolin Reyes (San Pedro de Macoris, Dom. Rep.), Pat Rigby (Dallas, TX), Rodolfo Rosario (Santo Domingo, Dom. Rep.), Don Shwery (West Vancouver, B.C.), Randy Taylor (Houston, TX), Rudy Terrasas (Pasadena, TX), Danilo Troncoso (La Romana, Dom. Rep.), George Urribarri (Bolivar, Venezuela), Juan Valera (Juan Baron, Dom. Rep.), Boris Villa (Barranquilla, Colombia).

Spring Training Information

Major League Club
Hotel Address: Palm Island Resorts, 7092 Placida Rd., Cape Haze, FL 33946. Telephone: (813) 697-4800. **Stadium Address:** Charlotte County Stadium, 2300 El Jobean Rd., P.O. Box 3609, Port Charlotte, FL 33949. Telephone: (813) 625-9500.

Minor League Clubs
Hotel Address: Days Inn, Tamiami Trail, Murdock, FL 33938. Telephone: (813) 627-8900. **Complex Address:** same as major league stadium.

TORONTO

Office Address: 300 Bremner Blvd., Suite 3200, SkyDome, Toronto, Ontario, Canada M5V 3B3. **Mailing Address:** same. **Telephone:** (416) 341-1000. **FAX:** (416) 341-1250.
Operated by: Toronto Blue Jays Baseball Club.

Ownership, Management

Honorary Chairman: N.E. Hardy. **Chairman:** P.N.T. Widdrington.
Board of Directors: Paul Beeston, Peter Bronfman, John Craig Eaton, N.E. Hardy, John Morgan, Sidney Oland, G.W. Radford, Herb Solway, George Taylor, P.N.T. Widdrington.
President/Chief Executive Officer: Paul Beeston.
Vice President, Business: Bob Nicholson.

Pat Gillick

General Administration

Director of Public Relations: Howard Starkman. **Assistant Director of Public Relations:** Mark Leno.
Director of Stadium and Ticket Operations: George Holm. **Assistant Director of Ticket Operations, Box Office Manager:** Randy Low. **Manager of Ticket Vault Services:** Paul Goodyear. **Manager of Subscriber Services:** Mike Maunder. **Manager of Event Ticket Services:** Allan Koyanagi. **Manager of Mail Order Services:** Doug Barr.
Assistant Director and Manager of Field Operations: Len Frejlich.
Director of Marketing: Paul Markle.
Manager of Promotions and Advertising: Rick Amos.
Director of Finance: Susan Quigley.
Manager of Group Sales: Maureen Haffey.
Manager of Team Travel: John Brioux.
Manager of Game Operations: Mario Coutinho. **Supervisor of Grounds:** Brad Bujold. **Manager of Security:** Fred Wootton. **Supervisor of Game Services:** Mick Bazinet.
Trainer: Tommy Craig. **Assistant Trainer:** Brent Andrews.
Clubhouse Managers: Jeff Ross (Blue Jays), Ian Duff (visitors).
Team Physician: Dr. Ron Taylor. **Consulting Orthopedic Surgeons:** Dr. James Andrews, Dr. Allan Gross, Dr. Martin Kornreich.

Radio, TV

Radio Announcers: Tom Cheek, Jerry Howarth. **Flagship Station:** CJCL-AM 1430.
TV Announcers: Don Chevrier, Jim Hughson, Buck Martinez, Fergie Oliver. **Flagship Stations:** CFTO-TV 9, TSN Cable TV.

1992 Schedule

APRIL
6-8-9 .... at Detroit
10-11-12 .... Baltimore
13-14-15-16 .... New York
17-18-19-20 .... at Boston
21-22-23 .... Cleveland
24-25-26 ..... Kansas City
28-29 .... California
30 .... at Milwaukee

MAY
1-2-3 .... at Milwaukee
4-5 .... at Oakland
6-7 .... at Seattle
8-9-10 .... at California
12-13 .... Oakland
14-15-16-17 .... Seattle
18-19-20 .... Minnesota
22-23-24 .... at Chicago
26-27 .... Milwaukee
29-30-31 .... Chicago

JUNE
1-2-3 .... at Minnesota
5-6-7 .... at Baltimore
8-9-10 .... at New York
11-12-13-14 .... Boston
16-17-18 .... Detroit
19-20-21 .. at Kansas City
22-23-24 .... at Texas
26-27-28 ... at Cleveland
29-30 .... Texas

JULY
1 .... Texas
3-4-5-6 .... California
7-8 .... Seattle
9-10-11-12 .... Oakland
16-17-18-19 ... at Seattle
20-21-22 ..... at California
23-24-25-26 ... at Oakland
28-29-30 ..... Kansas City
31 .... New York

AUGUST
1-2 .... New York
3-4-5 .... at Boston
6-7-8-9 .... at Detroit
10-11-12-13 .... Baltimore
14-15-16 ..... at Cleveland
18-19-20 .... at Milwaukee
21-22-23 .... at Minnesota
24-25-26 ...... at Chciago
27-28-29-30 ... Milwaukee
31 .... Chicago

SEPTEMBER
1-2 .... Chicago
4-5-6 .... Minnesota
7-8-9 ...... at Kansas City
11-12-13 .... at Texas
14-15-16-17 .... Cleveland
18-19-20 .... Texas
22-23-24 ..... at Baltimore
25-26-27 .... at New York
29-30 .... Boston

OCTOBER
2-3-4 .... Detroit

BLUE JAYS

Major League Staff
Manager: Cito Gaston.
Coaches: Bob Bailor, Galen Cisco, Rich Hacker, Larry Hisle, John Sullivan, Gene Tenace.

Baseball Operations
Executive Vice President, Baseball: Pat Gillick.
Special Assistant to Executive Vice President: Al Widmar.
Vice Presidents, Baseball: Al LaMacchia, Bob Mattick.
Assistant General Manager: Gord Ash.
Administrator, Player Personnel: Bob Nelson.
Administrative Assistants: Heather Connolly, Donna Kuzoff, Trina Hiscock.
Director, Player Development: Mel Queen.
Roving Instructors: Scott Breeden (pitching), Bill Buckner (hitting), Bob Didier (catching), Jim Hoff (infield, baserunning), Willie Upshaw (hitting).

Cito Gaston

Minor League Affiliates:
Class	Farm Team	Manager	Coach(es)
AAA	Syracuse	Nick Leyva	Rocket Wheeler, John Poloni
AA	Knoxville	Garth Iorg	Mike McAlpin, Steve Mingori
A	Dunedin	Dennis Holmberg	Hector Torres, Bill Monbouquette
A	Myrtle Beach	Doug Ault	Darren Balsley, Leroy Stanton
A	St. Catharines	J.J. Cannon	Rolando Pino, Reggie Cleveland
Rookie	Medicine Hat	Jim Nettles	Gilbert Rondon
Rookie	Charlotte	Omar Malave	Randy Phillips

Scouting
Director of Scouting: Bob Engle (Manheim, PA).
Director of International Scouting: Wayne Morgan (Morgan Hill, CA). **Director of Canadian Scouting:** Bob Prentice (Toronto). **Coordinator of Latin American Scouting:** Epy Guerrero (Santo Domingo, D.R.).
Major League Advance Scout: Don Welke (Louisville, KY).
Special Assignment Scouts: Moose Johnson (Arvada, CO), Tim Wilken (Dunedin, FL), Gordon Lakey (Houston, TX).
Scouts: David Blume (Elk Grove, CA), Chris Bourjos (Chicago, IL), Chris Buckley (Temple Terrace, FL), Ellis Clary (Valdosta, GA), John Cole (Irvine, CA),

Gord Ash

Ellis Dungan (Pensacola, FL), Joe Ford (Yukon, OK), Tim Hewes (Bakersfield, CA), Tom Hinkle (Atascadero, CA), Jim Hughes (McKinney, TX), Duane Larson (Harrisburg, NC), Ted Lekas (Worcester, MA), Ben McLure (Palmyra, PA), Andy Pienovi (Portland, OR), Jorge Rivera (Puerto Nuevo, PR), Mark Snipp (Fort Worth, TX), Jerry Sobeck (San Jose, CA), Neil Summers (Merrick, NY), Ron Tostenson (Stanton, CA).

Spring Training Information

Major League Club
Hotel Address: Ramada Inn Countryside, 2560 U.S. 19 North, Clearwater, FL 34621. Telephone: (813) 796-1234. **Stadium Address:** Dunedin Stadium, 350 Douglas Ave., Dunedin, FL 34698. Telephone: (813) 733-9302.

Minor League Clubs
Hotel Address: same as major league club. **Complex Address:** Cecil P. Englebert Recreational Complex, 1700 Solon Ave., Dunedin, FL 34698. Telephone: (813) 733-9302.

NATIONAL LEAGUE

NATIONAL LEAGUE

Mailing Address: 350 Park Ave., New York, NY 10022.
Telephone: (212) 339-7700.
President and Treasurer: Bill White.
Senior Vice President and Secretary: Phyllis Collins.
Executive Committee: Houston, Pittsburgh, St. Louis.
Director of Umpiring Supervision: Ed Vargo.
Vice President, Director of Media and Public Affairs: Katy Feeney.
Executive Secretary: Valerie Dietrich.
Assistant Secretary and Manager, Player Records: Nancy Crofts.
Administrative Assistant: Cathy Davis.
Public Relations Assistant: Dorsey Parker.
Years League Active: 1876-1992.
1992 Opening Date: April 6. **Closing Date:** Oct. 4.
No. of Games: 162.
Division Structure: East—Chicago, Montreal, New York, Philadelphia, Pittsburgh, St. Louis. **West**—Atlanta, Cincinnati, Houston, Los Angeles, San Diego, San Francisco.
Roster Limit: 25.
Umpires: Greg Bonin (Lafayette, LA), Gerry Crawford (Havertown, PA), Gary Darling (Gilbert, AZ), Bob Davidson (Altoona, IA), Gerry Davis (Appleton, WI), Dana DeMuth (Upland, CA), Bruce Froemming (Brown Deer, WI), Eric Gregg (Philadelphia, PA), Tom Hallion (Louisville, KY), Doug Harvey (San Diego, CA), Mark Hirschbeck (Stratford, CT), Bill Hohn (Trappe, PA), Jerry Layne (Winter Haven, FL), Randy Marsh (Edgewood, KY), John McSherry (Santee, CA), Ed Montague (San Mateo, CA), Frank Pulli (Palm Harbor, FL), Jim Quick (Incline Village, CA), Ed Rapuano (North Haven, CT), Charlie Reliford (Ashland, KY), Dutch Rennert (Oshkosh, WI), Steve Rippley (Largo, FL), Paul Runge (El Cajon, CA), Terry Tata (Cheshire, CT), Harry Wendelstedt (Ormond Beach, FL), Joe West (Greenville, NC), Charles Williams (Chicago, IL), Mike Winters (San Diego, CA).

Bill White

1991 Standings

East	W	L	Pct.	GB
Pittsburgh	98	64	.605	—
St. Louis	84	78	.519	14
Philadelphia	78	84	.481	20
Chicago	77	83	.481	20
New York	77	84	.475	20½
Montreal	71	90	.441	26½

West	W	L	Pct.	GB
*Atlanta	94	68	.580	—
Los Angeles	93	69	.574	1
San Diego	84	78	.519	10
San Francisco	75	87	.463	19
Cincinnati	74	88	.457	20
Houston	65	97	.401	29

*Won League Championship Series

Stadium Information

City	Stadium	LF	CF	RF	Capacity	'91 Att.
Atlanta	Fulton County	330	402	330	52,007	2,140,217
Chicago	Wrigley Field	355	400	353	38,710	2,314,250
Cincinnati	Riverfront	330	404	330	52,392	2,372,377
Houston	Astrodome	330	400	330	54,816	1,196,152
Los Angeles	Dodger	330	400	330	56,000	3,348,170
Montreal	Olympic	325	404	325	60,011	978,045
New York	Shea	338	410	338	55,601	2,284,484
Philadelphia	Veterans	330	408	330	62,382	2,050,012
Pittsburgh	Three Rivers	335	400	335	58,729	2,065,302
St. Louis	Busch	330	414	330	54,224	2,449,537
San Diego	SD Jack Murphy	327	405	327	59,022	1,804,289
San Francisco	Candlestick Park	335	400	335	58,000	1,737,479

ATLANTA

Office Address: 521 Capitol Ave., Atlanta, GA 30312. **Mailing Address:** P.O. Box 4064, Atlanta, GA 30302. **Telephone:** (404) 522-7630. **FAX:** (404) 614-1391.

Operated by: Atlanta National Baseball Club, Inc.

Ownership, Management

Chairman of the Board: Bill Bartholomay.
Board of Directors: Henry Aaron, Bill Bartholomay, Bobby Cox, Bob Hope, Stan Kasten, Rubye Lucas, Terence McGuirk, John Schuerholz, M.B. Seretean, Allison Thornwell, Ted Turner.
President: Stan Kasten.
Senior Vice President and Assistant to President: Hank Aaron.
Senior Vice President of Administration and Finance: Charles Sanders.
Vice President, Director of Marketing and Broadcasting: Wayne Long.

John Schuerholz

General Administration

Director of Public Relations: Jim Schultz. **Media Relations Manager:** Glen Serra. **Publications Manager:** Mike Ringering.
Director, Community Relations: Danny Goodwin.
Director of Stadium Operations and Security: Terri Brennan.
Director of Ticket Sales: Jack Tyson.
Ticket Distribution Manager: Ed Newman.
Director of Promotions: Miles McRea.
Assistant Controller: Chip Moore.
Equipment Manager and Traveling Secretary: Bill Acree. **Assistant Equipment Manager:** Casey Stephenson. **Visiting Clubhouse Manager:** John Holland.
Trainer: Dave Pursley. **Assistant Trainer:** Jeff Porter.
Team Physician: Dr. David Watson. **Associate Physicians:** Dr. Robert Crow, Dr. John Cantwell.

Radio, TV

Radio-TV Announcers: Skip Caray, Pete Van Wieren, Don Sutton, Joe Simpson. **Flagship Stations:** WGST 640-AM, WPCH 95-FM, TBS Channel 17, SportSouth.

1992 Schedule

APRIL
- 7-8 .... at Houston
- 9-10-11-12 . San Francisco
- 13-14-15 ..... at Cincinnati
- 16-17-18-19 .... at L.A.
- 20-21-22 ... at San Diego
- 24-25-26 .... Houston
- 27-28-29 .... Chicago

MAY
- 1-2-3 .... New York
- 4-5 .... at Chicago
- 6-7 .... at Pittsburgh
- 8-9-10-11 ..... at St. Louis
- 12-13-14 .... Pittsburgh
- 15-16-17 .... Montreal
- 18-19-20 .... St. Louis
- 22-23-24 ...... at Montreal
- 25-26-27 .. at Philadelphia
- 29-30-31 ..... at New York

JUNE
- 1-2-3 .... Philadelphia
- 5-6-7 .... at San Diego
- 8-9-10 ..... at Los Angeles
- 12-13-14 .... San Diego
- 15-16-17 ..... Los Angeles
- 18-19-20-21 .... Cincinnati
- 23-24 .... San Francisco
- 26-27-28 .... at Cincinnati
- 29-30 ... at San Francisco

JULY
- 1 .... at San Francisco
- 3-4-5 .... Chicago
- 6-7-8 .... New York
- 9-10-11-12 .... at Chicago
- 16-17-18-19 ... at Houston
- 21-22 .... at St. Louis
- 24-25-26 .... Pittsburgh
- 27-28-29 .... Houston
- 30-31 ... at San Francisco

AUGUST
- 1-2 ...... at San Francisco
- 4-5-6 .... Cincinnati
- 7-8-9-10 ..... Los Angeles
- 11-12-13 .... San Diego

(continued)
- 14-15-16-17 . at Pittsburgh
- 18-19-20 ...... at Montreal
- 21-22-23 .... St. Louis
- 25-26-27 .... Montreal
- 28-29-30 .. at Philadelphia
- 31 .... at New York

SEPTEMBER
- 1-2 .... at New York
- 4-5-6 .... Philadelphia
- 7-8 .... Los Angeles
- 9-10 .... Cincinnati
- 11-12-13 ..... at Houston
- 15-16-17 ..... at Cincinnati
- 18-19-20 .... Houston
- 21-22 ...... at Los Angeles
- 23-24 .... at San Francisco
- 25-26-27 .... at San Diego
- 29-30 ...... San Francisco

OCTOBER
- 1 .... San Francisco
- 2-3-4 .... San Diego

BRAVES

Major League Staff
Manager: Bobby Cox.
Coaches: Jim Beauchamp, Pat Corrales, Clarence Jones, Leo Mazzone, Jimy Williams, Ned Yost.

Baseball Operations
Executive Vice President and General Manager: John Schuerholz. **Assistant General Manager:** Dean Taylor. **Special Assistant to General Manager:** Paul Snyder
Director of Player Development and Scouting: Chuck LaMar. **Assistant Director of Player Development:** Rod Gilbreath. **Secretary:** Susan Bailey.
Minor League Field Coordinator: Bobby Dews.
Roving Instructors: Bruce Benedict (catching), Bill Fischer (pitching), Frank Fultz (strength and conditioning), Willie Stargell (hitting), Tack Wilson (hitting).

Bobby Cox

Minor League Affiliates:

Class	Farm Team	Manager	Coach(es)
AAA	Richmond	Chris Chambliss	Bruce Dal Canton, Sonny Jackson
AA	Greenville	Grady Little	Bill Slack, Mark Ross
A	Durham	Leon Roberts	Matt West, George Threadgill
A	Macon	Brian Snitker	Larry Jaster, Glenn Hubbard
Rookie	Pulaski	Randy Ingle	Cloyd Boyer, Fred Koenig
Rookie	Idaho Falls	Dave Hilton	Jerry Nyman, Phil Dale
Rookie	West Palm Beach	Jim Saul	Rick Albert, Ino Guerrero

Scouting
Assistant Scouting Director: Scott Proefrock. **Secretary:** Bobbie Cranford.
National Crosscheckers: Mike Arbuckle (Trenton, MO), Bart Braun (Vallejo, CA).
Regional Supervisors: Sonny Bowers (Waco, TX), Dean Jongewaard (Fountain Valley, CA), Paul Snyder (Lilburn, GA).
International Supervisor: Bill Clark (Columbia, MO).
Advance Scouts: Bill Lajoie (Osprey, FL), Fred Shaffer (New Castle, PA), Wes Westrum (Mesa, AZ), Bill Wight (Carmichael, CA), Don Williams (Paragould, AR), Bobby Wine (Morristown, PA).

Chuck LaMar

Scouts: Butch Baccala (Lake Oswego, OR), Stu Cann (Bradley, IL), Joe Caputo (Royersford, PA), Roy Clark (Martinsville, VA), Ray Corbett (Bryan, TX), Hep Cronin (Cincinnati, OH), Rob English (Duluth, GA), John Flannery (Lakewood, CA), Ralph Garr (Missouri City, TX), Steve Givens (Tallahassee, FL), Pedro Gonzalez (San Pedro de Macoris, Dom. Rep.), John Hagemann (Staten Island, NY), Jim Johnson (Alta Loma, CA), Brian Kohlscheen (York, NE), Deric Ladnier (Baton Rouge, LA), Scott Littlefield (Shrewsbury, MA), Robert Lucas (East Point, GA), Robyn Lynch (Albuquerque, NM), Scott Nethery (Tampa, FL), Jack Pierce (Leon, Mexico), Carlos Rios (Lantana, FL), Alex Smith (Jarrettsville, MD), Charlie Smith (Austin, TX), Ted Sparks (Atlanta, GA), Tony Stiel (Pontiac, MI), Bob Turzilli (Kinnelon, NJ), Dave Wilder (Berkeley, CA).

Spring Training Information

Major League Club
Hotel Address: Palm Beach Garden Marriott, 4000 RCA Blvd., Palm Beach Gardens, FL 33410. Telephone: (407) 622-8888. **Stadium Address:** Municipal Stadium, 715 Hank Aaron Drive, West Palm Beach, FL 33401. Telephone: (407) 683-6100.

Minor League Clubs
Hotel Address: Unavailable. **Complex Address:** same as major league stadium.

CHICAGO

Office Address: Wrigley Field, 1060 West Addison St., Chicago, IL 60613. **Mailing Address:** same. **Telephone:** (312) 404-2827. **FAX:** (312) 404-4000.

Operated by: Chicago National League Ball Club, Inc.

Ownership, Management

Board of Directors: Stanton Cook, chairman; Thomas Ayers; Charles Brumback; Donald Grenesko; Walter Massey; Andrew McKenna.

Executive Vice President, Business Operations: Mark McGuire.

Vice President, Marketing and Broadcasting: John McDonough.

Larry Himes

Vice President, Finance and Information Systems: Keith Bode.

Corporate Secretary: Stanley Gradowski.

Corporate Counsel: Geoff Anderson.

General Administration

Director of Media Relations: Sharon Pannozzo. **Assistant Director of Publications:** Ernie Roth.

Assistant Director of Marketing: Connie Kowal.

Director of Human Resources: Wendy Lewis.

Director of Stadium Operations: Tom Cooper. **Assistant Director of Stadium Operations:** Paul Rathje.

Director of Ticket Operations: Frank Maloney. **Assistant Director of Ticket Sales:** Bill Galante. **Assistant Director of Ticket Services:** Joe Kirchen.

Traveling Secretary: Peter Durso.

Equipment Manager: Yosh Kawano.

Team Physician: Dr. John Marquardt.

Head Trainer: John Fierro. **Assistant Trainer:** Dave Cilladi.

Radio, TV

Radio Announcers: Ron Santo, Thom Brennaman, Harry Caray. **TV Announcers:** Harry Caray, Thom Brennaman, Steve Stone. **Flagship Stations:** WGN 720 AM, WGN Channel 9.

1992 Schedule

APRIL		
7-8-9	at Philadelphia	
10-11-12	St. Louis	
14-15	at Pittsburgh	
17-18-19	at St. Louis	
20-21-22-23	Philadelphia	
24-25-26	Pittsburgh	
27-28-29	at Atlanta	

MAY	
1-2-3	at Cincinnati
4-5	Atlanta
6-7	Houston
8-9-10	Cincinnati
11-12-13	at Houston
15-16-17	at San Francisco
18-19-20	at Los Angeles
22-23-24	at San Diego
26-27-28	San Francisco
29-30-31	Los Angeles

JUNE	
1-2-3	San Diego
5-6-7	at Montreal
8-9-10	at St. Louis
12-13-14	Montreal
15-16-17	St. Louis
18-19-20-21	at Phil.
22-23-24-25	at New York
26-27-28	Philadelphia
29-30	New York

JULY	
1	New York
3-4-5	at Atlanta
6-7-8	Cincinnati
9-10-11-12	Atlanta
16-17-18-19	at Pittsburgh
20-21-22	at Cincinnati
24-25-26	at Houston
27-28-29	Pittsburgh
31	at New York

AUGUST	
1-2	at New York
3-4-5	at Montreal
6-7-8-9	New York
10-11-12	Montreal
13-14-15-16	Houston
18-19-20	at S.F.
21-22-23	at Los Angeles
24-25-26	at San Diego
28-29-30	San Francisco
31	Los Angeles

SEPTEMBER	
1-2	Los Angeles
4-5-6	San Diego
7-8-9	at Pittsburgh
11-12-13	at St. Louis
14-15	New York
16-17	Philadelphia
18-19-20	St. Louis
21-22	at New York
23-24	at Philadelphia
25-26-27	at Montreal
28-29-30	Pittsburgh

OCTOBER	
2-3-4	Montreal

CUBS

Major League Staff
Manager: Jim Lefebvre.
Coaches: Sammy Ellis, Chuck Cottier, Jose Martinez, Billy Connors, Tom Trebelhorn.

Baseball Operations
Executive Vice President, Baseball Operations: Larry Himes.
Senior Vice President, Baseball Operations: Jim Frey.
Assistant General Manager: Syd Thrift.
Director of Baseball Administration: Ned Colletti.
Director of Minor League Operations: Bill Harford Jr. **Administrative Assistant:** Patti Kargakis.
Minor League Coordinator/Hitting Instructor: Richie Zisk. **Pitching Coordinator:** Chuck Estrada.
Latin Coordinator: Sandy Alomar.
Roving Instructors: Mick Kelleher (infield), Jay Loviglio (infield, baserunning), Jimmy Piersall (outfield), Julio Valdez, Billy Williams.

Jim Lefebvre

Minor League Affiliates:
Class	Farm Team	Manager	Coach(es)
AAA	Iowa	Brad Mills	Rick Kranitz
AA	Charlotte	Marv Foley	Bill Earley
A	Winston-Salem	Bill Hayes	Lester Strode
A	Peoria	Steve Roadcap	Ray Sadecki
A	Geneva	Greg Mahlberg	Stan Kyles
A	Huntington	Phil Hannon	Joe Housey, Gil Kubski

Scouting
Vice President, Scouting and Player Development: Dick Balderson.
Assistant Director of Scouting: Scott Nelson.
Special Player Consultants: Hugh Alexander (Palm Harbor, FL), Jim Essian (Troy, MI), Eddie Lyons (Winston-Salem, NC).
National Supervisor: Larry Maxie (Upland, CA).
Regional Supervisors: Frank DeMoss (Fairmont, WV), Doug Mapson (Palmdale, CA), Earl Winn (Hattiesburg, MS).
Latin America Coordinator: Luis Rosa (Luquillo, PR).
Scouts: Bill Blitzer (Brooklyn, NY), Jeff Brookens (Chambersburg, PA), Bill Capps (Arlington, TX), Billy Champion (Shelby, NC), Bobby Gardner (Oviedo, FL), John Gracio (Mesa, AZ), Gene Handley (Huntington Beach, CA), Elmore Hill (Gastonia, NC), Joe Housey (Hollywood, FL), Toney Howell (Calumet City, IL), Spider Jorgensen (Cucamonga, CA), Gil Kubski (Granada Hills, CA), Dave Lottsfeldt (Mahtomedi, MN), Gregg Patterson (Baton Rouge, LA), Paul Provas (Houston, TX), John Stockstill (Overland Park, KS) Julio Valdez (Bani, Dom. Rep.).

Dick Balderson

Spring Training Information

Major League Club
Hotel Address: Mezona Motor Hotel, 250 W. Main St., Mesa, AZ 85201. Telephone: (602) 834-9233. **Stadium Address:** Ho Ho Kam Park, 1235 N. Center St., Mesa, AZ 85201. Telephone: (602) 461-0061.

Minor League Clubs
Hotel Address: Maricopa Motor Inn, 3 E. Main St., Mesa, AZ 85201. Telephone: (602) 834-6060. **Complex Address:** Fitch Park, 655 N. Center St., Mesa, AZ 85201. Telephone: (602) 844-2391.

CINCINNATI

Office Address: 100 Riverfront Stadium, Cincinnati, OH 45202. **Mailing Address:** same. **Telephone:** (513) 421-4510. **FAX:** (513) 421-7342.
Operated by: The Cincinnati Reds.

Ownership, Management
General Partner: Marge Schott. **Partners:** Frisch's Restaurants, Inc.; Carl Kroch; Carl Lindner; Multimedia, Inc.; Louis Nippert; Mrs. Louis Nippert; William Reik Jr.; George Strike.

General Administration
Publicity Director: Jon Braude. **Assistant Publicity Director:** Joe Kelley.

Bob Quinn

Director of Stadium Operations: Tim O'Connell.
Director of Marketing: Chip Baker. **Director of Speakers Bureau:** Gordy Coleman.
Controller: Ernie Brubaker.
Director of Ticket Department: John O'Brien. **Director of Season Ticket Sales:** Pat McCaffrey. **Director of Group Sales:** Susan Toomey.
Traveling Secretary: Joel Pieper.
Field Superintendent: Tony Swain.
Trainer: Larry Starr. **Assistant Trainer:** Doug Spreen.
Equipment Manager: Bernie Stowe.

Radio, TV
Radio-TV Announcers: Marty Brennaman, Gordy Coleman, Steve LaMar, Joe Nuxhall. **Flagship Stations:** WLW 700 AM, WLWT Channel 5.

1992 Schedule

APRIL		
6-7-8	....	San Diego
9-10-11-12	....	at Houston
13-14-15	....	Atlanta
17-18-19	......	at S.F.
20-21-22	..	at Los Angeles
24-25-26	....	at San Diego
28-29	....	Pittsburgh

MAY		
1-2-3	....	Chicago
4-5	....	at Pittsburgh
6-7	....	New York
8-9-10	......	at Chicago
12-13	......	at St. Louis
15-16-17	....	Philadelphia
18-19-20	.....	at Montreal
22-23-24	..	at Philadelphia
25-26-27	....	at New York
29-30-31	....	Montreal

JUNE		
2-3	....	St. Louis
4-5-6-7	....	at Los Angeles
8-9-10	...	at San Francisco
12-13-14	.....	Los Angeles
15-16-17	.....	San Francisco
18-19-20-21	....	at Atlanta
22-23-24	....	Houston
26-27-28	....	Atlanta
29-30	....	at Houston

JULY		
1	....	at Houston
2-3-4-5	....	at Pittsburgh
6-7-8	....	at Chicago
9-10-11-12	....	at Atlanta
16-17-18-19	....	St. Louis
20-21-22	....	Chicago
23-24-25-26	...	at St. Louis
27-28-29	...	at San Diego
31	....	Houston

AUGUST		
1-2-3	....	Houston
4-5-6	....	at Atlanta
7-8-9	.....	San Francisco
11-12-13	.....	Los Angeles
14-15-16	....	San Diego
17-18-19	..	at Philadelphia
21-22-23	......	at Montreal
24-25-26	....	Philadelphia
28-29-30	.....	at New York
31	....	Montreal

SEPTEMBER		
1-2	....	Montreal
3-4-5-6	....	New York
7-8	....	at Houston
9-10	....	at Atlanta
11-12-13	...	at San Diego
15-16-17	....	Atlanta
18-19-20	....	San Diego
21-22	....	Houston
23-24	......	at Los Angeles
25-26-27	....	at S.F.
29-30	....	Los Angeles

OCTOBER		
1	....	Los Angeles
2-3-4	......	San Francisco

REDS

Major League Staff
Manager: Lou Piniella.
Coaches: John McLaren, Jackie Moore, Tony Perez, Sam Perlozzo, Larry Rothschild.

Baseball Operations
Vice President and General Manager: Bob Quinn.
Administrative Assistant to General Manager: Joyce Pfarr.
Special Player Consultant: Chief Bender.
Director of Player Development: Jim Bowden.
Administrative Assistant: Lois Schneider.
Minor League Field Coordinator: Jim Tracy.
Roving Instructors: Jose Cardenal (outfield and baserunning), Don Gullett (pitching), Jim Hickman (hitting), Ron Oester (infield).

Lou Piniella

Minor League Affiliates:
Class	Farm Team	Manager	Coach(es)
AAA	Nashville	Pete Mackanin	Frank Funk, Jim Lett
AA	Chattanooga	Dave Miley	Mike Griffin
A	Cedar Rapids	Mark Berry	Mack Jenkins
A	Charleston, W.Va.	P.J. Carey	Derek Botelho
Rookie	Princeton	Sam Mejias	Doc Rodgers
Rookie	Billings	Donnie Scott	Terry Abbott

Scouting
Director of Scouting: Julian Mock (Daphne, AL).
Administrative Assistant, Scouting: Wilma Mann.
Consulting Scouts: Paul Campbell (Fairfield Glade, TN), Tony Robello (Ft. Worth, TX).
Scouting Supervisors: Johnny Almaraz (San Antonio, TX), Jeff Barton (Santa Ana, CA), Larry Barton Jr. (Fontana, CA), Ray Bellino (Jersey City, NJ), Gene Bennett (Wheelersburg, OH), Jack Bowen (Bethel Park, PA), George Brill (Tigard, OR), Dave Calaway (Rosamond, CA), Clay Daniel (Orlando, FL), Cal Emery (Centre Hall, PA), Paul Faulk (Laurinburg, NC), Les Houser (Albuquerque, NM), David Jennings (St. Charles, MO), Eddie Kolo (Liverpool, NY), Kevin Pearson (Muskogee, OK), Tom Severtson (Denver, CO), Bob Szymkowski (Riverdale, IL), Marion Trumbo (Bluemont, VA), Tom Wilson (Tuscaloosa, AL), Jeff Zimmerman (Rancho Cordova, CA).

Jim Bowden

Scouts: Bill Baker (Rosamond, CA), Joe Bellino (Edison, NJ), Jim Connor (Florence, KY), Ed DeBenedetti (Lodi, CA), Craig Gambs (Richmond, CA), Jim Grief (Paducah, KY), Don Gust (West Jordan, UT), Fred Hayes (Battle Creek, MI), Gordon Kelly (Magalia, CA), Steve Kring (Beavercreek, OH), Fred Leone (Brooklyn, NY), Dion Lowe (Decatur, GA), Ramon Morales (Levittown, PR), Miguel Nava (Miami, FL), Jerry Raddatz (Winona, MN), Doug Stuart (Brentwood, TN), Rob Symonds (Buffalo Grove, IL), Jim Vennari (Pomeroy, OH), John Walsh (Windsor, CT), Murray Zuk (Souris, Manitoba).

Spring Training Information
Major League Club
Hotel Address: Holiday Inn, Exit 13 at I-4, Plant City, FL. Mailing Address: P.O. Box 1120, Plant City, FL 34289. Telephone: (813) 752-3141. **Stadium Address:** Plant City Stadium, 1900 S. Park Rd., Plant City, FL. Telephone: (813) 752-1878.
Minor League Clubs
Hotel Address: Econo Lodge, 301 S. Frontage Rd., Plant City, FL 33566. Telephone: (813) 752-0570. **Complex Address:** same as major league stadium.

HOUSTON

Office Address: 8400 Kirby Dr., Houston, TX 77054. **Mailing Address:** P.O. Box 288, Houston, TX 77001. **Telephone:** (713) 799-9500. **FAX:** (713) 799-9562.

Operated by: Houston Sports Association, Inc.

Ownership, Management

Chairman of the Board: John McMullen.

Board of Directors: Mrs. James Blake, H.L. Brown Jr., Mrs. Thomas Dompier, James Elkins Jr., Alfred Glassell Jr., Jacqueline McMullen, John McMullen Jr., Peter McMullen, Mrs. Stephen Mochary, Estate of Vivian Smith, Jack Trotter.

General Administration

Bill Wood

Director of Public Relations: Rob Matwick. Assistant Director of Public Relations: Chuck Pool. **Staff Publicist:** Tyler Barnes.

Vice President, Marketing: Ted Haracz.
Director of Community Services: Gayle Mongan.
Markeing Operations Manager: Matt Kastel.
Director of Broadcasting: Jamie Hildreth.
Director of Advertising Sales/Promotions: Norm Miller.
Director of Communications: Pam Gardner.
Director of Sales: David Matlin.
Director of Group Sales: Debra Fulmer.
Director of Season Ticket Services: John Sorrentino.
Director of Scoreboard Operations: Paul Darst.
Traveling Secretary: Barry Waters.
Team Physicians: Dr. Bill Bryan, Dr. Michael Feltovich.

Radio, TV

Radio-TV Announcers: Bill Brown, Enos Cabell, Vince Cotroneo, Larry Dierker, Milo Hamilton, Bill Worrell. **Flagship Stations:** KPRC 950 AM, KTXH Channel 20, Home Sports Entertainment Cable.

1992 Schedule

APRIL
7-8 .... Atlanta
9-10-11-12 ..... Cincinnati
13-14-15 ..... Los Angeles
17-18-19 .... San Diego
20-21-22 ... San Francisco
24-25-26 .... at Atlanta
28-29-30 .... at New York

MAY
1-2-3 .... Pittsburgh
4-5 .... New York
6-7 .... at Chicago
8-9-10 ...... at Pittsburgh
11-12-13 .... Chicago
15-16-17 .... St. Louis
18-19-20 .. at Philadelphia
22-23-24 ..... at St. Louis
25-26-27 ...... at Montreal
29-30-31 ..... Philadelphia

JUNE
1-2-3 .... Montreal
4-5-6-7 .. at San Francisco
8-9-10 ...... at San Diego
12-13-14 ... San Francisco
15-16-17 .... San Diego
19-20-21 .... Los Angeles
22-23-24 ..... at Cincinnati
25-26-27-28 .... at L.A.
29-30 .... Cincinnati

JULY
1 .... Cincinnati
3-4-5 .... at New York
6-7-8 .... at Pittsburgh
9-10-11-12 ..... New York
16-17-18-19 .... Atlanta
20-21-22 .... Pittsburgh
24-25-26 .... Chicago
27-28-29 .... at Atlanta
31 .... at Cincinnati

AUGUST
1-2-3 .... at Cincinnati
4-5 .... at Los Angeles
6-7-8-9 ...... at San Diego
10-11-12 .... at S.F.
13-14-15-16 ... at Chicago
18-19-20 ...... at St. Louis
21-22-23 .. at Philadelphia
25-26-27 .... St. Louis
28-29-30 .... Montreal
31 .... Philadelphia

SEPTEMBER
1-2 .... Philadelphia
4-5-6 .... at Montreal
7-8 .... Cincinnati
9-10 ..... at San Francisco
11-12-13 .... Atlanta
14-15-16 ... San Francisco
18-19-20 ...... at Atlanta
21-22 .... at Cincinnati
23-24 .... at San Diego
25-26-27 .. at Los Angeles
29-30 .... San Diego

OCTOBER
1 .... San Diego
2-3-4 .... Los Angeles

48 • 1992 DIRECTORY

ASTROS

Major League Staff
Manager: Art Howe.
Coaches: Bob Cluck, Matt Galante, Rudy Jaramillo, Ed Ott, Tom Spencer.

Baseball Operations
General Manager: Bill Wood. **Assistant General Manager:** Bob Watson. **Assistant to General Manager:** Tim Hellmuth.
Administrative Assistant, Major League Operations: Beverly Rains.
Director of Minor League Operations: Fred Nelson. **Assistant Director of Minor Leagues and Scouting:** Lew Temple. **Administrative Assistant:** Carol Wogsland.

Art Howe

Director of Instruction: Jimmy Johnson.
Roving Instructors: Jim Coveney (hitting), Steve Dillard (infield), Dave Hudgens (hitting), Tom Wiedenbauer (outfield, baserunning).

Minor League Affiliates:
Class	Farm Team	Manager	Coach(es)
AAA	Tucson	Bob Skinner	Brent Strom, Dave Engle
AA	Jackson	Rick Sweet	Charlie Taylor, Don Reynolds
A	Osceola	Sal Butera	Jack Billingham, Frank Cacciatore
A	Burlington	Steve Curry	Rick Aponte, Rick Peters
A	Asheville	Tim Tolman	Jim Hickey, Bob Robertson
A	Auburn	Steve Dillard	Bill Kelso, Clark Crist
Rookie	Kissimmee	Julio Linares	Cesar Cedeno, Don Alexander

Scouting
Director of Scouting: Dan O'Brien.
Assistant Director of Scouting/International Development: David Rawnsley. **Administrative Assistant:** Myrtha Campbell.
National Supervisors: David Lakey (Austin, TX), Paul Weaver (Carpinteria, CA).
Regional Supervisors: Jack Bloomfield (McAllen, TX), Gerry Craft (St. Clairsville, OH), Walt Matthews (Texarkana, TX), Ross Sapp (Moreno Valley, CA), Lynwood Stallings (Kingsport, TN).
Major League Scouts: Stan Benjamin (Greenfield, MA), George Brophy (Minneapolis, MN), Dick Hager (Sunnyvale, CA), Charlie Fox (San Mateo, CA), Howie Haak (Palm Springs, CA).

Fred Nelson

Scouts: Stan Boroski (Kissimmee, FL), Ralph Bratton (Austin, TX), Clark Crist (Tucson, AZ), F.H. DeFord (Manchester, TN), Chuck Edmondson (Texarkana, AR), Orlando Estevez (Miami, FL), Ben Galante (Houston, TX), Carl Greene (Vilas, NC), Sterling Housley (Canoga Park, CA), Dan Huston (Bellevue, WA), Bill Kelso (Kansas City, MO), Bob King (La Mesa, CA), Julio Linares (San Pedro de Macoris, Dom. Rep.), Mike Maggart (Penn Yan, NY), Tom Mooney (Pittsfield, MA), Carlos Muro (Puebla, Mexico), Joe Pittman (Columbus, GA), Jim Pransky (Carlisle, PA), Andres Reiner (Valencia, Venez.), Ramee Richards (Los Angeles, CA), Rick Schroeder (San Jose, CA), Tad Slowik (Skokie, IL), Kevin Stein (Reynoldsburg, OH), Frankie Thon (Guaynabo, PR), Greg Whitworth (Nuevo, CA).

Spring Training Information
Major League Club
Hotel Address: Sol Orlando, 4787 W. Irlo Bronson Hwy., Kissimmee, FL 34746. Telephone (407) 397-0553. **Stadium Address:** Osceola County Stadium, 1000 Osceola Blvd., Kissimmee, FL 34744. Telephone: (407) 933-6500.

Minor League Clubs
Hotel Address: Save Inn, 2225 Irlo Bronson Hwy., Kissimmee, FL 34743. Telephone: (407) 846-0777. **Complex Address:** same as major league stadium.

LOS ANGELES

Office Address: Dodger Stadium, 1000 Elysian Park Ave., Los Angeles, CA 90012. **Mailing Address:** same. **Telephone:** (213) 224-1500. **FAX:** (213) 224-1269.
Operated by: Los Angeles Dodgers, Inc.

Ownership, Management
President: Peter O'Malley.
Board of Directors: Peter O'Malley, president; Harry Bardt; Roland Seidler, vice president/treasurer; Mrs. Roland Seidler, secretary.
Vice President, Communications: Tom Hawkins.
Vice President, Finance: Bob Graziano.
Vice President, Marketing: Barry Stockhamer.
Assistant Secretary and General Counsel: Santiago Fernandez.
Assistant to the President: Ike Ikuhara.
Vice President, Stadium Operations: Bob Smith.
Vice President, Ticket Operations: Walter Nash.
Vice President, Campo las Palmas: Ralph Avila.

Fred Claire

General Administration
Director of Publications and Broadcasting: Brent Shyer. **Director of Publicity:** Jay Lucas. **Assistant Director of Publicity:** Chuck Harris.
Director of Community Relations: Don Newcombe. **Community Relations:** Roy Campanella.
Director of Management Information Systems: Mike Mularky.
Director of Human Resources and Administration: Irene Tanji.
Director of Advertising and Special Events: Paul Kalil.
Director of Ticket Operations: Debra Duncan.
Director of Ticket Marketing: Allan Erselius.
Director of Stadium Operations: Jim Italiano.
Traveling Secretary: Bill DeLury.
Team Physicians: Dr. Frank Jobe, Dr. Michael Mellman.

Radio, TV
Radio-TV Announcers: Vin Scully, Don Drysdale, Ross Porter (KABC, KTTV); Jaime Jarrin, Rene Cardenas (KWKW). **Flagship Stations:** KABC 790 AM, KTTV Channel 11, KWKW 1330 AM (Spanish).

1992 Schedule

APRIL
6-7 ....San Francisco
9-10-11-12 ..at San Diego
13-14-15 ......at Houston
16-17-18-19 ....Atlanta
20-21-22 ....Cincinnati
24-25-26 ....at S.F.
27-28 ....St. Louis
29-30 ....Philadelphia

MAY
1-2-3 ....Montreal
5-6 ....at Philadelphia
8-9-10 ....at New York
11-12-13 ......at Montreal
15-16-17 ....New York
18-19-20 ....Chicago
22-23-24 ....Pittsburgh
25-26-27 .....at St. Louis
29-30-31 ......at Chicago

JUNE
1-2-3 ....at Pittsburgh
4-5-6-7 ....Cincinnati

8-9-10 ....Atlanta
12-13-14 .....at Cincinnati
15-16-17 ....at Atlanta
19-20-21 .....at Houston
22-23.........at San Diego
25-26-27-28 .....Houston
29-30 ....San Diego

JULY
1 ....San Diego
2-3-4-5 .....Philadelphia
6-7-8 ....Montreal
9-10-11-12 ......St. Louis
16-17-18-19 ....at Phil.
20-21-22 .....at New York
24-25-26 ....at Montreal
27-28-29 ....at S.F.
30-31 ....San Diego

AUGUST
1-2 ....San Diego
4-5 ....Houston
7-8-9-10 ....at Atlanta
11-12-13 .....at Cincinnati

14-15-16-17 ..........S.F.
18-19-20 ....New York
21-22-23 ....Chicago
24-25-26 ....Pittsburgh
28-29-30 .....at St. Louis
31 ....at Chicago

SEPTEMBER
1-2 ....at Chicago
4-5-6 ....at Pittsburgh
7-8 ....at Atlanta
9-10 ....San Diego
11-12-13 ...San Francisco
14-15-16 ....at San Diego
18-19-20............at S.F.
21-22 ....Atlanta
23-24...........Cincinnati
25-26-27 ....Houston
29-30 ......at Cincinnati

OCTOBER
1.............at Cincinnati
2-3-4 ....at Houston

50 • 1992 DIRECTORY

DODGERS

Major League Staff
Manager: Tommy Lasorda.
Coaches: Joe Amalfitano, Mark Cresse, Joe Ferguson, Ben Hines, Ron Perranoski.

Baseball Operations
Executive Vice President, Player Personnel: Fred Claire.
Director of Minor Leagues Operations: Charlie Blaney. **Minor League Administrator:** Julie Parker. **Secretary:** Rebecca Aguilar. **Data Processing:** John Hesket.
Minor League Field Coordinator: Steve Boros. **Assistant Field Coordinator:** Joe Vavra. **Pitching Coordinator:** Dave Wallace. **Hitting Coordinator:** Reggie Smith.

Tom Lasorda

Roving Instructors: Chico Fernandez (infield), Dick McLaughlin (bunting, outfield), Leo Posada (hitting), John Roseboro (catching), Maury Wills (baserunning).
Physical Therapist: Kevin Tollefson.

Minor League Affiliates:

Class	Farm Team	Manager	Coach(es)
AAA	Albuquerque	Bill Russell	Von Joshua, Claude Osteen, Mickey Hatcher
AA	San Antonio	Jerry Royster	Burt Hooton, Ron Roenicke
A	Bakersfield	Tom Beyers	Dino Ebel, Goose Gregson
A	Vero Beach	Glenn Hoffman	Jon Debus, Denny Lewallyn
A	Yakima	Joe Vavra	Tony Arnold, Garrett Teel
Rookie	Great Falls	Unavailable	Guy Conti, Helms Bohringer
Rookie	St. Lucie	John Shoemaker	Luis Tiant, Doug Simunic

Scouting
Director of Scouting: Terry Reynolds.
Advance Scouts: Mel Didier (Arlington, TX), Phil Regan (Byron Center, MI), Jerry Stephenson (Fullerton, CA), Gary Sutherland (Monrovia, CA).
Scouts: Eddie Bane (Phoenix, AZ), William Barkley (Waco, TX), Gil Bassetti (Brooklyn, NY), Bob Bishop (San Dimas, CA), Gib Bodet (San Clemente, CA), Mike Brito (Los Angeles, CA), Joe Campbell (Leeds, AL), Bob Darwin (Cerritos, CA), Eddie Fajardo (Anasco, PR), Lin Garrett (Zephyrhills, FL), Michael Hankins (Lee's Summit, MO), Dick Hanlon (Millbrae, CA), Dennis Haren (San Diego, CA), Gail Henley (Temple City, CA), Hank Jones (Vancouver, WA), Lon Joyce (Spartanburg, SC), John Keenan (Great Bend, KS),

Charlie Blaney

Gary LaRocque (Greensboro, NC), Don LeJohn (Brownsville, PA), Carl Loewenstine (Hamilton, OH), Dale McReynolds (Walworth, WI), Bob Miske (Amherst, NY), Tommy Mixon (Macon, GA), Deni Pacini (Kerman, CA), Bill Pleis (Parrish, FL), Mark Sheehy (Sacramento, CA), Jim Stoeckel (Vero Beach, FL), Dick Teed (Windsor, CT), Thomas Thomas (Lee's Summit, MO), Glen Van Proyen (West Chicago, IL).

Spring Training Information
Major League Club
Hotel Address: Dodgertown, 4001 26th St., Vero Beach, FL 32961. Telephone: (407) 569-4900. **Stadium Address:** same.
Minor League Clubs
Hotel Address: same as major league club. **Complex Address:** same as major league club.

MONTREAL

Office Address: 4545 De Coubertin Ave., Montreal, Que., Canada H1V 3P2. **Mailing Address:** P.O. Box 500, Station M, Montreal, Que., Canada H1V 3P2. **Telephone:** (514) 253-3434. **FAX:** (514) 253-8282.

Operated by: Montreal Baseball Club, Inc.

Ownership, Management
President and General Partner: Claude Brochu.
Vice President, Business Operations: Gerry Trudeau.
Vice President, Marketing: Michel Lagace.
Vice President, Communications: Richard Morency.

Dan Duquette

General Administration
Director of Media Services: Monique Giroux. **Director of Media Relations:** Richard Griffin.
Controller: Raymond St. Pierre. **Assistant Controller:** Michel Bussiere.
Director, Advertising: Johanne Heroux.
Director of Marketing and Communications: Carole Boivin.
Director of Team Travel: Erik Ostling.
Director of Stadium Operations: Monique Lacas. **Assistant Director of Stadium Operations:** Pierre Touzin.
Director of Food Concessions: Claude Delorme.
Director of Ticket Sales: Ronald Martineau. **Managers of Ticket Sales:** Ginette Bourgon, Suzanne Lemoignan. **Director of Ticket Office:** Luigi Carolo.
Director of Corporate Affairs: Pierre Touchette.
Director of Retailing: Susan LeBlanc.

Radio, TV
Radio Announcers: Jacques Doucet, Rodger Brulotte (French); Dave Van Horne, Ken Singleton, Elliott Price, Bobby Winkles (English). **Flagship Stations:** CKAC 730-AM (French); CFCF 600-AM (English).

TV Announcers: Raymond Lebrun, Claude Raymond, Denis Casavant, Rodger Brulotte (French); Dave Van Horne, Ken Singleton (English). **Flagship Stations:** CBFT 2, RDS (French); CBMT 6, TSN, CFCF-TV 12 (English).

1992 Schedule

APRIL
- 6-8-9 ....at Pittsburgh
- 10-11-12 .....at New York
- 13-14-15 ....St. Louis
- 17-18-19 ....New York
- 20-21-22-23 ....Pittsburgh
- 24-25-26 ......at St. Louis
- 27-28 ....at San Francisco
- 29-30........at San Diego

MAY
- 1-2-3 .....at Los Angeles
- 5-6 ....San Diego
- 8-9-10 .....San Francisco
- 11-12-13 .....Los Angeles
- 15-16-17 ....at Atlanta
- 18-19-20 ......Cincinnati
- 22-23-24 ....Atlanta
- 25-26-27 ....Houston
- 29-30-31 .....at Cincinnati

JUNE
- 1-2-3 ....at Houston
- 5-6-7 ....Chicago
- 8-9-10 ....New York
- 12-13-14 .....at Chicago
- 15-16-17 ....at New York
- 18-19-20-21 ..at Pittsburgh
- 22-23-24 ....Philadelphia
- 26-27-28 ......Pittsburgh
- 29-30 ....at Philadelphia

JULY
- 1 ....at Philadelphia
- 2-3-4-5 .....at San Diego
- 6-7-8 ....at Los Angeles
- 9-10-11-12.........at S.F.
- 16-17-18-19 ...San Diego
- 20-21-22...San Francisco
- 24-25-26 ....Los Angeles
- 27-28-29 .....at St. Louis
- 30-31 ....Philadelphia

AUGUST
- 1-2............Philadelphia
- 3-4-5 ....Chicago
- 6-7-8-9 ....at Philadelphia
- 10-11-12 ......at Chicago
- 14-15-16 ....St. Louis
- 18-19-20 ....Atlanta
- 21-22-23 ....Cincinnati
- 25-26-27........at Atlanta
- 28-29-30 ......at Houston
- 31 ....at Cincinnati

SEPTEMBER
- 1-2............at Cincinnati
- 4-5-6 ....Houston
- 7-8-9 ....St. Louis
- 11-12-13 ....New York
- 14-15.......at Philadelphia
- 16-17 ....at Pittsburgh
- 18-19-20 .....at New York
- 21-22 ....Philadelphia
- 23-24 ....Pittsburgh
- 25-26-27 ....Chicago
- 28-29-30 ......at St. Louis

OCTOBER
- 2-3-4 ....at Chicago

52 • 1992 DIRECTORY

EXPOS

Major League Staff
Manager: Tom Runnells.
Coaches: Felipe Alou, Tommy Harper, Joe Kerrigan, Jerry Manuel, Jay Ward.

Baseball Operations
Vice President, Baseball Operations: Bill Stoneman.
Vice President and General Manager: Dan Duquette. **Executive Advisor, Baseball Operations:** Eddie Haas. **Special Consultant, Baseball Operations:** Jim Fanning.
Director, Latin American Operations: Fred Ferreira.
General Manager of West Palm Beach Operations: Rob Rabenecker.
Director of Minor League Operations: Kent Qualls. **Scouting and Player Development Assistant:** Rene Marchand.
Director, Minor League Field Operations: Kevin Kennedy.
Roving Instructors: Nardi Contreras (pitching), Pete Dalena (hitting), Dave Machemer (infield), Luis Pujols (catching).

Tom Runnells

Minor League Affiliates:

Class	Farm Team	Manager	Coach(es)
AAA	Indianapolis	Pat Kelly	Gomer Hodge, Rich Dubee
AA	Harrisburg	Mike Quade	Mike Parrott
A	W. Palm Beach	David Jauss	Chuck Kniffin
A	Rockford	Rob Leary	Herman Starrette
A	Albany	Lorenzo Bundy	Keith Snider, Gary Lance
A	Jamestown	Q.V. Lowe	Jim Fleming
Rookie	W. Palm Beach	Nelson Norman	Tim Toricelli, Dave Tomlin

Scouting
Office Address: Expos Minor League Development Center, 6850 Lawrence Road, Lantana, FL 33462. **Mailing Address:** P.O. Box 6808, Lake Worth, FL 33466. **Telephone:** (407) 433-1990. **FAX:** (407) 433-3481.

Director of Scouting: Kevin Malone.
Baseball Operations Administrator: Roberta Mazur. **Administrative Assistant to the Scouting Director:** Gregg Leonard.
National Crosschecker: David Littlefield (Manassas, VA).
Scouting Supervisors: Jim Holden (Yucaipa, CA), Bob Oldis (Iowa City, IA), Ed Creech (Moultrie, GA).
Advance Scout: Tim Johnson.

Kevin Malone

Major League Scouts: Eddie Haas (Paducah, KY), Whitey DeHart (Molalla, OR).
Scouts: Jesus Alou (Santo Domingo, Dom. Rep.), Dennis Cardoza (Santa Clarita, CA), Doug Carpenter (Boca Raton, FL), Emilio Carrasquel (Caracas, Venez.), Carl Cassell (Las Vegas, NV), Pepito Centeno (Bayamon, PR), Arturo DeFreites (San Pedro de Macoris, Dom. Rep.), Phil Favia (Apache Junction, WY), Jim Fleming (Purcell, OK), Joe Frisina (Tidioute, PA), Bert Holt (Visalia, CA), Bob Johnson (Rockaway, NJ), Jeff Kahn (Mobile, AL), Bill McKenzie (Ottawa, Ont.), Rene Marchand (Three Rivers, Que.), Roy McMillan (Bonham, TX), Tomas Morales (Mexico City, Mex.), Carlos Moreno (La Guaira, Venez.), Mike Murphy (San Diego, CA), Rene Picota (Panama City, Panama), Mark Servais (LaCrosse, WI), Keith Snider (Stockton, CA), Pat Sullivan (Chattanooga, TN), Fred Wright (Charlotte, NC), Stan Zielinski (Winfield, IL).

Spring Training Information

Major League Club
Hotel Address: Holiday Inn, 3700 N. Ocean Dr., Singer Island, FL 33402. Telephone: (407) 443-4066. **Stadium Address:** Municipal Stadium, 715 Hank Aaron Drive, West Palm Beach, FL 33401. Telephone: (407) 684-6801.

Minor League Clubs
Hotel Address: Courtyard by Marriott, 600 Northpointe Pkwy., West Palm Beach, FL 33407. Telephone: (407) 640-9000. **Complex Address:** Expos Minor League Development Center, 6850 Lawrence Rd., Lantana, FL 33462. Telephone: (407) 433-1990.

NEW YORK

Office Address: Shea Stadium, 126th St. and Roosevelt Ave., Flushing, NY 11368. Mailing Address: same. Telephone: (718) 507-6387. FAX: (718) 565-4382.

Operated by: New York National League Baseball Club.

Ownership, Management

Chairman of the Board: Nelson Doubleday.

Board of Directors: Nelson Doubleday, J. Frank Cashen, Saul Katz, Marvin Tepper, Fred Wilpon.

Special Advisor to the Board of Directors: Richard Cummins.

President and Chief Executive Officer: Fred Wilpon.

Al Harazin

Executive Vice President and General Manager: Al Harazin. **Executive Assistant to the General Manager:** Jean Coen.

Chief Operating Officer and Senior Executive Vice President: Frank Cashen.

Vice President, Operations: Robert Mandt.
Vice President, Treasurer: Harold O'Shaughnessy.
Vice President, Marketing: Jim Ross.
Vice President, Broadcasting: Mike Ryan.

General Administration

Director of Public Relations: Jay Horwitz. **Assistant, Public Relations:** Craig Sanders.

Controller: Rick Iandoli.
Stadium Manager: John McCarthy.
Traveling Secretary: Bob O'Hara
Promotions Administrator: James Plummer.

Director of Ticket Operations: William Ianniciello. **Season Ticket Manager:** Marie Melluso. **Sales Manager:** Randye Ringler.

Equipment Manager: Charlie Samuels.
Team Physician: Dr. David Altchek.

Radio, TV

Radio Announcers: Bob Murphy, Gary Cohen. **Flagship Station:** WFAN 660 AM.

TV Announcers: Ralph Kiner, Tim McCarver, Fran Healy, Rusty Staub. **Flagship Stations:** WWOR Channel 9, Sportschannel America.

1992 Schedule

APRIL
6-7-8-9 . . . . at St. Louis
10-11-12 . . . . Montreal
13-14-15 . . . . . Philadelphia
17-18-19 . . . . . . at Montreal
21-22-23 . . . . St. Louis
24-25-26 . . at Philadelphia
28-29-30 . . . . Houston

MAY
1-2-3 . . . . at Atlanta
4-5 . . . . at Houston
6-7 . . . . at Cincinnati
8-9-10 . . . . . . Los Angeles
11-12-13 . . . . San Diego
15-16-17 . . at Los Angeles
18-19-20-21 . at San Diego
22-23-24 . . . . at S.F.
25-26-27 . . . . . . Cincinnati
29-30-31 . . . . Atlanta

JUNE
1-2 . . . . San Francisco

4-5-6-7 . . . . . . at Pittsburgh
8-9-10 . . . . at Montreal
12-13-14 . . . . . . Pittsburgh
15-16-17 . . . . Montreal
18-19-20-21 . . . . . St. Louis
22-23-24-25 . . . . . Chicago
26-27-28 . . . . . at St. Louis
29-30 . . . . at Chicago

JULY
1 . . . . at Chicago
3-4-5 . . . . Houston
6-7-8 . . . . at Atlanta
9-10-11-12 . . . . at Houston
16-17-18-19 . . . . S.F.
20-21-22 . . . . . Los Angeles
24-25-26 . . . . San Diego
27-28-29 . . at Philadelphia
31 . . . . Chicago

AUGUST
1-2 . . . . Chicago
4-5 . . . . at Pittsburgh
6-7-8-9 . . . . at Chicago

10-11-12 . . . . Pittsburgh
14-15-16 . . . . . Philadelphia
18-19-20 . . at Los Angeles
22-23 . . . . at San Diego
24-25-26 . . . . at S.F.
28-29-30 . . . . . . Cincinnati
31 . . . . Atlanta

SEPTEMBER
1-2 . . . . Atlanta
3-4-5-6 . . . . . . at Cincinnati
7-8-9 . . . . . . at Philadelphia
11-12-13 . . . . . . at Montreal
14-15 . . . . at Chicago
16-17 . . . . St. Louis
18-19-20 . . . . Montreal
21-22 . . . . Chicago
23-24 . . . . at St. Louis
25-26-27 . . . . . at Pittsburgh
28-29-30 . . . . . Philadelphia

OCTOBER
2-3-4 . . . . Pittsburgh

METS

Major League Staff
Manager: Jeff Torborg.
Coaches: Mike Cubbage, Barry Foote, Dave LaRoche, Tom McCraw, Mel Stottlemyre.

Baseball Operations
Assistant Vice President, Baseball Operations: Gerry Hunsicker.
Director of Minor League Operations: Steve Phillips. **Administrative Assistant, Minor Leagues:** James Duquette. **Administrator, Minor Leagues and Scouting:** Maureen Cooke.
Minor League Field Coordinator: Bobby Floyd. **Assistant Coordinator:** Chuck Hiller. **Training and Fitness Coordinator:** Scott Lawrenson.
Roving Instructors: John Gibbons (catching), Al Jackson (pitching), Rafael Landestoy (infield), Rich Miller (baserunning and outfield), Greg Pavlick (pitching), Ernie Rosseau (hitting).

Jeff Torborg

Minor League Affiliates:
Class	Farm Team	Manager	Coach(es)
AAA	Tidewater	Clint Hurdle	Bob Apodaca, Ron Washington
AA	Binghamton	Steve Swisher	Randy Niemann, Ron Gideon
A	St. Lucie	John Tamargo	Bill Latham, Bill Gardner Jr.
A	Columbia	Tim Blackwell	Jerry Koosman, Marlin McPhail
A	Pittsfield	Jim Thrift	Jeff Morris, Geary Jones
Rookie	Kingsport	Andre David	Jesus Hernaiz, Howie Freiling
Rookie	St. Lucie	Junior Roman	Felix Millan

Scouting
Director of Scouting: Roland Johnson. **Administrative Assistant, Scouting:** Scott Brow.
Scouting Supervisors: Joe Mason (Millbrook, AL), Bob Minor (Long Beach, CA), Paul Ricciarini (Pittsfield, MA).
Major League Scouts: Dick Gernert (Reading, PA), Dallas Green (West Grove, PA), Buddy Harrelson (Hauppauge, NY), Darrell Johnson (Ord, NE), Buddy Kerr (Oradell, NJ), Harry Minor (Long Beach, CA).
Scouts: Paul Baretta (Kensington, CT), Larry Chase (Pearcy, AR), Jim Eschen (Jacksonville, FL), Rob Guzik (Latrobe, PA), R.J. Harrison (Phoenix, AZ), Marty Harvat (Aurora, CO), Ken Houp (Seal Beach, CA), Reginald Jackson (Islip, NY), Andy Korenek (Houston, TX), Craig Kornfeld (Durham, NC), Jim Marshall (Clearwater, FL), Carlos Pascual (Miami, FL), Jim Reeves (Milwaukie, OR), Junior Roman (San Sebastian, PR), Tom Romenesko (Santee, CA), Bob Rossi (Baton Rouge, LA), Daraka Shaheed (Vallejo, CA), Eddy Toledo (Santo Domingo, Dom. Rep.), Terry Tripp (Harrisburg, IL), Bob Wellman (Covington, KY), Jim Woodward (Whittier, CA).

Gerry Hunsicker

Spring Training Information
Major League Club
Hotel Address: Radisson Inn, 10120 South Federal Highway, Port St. Lucie, FL 34952. Telephone: (407) 337-2200. **Stadium Address:** St. Lucie County Sports Complex, 525 NW Peacock Blvd., Port St. Lucie, FL 34986. Telephone: (407) 871-2100.
Minor League Clubs
Hotel Address: Same as major league hotel. **Complex Address:** Same as major league stadium. Telephone: (407) 340-0446.

PHILADELPHIA

Office Address: Veterans Stadium, Broad St. and Pattison Ave., Philadelphia, PA 19148. **Mailing Address:** P.O. Box 7575, Philadelphia, PA 19101. **Telephone:** (215) 463-6000. **FAX:** (215) 389-3050.
Operated by: The Phillies.

Ownership, Management
President, Chielf Executive Officer and General Partner: Bill Giles.
Partners: Claire Betz; Estate of John Drew Betz; Fitz Eugene Dixon Jr.; Mrs. Rochelle Levy; Tri-Play Associates: Alexander Buck, J. Mahlon Buck Jr., William Buck.
Executive Vice President and Chief Operating Officer: David Montgomery.
Secretary and Legal Counsel: William Webb.
Executive Secretary: Nancy Deren.

Lee Thomas

General Administration
Vice President, Public Relations: Larry Shenk.
Manager, Media Relations: Gene Dias. **Manager, Publicity:** Leigh McDonald. **Director of Community Relations:** Regina Castellani. **Assistant Director of Community Relations:** Karen Howard.
Senior Vice President, Finance and Planning: Jerry Clothier. **Controller:** Lou Perez.
Director, Planning/Development and Super Boxes: Tom Hudson.
Director of Speakers Bureau: Chris Wheeler.
Vice President, Marketing: Dennis Mannion. **Director of Promotions:** Frank Sullivan. **Assistant Director of Promotions:** Chris Legault. **Manager of Advertising and Broadcasting:** Jo-Anne Levy-Lamoreaux.
Vice President, Ticket Operations: Richard Deats. **Director, Sales:** Rory McNeil. **Director, Ticket Department:** Dan Goroff. **Manager of Group Sales:** Kathy Killian. **Manager of Sales Operations:** John Weber.
Traveling Secretary: Eddie Ferenz.
Director, Information Systems: Brian Lamoreaux.
Director, Stadium Operations: Mike DiMuzio. **Director, Office Operations:** Pat Cassidy.
Team Physician: Dr. Phillip Marone.
Trainers: Jeff Cooper, Mark Andersen.
Equipment Manager: Frank Coppenbarger.

Radio, TV
Radio-TV Announcers: Richie Ashburn, Harry Kalas, Garry Maddox, Andy Musser, Kent Tekulve, Chris Wheeler. **Flagship Stations:** WOGL 1210-AM, WTXF-TV Channel 29, Prism, SportsChannel.

1992 Schedule

APRIL		
7-8-9	Chicago	
10-11-12	Pittsburgh	
13-14-15	at New York	
17-18-19	at Pittsburgh	
20-21-22-23	at Chicago	
24-25-26	New York	
27-28	ar San Diego	
29-30	at Los Angeles	

MAY	
1-2-3	at San Francisco
5-6	Los Angeles
8-9-10	San Diego
11-12-13	San Francisco
15-16-17	at Cincinnati
18-19-20	Houston
22-23-24	Cincinnati
25-26-27	Atlanta
29-30-31	at Houston

JUNE	
1-2-3	at Atlanta
5-6-7	St. Louis
8-9-10	Pittsburgh
12-13-14	at St. Louis
15-16-17	at Pittsburgh
18-19-20-21	Chicago
22-23-24	at Montreal
26-27-28	at Chicago
29-30	Montreal

JULY	
1	Montreal
2-3-4-5	at Los Angeles
6-7-8	at San Francisco
9-10-11-12	at San Diego
16-17-18-19	Los Angeles
20-21-22	San Diego
24-25-26	San Francisco
27-28-29	New York
30-31	at Montreal

AUGUST	
1-2	at Montreal
3-4-5	at St. Louis
6-7-8-9	Montreal
11-12-13	St. Louis
14-15-16	at New York
17-18-19	Cincinnati
21-22-23	Houston
24-25-26	at Cincinnati
28-29-30	Atlanta
31	at Houston

SEPTEMBER	
1-2	at Houston
4-5-6	at Atlanta
7-8-9	New York
11-12-13	Pittsburgh
14-15	Montreal
16-17	at Chicago
18-19-20	at Pittsburgh
21-22	at Montreal
23-24	Chicago
25-26-27	St. Louis
28-29-30	at New York

OCTOBER	
2-3-4	at St. Louis

PHILLIES

Major League Staff
Manager: Jim Fregosi.
Coaches: Larry Bowa, Denis Menke, Johnny Podres, Mel Roberts, Mike Ryan, John Vukovich.

Baseball Operations
Vice President, General Manager: Lee Thomas.
Player Personnel Administrator: Ed Wade.
Assistant to the President: Paul Owens.
Director of Player Development: Del Unser.
Business Manager of Minor Leagues: Bill Gargano.
Computer Analyst: Jay McLaughlin. **Secretary, Baseball Administration:** Susan Ingersoll. **Secretary, Minor Leagues:** Maryann Skedzielewski.
Minor League Field Coordinator: Don Blasingame.
Roving Instructors: Glenn Brummer (catching), Dave Cash (infield), George Culver (pitching), Jerry Martin (hitting).

Jim Fregosi

Minor League Affiliates:

Class	Farm Team	Manager	Coach(es)
AAA	Scranton/W-B	Lee Elia	Al Leboeuf, Jim Wright
AA	Reading	Don McCormack	Kelly Heath, Carlos Arroyo
A	Clearwater	Bill Dancy	Darold Knowles
A	Spartanburg	Roy Majtyka	Buzz Capra, Tony Scott
A	Batavia	Ramon Aviles	John Martin, Floyd Rayford
Rookie	Martinsville	Roly DeArmas	Ramon Handerson, Ray Rippelmeyer

Scouting
Director of Scouting: Jay Hankins (Raytown, MO).
National Crosschecker: Randy Waddill (Valrico, FL).
Regional Crosscheckers: Dick Lawlor (Windsor, CT), Bob Reasonover (Clearwater, FL), Larry Reasonover (Dunwoody, GA), Tony Roig (Liberty Lake, WA).
Special Assignment Scouts: Ray Shore (Cincinnati, OH), Jimmy Stewart (Lafayette, LA).
Major League Scouts: Jim Baumer (Paoli, PA), Bing Devine (St. Louis, MO), Hank King (Limerick, PA), Larry Rojas (Clearwater, FL).

Del Unser

Scouts: Emil Belich (West Allis, WI), Ollie Bidwell (Fresno, CA), Jim Bierman (Cincinnati, OH), Carlos Cuervo (Phoenix, AZ), Tommy Ferguson (Santa Ana, CA), Jimmy Fregosi Jr. (Yorba Linda, CA), Eli Grba (Nashville, TN), Bill Harper (Corvallis, OR), Ken Hultzapple (Newport, PA), Jerry Jordan (Wise, VA), John Kennedy (Peabody, MA), Jerry Lafferty (Trenton, MO), George Lauzerique (West Palm Beach, FL), Terry Logan (Brenham, TX), Fred Mazuca (Orange, CA), Willie Montanez (Caguas, PR), Cotton Nye (Greenwood, AR), Art Parrack (Winter Park, FL), Jack Pastore (Wallingford, PA), Bob Poole (Redwood City, CA), Gerald Sanders (Philadelphia, PA), Roy Tanner (Charleston, SC), Scott Trcka (Hobart, IN).

Spring Training Information
Major League Club
Hotel: None. **Stadium Address:** Jack Russell Stadium, 800 Phillies Dr., Clearwater, FL 34615. Telephone: (813) 441-8638.
Minor League Clubs
Hotel Address: Best Western, 120 U.S. Hwy. North, Clearwater, FL 34625. Telephone: (813) 799-1565. Howard Johnsons, 410 US Hwy. South, Clearwater, FL 34625. Telephone: (813) 797-5021. Holiday Inn, 21030 U.S. Hwy. 19 N., Clearwater, FL 34625. Telephone: (813) 797-8173. **Complex Address:** Carpenter Complex, 651 Old Coachman Rd., Clearwater, FL 34625. Telephone: (813) 799-0503.

PITTSBURGH

Office Address: 600 Stadium Circle, Pittsburgh, PA 15212. **Mailing Address:** P.O. Box 7000, Pittsburgh, PA 15212. **Telephone:** (412) 323-5000. **FAX:** (412) 323-5024.

Operated by: Pittsburgh Associates.

Ownership, Management

Chairman of the Board: Douglas Danforth.
Board of Directors: Joe Brown, Frank Cahouet, Richard Cyert, Douglas Danforth, Eugene Litman, John Marous, Sophie Masloff, John McConnell, Thomas O'Brien, Paul O'Neill, David Roderick, Vincent Sarni, Mark Sauer, Harvey Walken.
President and Chief Executive Officer: Mark Sauer. **Assistant to the President:** Ken Wilson.
Senior Vice President, Business Operations: Doug Bureman.
Vice President, Marketing and Operations: Steve Greenberg.
Vice President, Finance and Administration: Ken Curcio.
Vice President, Public Relations: Rick Cerrone.

Mark Sauer

General Administration

Director of Media Relations: Jim Trdinich. **Assistant Director of Public Relations:** Sally O'Leary.
Director of Publications and Special Projects: Jim Lachimia.
Executive Director, Broadcasting and Advertising Sales: Mark Driscoll.
Director of Community Relations: Patty Paytas.
Director of Sales and Marketing: Bob Derda.
Director of Stadium Operations: Dennis Dapra.
Traveling Secretary: Greg Johnson.
Manager of Ticket Operations: Gary Remlinger. **Director of Ticket Services:** Robin Lysinger.
Director of Community Services and Sales: Al Gordon.
Director of Merchandising: Joe Billetdeaux.
Director of Promotions: Kathy Guy.
Team Physician: Dr. Joe Coroso. **Team Orthopedist:** Dr. Jack Failla.
Trainer: Kent Biggerstaff. **Assistant Trainer:** Dave Tumbas.
Equipment Manager: Roger Wilson.

Radio, TV

Radio-TV Announcers: Lanny Frattare, Jim Rooker, Kent Derdivanis, Steve Blass. **Flagship Stations:** KDKA 1020 AM, KDKA Channel 2, KBL Cable.

1992 Schedule

APRIL
6-8-9 .... Montreal
10-11-12 .. at Philadelphia
14-15 .... Chicago
17-18-19 ..... Philadelphia
20-21-22-23 ... at Montreal
24-25-26 ...... at Chicago
28-29 .... at Cincinnati

MAY
1-2-3 .... at Houston
4-5 .... Cincinnati
6-7 .... Atlanta
8-9-10 .... Houston
12-13-14 .... at Atlanta
15-16-17 ..... San Diego
19-20-21 .... at S.F.
22-23-24 .. at Los Angeles
25-26-27 .... at San Diego
29-30-31 ... San Francisco

JUNE
1-2-3 .... Los Angeles
4-5-6-7 .... New York
8-9-10 ..... at Philadelphia
12-13-14 ..... at New York
15-16-17 ..... Philadelphia
18-19-20-21 ..... Montreal
22-23-24 .... St. Louis
26-27-28 ..... at Montreal
29-30 .... at St. Louis

JULY
1 .... at St. Louis
2-3-4-5 .... Cincinnati
6-7-8 .... Houston
9-10-11-12 .. at Cincinnati
16-17-18-19 .... Chicago
20-21-22 ..... at Houston
24-25-26 ...... at Atlanta
27-28-29 ...... at Chicago
30-31 .... St. Louis

AUGUST
1-2 .... St. Louis
4-5 .... New York

6-7-8-9 .... at St. Louis
10-11-12 ..... at New York
14-15-16-17 ...... Atlanta
18-19-20 ...... San Diego
21-22-23 .... at S.F.
24-25-26 .. at Los Angeles
27-29-30 .... at San Diego

SEPTEMBER
1-2-3 ...... San Francisco
4-5-6 .... Los Angeles
7-8-9 .... Chicago
11-12-13 .. at Philadelphia
14-15 .... at St. Louis
16-17 .... Montreal
18-19-20 ..... Philadelphia
21-22 .... St. Louis
23-24 .... at Montreal
25-26-27 .... New York
28-29-30 ...... at Chicago

OCTOBER
2-3-4 .... at New York

58 • 1992 DIRECTORY

PIRATES

Major League Staff
Manager: Jim Leyland.
Coaches: Terry Collins, Rich Donnelly, Ray Miller, Milt May, Tommy Sandt.

Baseball Operations
Senior Vice President and General Manager: Ted Simmons. **Assistant General Manager:** Cam Bonifay.
Director of Minor League Operations: Chet Montgomery. **Assistant, Baseball Operations:** John Sirignano. **Administrative Assistant, Minor Leagues and Scouting:** Tom Treece. **Secretary:** Diane Grimaldi.
Director of Bradenton Baseball Operations: Jeff Podobnik.
Minor League Field Coordinator: Jack Lind.
Roving Instructors: Rocky Bridges (infield), Steve Henderson (hitting), Bill Henry (fitness), Joe Lonnett (catching), Paul Noce (baserunning), Bill Virdon.

Jim Leyland

Minor League Affiliates:

Class	Farm Team	Manager	Coach(es)
AAA	Buffalo	Marc Bombard	Spin Williams, Doc Edwards
AA	Carolina	Don Werner	Tom Dettore, Rich Chiles
A	Salem	John Wockenfuss	Rick Keeton
A	Augusta	Scott Little	Dave Rajsich, Julio Garcia
A	Welland	Trent Jewett	Tom Barnard
Rookie	Bradenton	Woody Huyke	Steve Watson

Scouting
Director of Scouting: Jack Zduriencik.
Scouting Supervisors: Ron King (Sacramento, CA), Don Mitchell (Union City, TN), Kevin Towers (Ausitn, TX).
Major League Scouts: Lenny Yochim (River Ridge, LA), Ken Parker (Pensacola, FL).
Scouts: Joe L. Brown (Monarch Beach, CA), Bill Bryk (Schererville, IN), Pablo Cruz (Santo Domingo, Dom. Rep.), Larry D'Amato (Tualatin, OR), Steve Demeter (Cleveland, OH), Angel Figueroa (Hacienda Heights, CA), Steve Fleming (Radford, VA), Jesse Flores (Sacramento, CA), Jerry Gardner (Los Alamitos, CA), Dave Holliday (Stillwater, OK), Carlos Loreto (Caracas, Ven.), Jose Luna (Bayamon, PR), Leland Maddox (Greensboro, NC), Rene Mons (Manchester, NH), Phil Morgan (Manhattan, KS), Boyd Odom (Decatur, GA), Ed Roebuck (Lakewood, CA), Paul Tinnell (Brandon, FL).

Chet Montgomery

Spring Training Information
Major League Club
Hotel Address: Pirate City, 1701 Roberto Clemente Memorial Dr. (27th St. East), Bradenton, FL 34208. Telephone: (813) 747-3031. **Stadium Address:** McKechnie Field, 17th Ave. West and 9th St. West, Bradenton, FL 34205. Telephone: (813) 748-4610.
Minor League Clubs
Hotel Address: Same as major league club. **Complex Address:** Same as major league club.

ST. LOUIS

Office Address: 250 Stadium Plaza, St. Louis, MO 63102. **Mailing Address:** same. **Telephone:** (314) 421-3060. **FAX:** (314) 425-0640.
Operated by: St. Louis National Baseball Club, Inc.

Ownership, Management
Chairman of the Board: August A. Busch III.
Vice Chairman: Fred Kuhlmann. **Administrative Assistant to Vice Chairman:** Pat Larson.
President and Chief Executive Officer: Stuart Meyer. **Administrative Assistant to President and CEO:** Elaine Milo.
Vice President, Business Operations: Mark Gorris. **Administrative Assistant to VP/Business Operations:** Renee Garrett.
Vice President, Marketing: Marty Hendin.
Controller: Brad Wood. **Secretary:** John Hayward.

Dal Maxvill

General Administration
Director of Public Relations: Jeff Wehling. **Manager of Public Relations:** Brian Bartow.
Director of Market Development and Broadcasting: Dan Farrell.
Director of Community Relations: Joe Cunningham. **Director of Sales:** Sue Ann McClaren.
Director of Tickets: Colin Allsop.
Traveling Secretary: C.J. Cherre.
Team Doctor: Dr. Stan London.
Trainer: Gene Gieselmann.
Equipment Manager: Buddy Bates.

Radio, TV
Radio Announcers: Jack Buck, Joe Buck, Mike Shannon. **Flagship Station:** KMOX 1120 AM.
TV Announcers: George Grande, Al Hrabosky. **Flagship Station:** KPLR Channel 11.

1992 Schedule

APRIL		
6-7-8-9	New York
10-11-12	at Chicago
13-14-15	at Montreal
17-18-19	Chicago
21-22-23	at New York
24-25-26	Montreal
27-28	at Los Angeles
29-30	at San Francisco

MAY	
1-2-3	at San Diego
5-6-7	San Francisco
8-9-10-11	Atlanta
12-13	Cincinnati
15-16-17	at Houston
18-19-20	at Atlanta
22-23-24	Houston
25-26-27	Los Angeles
29-30-31	San Diego

JUNE	
2-3	at Cincinnati
5-6-7	at Philadelphia
8-9-10	Chicago
12-13-14	Philadelphia
15-16-17	at Chicago
18-19-20-21	at New York
22-23-24	at Pittsburgh
26-27-28	New York
29-30	Pittsburgh

JULY	
1	Pittsburgh
2-3-4-5	at San Francisco
6-7-8	at San Diego
9-10-11-12	at L.A.
16-17-18-19	at Cincinnati
21-22	Atlanta
23-24-25-26	Cincinnati
27-28-29	Montreal
30-31	at Pittsburgh

AUGUST	
1-2	at Pittsburgh
3-4-5	Philadelphia
6-7-8-9	Pittsburgh
11-12-13	at Philadelphia
14-15-16	at Montreal
18-19-20	Houston
21-22-23	at Atlanta
25-26-27	at Houston
28-29-30	Los Angeles
31	San Diego

SEPTEMBER	
1-2	San Diego
4-5-6	San Francisco
7-8-9	at Montreal
11-12-13	Chicago
14-15	Pittsburgh
16-17	at New York
18-19-20	at Chicago
21-22	at Pittsburgh
23-24	New York
25-26-27	at Philadelphia
28-29-30	Montreal

OCTOBER	
2-3-4	Philadelphia

CARDINALS

Major League Staff
Manager: Joe Torre.
Coaches: Don Baylor, Joe Coleman, Dave Collins, Bucky Dent, Gaylen Pitts, Red Schoendienst.

Baseball Operations
Vice President and General Manager: Dal Maxvill.
Administrative Assistant to General Manager: Judy Carpenter-Barada.
Director of Player Development: Mike Jorgensen.
Assistant Player Development/Scouting: Scott Smulczenski. **Staff Assistant:** John Vuch. **Administrative Assistant:** Judy Francis.
Field Coordinator, Player Development: George Kissell.
Roving Instructors: Hub Kittle (pitching), Johnny Lewis (hitting), Bake McBride (hitting and baserunning), Luis Melendez (outfield), Bob Milliken (pitching), Dave Ricketts (catching).

Joe Torre

Minor League Affiliates:
Class	Farm Team	Manager	Coach(es)
AAA	Louisville	Jack Krol	Mark Riggins
AA	Arkansas	Joe Pettini	Marty Mason
A	St. Petersburg	Dave Bialas	John Stuper
A	Springfield	Rick Colbert	Roy Silver
A	Savannah	Mike Ramsey	Ramon Ortiz
A	Hamilton	Chris Maloney	Scott Melvin
Rookie	Johnson City	Steve Turco	Orlando Thomas
Rookie	Chandler	Joe Cunningham	Mauricio Nunez

Scouting
Director of Scouting: Fred McAlister (St. Petersburg, FL). **Assistant Scouting Director:** Marty Maier (Hollywood, FL).
Scouting Supervisor/Special Assignments: Marty Keough (Irvine, CA).
Advance Scout: Jack Hubbard (Safety Harbor, FL).
Special Assignment Scout: Rube Walker (Smyrna, GA).
Scouting Supervisors: Jorge Aranzamendi (Cabo Rojo, PR), Jim Bayens (Richmond Hills, GA), Jim Belz (Springfield, IL), Randy Benson (Granite Quarry, NC), Vern Benson (Granite Quarry, NC), Roberto Diaz (Santo Domingo, Dom. Rep.), Manny Guerra (N. Las Vegas, NV), Jim Johnston (San Leandro, CA), Tom McCormack (St. Louis, MO), Joe Morlan (New Albany, OH), Mel Nelson (Highland, CA), Scott Nichols (Timberville, VA), Jay North (Concord, CA), Jim Pamlanye (Orlando, FL), Joe Rigoli (Hopatcong, NJ), Mike Roberts (Raytown, MO), Hal Smith (Hilltop Lakes, TX), Roger Smith (Eastman, GA), Tim Thompson (Lewistown, PA).
Scouts: James Brown (Newport, KY), Roy Cromer (Lexington, SC), John DiPuglia (Miami, FL), Manuel Espinosa (Boca Chica, Dom. Rep.), Cecil Espy (San Diego, CA), Juan Melo (Bani, Dom. Rep.), Chuck Menzhuber (Costa Mesa, CA), Joe Popek (Clifton, NJ), Ken Thomas (Nashville, TN).

Spring Training Information
Major League Club
Hotel Address: St. Petersburg Hilton Towers, 333 1st St. South, St. Petersburg, FL 33701. Telephone: (813) 894-5000. **Stadium Address:** Al Lang Stadium, 180 2nd Ave. SE, St. Petersburg, FL 33701. Telephone: (813) 896-4641.

Minor League Clubs
Hotel Address: The Inn at St. Petersburg, 5005 34th St. N., St. Petersburg, FL 33714. Telephone: (813) 525-1181. **Complex Address:** Busch Complex, 7901 30th Ave. N., P.O. Box 41027, St. Petersburg, FL 33733. Telephone: (813) 345-5300.

SAN DIEGO

Office Address: 9449 Friars Rd. (Jack Murphy Stadium), San Diego, CA 92108. **Mailing Address:** P.O. Box 2000, San Diego, CA 92112. **Telephone:** (619) 282-4494. **FAX:** (619) 282-2228.
Operated by: The San Diego Padres Baseball Partnership.

Ownership, Management
Chairman: Tom Werner.
Vice Chaimen: Art Engel, Art Rivkin, Russell Goldsmith.
Partners: Malin Burnham, Bruce Corwin, John Earhart, Jack Goodall, Keith Matson, Michael Monk, Leon Parma, Bob Payne, Peter Peckham, Ernest Rady, Scott Wolfe.
President: Dick Freeman.
Vice President, Business Operations: Bill Adams.
Vice President, Public Relations: Andy Strasberg.
Vice President, Finance: Bob Wells.

Joe McIlvaine

General Administration
Director of Media Relations: Jim Ferguson. **Assistant Director of Media Relations:** Roger Riley.
Director of Community Relations and Publications: Jim Geschke.
Coordinator of Community Relations: Darla Davis.
Director of Administrative Services: Lucy Freeman.
Director of Marketing: Don Johnson.
Director of Promotions: Tom Ryba.
Director of Scoreboard Operations: Mark Guglielmo.
Director of Stadium Operations: Doug Duennes.
Director of Ticket Operations: Dave Gilmore.
Director of Ticket Sales: Jack Autry.
Manager of Accounting: Bob Croasdale.
Traveling Secretary: John "Doc" Mattei.
Equipment Manager: Brian Prilaman.
Trainer: Bob Day. **Assistant Trainer:** Todd Hutcheson.

Radio, TV
Radio-TV Announcers: Bob Chandler, Jerry Coleman, Ted Leitner, Rick Monday (KFMB-AM Radio, KUSI-TV, Cox Cable); Mario Thomas Zapiain, Eduardo Ortega, Santos Perez (XEXX Radio-Tijuana). **Flagship Stations:** KFMB 760 AM, XEXX AM, KUSI Channel 51, Cox Cable.

1992 Schedule

APRIL
6-7-8	at Cincinnati
9-10-11-12	Los Angeles
14-15-16	at S.F.
17-18-19	at Houston
20-21-22	Atlanta
24-25-26	Cincinnati
27-28	Philadelphia
29-30	Montreal

MAY
1-2-3	St. Louis
5-6	at Montreal
8-9-10	at Philadelphia
11-12-13	at New York
15-16-17	at Pittsburgh
18-19-20-21	New York
22-23-24	Chicago
25-26-27	Pittsburgh
29-30-31	at St. Louis

JUNE
1-2-3	at Chicago
5-6-7	Atlanta
8-9-10	Houston
12-13-14	at Atlanta
15-16-17	at Houston
18-19-20-21	at S.F.
22-23	Los Angeles
25-26-27-28	S.F.
29-30	at Los Angeles

JULY
1	at Los Angeles
2-3-4-5	Montreal
6-7-8	St. Louis
9-10-11-12	Philadelphia
16-17-18-19	at Montreal
20-21-22	at Philadelphia
24-25-26	at New York
27-28-29	Cincinnati
30-31	at Los Angeles

AUGUST
1-2	at Los Angeles
3-4-5	San Francisco
6-7-8-9	Houston
11-12-13	at Atlanta
14-15-16	at Cincinnati
18-19-20	at Pittsburgh
22-23	New York
24-25-26	Chicago
27-29-30	Pittsburgh
31	at St. Louis

SEPTEMBER
1-2	at St. Louis
4-5-6	at Chicago
7-8	at San Francisco
9-10	at Los Angeles
11-12-13	Cincinnati
14-15-16	Los Angeles
18-19-20	at Cincinnati
21-22	San Francisco
23-24	Houston
25-26-27	Atlanta
29-30	at Houston

OCTOBER
1	at Houston
2-3-4	at Atlanta

PADRES

Major League Staff
Manager: Greg Riddoch.
Coaches: Bruce Kimm, Rob Picciolo, Merv Rettenmund, Mike Roarke, Jim Snyder.

Baseball Operations
Executive Vice President, Baseball Operations and General Manager: Joe McIlvaine. **Assistant Vice President, Baseball Operations and Assistant General Manager:** John Barr.
Director of Minor Leagues: Ed Lynch. **Minor League Administrator:** Priscilla Oppenheimer.
Minor League Field Coordinator: Tom Gamboa. **Roving Instructor:** Tye Waller.

Greg Riddoch

Minor League Affiliates:

Class	Farm Team	Manager	Coach(es)
AAA	Las Vegas	Jim Riggleman	Jon Matlack, Tony Torchia
AA	Wichita	Bruce Bochy	Danny Garcia
A	High Desert	Bryan Little	Bruce Tanner, Lonnie Keeter
A	Waterloo	Keith Champion	Sonny Siebert
A	Charleston, SC	Dave Trembley	Jaime Moreno, Fred Cambria
A	Spokane	Ed Romero	Barry Moss, Jack Lamabe
Rookie	Scottsdale	Ken Berry	Manny Lantigua, Charlie Greene

Scouting
Scouting Director: Reggie Waller.
Scouting Coordinators: Ray Coley (Tucson, AZ), Andy Hancock (Buford, GA), Larry Harper (San Francisco, CA), Joe Henderson (San Diego, CA), John Kosciak (Milford, MA), Damon Oppenheimer (St. Petersburg, FL).
National Crosschecker: Brad Sloan (Peoria, IL).
Major League Scouts: Ken Bracey (Morton, IL), Carmen Fusco (Camp Hill, PA).
Special Assignment Scout: Dick Williams (Las Vegas, NV).
Advance Scout: Steve Lubratich (San Diego, CA).
Full-Time Scouts: Dave Bartosch (Newhall, CA), Dave Finley (San Diego, CA), Denny Galehouse (Doylestown, OH), Ronquito Garcia (Caguas, PR), Brian Granger (Dickson, TN), Kasey McKeon (Burlington, NC), Bobby Malkmus (Union, NJ), Jim Miller (San Jose, CA), Pat Murtaugh (Crown Point, IN), Hosken Powell (Pensacola, FL), Greg Smith (Antioch, TN), Van Smith (Belleville, IL), Scipio Spinks (Oklahoma City, OK), Craig Weissman (San Diego, CA).

Reggie Waller

Spring Training Information
Major League Club
Hotel Address: Park Inn International, 2600 S. Fourth Ave., Yuma, AZ 85364. **Telephone:** (602) 726-4830. **Stadium Address:** Ray Kroc Baseball Complex/Desert Sun Stadium, 1440 Desert Hills Dr., Yuma, AZ 85364. **Telephone:** (602) 726-6040.

Minor League Clubs
Hotel Address: Motel 10 Inn, 2730 S. Fourth Ave., Yuma, AZ 85364. Telephone: (602) 344-3550. **Complex Address:** same as major league stadium.

SAN FRANCISCO

Office Address: Candlestick Park, San Francisco, CA 94124. **Mailing Address:** same. **Telephone:** (415) 468-3700. **FAX:** (415) 467-0485.
Operated by: The San Francisco Giants.

Ownership, Management
Chairman: Bob Lurie.
Board of Directors: Corey Busch, James Hunt, Michael Kurzman, Bob Lurie, Connie Lurie, Peter Magowan, Al Rosen, Eugene Valla.
President and General Manager: Al Rosen.
Executive Vice President: Corey Busch.
Senior Vice President: Pat Gallagher.
Staff Counsel: Michael Shapiro.

Al Rosen

General Administration
Vice President, Public Relations: Duffy Jennings. **Director, Media Relations:** Matt Fischer. **Director of Communications:** Robin Carr Locke. **Administrative Assistant, Media Relations:** Maria Jacinto. **Media Relations Assistant:** Jim Moorehead.
Community Services Director: Dave Craig. **Assistant Director, Community Services:** Mike Sadek.
Director of Publications: Mark Ray.
Special Assistants to the President: Willie Mays, Willie McCovey.
Director of Marketing: Mario Alioto.
Promotions Manager: Valerie McGuire.
Vice President, Stadium Operations: Jorge Costa. **Director of Stadium Operations:** Gene Telucci.
Vice President, Finance/Administration: John Yee. **Controller:** Jeannie Hurley.
Vice President, Ticket Operations: Arthur Schulze. **Director of Ticket Operations:** Judy Jones.
Retail Sales Director: Bob Tolifson.
Director of Travel: Dirk Smith.
Team Physicians: Dr. Gordon Campbell, Dr. William Straw.
Trainers: Mark Letendre, Greg Lynn.
Home Clubhouse: Mike Murphy. **Visiting Clubhouse:** Harvey Hodgerney.

Radio, TV
Radio-TV Announcers: Ron Fairly, Hank Greenwald, Duane Kuiper, Joe Morgan. **Flagship Stations:** KNBR 680 AM, KTVU Channel 2.

1992 Schedule

APRIL
6-7 . . . . at Los Angeles
9-10-11-12 . . . . . . at Atlanta
14-15-16 . . . . San Diego
17-18-19 . . . . . . Cincinnati
20-21-22 . . . . . . at Houston
24-25-26 . . . . . Los Angeles
27-28 . . . . Montreal
29-30 . . . . St. Louis

MAY
1-2-3 . . . . Philadelphia
5-6-7 . . . . at St. Louis
8-9-10 . . . . at Montreal;
11-12-13 . . at Philadelphia
15-16-17 . . . . Chicago
19-20-21 . . . . . . Pittsburgh
22-23-24 . . . . . . New York
26-27-28 . . . . . at Chicago
29-30-31 . . . . at Pittsburgh

JUNE
1-2 . . . . at New York
4-5-6-7 . . . . Houston
8-9-10 . . . . Cincinnati
12-13-14 . . . . . at Houston
15-16-17 . . . . at Cincinnati
18-19-20-21 . . . San Diego
23-24 . . . . at Atlanta
25-26-27-28 . at San Diego
29-30 . . . . Atlanta

JULY
1 . . . . Atlanta
2-3-4-5 . . . . St. Louis
6-7-8 . . . . Philadelphia
9-10-11-12 . . . . . Montreal
16-17-18-19 . . at New York
20-21-22 . . . . . at Montreal
24-25-26 . . at Philadelphia
27-28-29 . . . . . Los Angeles
30-31 . . . . Atlanta

AUGUST
1-2 . . . . Atlanta
3-4-5 . . . . at San Diego
7-8-9 . . . . . . at Cincinnati
10-11-12 . . . . Houston
14-15-16-17 . . . . . . at L.A.
18-19-20 . . . . Chicago
21-22-23 . . . . . . Pittsburgh
24-25-26 . . . . . . New York
28-29-30 . . . . . at Chicago

SEPTEMBER
1-2-3 . . . . at Pittsburgh
4-5-6 . . . . at St. Louis
7-8 . . . . San Diego
9-10 . . . . Houston
11-12-13 . . at Los Angeles
14-15-16 . . . . . at Houston
18-19-20 . . . . Los Angeles
21-22 . . . . . . at San Diego
23-24 . . . . Atlanta
25-26-27 . . . . . Cincinnati
29-30 . . . . at Atlanta

OCTOBER
1 . . . . at Atlanta
2-3-4 . . . . at Cincinnati

GIANTS

Major League Staff
Manager: Roger Craig.
Coaches: Carlos Alfonso, Dusty Baker, Bob Brenly, Wendell Kim, Bob Lillis.

Baseball Operations
Vice President and Assistant General Manager: Ralph Nelson.
Vice President, Baseball Operations: Bob Kennedy.
Director of Minor League Operations: Tony Siegle. **Assistant Director of Minor League Operations:** Scot Asher. **Administrative Assistant, Minor Leagues:** Lucia McNally.
Director of Player Development: Jack Hiatt. **Assistant Director of Player Development:** Jack Mull.
Roving Instructors: Duane Espy (hitting), Les Moss (pitching).

Roger Craig

Minor League Affiliates:

Class	Farm Team	Manager	Coach(es)
AAA	Phoenix	Bill Evers	Tony Taylor, Todd Oakes
AA	Shreveport	Bill Robinson	Dick Dietz, Steve Cline
A	San Jose	Ron Wotus	Rick Miller, Frank Reberger
A	Clinton	Bill Stein	Nelson Rood, Gary Lucas
A	Everett	Norm Sherry	Mike Bubalo, Kevin Higgins
Rookie	Scottsdale	Alan Bannister	Diego Segui, Juan Lopez

Scouting
Vice President, Scouting: Bob Fontaine.
Director of Scouting: Dave Nahabedian. **Administrative Assistants:** Matt Nerland, Karen Sweeney.
Major League Scouts: Harry Craft (Conroe, TX), Hank Sauer (Millbrae, CA), John Van Ornum (Fresno, CA).
National Crosscheckers: Al Heist (Cookson, OK), , Mike Russell (Pensacola, FL).
Special Assignment Scout: Bob Miller (Carlsbad, CA).
Scouts: Bob Cummings (Oaklawn, IL), Nino Escalera (Carolina, PR), George Genovese (North Hollywood, CA), Herman Hannah (Dearborn, MI), Chuck Hensley Jr. (Foster City, CA), Elvio Jimenez (San Pedro de Macoris, Dom. Rep.), Mike Keenan (Manhattan, KS), Richard Klaus (Decatur, IL) Tom Korenek (Houston, TX), Alan Marr (Bellmore, NY), Doug McMillan (Cameron Park, CA), Tony Michalak (Covington, KY), Rick Ragazzo (Irvine, CA), Gary Robinson (Charlotte, NC), John Shafer (Portland, OR), Joe Strain (Englewood, CO), Todd Thomas (St. Louis, MO), Gene Thompson (Scottsdale, AZ), Mike Toomey (Hyattsville, MD), Elanis Westbrooks (Hattiesburg, MS), Tom Zimmer (St. Petersburg, FL).

Dave Nahabedian

Spring Training Information
Major League Club
Hotel Address: Scottsdale Plaza Resort, 7200 N. Scottsdale Rd., Scottsdale, AZ 85253. Telephone: (602) 948-5000. **Stadium Address:** Scottsdale Stadium, 7402 E. Osborn Rd., Scottsdale, AZ 85251. Telephone: (602) 990-7972.

Minor League Clubs
Hotel Address: Wooley's Suites, 1635 N. Scottsdale Rd., Tempe, AZ 85281. Telephone: (602) 947-3711. **Complex Address:** Indian School Park, Hayden and Camelback Rds., Scottsdale, AZ 85251. Telephone: (602) 990-3341.

COLORADO ROCKIES

Office Address: 1700 Broadway, Suite 2100, Denver, CO 80290. **Mailing Address:** Same. **Telephone:** (303) 292-0200. **FAX:** (303) 830-8977.

Operated by: Colorado Rockies Baseball, Inc.

Ownership, Management

Chairman and Chief Executive Officer: John Antonucci.
President and Chief Operating Officer: Steve Ehrhart.
Executive Vice President and General Counsel: Paul Jacobs.
Vice President, Finance: Michael Kent.
Senior Vice President, Public Affairs: Dean Peeler.
Executive Administrator: Wendy Jobe

General Administration

Bob Gebhard

Director, Public Relations: Mike Swanson.
Administrative Assistant, Public Affairs: Barb Maniscalco.
Director, Merchandising: Mark Ehrhart.
Director of Corporate Marketing: Dave Glazier.
Director, Community Services: Roger Kinney. **Manager, Community Relations:** Jackie Sarmiento.
Special Events Coordinator: Alan Bossart.
Director, Ticket Operations: Chuck Javernick.

Baseball Operations

Senior Vice President and General Manager: Bob Gebhard.
Executive Vice President, Baseball Operations: John McHale.
Senior Vice President, Baseball Operations: Bernie Mullin.
Assistant General Manager/Minor League Director: Randy Smith.
Administrators, Baseball Operations: Mark Cheney, Jeff Tamarkin.
Administrative Assistant, Baseball Operations: Chris Rice.
Roving Instructor: Amos Otis (hitting/baserunning).

Minor League Affiliates:

Class	Farm Team	Manager	Coach(es)
A	Bend	Gene Glynn	Joe Niekro, Johnny Zizzo
Rookie	Mesa	Paul Zuvella	Rick Mathews

Scouting

Director of Scouting: Pat Daugherty.
Assistant Director of Scouting: Paul Egins.
National Crosscheckers: Herb Hippauf (Sunnyvale, CA), Randy Smith (Denver, CO).
Major League Scouts: Bob Gebhard (Denver, CO), Larry Bearnarth (Denver, CO), Eddie Robinson (Ft. Worth, TX).
Full-Time Scouts: Ty Coslow (Louisville, KY), Dar Cox (Red Oak, TX), Mike Garlatti (Highland Park, NJ), Gene Glynn (Mankato, MN), Julian Gonzalez (Dominican Republic), Al Hargesheimer (Arlington Heights, IL), Randy Johnson (Escondido, CA), Pat Jones (Davie, FL), Jimmy Lester (Columbus, GA), Frank Mattox (Los Angeles, CA), Danny Montgomery (Charlotte, NC), Lance Nichols (Dodge City, KS), Jorge Posada (Rio Piedras, PR), Ed Santa (Columbus, OH), Tom Wheeler (Pleasant Hill, CA), Johnny Zizzo (Youngstown, OH).

Pat Daugherty

FLORIDA MARLINS

Office Address: 100 NE 3rd Ave., Ft. Lauderdale, FL 33301. **Mailing Address:** Same. **Telephone:** (305) 779-7070. **FAX:** (305) 779-7130.

Operated by: The Florida Marlins, Inc.

Ownership, Management
Owner: H. Wayne Huizenga.
President: Carl Barger.

General Administration
Vice President of Business Operations: Richard Andersen.
Vice President of Communications: Dean Jordan.
Vice President/Expansion Coordinator: Don Smiley.
Director of Season and Group Sales: Bill Galante.
Archivist: Margo Malone.

David Dombrowski

Baseball Operations
Executive Vice President and General Manager: David Dombrowski.
Assistant General Manager: Frank Wren.
Special Assistant to the General Manager: Cookie Rojas.
Senior Advisor, Player Personnel: Whitey Lockman.
Director of Player Development: John Boles. **Director of Minor League Administration:** Dan Lunetta. **Executive Secretary, Player Development:** Amy Grubbs.
Coordinator of Team Development: Jim Hendry.
Roving Instructors: Joe Breeden (catching), Jack Maloof (hitting), Sal Rende (defense). **Trainer and Equipment Manager:** Vince Scavo.

Minor League Affiliates:

Class	Farm Team	Manager	Coach(es)
A	Erie	Fredi Gonzalez	Jose Castro, Marty DeMerritt
Rookie	GCL Marlins	Carlos Tosca	Fernando Arroyo, Carlos Ponce

Scouting
Director of Scouting and Special Assistant to the General Manager: Gary Hughes.
Director of Latin American Operations and Special Consultant to the General Manager: Angel Vasquez.
National Crosscheckers: Murray Cook (Cincinnati, OH), Dick Egan (Reno, NV), Orrin Freeman (LaJolla, CA), Jax Robertson (Dearborn, MI), Greg Zunino (Cape Coral, FL).
Major League Scouts: Ken Kravec (Sarasota, FL), Scott Reid (Phoenix, AZ), John Young (Diamond Bar, CA).
Scouts: Eddie Bockman (Millbrae, CA), Rich Bordi (Rohnert Park, CA), Edmundo Borrome (Santo Domingo, Dom. Rep.), Kelvin Bowles (Rocky Mount, VA), Ty Brown (Ruther Glen, VA), Julian Camilo (Santo Domingo, Dom. Rep.), Joe Campise (Houston, TX), John Castleberry (Fairfax, VA), Brad Del Barba (Covington, KY), Scott Diez (Delray Beach, FL), Lou Fitzgerald (Cleveland, TN), Al Geddes (Canby, OR), Will George (Pennsauken, NJ), Matt King (Aptos, CA), Bob Laurie (Carmel, IN), Grady Mack (Hermosa Beach, CA), Steve Minor (Long Beach, CA), Jim Moran (Davenport, FL), Levy Ochoa (Cabimas, Venezuela), Fran Oneto (Merced, CA), Jeff Pentland (Tempe, AZ), Cucho Rodriguez (Santurce, PR), Bill Scherrer (Buffalo, NY), Tim Schmidt (San Bernardino, CA), William Serena (Hayward, CA), Bill Singer (Decatur, AL), Birdie Tebbetts (Anna Maria, FL), Wally Walker (Reno, NV), DeJon Watson (Baldwin Hills, CA), Jeff Wren (Ocala, FL).

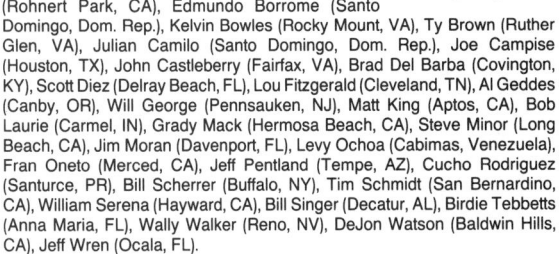

Gary Hughes

MAJORS
OTHER INFORMATION

Major League Baseball Productions
THE PHOENIX COMMUNICATIONS GROUP, INC.

Mailing Address: 3 Empire Boulevard, South Hackensack, NJ 07606.
Telephone: (201) 807-0888. **FAX:** (201) 807-0272.
Chairman: Joe Podesta. **President:** James Holland. **Senior Vice President, Executive Producer:** Geoff Belinfante. **Vice President, Director of Baseball Programming:** Mike Kostel.

Major League Players Association

Mailing Address: 805 3rd Ave., New York, NY 10022. **Telephone:** (212) 826-0808. **FAX:** (212) 752-3649.
Executive Director and General Counsel: Donald Fehr. **Special Assistant:** Mark Belanger.
Associate General Counsel: Eugene Orza. **Assistant General Cousel:** Lauren Rich, Michael Weiner.
Director of Marketing: Allyne Price.
Executive Board: Player representatives of the 26 major league clubs.
League Representatives: Paul Molitor (A.L.), Jay Bell (N.L.).

Major League Scouting Bureau

Mailing Address: 23712 Birtcher Dr., Suite A, El Toro, CA 92630. **Telephone:** (714) 458-7600. **FAX:** (714) 458-9454.
Director: Don Pries.
Assistant Director: Frank Marcos. **Administrator:** RoseMary Durgin. **Administrative Assistant:** Mike Wilson. **Computer Operations:** Lisa Harryman.
Board of Directors: Bill Murray, chairman; Sandy Alderson (A's), Dick Balderson (Cubs), Lou Gorman (Red Sox), Jay Hankins (Phillies), Roland Hemond (Orioles), Joe McIlvaine (Padres), Art Stewart (Royals), Don Pries.
Scouts: Bruce Andrew (Northridge, CA), Jim Baba (Saskatoon, Sask.), Richard Baurle (Carnegie, PA), James Beavers (Roswell, GA), William Beezer (Philipsburg, PA), Ron Betts (Edmonton, Alta.), Brannon Bonifay (Okeechobee, FL), Tom Bourque (Cambridge, MA), Russ Bove (Apopka, FL), Stan Brzezicki (Erie, PA), Tom Burkert (Howell, MI), Walt Burrows (Brentwood Bay, B.C.), Rudy Camejo (Hialeah, FL), Art Chapman (Lutherville, MD), Mike Childers (Oklahoma City, OK), Dick Cole (Costa Mesa, CA), Dick Colpaert (Utica, MI), Jeff Cornell (Kansas City, MO), Robby Corsaro (Upland, CA), Jerry Cunningham (Cuba, MO), Ralph DiLullo (Paterson, NJ), Dan Dixon (San Diego, CA), John Dunsford (Charlottetown P.E.I.), Pal Eldredge (Honolulu, HI), Gerry Falk (Carman, Man.), Walt Fields (Fulton, IL), Art Gardner (Walnut Grove, MS), Rusty Gerhardt (Arlington, TX), Bill Green (Vancouver, B.C.), Sean Gulliver (St. Johns, Nfld.), Randy Gumpert (Berks County, PA), Mike Hamilton (Arlington, TX), Rich Hinell (Dryden, NY), Lowell Hodges (Sidney, B.C.), Doug Horning (Schererville, IN), Lee Irwin (Fresno, CA), Larry Izzo (Deer Park, NY), Bill Jackson (Peoria, AZ), Brad Kohler (Easton, PA), Don Kohler (Plainfield, NJ), Don Koonce (Fayetteville, NC), Mick Kozlowski (Kitchener, Ont.), Mike Larson (Waseca, MN), Herb Mancini (Youngstown, OH), Jim Martz (Lima, OH), Glen Matheson (Truro, N.S.), Ed McCarthy (West Haven, CT), Jethro McIntyre (Oakland, CA), Dave McManus (Fredericton, N.B.), Bob Meisner (Golden, CO), Lenny Merullo (Reading, MA), Joseph McGillen (Philadelphia, PA), Leon McGraw (Baton Rouge, LA), Paul Mirocke (Tampa, FL), Rick Oliver (LaVerne, CA), Larry Osborne (Atlanta, GA), Tim Osborne (Marietta, GA), Buddy Peterson (Sacramento, CA), Ed Pienta (Chicago, IL), Elmo Plaskett (St. Croix, Virgin Islands), Cesar Presbot (Bronx, NY), Bud Pritchard (Fullerton, CA), Gary Rajsich (Beaverton, OR), Gary Randall (Nashville, TN), Doug Robbins (Bridgeport, WV), Jim Robinson (Kirkland, WA), Al Ronning (Sunnyvale, CA), George Santiago (Santurce, PR), Kevin Saucier (Pensacola, FL), Carroll Sembera (Shiner, TX), Pat Shortt (Rockville Centre, NY), Craig Smajstrla (Pearland, TX), Ralph Smith (Fairfield, OH), Steve Stocker (Indianapolis, IN), Ed Sukla (Irvine, CA), Jim Terrell (Beaverton, MI), Steve Terry (Peterborough, Ont.), Tom Valcke (Windsor, Ont.), Joaquin Velilla (Toa Alta, PR), Jim Walton (Shattuck, OK).

Major League Umpires Association

Mailing Address: 1735 Market St., Suite 3420, Philadelphia, PA 19103.
Telephone: (215) 979-3200.
General Counsel: Richard Phillips.

Major League Baseball Umpire Development Program

Mailing Address: P.O. Box A, St. Petersburg, FL 33731. **Telephone:** (813) 823-1286. **FAX:** (813) 821-5819.
Executive Director: Edwin Lawrence.
Administrative Assistant: Barbara Douglas.
Director of Field Supervision: Mike Fitzpatrick (Kalamazoo, MI).
Supervisors: Dennis Cregg (Webster, MA), Mike Felt (Tarpon Springs, FL), Tom Lepperd (Des Moines, IA), Dick Nelson (Perryville, AR), Michael Pilato (Yorba Linda, CA).
Area Observers: Joe Linsalata (Hollywood, FL), Jerry Neudecker (Mary Esther, FL).

National Baseball Hall of Fame

Mailing Address: P.O. Box 590, Cooperstown, NY 13326. **Telephone:** (607) 547-9988. **FAX:** (607) 547-5980.
President: Edward Stack. **Vice President:** Stephen Clark Jr. **Secretary:** William Burdick.
Treasurer/Director: Howard Talbot Jr. **Associate Director:** Bill Guilfoile.
Merchandising Director: Jeffrey Stevens.
Curator: William Spencer. **Registrar:** Peter Clark. **Controller:** Frances Althiser. **Librarian, National Baseball Library:** Tom Heitz.

Major League Baseball Players Alumni Association

Mailing Address: 3637 4th St. No., Suite 101, St. Petersburg, FL 33704. **Telephone:** (813) 822-3399. **FAX:** (813) 822-6300.
Chairman of the Board: Bob Miller. **Vice Chairman:** Jim Hannan. **Board of Directors:** Bob Boone, Darrel Chaney, Jim "Mudcat" Grant, Rich Hand, Lou Klimchock, Tug McGraw, Jim Price, Dick Radatz, Ken Sanders, Fred Valentine, Carl Warwick.
President: Brooks Robinson. **Vice Presidents:** Hank Aguirre, Carl Erskine, Mike Hegan, Chuck Hinton, Al Kaline, Eddie Robinson, Mike Schmidt, Rusty Staub, Billy Williams.
Vice President, Administration: Dan Foster. **Manager, Member Services:** Peggy Heine.

Association of Professional Baseball Players of America

Mailing Address: 12062 Valley View St., Suite 211, Garden Grove, CA 92645. **Telephone:** (714) 892-9900. **FAX:** (714) 897-0233.
President: John McHale.
Secretary-Treasurer: Chuck Stevens.
1st Vice President: Joe DiMaggio. **2nd Vice President:** Arthur Richman. **3rd Vice President:** Bob Kennedy.
Advisory Council: Calvin Griffith, Eddie Sawyer.

Baseball Assistance Team (BAT)

Mailing Address: 350 Park Ave., New York, NY 10022. **Telephone:** (212) 339-7884. **FAX:** (212) 355-0007.
Chairman: Ralph Branca. **President:** Joe Garagiola. **Vice Presidents:** Rusty Staub, Joe Black, Earl Wilson. **Secretary and Treasurer:** Tom Ostertag.

Baseball Chapel

Mailing Address: P.O. Box 300, Bloomingdale, NJ 07403. **Telephone:** (201) 838-8111 or 838-7070.
President: Bobby Richardson.
Executive Director: Dave Swanson.
Area Representatives: Sam Bender (Pt. Clinton, OH), David Fisher (Toronto, Ontario), Bruce Reynolds (Clearwater, FL), John Werhas (Anaheim Hills, CA).
Minor League Coordinator: Rip Kirby (Phoenix, AZ).
Latin America Coordinator: Carlos Rios (Lantana, FL)

MEDIA INFORMATION

Baseball Statistics Bureaus

Elias Sports Bureau, Inc.

Mailing Address: 500 Fifth Ave., New York, NY 10110. **Telephone:** (212) 869-1530.
General Manager: Seymour Siwoff.

Howe Sportsdata International

Mailing Address: Boston Fish Pier, West Bldg. #2, Suite 306, Boston, MA 02210. **Telephone:** (617) 951-0070. **Stats Service:** (617) 951-1379. **FAX:** (617) 737-9960.
President: Alan Goldfine. **Executive Vice President:** Jay Virshbo. **Vice President, Director of Records Bureau:** Bill Weiss.
Night Manager: Mike Walczak. **Communications Manager:** Tom Graham. **Verifications Manager:** Jim Keller. **Statisticians:** Bob Townsend, Chris Pollari, John Foley, Vinnie Vitro, Paul LaRocca, Mike Pogson, Jeff Newton, Brian Joura.

Television

ESPN

Mailing Address: Bristol Office—ESPN Plaza, Bristol, CT 06010. **Telephone:** (203) 585-2000. **FAX:** (203) 585-2422. **New York Office**—605 Third Ave., New York, NY 10016. Telephone: (212) 916-9260. FAX: (212) 9165-9312.
President and Chief Executive Officer: Steve Bornstein.
Senior Vice President, Communications: Rosa Gatti. **Vice President, Communications:** Chris LaPlaca. **Manager of Programming Information:** Mike Soltys.
Senior Vice President, Programming: Loren Matthews. **Coordinating Producer:** Jed Drake. **Executive Editor:** John Walsh. **Managing Editor:** Steve Anderson. **Coordinating Producer, Baseball Tonight:** Eric Schoenfeld.
Studio Hosts: Chris Berman, Gary Miller, John Saunders.
Play-by-Play Announcers: Chris Berman, Steve Zabriskie, Jon Miller, Steve Physioc, Gary Thorne.
Analysts: Dave Campbell, Peter Gammons, Tommy Hutton, Ray Knight, Joe Morgan, Jerry Reuss.

CBS

Mailing Address: 51 W. 52nd St., 30th Floor, New York, NY 10019. **Telephone:** (212) 975-4321.
President, CBS Sports: Neal Pilson.
Director of Communications: Susan Kerr. **Associate Director of Sports Publicity:** Lou D'Ermilio. **Director of Sports Publicity:** Sandy Genelius. **Sports Publicist:** Robin Daniels. **Press Coordinator:** Kris Kellam.

Radio

ESPN

Mailing Address: ESPN Plaza, Bristol, CT 06010. **Telephone:** (203) 585-2661. **FAX:** (203) 585-2213.
Executive Producer: Kevin Young. **Producers:** John Martin, Bruce Murray. **News Editor:** Larry Schwartz.

CBS

Mailing Address: 51 West 52nd St., New York, NY 10019. **Telephone:** (212) 975-8117. **FAX:** (212) 975-3515.
Vice President, Executive Producer: Frank Murphy. **Director, Sports and Features:** David Kurman. **Manager, Sports and Features, Producer:** Don Sabatini. **Director, Communications:** Helene Blueberg.,

Baseball Writers Assoc. of America

Mailing Address: 36 Brookfield Road, Fort Salonga, NY 11768. **Telephone:** (516) 757-0562. **FAX:** (516) 757-6817.
President: Pat Reusse (Minneapolis Star and Tribune).
Vice President: Neil Hohlfeld (Houston Chronicle).
Board of Directors: Paul Meyer (Pittsburgh Post-Gazette), Claire Smith (New York Times), Kit Stier (Oakland Tribune), Mark Whicker (Orange County Register).
Secretary-Treasurer: Vern Plagenhoef (Booth Newspapers, Michigan).
Executive Secretary: Jack Lang. **Assistant Secretary:** Red Foley.

National Assoc. of Baseball Writers & Broadcasters

Mailing Address: P.O. Box A, St. Petersburg, FL 33731. **Telephone:** (813) 823-4050. **FAX:** (813) 821-5819.
President: George Rorrer (Louisville Courier-Journal).
Vice President: Bill Weiss (Howe Sportsdata International).
Secretary-Treasurer: Bob Sparks (National Association).

Society for American Baseball Research

Mailing Address: P.O. Box 93183, Cleveland, OH 44101. **Telephone:** (216) 575-0500. **FAX:** (216) 575-0502.
President: Lloyd Johnson (Kansas City). **Vice President:** Jack Kavanagh (No. Kingstown, RI).
Executive Director: Morris Eckhouse (Cleveland). **Secretary:** Claudia Perry (Houston). **Treasurer:** Robert Ruland (Southfield, MI).

Baseball Tickers

SportsTicker

Mailing Address: Harborside Financial Center, 600 Plaza Two, Jersey City, NJ 07311. **Telephone:** (201) 309-1200. **FAX:** (201) 860-9742.
President: Peter Bavasi. **Vice President:** Rick Alessandri. **General Manager:** John Mastroberardino. **Managing Editor:** Joe Carnicelli.

Periodicals

USA Today

Mailing Address: 1000 Wilson Blvd., Arlington, VA 22209. **Telephone:** (703) 276-3400. **FAX:** (703) 558-3905.
Baseball Editors: Bob Velin, Matt Cimento. **Baseball Columnist:** Hal Bodley. **Major League Beat Writers:** Rod Beaton (NL), Mel Antonen (AL). **Baseball Reporters:** Chuck Johnson, Denise Tom.

USA Today Baseball Weekly

Mailing Address: 1000 Wilson Blvd., Arlington, VA 22229. **Telephone:** (703) 276-3400. **FAX:** (703) 558-4678.
Publisher: Tom Farrell. **Editor:** Paul White. **National Sales Manager:** Kevin McCarthy. **Classified Sales Manager:** Lynn Busby.

The Sporting News

Mailing Address: 1212 N. Lindbergh Blvd., St. Louis, MO 63132. **Telephone:** (314) 997-7111. **FAX:** (314) 993-7723.
Editor: John Rawlings. **Managing Editor:** Steve Meyerhoff.
Information Development: William Topaz (director), Gary Levy (editor), Mike Nahrstedt (managing editor), Joe Hoppel (senior editor).

Sports Illustrated

Mailing Address: Time & Life Building, New York, NY 10020. **Telephone:** (212) 522-1212. **FAX, Editorial:** (212) 522-0610. **FAX, Public Relations:** (212) 522-0610.
Managing Editor: John Papanek. **Senior Editor, Baseball:** David Bauer. **Associate Editor, Baseball:** Greg Kelly. **Editor-At-Large:** Steve Wulf. **Writers:** Tim Kurkjian, Steve Rushin. **Reporters:** Jeff Bradley, Albert Im, Jim Rodewald.
Director of Communications: Art Berke. **Publicity Director:** Roger Jackson.

Bill Mazeroski's Baseball

Mailing Address: 100 W. Harrison, North Tower, Fifth Floor, Seattle, WA 98119. **Telephone:** (206) 282-2322. **FAX:** (206) 284-2083.
Publisher: Shane O'Neill. **Editor:** Ken Leiker.

Beckett Publications

Mailing Address: 4887 Alpha Rd., Suite 200, Dallas, TX 75244. **Telephone:** (214) 991-2630. **FAX:** (214) 991-8930.
Managing Editor: Jay Johnson. **Assistant Editor, Baseball Card Monthly:** Mike Payne. **Associate Editor, Focus on Future Stars:** Gary Santaniello.

Krause Publications

Mailing Address: 700 E. State St., Iola, WI 54990. **Telephone:** (715) 445-2214. **FAX:** (715) 445-4087.
Publisher: Steve Ellingboe.
Editor, Fantasy Baseball: Greg Ambrosius. **Editor, Baseball Cards Magazine:** Kit Kiefer. **Editor, Sports Collectors Digest:** Tom Mortenson. **Editor, Baseball Card News:** Scott Kelnhofer.

MINOR LEAGUES

BUFFALO
BISONS

Office Address: 275 Washington St., Buffalo, NY 14205. **Mailing Address:** P.O. Box 450, Buffalo, NY 14205. **Telephone:** (716) 846-2000. **FAX:** (716) 846-2258.

Affiliation (first year): Pittsburgh Pirates (1988). **Years in League:** 1985-.

Operated by: Bison Baseball, Inc.

Chairman of the Board: Robert E. Rich Sr.

President: Robert E. Rich Jr. **Executive Vice Presidents:** Melinda Rich, Herbert Kusche. **Vice President/Secretary:** William Gisel Jr.

Vice President/General Manager: Michael Billoni. **Vice President/General Manager (SSI):** Jonathan Dandes. **Vice President/Administration:** Marta Hiczewski. **Assistant General Manager:** Mike Buczkowski. **Comptroller:** John Dougherty. **Executive Director, Sales:** James Mack. **Baseball Operations Manager:** Kenneth Lehner. **Advertising and Promotions Manager:** Robin Lenhard. **Merchandise Manager:** Nancy Martin.

Field Manager: Marc Bombard. **Coaches:** Doc Edwards, Spin Williams.

Trainer: Mike Sandoval.

Radio Announcer: Pete Weber. **No. of Games Broadcast:** Home-72, Away-72. **Flagship Station:** WGR 550-AM.

Stadium Name: Pilot Field. **Location:** I-190 to Elm St. exit, left on Swan St. **Standard Game Times:** 1:05 p.m.; 2:05; 7:05.

Visiting Club Hotel: Holiday Inn Buffalo, 620 Delaware Ave., Buffalo, NY 14202. Telephone: (716) 886-2121.

DENVER
ZEPHYRS

Office Address: 2850 W. 20th Ave., Denver, CO 80211. **Telephone:** (303) 433-2032. **FAX:** (303) 433-1428.

Affiliation (first year): Milwaukee Brewers (1987). **Years in League:** 1955-62, 1969-.

Operated by: Dikeou Enterprises

President and Managing Partner: John Dikeou. **Executive Vice President:** R.D. Betcke.

Director of Sales: Jack Swallow. **Director of Operations:** Meg Philpott. **Director of Media and Public Relations:** Brad Dunevitz. **Media Relations Assistant:** Steve Nickell. **Clubhouse Manager:** Keith Schulz. **Operation Assistants:** Katie Bell, Mike Thumim.

Field Manager: Tony Muser. **Coaches:** Lamar Johnson, Mike Campbell.

Trainer: Peter Kolb.

Radio: None.

Stadium Name: Mile High. **Location:** I-25 to exit 210B. **Standard Game Times:** 12:35 p.m., 2:05, 6:35.

Visiting Club Hotels: Unavailable.

INDIANAPOLIS
INDIANS

Office Address: 1501 W. 16th St., Indianapolis, IN 46202. **Telephone:** (317) 269-3545. **FAX:** (317) 269-3541.

Affiliation (first year): Montreal Expos (1984). **Years in League:** 1902-62, 1969-.

Operated by: Indianapolis Indians, Inc.

President and General Manager: Max Schumacher. **Assistant General Manager/Publicity Director:** Cal Burleson. **Business Manager:** Scott Doehrman. **Director of Special Projects:** Bruce Schumacher. **Ticket Manager:** Mike Schneider. **Promotions Coordinator:** Daryle Keith. **Stadium Director:** Dan Madden.

Field Manager: Pat Kelly. **Coaches:** Gomer Hodge, Rich Dubee.

Trainer: John Spinosa.

Radio Announcers: Howard Kellman, Tom Akins. **No. of Games Broadcast:** Home-72, Away-72. **Flagship Station:** WIRE 100.9-FM.

Stadium Name: Owen J. Bush. **Location:** 1½ miles west of Meridian St. on 16th St. **Standard Game Times:** Mon.-Sat. (April-May) 7 p.m., (June-Sept.) 7:35; Sun. (April-June) 2, (July-Sept.) 6.

Visiting Club Hotel: Speedway Motel, 4400 W. 16th St., Indianapolis, IN 46222. Telephone: (317) 241-2500.

IOWA
CUBS

Office Address: 350 SW 1st, Des Moines, IA 50309. **Telephone:** (515) 243-6111. **FAX:** (515) 243-5152.

Affiliation (first year): Chicago Cubs (1981). **Years in League:** 1969-.
Operated by: The Greater Des Moines Baseball Co.
President: Ken Grandquist.
General Manager: Sam Bernabe. **Assistant General Manager:** Todd Guske. **Public Relations Director:** Todd Weber. **Group Sales Director:** Paul Kemble. **Director of Merchandising:** Nick Willey. **Director of Broadcasting:** Deene Ehlis. **Controller:** Sue Tollefson. **Office Manager:** Sharlynn Thomsen. **Stadium Operations:** Steve Heimbach. **Groundskeeper:** Mike Andresen.

Field Manager: Brad Mills. **Coach:** Rick Kranitz.
Trainer: Brian McCann.
Radio Announcer: Deene Ehlis. **No. of Games Broadcast:** Home-72, Away-72. **Flagship Station:** KSO 1390-AM.

Stadium Name: Sec Taylor. **Location:** I-235 to 3rd St. exit, south on 3rd Street to Court, east on Court to 2nd, south on 2nd. **Standard Game Times:** Mon.-Sat. (April-May) 7 p.m., (June-Sept.) 7:30; Sun. (April-June) 2, (July-Sept.) 6.

Visiting Club Hotel: Kirkwood Civic Center, Downtown, 4th at Walnut, Des Moines, IA 50309. Telephone: (515) 244-9191.

LOUISVILLE
REDBIRDS

Office Address: Kentucky State Fairgrounds, Freedom Way and Phillips Lane, Louisville, KY 40213. **Mailing Address:** P.O. Box 36407, Louisville, KY 40233. **Telephone:** (502) 367-9121. **FAX:** (502) 368-5120.

Affiliation (first year): St. Louis Cardinals (1982). **Years in League:** 1902-62, 1982-.
Operated by: Louisville Baseball Club, Inc.
Directors: Daniel Ulmer, chairman; Gene Gardner, president; John Hillerich III, vice president and treasurer; Dale Owens, secretary; Edward Glasscock; James Morrissey; Thomas Musselman; Robert Stallings.
General Manager: Dale Owens. **Executive Secretary and Team Operations:** Mary Barney. **Controller:** Jane Hoben. **Director of Marketing:** Tab Brockman. **Director of Broadcasting:** Jim Kelch. **Ticket Manager:** Greg Galiette. **Group Sales Director:** Melissa Ackman. **Sales:** Doug Schutz, Dee Cordell, Theresa Shinault.

Field Manager: Jack Krol. **Coach:** Mark Riggins.
Trainer: Brad Bluestone.
Radio Announcers: Jim Kelch, Mark Neely. **No. of Games Broadcast:** Home-72, Away-72. **Flagship Station:** WAVG 970-AM.

Stadium Name: Cardinal. **Location:** Intersection of I-65 and I-264 at Kentucky Fair and Exposition Center. **Standard Game Times:** 7:15 p.m.; Sun., 2 & 6.

Visiting Club Hotels: Executive Inn, 978 Phillips Lane, Louisville, KY 40213. Telephone: (502) 367-6161; Seelbach Hotel, 500 Fourth Ave., Louisville, KY 40201. Telephone: (502) 585-3200.

NASHVILLE
SOUNDS

Office Address: 534 Chestnut St., Nashville, TN 37203. **Mailing Address:** P.O. Box 23290, Nashville, TN 37202. **Telephone:** (615) 242-4371. **FAX:** (615) 256-5684.

Affiliation (first year): Cincinnati Reds (1987). **Years in League:** 1985-.
Operated by: Nashville Sounds Baseball Club, Ltd.
President and General Manager: Larry Schmittou. **Director of Administration and Concessions:** Ron Schmittou. **Director of Marketing and Public Relations:** Jim Ballweg. **Director of Ticket Sales:** Dot Cloud. **Business Manager:** Susan Ross. **Director of Group Sales:** Kelly Nance. **Office Manager:** Sharon Carson. **Equipment Manager:** Tim Williamson.
Field Manager: Pete Mackanin. **Coaches:** Frank Funk, Jim Lett.
Trainer: John Young.
Radio Announcers: Steve Carroll, Mike Smithson. **No. of Games Broadcast:** Home-72, Away-72. **Flagship Station:** WWTN 99.7 FM.
Stadium Name: Herschel Greer. **Location:** I-65 to Wedgewood exit. Standard Game Times: 7:35 p.m., Sun (April-May) 2:05.
Visiting Club Hotels: Days Inn Vanderbilt, 1800 West End Ave., Nashville, TN 37203. Telephone: (615) 327-0922; Executive Plaza, 823 Murfreesboro, Rd., Nashville, TN 37210. Telephone: (615) 367-1234; Shoney's Inn, 1521 Demonbreun St., Nashville, TN 37203. Telephone: (615) 255-9977.

OKLAHOMA CITY
89ers

Office Address: State Fairgrounds, 89er Drive, Oklahoma City, OK 73107. **Mailing Address:** P.O. Box 75089, Oklahoma City, OK 73147. **Telephone:** (405) 946-8989. **FAX:** (405) 942-4198.
Affiliation (first year): Texas Rangers (1983). **Years in League:** 1962, 1969-.
Operated by: 89er Baseball Club of Oklahoma City.
Chairman and Chief Executive Officer: Jeffrey Loria. **President:** Bobby Murcer.
Vice President and General Manager: Jim Weigel. **Assistant General Manager:** Dorsena Picknell. **Busines Manager:** Dee Hood. **Media Coordinator:** Cathy Shank. **Director of Communications:** Nancy Samson Cohen. **Director of Operations:** Andrew Putnam. **Ticket Manager:** Lance Buckley. **Assistant Ticket Manager/Promotions:** Brad Tammen. **Director of Group Sales:** Glenn Popowitz. **Executive Secretary:** Nancy Haddock.
Field Manager: Tommy Thompson. **Coaches:** Oscar Acosta, Mike Berger.
Trainer: Ray Ramirez.
Radio Announcer: Brian Barnhart. **No. of Games Broadcast:** Home-72, Away-72. **Flagship Station:** KXXY 1340-AM.
Stadium Name: All Sports. **Location:** I-44 to NW 10th St., east to 89er Drive, on the State Fairgrounds. **Standard Game Times:** 7:05 p.m.; Sun. (April-May) 1:35, (June-Sept.) 7:05.
Visiting Club Hotel: Holiday Inn Northwest, 3535 NW 39th, Oklahoma City, OK 73112. Telephone: (405) 947-2351.

OMAHA
ROYALS

Office Address: 1202 Bert Murphy Ave., Omaha, NE 68107. **Mailing Address:** P.O. Box 3665, Omaha, NE 68103. **Telephone:** (402) 734-2550. **FAX:** (402) 734-7166.
Affiliation (first year): Kansas City Royals (1969). **Years in League:** 1955-59, 1961-62, 1969-.
Operated by: Omaha Royals, Inc.
President: Joe Adams.
Vice President and General Manager: Bill Gorman. **Assistant General Manager:** Terry Wendlandt. **Director of Marketing:** Rob Goodman. **Director of Customer Service:** Cindy Kiger. **Comptroller:** Sue Nicholson. **Corporate Sales Representatives:** Dick Beckius, Mike Mashanic, Mark Morris.
Field Manager: Jeff Cox. **Coaches:** Joel Horlen, Bob Herold.
Trainer: Mark Farnsworth.
Radio Announcer: Frank Adkisson. **No. of Games Broadcast:** Home-72, Away-72. **Flagship Station:** KKAR 1180-AM.
Stadium Name: Rosenblatt. **Location:** I-80 to South 13 St. exit, south one block. **Standard Game Times:** 7:05; Sun., 1:35.
Visiting Club Hotel: Ramada Inn Central, 7007 Grover St., Omaha, NE 68106. Telephone: (402) 397-7030

INTERNATIONAL LEAGUE

Class AAA

Office Address: 55 South High St., Suite 202, Dublin, OH 43017.

Telephone: (614) 791-9300. **FAX:** (614) 791-9009.

President/Treasurer: Randy Mobley.

Vice Presidents: Harold Cooper, Dave Rosenfield, George Sisler Jr. **Secretary:** Richard Davis.

Directors: Joe Altobelli (Rochester), Bruce Baldwin (Richmond), Gene Cook (Toledo), Dave Rosenfield (Tidewater), Ken Schnacke (Columbus), Anthony "Tex" Simone (Syracuse), Mike Tamburro (Pawtucket), Bill Terlecky (Scranton/Wilkes-Barre).

Office Secretary: Marcia Willison.

Years League Active: 1884-1992.

Randy Mobley

Division Structure: East—Pawtucket, Rochester, Scranton Wilkes-Barre, Syracuse. **West**—Columbus, Richmond, Tidewater, Toledo.

1992 Opening Date: April 9. **Closing Date:** Sept. 7.

No. of Games: 144.

Playoff Format: Division winners play best-of-5 series for league championship.

All-Star Game: July 15 at Richmond (joint Triple-A game).

Roster Limit: 23, until midnight Aug. 10 when roster can be expanded to 25.

Statistician: Howe Sportsdata International, Boston Fish Pier, West Bldg. #2—Suite 306, Boston MA 02210.

Umpires: Wally Bell (Youngstown, OH), Paul Bortolotti (Mansfield, MA), Perry Costello (Lansing, MI), Terry Craft (Osprey, FL), Phil Cuzzi (Belleville, NJ), Mike DuMont (Lansing, MI), Ed Hickox (DeLand, FL), Jeff Kellogg (Dearborn Heights, MI), Bob Long (Randolph, MA), Jerry Meals (Salem, OH), Kevin O'Connor (Oxford, MA), Brian O'Nora (Youngstown, OH), Jim Paylor (Harkers Island, NC), Jeff Thibodeau (East Longmeadow, MA).

1991 Standings (Overall)

Club (Affiliate)	W	L	Pct.	GB	'91 Manager
*†Columbus (Yankees)	85	59	.590	—	Rick Down
†Pawtucket (Red Sox)	79	64	.552	5½	Butch Hobson
Tidewater (Mets)	77	65	.542	7	Steve Swisher
Rochester (Orioles)	76	68	.528	9	Greg Biagini
Toledo (Tigers)	74	70	.514	11	Joe Sparks
Syracuse (Blue Jays)	73	71	.507	12	Bob Bailor
Scranton (Phillies)	65	78	.455	19½	Bill Dancy
Richmond (Braves)	65	79	.451	20	Phil Niekro

*Won playoffs † Won division title.

Stadium Information

Club	Stadium	LF	CF	RF	Capacity	'91 Att.
Columbus	Cooper	355	400	330	15,000	570,605
Pawtucket	McCoy	325	380	325	6,010	349,338
Richmond	The Diamond	330	402	330	12,148	434,994
Rochester	Silver	320	400	315	12,503	345,167
Scranton	Lackawanna Cty	330	408	330	10,776	535,725
Syracuse	MacArthur	320	434	320	8,408	307,993
Tidewater	Metropolitan Park	341	410	341	6,150	196,998
Toledo	Ned Skeldon	325	410	325	10,025	217,662

COLUMBUS
CLIPPERS

Office Address: 1155 W. Mound St., Columbus, OH 43223. **Mailing Address:** Same. **Telephone:** (614) 462-5250. **FAX:** (614) 462-3271.

Affiliation (first year): New York Yankees (1979). **Years in League:** 1955-70, 1977-.

Operated by: Columbus Baseball Team, Inc.

General Manager: Ken Schnacke. **Assistant General Managers:** Dick Fitzpatrick, Mark Warren. **Director of Stadium Operations:** Steve Dalin. **Director of Ticket Sales:** Scott Ziegler. **Director of Media Relations:** Rob Butcher. **Director of Merchandising:** Gregg Kaye. **Director of Business Operations:** John Allen. **Director of Group Sales:** Brad Kullman. **Director of Community Relations:** Randy Parker. **Assistant Ticket Director:** Tom Baldwin. **Assistant Sales Director:** Chris Zieg.

Field Manager: Rick Down. **Coaches:** Mike Brown, Hop Cassady, Ted Uhlaender.

Trainer: Mike Heifferon.

Radio Announcer: Terry Smith. **No. of Games Broadcast:** Home-72, Away-72. **Flagship Station:** WBNS 1460-AM.

Stadium Name: Cooper. **Location:** I-70 West to Mound St. exit, left to stadium; I-70 East to Broad St. exit, left on Broad, right on Glenwood, right on Mound. **Standard Game Times:** Mon.-Sat. 7 p.m.; Sun. (April-June 7) 2, (June 28-Sept.) 6.

Visiting Club Hotel: Best Western-Columbus North, 888 E. Dublin-Granville Rd., Columbus, OH 43229. Telephone: (614) 888-8230.

PAWTUCKET
RED SOX

Office Address: 1 Columbus Ave., Pawtucket, RI 02860. **Mailing Address:** P.O. Box 2365, Pawtucket, RI 02861. **Telephone:** (401) 724-7300. **FAX:** (401) 724-2140.

Affiliation (first year): Boston Red Sox (1973). **Years in League:** 1973-.

Operated by: Pawtucket Red Sox Baseball Club, Inc.

Owner and Chairman of the Board: Ben Mondor. **President:** Mike Tamburro.

Vice President and General Manager: Lou Schwechheimer. **Director of Stadium Operations:** Mick Tedesco. **Director of Public Relations:** Bill Wanless. **Director of Clubhouse Operations:** Bill Broadbent. **Director of Sales:** Michael Gwynn. **Public Relations Assistant:** Greg McKinney. **Stadium Operations Assistant:** Jeff Goss. **Sales:** Larry Goldstein. **Office Manager:** Kathy Davenport. **Clubhouse Operations:** Chris Parent. **Secretary:** Linda Nason.

Field Manager: Rico Petrocelli. **Coaches:** Dick Pole, Mark Meleski.

Trainer: Peter Youngman.

Radio Announcer: Jack LeFaivre. **No. of Games Broadcast:** Home-72, Away-72. **Flagship Station:** WARA 1320-AM.

Stadium Name: McCoy. **Location:** I-95 N to exit 28 (School St.); I-95 S to exit 2A (Newport Ave.). **Standard Game Times:** 7 p.m.; Sun., 1

Visiting Club Hotel: Comfort Inn, 2 George St., Pawtucket, RI 02860. Telephone: (401) 723-6700.

RICHMOND
BRAVES

Office Address: 3001 N. Boulevard, Richmond, VA 23230. **Mailing Address:** P.O. Box 6667, Richmond, VA 23230. **Telephone:** (804) 359-4444. **FAX:** (804) 359-0731.

Affiliation (first year): Atlanta Braves (1966). **Years in League:** 1884, 1915-17, 1954-64, 1966-.

Operated by: Atlanta National League Baseball, Inc.

General Manager: Bruce Baldwin. **Director of Stadium Operations:**

Dan Hoffman. **Marketing Director:** Ken Clary. **Assistant Marketing Director & Director of Group Sales:** CeCe Perkins. **Ticket Manager:** Chris Pizzini. **Director of Public Relations:** Eric Johnson. **Director of Field Maintenance:** Barney Lopas. **Office Manager:** Joanne Curnutt.

Field Manager: Chris Chambliss. **Coaches:** Bruce Dal Canton, Sonny Jackson.

Trainer: Jim Lovell.

Radio Announcers: Bob Black, Steve Melewski. **No. of Games Broadcast:** Home-72, Away-72. **Flagship Station:** WRNL 910-AM.

Stadium Name: The Diamond. **Location:** I-64 & I-95 Junction, Exit 78. **Standard Game Times:** 7 p.m.; DH, 6; Sun., 2.

Visiting Club Hotels: Holiday Inn-Midtown, 3200 W. Broad St., Richmond, VA 23230. Telephone: (804) 359-4061. Holiday Inn-Crossroads, 2000 Staples Mill Rd., Richmond, VA 23230. Telephone: (804) 359-6061.

ROCHESTER
RED WINGS

Office Address: 500 Norton St., Rochester, NY 14621. **Telephone:** (716) 467-3000. **FAX:** (716) 467-6732.

Affiliation (first year): Baltimore Orioles (1961). **Years in League:** 1885-89, 1891-92, 1895-.

Operated by: Rochester Community Baseball, Inc.

General Manager: Joe Altobelli. **Assistant General Manager:** Bruce Leichtman. **Director of Baseball Operations:** Russ Brandon. **Director of Community Relations:** Will Rumbold. **Director of Promotions/Group Sales:** Dan Mason. **Director of Communications:** Bob Socci. **Business Manager:** Darlene Giardina. **Executive Secretary:** Pat Santillo.

Field Manager: Jerry Narron. **Coach:** Steve Luebber.

Trainer: Jeff Wood.

Radio Announcers: Josh Lewin, Bob Socci. **No. of Games Broadcast:** Home-72, Away-72. **Flagship Station:** WPXY 1280-AM.

Stadium Name: Silver. **Location:** 2 blocks south of Rt. 104, between Seneca and Clinton Ave. **Standard Game Times:** 2:05 p.m., 7:05.

Visiting Club Hotel: Holiday Inn-Downtown, 120 E. Main St., Rochester, NY 14604. Telephone: (716) 546-6400.

SCRANTON/W-B
RED BARONS

Office Address: 235 Montage Mountain Road, Moosic, PA 18507. **Mailing Address:** P.O. Box 3449, Scranton, PA 18505. **Telephone:** (717) 963-6556. **FAX:** (717) 963-6564.

Affiliation (first year): Philadelphia Phillies (1989). **Years in League:** 1989-.

Operated by: Lackawanna County Multi-Purpose Stadium Authority.

General Manager: Bill Terlecky. **Assistant General Manager:** Rick Muntean. **Controller:** Tom Durkin. **Group Sales:** Mary Ann Dziak. **Public Relations Director:** Mike Cummings. **Season Tickets Manager:** Norine Legg. **Office Manager:** Donna McDonald. **Box Office Manager:** Todd Peters. **Administrative Assistant:** Cathy Kacer.

Field Manager: Lee Elia. **Coaches:** Al Leboeuf, Jim Wright.

Trainer: Barney Nugent.

Radio Announcers: Mike Remish, Kent Westling. **No. of Games Broadcast:** Home-72; Away-72. **Flagship Station:** WICK 1400-AM.

Stadium Name: Lackawanna County Multi-Purpose. **Location:** I-81 to exit 51, Davis St. east, right on Montage Mountain Road. **Standard Game Times:** 7:30 p.m.; Sun. 6.

Visiting Club Hotel: Royce Hotel, 700 Lackawanna Ave., Scranton, PA 18503. Telephone: (717) 342-8300.

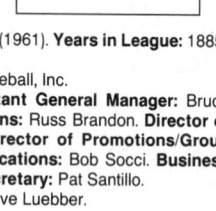

SYRACUSE
CHIEFS

Office Address: MacArthur Stadium, Syracuse, NY 13208. **Telephone:** (315) 474-7833. **FAX:** (315) 474-2658.

Affiliation (first year): Toronto Blue Jays (1978). **Years in League:** 1885-89, 1891-92, 1894-1901, 1918, 1920-27, 1934-55, 1961-.

Operated by: Community Baseball Club of Central New York, Inc.

President: Donald Waful.

General Manager and Executive Vice President: Anthony "Tex" Simone. **Assistant General Manager:** John Simone. **Director of Sales and Marketing:** Lu Ann Wall. **Director of Finance:** Vince Testa. **Director of Stadium Maintenance:** Mark Watson. **Group Sales:** Vic Gallucci.

Field Manager: Nick Leyva. **Coaches:** John Poloni, Rocket Wheeler.

Trainer: Randy Holland.

Radio Announcers: Dan Hoard, Joel Mareiniss. **No. of Games Broadcast:** Home-72, Away-72. **Flagship Station:** WHEN 620-AM.

Stadium Name: MacArthur. **Location:** Exit 22 (Hiawatha Blvd.) on westbound Route 81; Exit 7 (Court St.) on eastbound Route 690. **Standard Game Times:** 7 p.m., Sun. 6; Sat.-Sun. (April-May 16) 2.

Visiting Club Hotel: Unavailable.

TIDEWATER
TIDES

Office Address: 6000 Northampton Blvd., Norfolk, VA 23502. **Mailing Address:** P.O. Box 12111, Norfolk, VA 23502. **Telephone:** (804) 461-5600. **FAX:** (804) 461-0405.

Affiliation (first year): New York Mets (1969). **Years in League:** 1969-.

Operated by: Tidewater Professional Sports, Inc.

President: Richard J. Davis.

Executive Vice President, General Manager: Dave Rosenfield. **Assistant General Manager-Administration:** Mark Brown. **Assistant General Manager-Sales:** Kevin Greene. **Director of Corporate/Group Sales:** Ed Nagourney. **Concessions Manager:** Joe Gorza. **Administrative Assistant:** Shon Sbarra. **Bookkeeper/Secretary:** Mary Gardner.

Field Manager: Clint Hurdle. **Coaches:** Bob Apodaca, Ron Washington.

Trainer: Fred Hina.

Radio Announcers: Charlie Slowess, Jay Colley. **No. of Games Broadcast:** Home-72, Away-72. **Flagship Station:** WTAR 790-AM.

Stadium Name: Metropolitan Memorial Park. **Location:** Adjacent to I-64 and Military Highway. **Standard Game Times:** Mon.-Sat., 7:15 p.m.; DH 6:15; Sun. (April-June 21) 1:15, (July 5-Sept.) 6:15.

Visiting Club Hotel: Days Inn, 5701 Chambers St., Norfolk, VA 23502. Telephone: (804) 461-0100;

TOLEDO
MUD HENS

Office Address: 2901 Key St., Maumee, OH 43537. **Mailing Address:** P.O. Box 6212, Toledo, OH 43614. **Telephone:** (419) 893-9483. **FAX:** (419) 893-5847.

Affiliation (first year): Detroit Tigers (1987). **Years in League:** 1965-.

Operated by: Toledo Mud Hens Baseball Club, Inc.

General Manager: Gene Cook. **Assistant General Manager:** Joe Napoli. **Community Relations:** Jeff Condon. **Media Relations:** Jim Konecny. **Bookkeeper:** Beth Keller. **Secretary:** Carol Hamilton.

Field Manager: Joe Sparks. **Coaches:** Kevin Bradshaw, Ralph Treuel.

Trainer: Steve McInerney.

Radio Announcers: Jim Weber, Frank Gilhooley. **No. of Games Broadcast:** Home-72, Away-72. **Flagship Station:** WMTR 96.1 FM.

Stadium Name: Ned Skeldon. **Location:** 1 mile east of Ohio Turnpike, exit 4 on Key St. **Game Times:** 7 p.m.; DH 6; Sun., 2.

Visiting Club Hotel: Ramada Inn, 2340 S. Reynolds Rd., Toledo, OH 43614. Telephone: (419) 865-1361

PACIFIC COAST LEAGUE

Class AAA

Mailing Address: 2101 E. Broadway, Suite 35, Tempe, AZ 85282.
Telephone: (602) 967-7679. **FAX:** (602) 968-8141.
President/Secretary-Treasurer: William Cutler.
Vice President: Mel Kowalchuck.
Directors: Joe Buzas (Portland), George Foster (Tacoma), Bob Goughan (Colorado Springs), Rick Holtzman (Tucson), Brent Imlach (Vancouver), Larry Koentopp (Las Vegas), Mel Kowalchuk (Edmonton), Pat McKernan (Albuquerque), Craig Pletenik (Phoenix), Russ Parker (Calgary).
Executive Committee: Joe Buzas, Rick Holtzman, Craig Pletenik.
Office Secretaries: Jeannie Bordes, Kathy Cutler.

Bill Cutler

Years League Active: 1903-1992.
1992 Opening Date: April 9. **Closing Date:** Sept. 7. **First Half Ends:** June 23.
No. of Games: 144.
Division Structure: Northern—Calgary, Edmonton, Portland, Tacoma, Vancouver. **Southern**—Albuquerque, Colorado Springs, Las Vegas, Phoenix, Tucson.
Playoff Format: First-half first-place teams play second-half first-place teams in best-of-5 semifinals, winners meet in best-of-5 final.
All-Star Game: July 15 at Richmond, Va. (joint Triple-A game).
Roster Limit: 23.
Statistician: Howe Sportsdata International, Boston Fish Pier, West Bldg. #2—Suite 306, Boston MA 02210.
Umpires: Ron Barnes (El Cerrito, CA), David Buck (Stevensville, MI), Joe Burleson (Las Vegas, NV), Craig Compton (Morrisville, PA), Field Culbreth (Inman, SC), Kerwin Danley (Los Angeles, CA), Todd Freese (Denver, CO), Ray Leible (Midland, TX), John Lipsey (Mesa, AZ), Matt Malone (O'Fallon, MO), Darrel Mason (Edmonds, WA), Steven Morrow (Marana, AZ), Larry Poncino (San Clemente, CA), Hank Schwarz (Bellingham, WA), Dan Wickham (Chandler, AZ).

1991 Standings (Overall)

Club (Affiliate)	W	L	Pct.	GB	'91 Manager
Albuquerque (Dodgers)	80	58	.580	—	Kevin Kennedy
†*Tucson (Astros)	79	61	.564	2	Bob Skinner
†Calgary (Mariners)	72	64	.529	7	Keith Bodie
†Colorado Springs (Indians)	72	67	.518	8½	Charlie Manuel
Edmonton (Angels)	70	66	.515	9	Max Oliveras
†Portland (Twins)	70	68	.507	10	Russ Nixon
Phoenix (Giants)	68	70	.493	12	Duane Espy
Las Vegas (Padres)	65	75	.464	16	Jim Riggleman
Tacoma (Athletics)	63	73	.463	16	Jeff Newman
Vancouver (White Sox)	49	86	.363	29½	Marv Foley, Rick Renick

*Won playoffs †Won split-season pennant.

Stadium Information

Club	Stadium	LF	CF	RF	Capacity	'90 Att.
Albuquerque	Albuq. Sports	360	410	340	10,510	340,685
Calgary	Foothills	345	400	345	7,500	325,965
Colo. Springs	Sky Sox	335	410	335	6,000	174,731
Edmonton	John Ducey Park	335	405	320	6,200	252,813
Las Vegas	Cashman Field	328	433	328	9,370	330,699
Phoenix	Scottsdale	360	420	345	7,000	247,791
Portland	Civic	309	407	348	26,500	181,116
Tacoma	Cheney	325	425	325	8,500	293,418
Tucson	Hi Corbett Field	366	392	348	8,000	317,347
Vancouver	Nat Bailey	335	395	335	6,500	288,978

ALBUQUERQUE
DUKES

Office Address: 1601 Stadium Blvd. SE, Albuquerque, NM 87106. **Mailing Address:** P.O. Box 26267, Albuquerque, NM 87125. **Telephone:** (505) 243-1791. **FAX:** (505) 842-0561.

Affiliation (first year): Los Angeles Dodgers (1972). **Years in League:** 1972-.

Operated by: Albuquerque Professional Baseball Club, Inc.

Chairman of the Board: Robert Lozinak.

President and General Manager: Pat McKernan. **Director of Administration:** Mark Rupert. **Director of Publicity:** David Sheriff. **Director of Group Sales and Tickets:** Duane Miller. **Assistant Ticket Manager:** Paul Lanning. **Secretary to the President:** Dawnene Shoup. **Assistant to the President:** Scott Jacobson. **Director of Sales:** James Guscott. **Director of Stadium Operations:** Steve Brainard. **Director of Marketing:** Paul Fetz. **Administrative Assistants:** Glenn Kaiser, Steve Powderly. **Concessions Manager:** Charles Ditzenberger.

Field Manager: Bill Russell. **Coaches:** Von Joshua, Claude Osteen.

Trainer: Stan Johnston.

Radio Announcers: Jim Lawwill, Mike Roberts. **No. of Games Broadcast:** Home-72, Away-72. **Flagship Station:** KKOB 770-AM.

Stadium Name: Albuquerque Sports. **Location:** I-25 to Stadium Blvd. exit, east onto Stadium Blvd. **Standard Game Times:** 7 p.m., DH 5; Sun. 1

Visiting Club Hotel: Howard Johnson Plaza Hotel North, 6000 Pan American Freeway NE, Albuquerque, NM 87109. Telephone: (505) 821-9451.

CALGARY
CANNONS

Office Address: Foothills Baseball Stadium, Crowchild Trail N.W. and 24th Ave., Calgary, Alberta. **Mailing Address:** P.O. Box 3690, Station B, Calgary, Alberta T2M 4M4. **Telephone:** (403) 284-1111. **FAX:** (403) 284-4343.

Affiliation (first year): Seattle Mariners (1985). **Years in League:** 1985-.

Operated by: Calgary Cannons Baseball Club Ltd.

President: Russ Parker.

Vice President and General Manager: Gary Arthur. **Executive Assistant to President:** Bill Cragg. **Assistant General Manager-Operations:** Brent Parker. **Director of Media and Public Relations:** John Traube. **Director of Ticketing:** Greg Winthers. **Director of Accounting:** Chris Poffenroth. **Director of Marketing:** Doug Young. **Secretary/Receptionist:** Colette Longmuir.

Field Manager: Keith Bodie. **Coach:** Ross Grimsley.

Trainer: Randy Roetter.

Radio: Unavailable.

Stadium Name: Foothills. **Location:** Intersection of 24th Ave. and Crowchild Trail NW. **Standard Game Times:** 7:05 p.m. (except April, 6:05), 1:35, 12:05.

Visiting Club Hotel: Sandman Hotel, 888 7th Ave. S.W., Calgary, Alberta T2P 3V3. Telephone: (403) 237-8626.

COLORADO SPRINGS
SKY SOX

Office Address: 4385 Tutt Ave., Colorado Springs, CO 80922. **Telephone:** (719) 597-1449. **FAX:** (719) 597-2491.

Affiliation (first year): Cleveland Indians (1988). **Years in League:** 1988-.

Operated by: Colorado Springs Sky Sox, Inc.

Principal Owners: David G. Elmore, D.G. Elmore.

President and General Manager: Bob Goughan. **Vice President for Administration:** Sam Polizzi. **Assistant General Managers:** Dwight Hall, Rai Henninger. **Director of Communications:** Chad Starbuck. **Director of Merchandising:** Jay Kranchalk. **Ticket Manager:** Andy Berg. **Director**

of Public Relations: Chris Costello. **Business Manager:** Carroll Payne. **Director of Stadium Operations:** Mark Leasure. **Sales Representatives:** Mark Cusumano, Bill McCormick, Steve Nitzel.

Field Manager: Charlie Manuel. **Coaches:** Dyar Miller, Luis Isaac.
Trainer: Steve Ciszczon.
Radio Announcers: Dan Karcher, Dick Chase. **No. of Games Bradcast:** Home-72, Away-72. **Flagship Station:** KSSS 740-AM.
Stadium Name: Sky Sox. **Location:** From airport, Powers Blvd. to Barnes Rd., right on Tutt. **Standard Game Times:** 6:35 p.m., 1:35.
Visiting Club Hotel: Sheraton Colorado Springs, 2886 S. Circle Dr., Colorado Springs, CO 80906. Telephone: (719) 576-5900.

EDMONTON
TRAPPERS

Office Address: 10233 96th Ave., Edmonton, Alberta T5K 0A5. **Telephone:** (403) 429-2934. **FAX:** (403) 426-5640.
Affiliation (first year): California Angels (1983). **Years in League:** 1981-.
Operated by: Edmonton Trappers Baseball Club.
President and General Manager: Mel Kowalchuk. **Assistant General Manager and Public Relations Director:** Dennis Henke. **Stadium Manager:** Richard Henke. **Sales Manager:** Rob McGillis. **Ticket Manager and Accountant:** Gabrielle Hampel. **Account Executive:** Al Coates. **Office Manager:** Nancy Yeo. **Administrative Assistant:** Colin MacPhail.
Field Manager: Max Oliveras. **Coaches:** Gary Ruby, Lenn Sakata.
Trainer: Don McGann.
Radio Announcer: Al Coates. **No. of Games Broadcast:** Unavailable. **Flagship Station:** Unavailable.
Stadium Name: John Ducey Park. **Location:** 102 St. and 96 Ave. **Standard Game Times:** 7:05 p.m.; Sun. 2:05.
Visiting Club Hotel: Inn on 7th, 10001 107th Ave., Edmonton, Alberta T5J 1J1. Telephone: (403) 429-2861.

LAS VEGAS
STARS

Office Address: 850 Las Vegas Blvd N., Las Vegas, NV 89101. **Telephone:** (702) 386-7200. **FAX:** (702) 386-7214.
Affiliation (first year): San Diego Padres (1983). **Years in League:** 1983-.
Operated by: Las Vegas Stars Baseball Club, Inc.
President: Larry Koentopp.
General Manager: Don Logan. **Senior Administrative Assistant:** Bob Blum. **Assistant General Managers:** Mark Grenier, Kevin Koentopp. **Director of Public Relations:** Bryan Dangerfield. **Comptroller:** Jan Jaeger. **Office Manager:** Marie Schenk.
Field Manager: Jim Riggleman. **Coaches:** Jon Matlack, Tony Torchia.
Trainer: Larry Duensing.
Radio Announcers: Ken Korach, Rich Waltz. **No. of Games Broadcast:** Home-72, Away-72. **Flagship Station:** KENO 1460-AM.
Stadium Name: Cashman Field. **Location:** Two miles north of downtown on Las Vegas Blvd., or Cashman Field exit off U.S. 95. **Standard Game Times:** 7:05 p.m.; Sun. 1:05.
Visiting Club Hotel: Las Vegas Club Hotel, 18 E. Fremont St., Las Vegas, NV 89101. Telephone: (702) 385-1664.

PHOENIX
FIREBIRDS

Office Address: Scottsdale Stadium, 7408 E. Osborn Rd., Scottsdale, AZ 85251. **Mailing Address:** P.O. Box 8303, Scottsdale, AZ 85252. **Telephone:** (602) 275-0500. **FAX:** (602) 220-9425.
Affiliation (first year): San Francisco Giants (1966). **Years in League:** 1958-59, 1966-.
Operated by: Professional Sports, Inc.

President: Larry Yount.
General Manager: Craig Pletenik. **Director of Sales:** William Gatlin. **Director of Tickets and Operations:** Bryan Milbourn. **Director of Broadcasting:** Russ Langer. **Director of Promotions and Public Relations:** T.R. Osborne. **Comptroller:** Mary Jo Balthasar.
Field Manager: Bill Evers. **Coaches:** Tony Taylor, Todd Oakes.
Trainer: Bruce Graham.
Radio Announcer: Russ Langer. **No. of Games Broadcast:** Home-72, Away-72. **Flagship Station:** KXAM 1310-AM.
Stadium Name: Scottsdale. **Location:** North on Scottsdale Rd. to Osborn, east to stadium. **Standard Game Times:** 7:05 p.m.; Sun. 6:05.
Visiting Club Hotel: Unavailable.

PORTLAND
BEAVERS

Office Address: 1844 SW Morrison Ave., Portland, OR 97205. **Mailing Address:** P.O. Box 1659, Portland, OR 97207. **Telephone:** (503) 223-2837. **FAX:** (503) 274-0316.
Affiliation (first year): Minnesota Twins (1987). **Years in League:** 1903-72, 1978-.
Operated by: Buzas Baseball, Inc.
Cheif Executive Officer and Owner: Joe Buzas.
Executive Vice President and Co-General Manager: Mark Helminiak.
Vice President and Co-General Manager: Tammy Felker-White. **Director of Marketing and Promotions:** Yoshi Okamoto.
Field Manager: Scott Ullger. **Coaches:** Gorman Heimueller, Paul Kirsch.
Trainer: Jim Kahmann.
Radio Announcers: Mike Parker, Dale McConachie. **No. of Games Broadcast:** Home-72, Away-72. **Flagship Station:** KFXX 1520-AM.
Stadium Name: Civic. **Location:** I-405 to West Burnside, left on 20th Street. **Standard Game Times:** 7:05 p.m., Sun. 1:35.
Visiting Club Hotel: Red Lion Inn-Coliseum, 1225 N. Thunderbird Way, Portland OR 97207. Telephone: (503) 235-8311.

TACOMA
TIGERS

Office Address: 2525 Bantz Blvd., Tacoma, WA 98405. **Office Address:** P.O. Box 11087, Tacoma, WA 98411. **Telephone:** (206) 752-7707. **FAX:** (206) 752-7135.
Affiliation (first year): Oakland Athletics (1981). **Years in League:** 1904-05, 1960-.
Operated by: George's Pastime, Inc.
President: George Foster.
General Manager: Frank Colarusso. **Assistant General Manager:** Ron Zollo. **Director of Marketing Operations:** Tom Bordeaux. **Director of Sales and Marketing:** David Carl. **Public Relations:** Kevin Kalal. **Ticket Manager:** Betty Howes. **Assistant Ticket Manager:** Dan Graham. **Office Manager:** Maureen Mayo. **Secretary/Receptionist:** Jan Plein. **Clubhouse Manager:** Steve Spry.
Field Manager: Bob Boone. **Coaches:** Glenn Abbott, Mitchell Page.
Trainer: Walt Horn.
Radio Announcer: Bob Robertson. **No. of Games Broadcast:** Home-72, Away-72. **Flagship Station:** KLAY 1180-AM.
Stadium Name: Cheney. **Location:** Exit 19th St. from Highway 16. **Standard Game Times:** 7:05 p.m., Sun. 1:35, DH 6:05.
Visiting Club Hotel: Days Inn, 6802 Tacoma Mall Blvd., Tacoma, WA 98409. Telephone: (206) 475-5900.

TUCSON
TOROS

Office Address: 3400 East Camino Campestre, Tucson, AZ 85716. **Mailing Address:** P.O. Box 27045, Tucson, AZ 85726. **Telephone:** (602) 325-2621. **FAX:** (602) 327-2371.

Affiliation (first year): Houston Astros (1980). **Years in League:** 1969-.
Operated by: Tucson Toros, Inc.
President, Owner: Rick Holtzman.
General Manager: Mike Feder. **Assistant General Manager:** Jim Wehmeier. **Business Manager:** Pattie Feder. **Director of Sales:** Tom Cutler. **Director of Group Sales:** Diane Yasutake. **Director of Marketing:** Doug Leary. **Director of Broadcasting:** Mario Impemba.
Field Manager: Bob Skinner. **Coaches:** Brent Strom, Dave Engle.
Trainer: Larry Lasky.
Radio Announcer: Mario Impemba. **No. of Games Broadcast:** Home-72, Away-72. **Flagship Station:** KMRR 1330-AM.
Stadium Name: Hi Corbett Field. **Location:** I-10 to Broadway exit, east to Randolph Way, south 1 mile. **Standard Games Times:** Mon.-Thur. (April-May) 7 p.m., Fri.-Sat. 7:30, Sun. 2; All games (June-Aug.) 7:30.
Visiting Club Hotel: Ramada Inn-Foothills, 6944 E. Tanque Verde, Tucson AZ 85715. Telephone (602) 886-9595.

VANCOUVER
CANADIANS

Office Address: 4601 Ontario St., Vancouver, B.C. V5V 3H4. **Telephone:** (604) 872-5232. **FAX:** (604) 872-1714.

Affiliation (first year): Chicago White Sox (1989). **Years in League:** 1956-62, 1965-69, 1978-.
Operated by: JSS Sports, Inc.
President: John McHale.
Vice President and General Manager: Brent Imlach. **Assistant General Manager:** Dick Phillips. **Manager of Accounting and Administration:** Shane Jones. **Advertising and Promotions:** Ken Cooper, Gerry Dean. **Marketing and Promotions:** Torchy Pechet.
Field Manager: Rick Renick. **Coaches:** Rick Peterson, Roger LaFrancois.
Trainer: Greg Latta.
Radio Announcer Brook Ward. **No. of Games Broadcast:** Home-72, Away-select. **Flagship Station:** CFVR 850-AM.
Stadium Name: Nat Bailey. **Location:** Highway 99 to Oak St., right on 41st Ave., left on Ontario St. **Standard Game Times:** 7:05 p.m.; Sun. 1:30.
Visiting Club Hotel: Coast Vancouver Hotel, 1041 S.W. Marine Dr., Vancouver, B.C. V6P 6L6. Telephone: (604) 263-1555.

EASTERN LEAGUE

Class AA

Mailing Address: P.O. Box 716, Plainville, CT 06062.
Telephone: (203) 747-9332. **FAX:** (203) 747-9463.
President, Treasurer: Charles Eshbach.
Vice Presidents: Joseph Buzas, Craig Stein.
Secretary: Joseph Buzas.
Directors: Ralph Acampora (Albany), Gregory Agganis (Canton), Joseph Buzas (New Britain), Gerry Hunsicker (Binghamton), Peter Kirk (Hagerstown), Jerome Mileur (Harrisburg), Richard Stanley (London), Craig Stein (Reading).
Years League Active: 1923-1992.
1992 Opening Date: April 9. **Closing Date:** Sept. 1.
No. of Games: 140.
Division Structure: None.

Charles Eshbach

Playoff Format: First-place team plays fourth-place team and second-place team plays third-place team in best-of-5 semifinals. Semifinals winners play best-of-5 series for league championship.
All-Star Game: July 13, at Charlotte, N.C. (joint Double-A game).
Roster Limit: Per National Association agreement.
Statistician: Howe Sportsdata International, Boston Fish Pier, West Bldg. #2—Suite 306, Boston MA 02210.
Umpires: Joe Caraco (Malden, MA), Pete Celestino (Copiague, NY), John Dezelan (Pittsburgh, PA), Brian King (Apopka, FL), Scott Simonides (Lakeland, FL), Greg Street (Wendell, NC), David Wilk (Darien, CT), Matt Winans (Watertown, CT).

1991 Standings (Overall)

Club (Affiliate)	W	L	Pct.	GB	'91 Manager
Harrisburg (Expos)	87	53	.621	—	Mike Quade
Hagerstown (Orioles)	81	59	.579	6	Jerry Narron
*Albany-Colonie (Yankees)	76	64	.543	11	Dan Radison
Canton-Akron (Indians)	75	65	.536	12	Ken Bolek
Reading (Phillies)	72	68	.514	15	Don McCormack
London (Tigers)	61	78	.439	25½	Gene Roof
Williamsport (Mets)	60	79	.432	26½	Clint Hurdle
New Britain (Red Sox)	47	93	.336	40	Gary Allenson

*Won playoffs

Stadium Information

Club	Stadium	LF	CF	RF	Capacity	'91 Att.
Albany	Heritage Park	325	410	335	5,500	171,466
Binghamton[1]	Binghamton Municipal	330	400	330	6,000	—
Canton-Akron	Thurman Munson Mem	330	400	330	5,760	218,397
Hagerstown	Municipal	335	400	335	6,000	193,753
Harrisburg	RiverSide	335	400	335	5,600	233,423
London	Labatt Park	330	405	330	5,400	150,435
New Britain	Beehive Field	320	388	320	4,178	146,632
Reading	Municipal	330	400	330	7,000	250,610

[1]Binghamton franchise operated in Williamsport in 1991.

ALBANY-COLONIE
YANKEES

Office Address: Heritage Park, Watervliet-Shaker Rd., Albany, NY 12211. **Telephone:** (518) 869-9236. **FAX:** (518) 869-9237.

Affiliation (first year): New York Yankees (1985). **Years in League:** 1920-32, 1937-59, 1983-.

Operated by: Keating Sports Group, Inc.

President: Paul Keating.

Vice President, General Manager: Ralph Acampora. **Vice President/Public Relations:** Rip Rowan. **Director of Broadcasting:** John Thomas. **Director of Administrative Services:** Isabelle Acampora.

Field Manager: Dan Radison. **Coaches:** Dave Jorn, Rob Thomson.

Trainer: Tim Weston.

Radio Announcer: John Thomas. **No. of Games Broadcast:** Home-70, Away-70. **Flagship Station:** Unavailable.

Stadium Name: Heritage Park. **Location:** From N.Y. Thruway, exit 24 to I-87 North, exit 4 and follow signs to Watervliet-Shaker Road (Rt. 155). **Standard Game Times:** 7:05 p.m., 2:05.

Visiting Club Hotel: Holiday Inn, 946 New Loudon Rd., Latham, NY 12110 Telephone: (518) 783-6161.

BINGHAMTON
METS

Office Address: Henry & Fayette Streets, Binghamton, NY 13901. **Mailing Address:** P.O. Box 598, Binghamton, NY 13902. **Telephone:** (607) 723-6387. **FAX:** (607) 723-7779.

Affiliation (first year): New York Mets (1992). **Years in League:** 1923-37, 1940-63, 1966-68, 1992-.

Operated by: Sterling Doubleday Enterprises.

Director: Gerry Hunsicker.

General Manager: R.C. Reuteman. **Assistant General Manager:** Mark White. **Director of Marketing:** Meghan Molnar. **Director of Operations:** Charles Carlson. **Business Manager:** Ann Morris.

Field Manager: Steve Swisher. **Coaches:** Randy Niemann, Ron Gideon.

Trainer: Joe Hawkins.

Radio Announcer: Rob Evans. **No. of Games Broadcast:** Home-70, Away-70. **Flagship Station:** WMRV 1430-AM.

Stadium Name: Binghamton Municipal. **Location:** I-81 to exit 4S (Binghamton), route 11 exit to Henry St. **Standard Game Times:** 7:00 p.m., Sun. 1:30.

Visiting Club Hotel: Unavailable.

CANTON-AKRON
INDIANS

Office Address: 2501 Allen Ave. SE, Canton, OH 44707. **Telephone:** (216) 456-5100. **FAX:** (216) 456-5450.

Affiliation (first year): Cleveland Indians (1989). **Years in League:** 1989-.

Operated by: Canton Professional Baseball, Inc.

President: Mike Agganis. **Director:** Greg Agganis.

General Manager: Glen Strong. **Assistant General Manager:** Jeff Auman. **Director of Ticket Operations:** Peter Thomas. **Director of Stadium Operations:** Greg Zink. **Assistant Publc Relations Director:** Steve Bozeka. **Publicity Coordinator:** Brent Horvath.

Field Manager: Brian Graham. **Coaches:** Ken Rowe, Jim Gabella.

Trainer: Lee Kuntz.

Radio: Unavailable.

Stadium Name: Thurman Munson Memorial. **Location:** I-77 to exit 103. **Standard Game Times:** 7:05 p.m.; Sun. 1:35.

Visiting Club Hotel: Parke Hotel, 4343 Everhard Rd. NW, Canton, OH 44718. Telephone: (216) 499-9410.

HAGERSTOWN
SUNS

Office Address: Municipal Stadium, 274 East Memorial Blvd., Hagerstown, MD 21740. **Mailing Address:** P.O. Box 230, Hagerstown, MD 21741. **Telephone:** (301) 791-6266. **FAX:** (301) 791-6066.

Affiliation (first year): Baltimore Orioles (1989). **Years in League:** 1989-.
Operated by: Maryland Baseball Limited Partnership.
Chairman: Peter Kirk.
General Manager: Bob Miller. **Assistant General Managers:** Carol Gehr, Mike Oravec. **Director of Public Relations:** Dave Collins. **Director of Special Projects:** Jennifer Blatt. **Director of Broadcasting:** John Price. **Controller:** Larry Martin..
Field Manager: Don Buford Sr. **Coaches:** Joe Durham, Moe Drabowsky.
Trainer: Kevin Harmon.
Radio Announcer: John Price. **No. of Games Broadcast:** Home-70, Away-70. **Flagship Station:** WJEJ 1240-AM.
Stadium Name: Municipal. **Location:** I-70 West, exit 32-B, turn left at Burger King to stadium. **Standard Game Times:** 7:05 p.m.; Sun., 2:05.
Visiting Club Hotel: Ramada Inn Convention Center, 901 Dual Highway, Hagerstown, MD 21740. Telephone: (301) 733-5100.

HARRISBURG
SENATORS

Office Address: RiverSide Stadium, City Island, Harrisburg, PA 17101. **Mailing Address:** P.O. Box 15757, Harrisburg, PA 17105. **Telephone:** (717) 231-4444. **FAX:** (717) 231-4445.

Affiliation (first year): Montreal Expos (1991). **Years in League:** 1924-35, 1987-.
Operated by: Harrisburg Senators Baseball Club, Inc.
Owner: Jerome Mileur. **President:** Scott Carter.
General Manager: Rick Redd. **Assistant General Manager:** Todd Vander Woude. **Marketing Director:** Mark Clarke. **Director of Public Relations:** Mark Mattern. **Ticket Manager:** Karen Hutter Sambo. **Groundskeeper:** Will Schnell.
Field Manager: Mike Quade. **Coach:** Mike Parrott.
Trainer: Jay Williams.
Radio Announcer: Mark Mattern. **No. of Games Broadcast:** Home-70, Away-70. **Flagship Station:** WMIX 1460-AM.
Stadium Name: RiverSide. **Location:** I-83, exit 23, Second St. to Market St., bridge to City Island. **Standard Game Times:** 7:05 p.m.; Sun. 2:05.
Visiting Club Hotel: Harrisburg Hilton, One N. Second St., Harrisburg, PA 17101. Telephone: (717) 233-6000..

LONDON
TIGERS

Office Address: 89 Wharncliffe Road N., London, Ontario N6H 2A7. **Telephone:** (519) 645-2255. **FAX:** (519) 673-1837.

Affiliation (first year): Detroit Tigers (1989). **Years in League:** 1989-.
Operated by: London Tigers Baseball Club.
President: Dan Ross. **Director:** Richard Stanley.
General Manager and Vice President, Operations: Bob Gilson. **Director of Operations:** Bob Eaman. **Director of Marketing and Public Relations:** Lisa Czach. **Business Manager:** Joan Lapkowski. **Merchandise Manager:** Dani Ouimet. **Stadium Operations:** Jeff Cousins.
Field Manager: Mark DeJohn. **Coaches:** Jeff Jones, Bruce Fields.
Trainer: Terry Smith.
Radio: None
Stadium Name: Labatt Park. **Location:** Highway 401 to Wellington Road N., north to Queens Avenue, west to ballpark. **Standard Game Times:** 7:05 p.m.; Sun. 1:35.

Visiting Club Hotel: The Sheraton Armouries Hotel, 325 Dundas St., London, Ontario N6B 1T9. Telephone: (519) 679-6111.

NEW BRITAIN
RED SOX

Office Address: Beehive Field, Willowbrook Park Complex, New Britain, CT 06051. **Mailing Address:** P.O. Box 1718, New Britain, CT 06050. **Telephone:** (203) 224-8383. **FAX:** (203) 225-6267.
Affiliation (first year): Boston Red Sox (1983). **Years in League:** 1983-.
Operated by: Buzas Enterprises, Inc.
Chairman: Joseph Buzas. **President:** Hilary Buzas-Drammis. **Vice President:** George Burkert.
General Manager: Gerry Berthiaume. **Assistant General Manager:** John Kameisha. **Business Manager:** Steven Archibald. **Administrative Assistant:** Jack Levine.
Field Manager: Jim Pankovits. **Coaches:** Rick Wise, Demarlo Hale.
Trainer: Gordon Hurlbert.
Radio: None.
Stadium Name: Beehive Field. **Location:** 84 East/West to 72 East (exit 35) to Ellis Street exit, left onto Ellis, left onto S. Main St. **Standard Game Times:** 7:15 p.m.; Sun., 2; Sat. (April) 2, (May-Aug.) 7:15.
Visiting Club Hotel: Ramada Hotel, 65 Columbus Blvd., New Britain, CT 06050. Telephone: (203) 224-9161.

READING
PHILLIES

Office Address: Rt. 61 South/Centre Ave., Reading, PA 19605. **Mailing Address:** P.O. Box 15050, Reading, PA 19612. **Telephone:** (215) 375-8469. **FAX:** (215) 373-5868.
Affiliation (first year): Philadelphia Phillies (1967). **Years in League:** 1933-35, 1952-61, 1963-65, 1967-.
Operated by: E&J Professional Baseball Club, Inc.
President: Craig Stein.
General Manager: Chuck Domino. **Director of Operations:** Andy Bortz. **Director of Sales and Marketing:** Todd Parnell. **Director of Publicity:** Mark Wallace. **Community Relations:** Jack Olson. **Business Manager:** Crystal Domino. **Stadium Grounds Superintendent:** Dan Douglas.
Field Manager: Don McCormack. **Coaches:** Carlos Arroyo, Kelly Heath.
Trainer: Mark Ruffner.
Radio Announcer: Randy Stevens. **No. of Games Broadcast:** Home-70, Away-70. **Flagship Station:** WRAW 1340-AM.
Stadium Name: Municipal Memorial. **Location:** Turnpike exit 21 to 222 North. At intersection of 222 and 61. **Standard Game Times:** 7:05 p.m.; Sun., 1:05.
Visiting Club Hotel: Wellesley Inn, 910 Woodland Rd., Wyomissing, PA 19610. Telephone: (215) 374-1500.

SOUTHERN LEAGUE

Class AA

Mailing Address: 235 Main Street, Suite 103, Trussville, AL 35173.
Telephone: (205) 655-7062. **FAX:** (205) 655-7512.
President, Secretary-Treasurer: Jimmy Bragan.
Directors: Paul Beeston (Knoxville), Peter Bragan Sr. (Jacksonville), Steve Bryant (Carolina), Rich DeVos (Orlando), Bill Hardekop (Birmingham), David Hersh (Memphis), Rick Holtzman (Chattanooga), Charles Sanders (Greenville), Larry Schmittou (Huntsville), George Shinn (Charlotte).
Years League Active: 1964-92.
1992 Opening Date: April 9. **Closing Date:** Sept. 5. **First half ends:** June 21.
No. of Games: 144.
Division Structure: East—Carolina, Charlotte, Greenville, Jacksonville, Orlando. **West**—Birmingham, Chattanooga, Huntsville, Knoxville, Memphis.
Playoff Format: First half division winners play second-half winners in best-of-5 playoff; winners meet for league championship in best-of-5 finals.
All-Star Game: July 13 at Charlotte (joint Double-A game).
Roster Limit: 23.
Statistician: Howe Sportsdata International, Boston Fish Pier, West Bldg. #2—Suite 306, Boston MA 02210.
Umpires: Ed Bean (Winter Haven, FL), Matt Bohn (Bakersfield, CA), Robert Brooks (Pleasanton, CA), Chuck Clabough (Overland, MO), Martin Foster (Denver, CO), Chris Hoffarth (Casselberry, FL), Michael Huber (Greenville, IL), Brian King (Apopka, FL), Paul Nauert (Shively, KY), John Powell (Alpharetta, GA), Vince Rainforth (Lincoln, IL), Jerry Schmitt (Chicago, IL), Mike Snader (Phoenix, AZ), Bennie Walton (Lake Worth, FL), Marvin Wright (Covington, KY).

Jimmy Bragan

1991 Standings (Overall)

Club (Affiliate)	W	L	Pct.	GB	'91 Manager
†Greenville (Braves)	88	56	.611	—	Chris Chambliss
†Birmingham (White Sox)	77	66	.538	10½	Tony Franklin
†*Orlando (Twins)	77	67	.535	11	Scott Ullger
Jacksonville (Mariners)	74	69	.517	13½	Jim Nettles
Charlotte (Cubs)	74	70	.514	14	Jay Loviglio
Chattanooga (Reds)	72	72	.500	16	Jim Tracy
Carolina (Pirates)	67	75	.472	20	Marc Bombard
†Knoxville (Blue Jays)	67	77	.465	21	John Stearns
Memphis (Royals)	61	83	.424	27	Jeff Cox
Huntsville (Athletics)	61	83	.424	27	Casey Parsons

*Won playoffs †Won split-season pennant

Stadium Information

Club	Stadium	LF	CF	RF	Capacity	'91 Att.
Birmingham	Hoover Metro.	340	405	340	10,000	313,412
Carolina	Five County	330	400	330	6,000	218,054
Charlotte	Knights Castle	330	405	330	10,000	313,791
Chattanooga	Engel	355	415	324	7,500	186,285
Greenville	Greenville Muni.	335	405	335	7,027	222,038
Huntsville	Joe W. Davis	345	405	330	10,200	224,208
Jacksonville	Wolfson Park	320	395	320	8,200	231,139
Knoxville	Bill Meyer	330	400	330	6,412	123,361
Memphis	Tim McCarver	323	398	325	10,000	185,409
Orlando	Tinker Field	340	412	320	5,104	110,131

BIRMINGHAM
BARONS

Office Address: 100 Ben Chapman Dr., Birmingham, AL 35244. **Mailing Address:** P.O. Box 360007, Birmingham, AL 35236.
Telephone: (205) 988-3200. **FAX:** (205) 988-9698.

Affiliation (first year): Chicago White Sox (1986). **Years in League:** 1964-65, 1967-75, 1981-.

Operated by: Birmingham Barons Baseball Club, Inc.
President: Bill Hardekopf.
General Manager: Joe Scrivner. **Assistant General Manager:** Tony Ensor. **Director of Public Relations/Diamond Club Coordinator:** Frank Buccieri. **Director of Group Sales:** Patrick Mulvihill. **Office Manager:** Norma Rosebrough. **Accounting Clerk:** Kecia Arnold. **Head Groundskeeper:** James Reach.

Field Manager: Tony Franklin. **Coaches:** Sam Hairston, Don Cooper, Pat Roessler.
Trainer: Steve Davis.
Radio Announcer: Curt Bloom. **No. of Games Broadcast:** Home-72, Away-72. **Flagship Station:** WYDE 850-AM.

Stadium Name: Hoover Metropolitan. **Location:** I-459 to Hwy. 150 (exit 10) in Hoover. **Standard Game Times:** 7:05 p.m.; Sun. 2.

Visiting Club Hotel: Riverchase Inn, 1800 Riverchase Dr., Hoover, AL 35244. Telephone: (205) 985-7500.

CAROLINA
MUDCATS

Office Address: 903 N. Arendell Ave., Zebulon, NC 27597. **Mailing Address:** P.O. Drawer 1218, Zebulon, NC 27597. **Telephone:** (919) 269-2287. **FAX:** (919) 269-4910.

Affiliation (first year): Pittsburgh Pirates (1991). **Years in League:** 1991-.

Operated by: Carolina Professional Baseball Club, Inc.
President: Steve Bryant.
General Manager: Joe Kremer. **Assistant General Manager:** Peter Fisch. **Secretary/Treasurer:** Cyndy Aremia. **Director of Promotions:** Dave Kotarba. **Director of Media Relations:** Stephen Staudigl. **Sales Manager:** Duke Sanders. **Office Manager:** Jackie DiPrimo.

Field Manager: Don Werner. **Coaches:** Tom Dettore, Rich Chiles.
Trainer: Sandy Krum.
Radio Announcer: Bob Licht. **No. of Games Broadcast:** Home-72, Away-72. **Flagship Station:** WKIX 850-AM.

Stadium Name: Five County. **Location:** U.S. 264 and Highway 39 in Zebulon. **Standard Game Times:** 7:35 p.m.; Sun. (April-May) 2:05, (June-Sept.) 6:05.

Visiting Club Hotel: North Raleigh Hilton, 3415 Wake Forest Rd., Raleigh, NC 27609. Telephone: (919) 872-2323.

CHARLOTTE
KNIGHTS

Office Address: 2280 Deerfield Dr., Fort Mill, SC 29715. **Mailing Address:** P.O. Box 1207, Fort Mill, SC 29716. **Telephone:** (803) 548-8051. **FAX:** (803) 548-8055.

Affiliation (first year): Chicago Cubs (1989). **Years in League:** 1964-72, 1976-.

Operated by: Charlotte Baseball, Inc.
Owner: George Shinn. **President:** Spencer Stolpen. **Vice President:** Roger Schweikert.
Vice President and General Manager: Bill Lavelle. **Director of Sales and Marketing:** Steve Lyons. **Media and Communications Director:** Pat McConnell. **Special Events:** Joby Giacalone. **Ticket Manager:** Chris Carroll. **Stadium Manager:** Marc Farha.
Field Manager: Marv Foley. **Coach:** Bill Earley.

Trainer: Bob Grimes.
Radio Announcer: Pat McConnell. **No. of Games Broadcast:** Home-72, Away-72. **Flagship Station:** Unavailable.
Stadium Name: Knights Castle. **Location:** I-77 South to exit 88 (Gold Hill Rd.), exit right onto Deerfield Lane. **Standard Game Times:** 7:30 p.m.; Sun. (April-May) 2, (May-Sept.) 7.
Visiting Club Hotel: Unavailable.

CHATTANOOGA
LOOKOUTS

Office Address: 1131 East Third St., Chattanooga, TN 37403. **Mailing Address:** P.O. Box 11002, Chattanooga, TN 37401.
Telephone: (615) 267-2208. **FAX:** (615) 267-4258.
Affiliation (first year): Cincinnati Reds (1988). **Years in League:** 1964-65, 1978-.
Operated by: Engel Stadium Corporation.
President: Richard Holtzman.
Vice President and General Manager: Bill Davidson. **Director of Operations:** Scott Bryant. **Director of Broadcasting:** Larry Ward. **Director of Marketing and Public Relations:** Matthew Riley. **Director of Promotions and Special Events:** Melissa Sparks. **Director of Facility Maintenance:** Tony Strickland. **Director of Ticket Operations:** Lori Clark. **Sales Representatives:** Michael Fabian, Susan McCoy.
Field Manager: Dave Miley. **Coach:** Mike Griffin.
Trainer: Jim Knudtson.
Radio Announcer: Larry Ward. **No. of Games Broadcast:** Home-72, Away-72. **Flagship Station:** WDEF 1370-AM.
Stadium Name: Engel. **Location:** I-24 to I-27 North to exit 4th St. exit; 1½ miles to ballpark. **Standard Game Times:** 7 p.m., DH 6; Wed. 12:30; Sun. 2.
Visiting Club Hotel: Best Western Heritage Inn, I-75 and Lee Hwy., Chattanooga, TN. Telephone: (615) 899-3311.

GREENVILLE
BRAVES

Office Address: One Braves Ave., Greenville, SC 29607. **Mailing Address:** P.O. Box 16683, Greenville, SC 29606.
Telephone: (803) 299-3456. **FAX:** (803) 277-7369.
Affiliation (first year): Atlanta Braves (1984). **Years in League:** 1984-.
Operated by: Atlanta National League Baseball, Inc.
Director: Charles Sanders.
General Manager: Steve DeSalvo. **Director of Public Relations and Marketing:** Geoff Wasserman. **Director of Broadcasting:** Mark Hauser. **Director of Stadium Operations:** Mike Dunn. **Director of Ticket Sales:** Dan Kable. **Ticket Manager:** Jimmy Moore. **Director of Food Services:** Tracey Vandiver.
Field Manager: Grady Little. **Coaches:** Mark Ross, Randy Ingle, Bill Slack.
Trainer: Bryan Butz.
Radio Announcers: Mark Hauser, Doug Holliday. **No. of Games Broadcast:** Home-72, Away-72. **Flagship Station:** WBFM 98.1 FM.
Stadium Name: Greenville Municipal. **Location:** I-85 to exit 46 (Mauldin Rd.), east 2 miles. **Standard Game Times:** 7:15 p.m.
Visiting Club Hotel: Best Western Ramada Inn, 412 Mauldin Rd. at I-85, Greenville, SC 29605. Telephone: (803) 277-6730.

HUNTSVILLE
STARS

Office Address: 3125 Leeman Ferry Rd., Huntsville, AL 35815. **Mailing Address:** P.O. Box 2769, Huntsville, AL 35804.
Telephone: (205) 882-2562. **FAX:** (205) 880-0801.
Affiliation (first year): Oakland Athletics (1985). **Years in League:** 1985-.

Operated by: Huntsville Baseball, Inc.
President: Larry Schmittou.
General Manager: David Demonbreun. **Director of Sales and Marketing:** Don Mincher. **Director of Public Relations:** Patrick Nichol. **Director of Operations:** Chad Bailey. **Director of Concessions:** Dave Stewart. **Director of Tickets and Administration:** Melissa Freedman. **Director of Broadcasting:** Jack Wiers.
Field Manager: Casey Parsons. **Coach:** Bert Bradley.
Trainer: Greg Hauck.
Radio Announcer: Jack Wiers. **No. of Games Broadcast:** Home-72, Away-72. **Flagship Station:** WKGL 1450-AM.
Stadium Name: Joe W. Davis. **Location:** I-65 to Hwy 20 east, south on Memorial Parkway. **Standard Game Times:** 7:35 p.m., DH 6:05; Sun. (April-May) 2:05, (June-Aug.) 7:35.
Visiting Club Hotels: LaQuinta Inn, 3141 University Dr., Huntsville, AL 35816. Telephone: (205) 533-0756; Holiday Inn, 3810 University Dr., Huntsville, AL 35816. Telephone: (205) 837-7171; Red Carpet Inn, 2700 S. Memorial Pkwy., Huntsville, AL 35801. Telephone: (205) 536-6661.

JACKSONVILLE
SUNS

Office Address: 1201 E. Duval St., Jacksonville, FL 32202. **Mailing Address:** P.O. Box 4756, Jacksonville, FL 32201.
Telephone: (904) 358-2846. **FAX:** (904) 358-2845.
Affiliation (first year): Seattle Mariners (1991). **Years in League:** 1970-.
Operated by: Baseball JAX., Inc.
President: Peter Bragan Sr. **Vice Presidents:** Mary Bragan, Jim Goodwin.
Vice President/General Manager: Peter Bragan Jr. **Assistant General Manager:** Mike Holmes. **Director of Broadcasting:** Kevin McNabb. **Director of Stadium Operations:** Mike Bezdek. **Director of Ticket Operations:** Susan Murphy. **Administrative Assistant:** Robyn Dixon. **Office Manager:** Cathy Wiggins. **Assistant to the President:** Jerry LeMoine.
Field Manager: Bob Hartsfield. **Coaches:** Jeff Andrews, Mike Goff.
Trainer: Paul Downing.
Radio Announcer: Kevin McNabb. **No. of Games Broadcast:** Home-72, Away-72. **Flagship Station:** WQIK 1320-AM.
Stadium Name: Wolfson Park. **Location:** I-95 to 20th St. East exit to the Gator Bowl complex; Mathews or Hart Bridges to Gator Bowl exits. **Standard Game Times:** 7:35 p.m.; Sun. (April-May) 2:35, (June-Aug.) 5:35.
Visiting Club Hotels: La Quinta Inn-Baymeadows, 8255 Dix Ellis Trail, Jacksonville, FL. Telephone: (904) 731-9940.

KNOXVILLE
BLUE JAYS

Office Address: 633 Jessamine St., Knoxville, TN 37917. **Telephone:** (615) 637-9494. **FAX:** (615) 523-9913.
Affiliation (first year): Toronto Blue Jays (1980). **Years in League:** 1964-67, 1972-.
Operated by: Knoxville Blue Jays Baseball Club, Inc.
President: Paul Beeston.
General Manager: Dan Rajkowski. **Assistant General Manager:** Bill Dyke. **Director of Public Relations:** Brian Cox.
Field Manager: Garth Iorg. **Coaches:** Steve Mingori, Mike McAlpin.
Trainer: Doug Merrifield.
Radio Announcer: Mike Johnson. **No. of Games Broadcast:** Home-72, Away-72. **Flagship Station:** WNOX 99.3 FM.
Stadium Name: Bill Meyer. **Location:** I-40 to business loop, exit onto Summit Hill Dr. and follow signs. **Standard Game Times:** 7 p.m., DH 6; Sun. 2.
Visiting Club Hotel: LaQuinta Inn, 258 N. Peters Rd., Knoxville, TN 37923. Telephone: (615) 690-9777.

MEMPHIS
CHICKS

Office Address: 800 Home Run Lane, Memphis, TN 38104 **Telephone:** (901) 272-1687. **FAX:** (901) 278-3354.

Affiliation (first year): Kansas City Royals (1984). **Years in League:** 1978-.

Operated by: PSET, Inc.

President: David Hersh. **Vice President:** Larry Rutstein.

General Manager: Gary McCune. **Director of Sales and Marketing:** Paul Hartlage. **Office Manager:** Kathy Miller. **Director of Promotions:** Shannon Black. **Director of Public Relations and Broadcasting:** Tom Stocker. **Stadium Manager:** Phil Goodwin. **Receptionist:** Carrie Aiken.

Field Manager: Brian Poldberg. **Coaches:** Mike Alvarez.

Trainer: Mike Leon.

Radio Announcer: Tom Stocker. **No. of Games Broadcast:** Home-72, Away-72. **Flagship Station:** WREC 600-AM.

Stadium Name: Tim McCarver. **Location:** In State Fairgrounds complex next to Liberty Bowl. **Standard Game Times:** 7:15 p.m.; Sun. (Apr.-May) 2:15, (June-Sept.) 6:15.

Visiting Club Hotels: Unavailable.

ORLANDO
SUNRAYS

Office Address: 287 S. Tampa Ave., Orlando, FL 32805. **Telephone:** (407) 872-7593. **FAX:** (407) 649-1637.

Affiliation (first year): Minnesota Twins (1973). **Years in League:** 1973-.

Operated by: Orlando SunRays, Ltd.

President and General Manager: Pat Williams. **Assistant General Manager:** Shereen Samonds. **Director of Accounting:** John Cody. **Director of Ticket Operations:** William Peirce. **Director of Sales:** Valerie Nash. **Director of Food Services:** Leslie Prather Jr. **Office Manager and Special Projects:** Lynn Barnette. **Director of Media and Communications:** Andrew Monaco. **Grounds Superintendent:** Doug Lopas.

Field Manager: Phil Roof. **Coaches:** Mark Funderburk, Jim Shellenback.

Trainer: Rick McWane.

Radio Announcer: Andrew Monaco. **No. Of Games Broadcast:** Home-72, Away-72. **Flagship Station:** WPRD 1440-AM.

Stadium Name: Tinker Field. **Location:** I-4 to Exit 37 (Gore St.), west to Tampa Ave., right on Tampa. **Standard Game Times:** 7:05 p.m.; Sun. 6:05.

Visiting Club Hotel: Omni Orlando Hotel at Centroplex, 400 W. Livingston St., Orlando, FL 32801. Telephone: (407) 843-6664.

TEXAS LEAGUE

Class AA

Office Address: Unavailable.
Telephone, FAX: Unavailable.
Vice President: J. Con Maloney.
Directors: Bob Beban (San Antonio), J. Con Maloney (Jackson), Taylor Moore (Shreveport), Jim Paul (El Paso), Miles Prentice (Midland), Joe Preseren (Tulsa), Steve Shaad (Wichita), Bill Valentine (Arkansas).
Secretary: Joe Preseren.
Years League Active: 1888-1942, 1946-1992.
1992 Opening Date: April 10. **Closing Date:** Aug. 31.
First Half Ends: June 19.
No. of Games: 136.
Division Structure: East—Arkansas, Jackson, Shreveport, Tulsa. **West**—El Paso, Midland, San Antonio, Wichita.
Playoff Format: First half divisional winners play second half divisional winners in best-of-3 divisional playoff. Divisional champions meet in a best-of-7 series to determine league champion.
1992 All-Star Game: July 20 at Jackson.
Roster Limit: 23.
Statistician: Howe Sportsdata International, Boston Fish Pier, West Bldg. #2—Suite 306, Boston MA 02210.
Umpires: Richard Fossa (Providence, RI), Brian Gibbons (South Bend, IN), Orlando Gutierrez (Sweetwater, FL), Cris Jones (Springfield, IL), Mitchell Kiker (Greer, SC), Darrel Mason (Edmonds, WA), Mike Matheson (San Francisco, CA), Red Morrow (Pueblo, CO), Richard Roder (Des Moines, IA), George Ulrich (San Diego, CA), Tim Vessey (Montesano, WA), Larry White (West Depthford, NJ).

1991 Standings (Overall)

Club (Affiliate)	W	L	Pct.	GB	'91 Manager
*†Shreveport (Giants)	86	50	.632	—	Bill Evers
†El Paso (Brewers)	81	55	.596	5	Dave Huppert
Wichita (Padres)	71	64	.526	14½	Steve Lubratich
Jackson (Astros)	70	66	.515	16	Rick Sweet
†Midland (Angels)	67	68	.496	18½	Don Long
San Antonio (Dodgers)	61	75	.449	25	John Shoemaker
Tulsa (Rangers)	58	78	.426	28	Bobby Jones
Arkansas (Cardinals)	49	87	.360	37	Joe Pettini

*Won playoffs †Won split-season pennant

Stadium Information

Club	Stadium	LF	CF	RF	Capacity	'91 Att.
Arkansas	Ray Winder Field	320	390	340	6,083	265,268
El Paso	Cohen	340	410	340	10,000	273,438
Jackson	Smith-Wills	330	400	330	5,200	114,660
Midland	Angels	333	392	333	4,000	180,616
San Antonio	V.J. Keefe	325	400	325	3,500	185,336
Shreveport	Fair Grounds Field	330	400	330	6,200	206,540
Tulsa	Drillers	335	390	340	10,744	260,864
Wichita	Lawrence-Dumont	344	401	312	6,723	200,217

ARKANSAS
TRAVELERS

Office Address: War Memorial Park, Little Rock, AR 72205. **Mailing Address:** P.O. Box 5599, Little Rock, AR 72215.
Telephone: (501) 664-1555. **FAX:** (501) 664-1834.
Affiliation (first year): St. Louis Cardinals (1966). **Years in League:** 1966-.
Operated by: Arkansas Travelers Baseball Club, Inc.
President: Bert Parke.
Executive Vice President, General Manager: Bill Valentine. **Assistant General Manager:** Michael Schiff. **Park Superintendent:** Greg Johnson. **Office Manager:** Becky Campbell.
Field Manager: Joe Pettini. **Coach:** Marty Mason.
Trainer: Mark O'Neal.
Radio Announcers: Jim Elder, Brady Gadberry. **No. of Games Broadcast:** Home-68. **Flagship Station:** KWNN 1050-AM.
Stadium Name: Ray Winder Field. **Location:** I-630 at Fair Park Blvd. exit. **Standard Game Times:** 7:30 p.m., DH 6:30.
Visiting Club Hotel: Markham Inn, 5120 West Markham, Little Rock, AR 72204. Telephone: (501) 666-0161.
Daily Newspapers/Beat Writers: Arkansas Democrat-Gazette (Pete Perkins).

EL PASO
DIABLOS

Office Address: 9700 Gateway North Blvd., El Paso, TX 79924. **Mailing Address:** P.O. Drawer 4797, El Paso, TX 79914.
Telephone: (915) 755-2000. **FAX:** (915) 757-0671.
Affiliation (first year): Milwaukee Brewers (1981). **Years in League:** 1962-70, 1972-.
Operated by: El Paso Diablos, Inc.
President: Jim Paul.
Vice President and General Manager: Rick Parr. **Vice President and Associate General Manager:** Ken Schrom. **Vice President and Business Manager:** Karen Paul. **Assistant General Managers:** Todd Ellzey, Fred Palmerino, Derrick Grubbs. **Ticket Manager:** Sue Serna. **Director of Broadcasting:** Jon Teicher. **Assistant to the President:** Naida Fordyce. **Assistant to the General Manager:** Heather Smith. **Head Groundskeeper:** Mike Varner. **Receptionist:** Lucy Chavez.
Field Manager: Chris Bando. **Coach:** Rob Derksen.
Trainer: Dan Dalen.
Radio Announcer: Jon Teicher. **No. of Games Broadcast:** Home-68, Away-68. **Flagship Station:** KHEY 690-AM.
Stadium Name: Cohen. **Location:** I-10 to US 54 North, Diana exit. **Standard Game Times:** 7 p.m.; Sun. and Wed. 6:30.
Visiting Club Hotel: Rodeway Inn, 6201 Gateway Blvd. West, El Paso, TX 79925. Telephone: (915) 778-6611.

JACKSON
GENERALS

Office Address: 1200 Lakeland Dr., Jackson, MS 39216. **Mailing Address:** P.O. Box 4209, Jackson, MS 39296. **Telephone:** (601) 981-4664. **FAX:** (601) 981-4669.
Affiliation (first year): Houston Astros (1991). **Years in League:** 1975-.
Operated by: Cowboy Maloney Supply Co., Inc.
President: J. Con Maloney.
General Manager: Bill Blackwell. **Assistant General Manager:** Flynn Harrell. **Director of Broadcasting:** Bill Walberg. **Office Manager:** Judy Blackwell. **Grounds Supervisor:** Joe Whipps. **Transportation:** Richard Cherry.
Field Manager: Rick Sweet. **Coaches:** Don Reynolds, Charley Taylor.

Trainer: Ron Porterfield.
Radio Announcer: Bill Walberg. **No. of Games Broadcast:** Home-68, Away-68. **Flagship Station:** WJDS 620-AM.
Stadium Name: Smith-Wills. **Location:** I-55 to Lakeland Drive exit, ¼ mile east. **Game Times:** 7 p.m.; Sun. (April-May) 2:30, (June-Aug.) 6.
Visiting Club Hotel: Passport Inn, 5035 I-55 North, Jackson, MS 39236. Telephone: (601) 982-1011.

MIDLAND
ANGELS

Office Address: 4300 N. LaMesa Rd., Midland, TX 79705. **Mailing Address:** P.O. Box 12, Midland, TX 79702. **Telephone:** (915) 683-4251. **FAX:** (915) 683-0994.
Affiliation (first year): California Angels (1985). **Years in League:** 1972-.
Operated by: Midland Sports, Inc.
President: Miles Prentice. **Executive Vice President:** Bob Richmond.
General Manager: Monty Hoppel. **Director of Sales and Marketing:** Rick Carden. **Business Manager:** Nancy Swallow. **Director of Operations:** Mike Deichert. **Director of Concessions and Publications:** Doug Stewart. **Administrative Assistants:** Jeff Corbett, Scott Seator.
Field Manager: Don Long. **Coaches:** Nate Oliver, Kernan Ronan.
Trainer: Scott Sowell.
Radio Announcer: Bob Hards. **No. of Games Broadcast:** Home-68, Away-68. **Flagship Station:** KCRS 550-AM.
Stadium Name: Angels. **Location:** Rankin Highway/Big Spring to Loop 250, exit right on LaMesa Rd. **Standard Game Times:** 7 p.m.; Sun. 6.
Visiting Club Hotel: Ramada Inn, 3100 W. Wall St., Midland, TX 79703. Telephone: (915) 699-4144.

SAN ANTONIO
MISSIONS

Office Address: NW 36th @ Culebra, San Antonio, TX 78228. **Mailing Address:** P.O. Box 28268, San Antonio, TX 78228.
Telephone: (512) 434-9311. **FAX:** (512) 434-9431.
Affiliation (first year): Los Angeles Dodgers (1977). **Years in League:** 1888, 1892, 1895-99, 1907-42, 1946-64, 1967-.
Operated by: San Antonio Missions Baseball Club, Inc.
President: Dave Elmore.
General Manager: Burl Yarbrough. **Assistant General Manager:** David Oldham. **Director of Operations:** Doug Campbell. **Office Manager:** Michele Dirck.
Field Manager: Jerry Royster. **Coaches:** Ron Roenicke, Burt Hooton.
Trainer: Brett Massie.
Radio Announcers: Roy Acuff, Bob Swoboda. **No. of Games Broadcast:** Home-68, Away-68. **Flagship Station:** KONO 860-AM.
Stadium Name: V.J. Keefe Memorial. **Location:** 5 miles from Culebra Rd. exit off I-10; 4 miles from Bandera Rd. exit off I-410. **Standard Game Times:** 7:05 p.m.; Sun. 6:05.
Visiting Club Hotel: Unavailable.

SHREVEPORT
CAPTAINS

Office Address: 2901 Pershing Blvd., Shreveport, LA 71109. **Mailing Address:** P.O. Box 3448, Shreveport, LA 71133.
Telephone: (318) 636-5555. **FAX:** (318) 636-5670.
Affiliation (first year): San Francisco Giants (1979). **Years in League:** 1895, 1908-10, 1915-32, 1938-42, 1946-57, 1968-.
Operated by: Shreveport Baseball, Inc.
President and General Manager: Taylor Moore.
Assistant General Managers: Linda Johnson, Ron Viskozki, Mike Mitchell. **Director of Food and Beverage:** Leroy Beasley. **Director of**

Facilities: Steve Bange. **Director of Broadcasting:** Dave Nitz. **Director of Video:** Gilbert Little.
Field Manager: Bill Robinson. **Coaches:** Dick Dietz, Steve Cline.
Trainer: Bill Wilson.
Radio Announcer: Dave Nitz. **No. of Games Broadcast:** Home-68, Away-68. **Flagship Station:** KEEL 710-AM.
Stadium Name: Fair Grounds Field. **Location:** Hearne Avenue (US 171) exit off I-20, at Louisiana State Fairgrounds. **Standard Game Times:** 7:05 p.m., Sun. (April-May) 2:05.
Visiting Club Hotel: Quality Inn-Bossier City, 3033 Hilton Dr., Bossier City, LA 71111. Telephone: (318) 747-2400.

TULSA
DRILLERS

Office Address: 4802 E. 15th, Tulsa, OK 74112. **Mailing Address:** P.O. Box 4448, Tulsa, OK 74159. **Telephone:** (918) 744-5901. **FAX:** (918) 747-3267.
Affiliation (first year): Texas Rangers (1977). **Years in League:** 1933-42, 1946-65, 1977-.
Operated by: Tulsa Baseball, Inc.
President: Went Hubbard.
General Manager: Joe Preseren. **Assistant General Manager:** Chuck Lamson. **Director of Public Relations:** Brian Carroll. **Director of Food and Beverage:** Chris Pound. **Ticket Manager:** Tina Burney. **Director of Operations:** Derek Leistra. **Bookkeeper:** Cheryl Moore.
Field Manager: Bobby Jones. **Coaches:** Jackson Todd, Randy Whisler.
Trainer: Greg Harrel.
Radio Announcer: Bruce Howard. **No. of Games Broadcast:** Home-68, Road-68. **Flagship Station:** KAKC 1300-AM.
Stadium Name: Drillers. **Location:** 3 miles north of I-44 and 1½ miles south of I-244 on Yale Ave. **Standard Game Times:** 7:35 p.m.; Sun. (April-May) 2:05, (June-Aug.) 6:05, DH 6:05.
Visiting Club Hotel: Embassy Suites. 3332 South 79 E. Ave., Tulsa, OK 74145. Telephone: (918) 622-4000.

WICHITA
WRANGLERS

Office Address: 300 S. Sycamore, Wichita, KS 67213. **Mailing Address:** P.O. Box 1420, Wichita, KS 67201. **Telephone:** (316) 267-3372. **FAX:** (316) 267-3382.
Affiliation (first year): San Diego Padres (1987). **Years in League:** 1987-.
Operated by: Wichita Baseball, Inc.
Chairman: Robert Rich, Sr. **President:** Robert Rich Jr.
General Manager: Steve Shaad. **Consultant to the General Manager:** Larry Davis. **Director of Administration:** Dian Overaker. **Stadium/Baseball Operations Manager:** Mark Schimming. **Business/Stadium Operations Assistant:** Darin Luman. **Business Operations Assistant:** Michael Weiner. **Business Manager:** Brad Eldridge. **Sales and Marketing Manager:** Bill Fanning. **Marketing/Media Relations Coordinator:** Rick Orienza. **Operations Manager:** Chris Taylor. **Office Coordinator:** Jan Wright. **Marketing Assistant:** Dave Schultz. **Stadium Manager:** Mark Viniard.
Field Manager: Bruce Bochy. **Coaches:** Unavailable.
Trainer: Steve Sayles.
Radio Announcer: Scott Masteller. **No. of Games Broadcast:** Home-68, Away-68. **Flagship Station:** KQAM 1410-AM.
Stadium Name: Lawrence-Dumont. **Location:** From I-135, to Kellogg Ave., to Sycamore exit. **Standard Game Times:** 7:15 p.m.; Sun. (April-May) 2:15, (June-Aug.) 6:15.
Visiting Club Hotel: Downtown Family Inn, 221 E. Kellogg, Wichita, KS. Telephone: (316) 267-9281.

CALIFORNIA LEAGUE

Class A

Mailing Address: 1060 Willow St. 6; P.O. Box 26400, San Jose, CA 95125.
Telephone: (408) 977-1977. **FAX:** (408) 294-6025.
President, Treasurer: Joe Gagliardi.
Vice President: Rick Smith.
Executive Committee: Joe Gagliardi, Allen Gilbert, Rick Smith, Harry Stavrenos.
Directors: Bobby Brett (High Desert), Bruce Bucz (Visalia), Alan Levin (Modesto), Don Nomura (Salinas), Jack Patton (Reno), Lowell Patton (Bakersfield), Harry Stavrenos (San Jose), Hank Stickney (San Bernardino), Ken Stickney (Palm Springs), Walt Winkelman (Stockton).
League Administrator: John Levenda.
Secretary: William Weiss.
Years League Active: 1941-1942, 1946-1992.

Joe Gagliardi

1992 Opening Date: April 9. **Closing Date:** Aug. 30. **First Half Ends:** June 16.
No. of Games: 136.
Division Structure: Northern—Modesto, Reno, Salinas, San Jose, Stockton. **Southern**—Bakersfield, High Desert, Palm Springs, San Bernardino, Visalia.
Playoff Format: First-half division winners play second-half division winners in best-of-5 division playoff. If one team wins both halves in either division they play the team in their division with the next best winning percentage. Division playoff winners play best-of-5 series for championship.
All-Star Game: June 19 at Modesto.
Roster Limit: 25.
Statistician: Howe Sportsdata International, Boston Fish Pier, West Bldg. #2—Suite 306, Boston MA 02210; P.O. Box 5061, San Mateo, CA 94402.

1991 Standings (Overall)

Club (Affiliate)	W	L	Pct.	GB	'91 Manager
†San Jose (Giants)	92	44	.676	—	Ron Wotus
†Bakersfield (Dodgers)	85	51	.625	7	Tom Beyers
†*High Desert (Padres)	73	63	.537	19	Bruce Bochy
Stockton (Brewers)	71	65	.522	21	Chris Bando
Modesto (Athletics)	68	68	.500	24	Ted Kubiak
Palm Springs (Angels)	65	71	.478	27	Nate Oliver
Reno (Independent)	59	77	.434	33	Mal Fichman
Visalia (Twins)	58	78	.426	34	Steve Liddle
Salinas (Independent)	55	81	.404	37	Hide Koga
San Bernardino (Mariners)	54	82	.397	38	Tommy Jones

*Won playoffs †Won split-season pennant

Stadium Information

Club	Stadium	LF	CF	RF	Capacity	'91 Att.
Bakersfield	Sam Lynn	328	354	328	3,200	147,655
High Desert	Maverick	330	400	310	3,500	204,438
Modesto	Thurman Field	325	370	300	2,500	77,287
Palm Springs	Angel	360	408	360	5,185	64,871
Reno	Moana Municipal	339	420	339	4,000	76,045
Salinas	Salinas Municipal	365	402	335	3,000	66,079
San Bern.	Fiscalini Field	330	387	330	3,600	187,895
San Jose	Municipal	340	390	340	5,000	123,965
Stockton	Hebert Field	325	392	325	3,500	90,126
Visalia	Recreation Park	320	405	320	2,000	67,386

BAKERSFIELD
DODGERS

Office Address: 4009 Chester Ave., Bakersfield, CA 93301. **Mailing Address:** P.O. Box 10031, Bakersfield, CA 93389. **Telephone:** (805) 322-1363. **FAX:** (805) 322-6199.

Affiliation (first year): Los Angeles Dodgers (1984). **Years in League:** 1941-42, 1946-75, 1978-79, 1982-.

Operated by: Bakersfield Dodgers Baseball Club.

President: Lowell Patton.

General Manager: Rick Smith. **Assistant General Manager:** Jerry Stipo. **Director of Group Ticket Sales:** Bob Levy. **Administrative Assistant:** Ron Siegel.

Field Manager: Tom Beyers. **Coach:** Glenn Gregson.

Trainer: Matt Wilson.

Radio: None.

Stadium Name: Sam Lynn Ballpark. **Location:** Hwy 99 to California Ave. exit, east on California Ave., left on Chester Ave. **Standard Game Times:** 7:30 p.m.

Visiting Club Hotel: Best Western, 2620 Pierce Rd., Bakersfield, CA 93308. Telephone: (805) 327-9651.

HIGH DESERT
MAVERICKS

Office Address: 12000 Stadium Way, Adelanto, CA 92301. **Telephone:** (619) 246-6287. **FAX:** (619) 246-3197.

Affiliation (first year): San Diego Padres (1991). **Years in League:** 1991-.

Operated by: High Desert Mavericks, Inc.

President: Bobby Brett.

Vice President and General Manager: Leanne Pagliai. **Director of Operations:** Dan Zusman. **Director of Promotions:** Laura Beeman. **Director of Administration:** Noreen Lange. **Account Executives:** David Gasaway, Pat Wilhelmi, Greg Rosen.

Field Manager: Bryan Little. **Coaches:** Lonnie Keeter, Bruce Tanner.

Trainer: Unavailable.

Radio Announcer: Matt Vasgerdsian. **No. of Games Broadcast:** Home-68, Away-36. **Flagship Station:** KVVQ 910-AM/103.1 FM.

Stadium Name: Maverick. **Location:** I-15 to Hwy. 395 to Adelanto Road. **Standard Game Times:** 7:05 p.m.; Sun. (April-June) 1:05, (July-Aug.) 6:05.

Visiting Club Hotel: Green Tree Inn, 14173 Green Tree Blvd., Victorville, CA 92392. Telephone: (619) 245-3461.

MODESTO
A's

Office Address: 501 Neece Dr. Modesto, CA 95351. **Mailing Address:** P.O. Box 2437, Modesto, CA 95351. **Telephone:** (209) 529-7368. **FAX:** (209) 529-7213.

Affiliation (first year): Oakland A's (1975). **Years in League:** 1946-64, 1966-.

Operated by: Modesto A's Baseball Club, Inc.

President: Alan Levin.

Vice President and General Manager: Tim Marting. **Director of Marketing:** Matt Ellis. **Director of Stadium Operations:** Charles Leone. **Office Manager and Director of Merchandising:** Gloria DeLeon.

Field Manager: Ted Kubiak. **Coach:** Pete Richert.

Trainer: Dave Hollenbeck.

Radio: None.

Stadium Name: Thurman Field. **Location:** Hwy. 99 to Tuolomne Street exit, 1 block west to Neece Drive, left 1/4 mile to ballpark. **Standard Game Times:** 7:15 p.m., Sun. (April-May) 1:15.

Visiting Club Hotel: Red Lion Hotel, 950 9th St., Modesto, CA 95354. Telephone: (209) 526-6000.

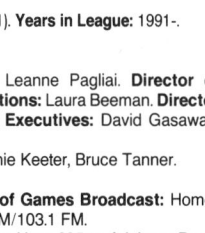

PALM SPRINGS
ANGELS

Office Address: Sunrise Way at Baristo Road, Palm Springs, CA 92263. **Mailing Address:** P.O. Box 1742, Palm Springs, CA 92263. **Telephone:** (619) 325-4487. **FAX:** (619) 325-9467.

Affiliation (first year): California Angels (1986). **Years in League:** 1986-.
Operated by: Quantum Entertainment.
General Manager: Kevin Haughian. **Assistant General Manager:** Steve Barth. **Director of Operations:** Buddy Meacham. **Director of Broadcasting:** Jon Sandler. **Publications Director:** Steve Pastorino. **Director of Sales and Marketing:** John Levine. **Director of Media and Public Relations:** David Louis.
Field Manager: Mario Mendoza. **Coaches:** Stewart Cliburn, Gene Richards.
Trainer: Derek Winchell.
Radio Announcer: Jon Sandler. **No. of Games Broadcast:** Home-68, Away-68. **Flagship Station:** KNWZ 1270-AM.
Stadium Name: Angels. **Location:** Hwy. 111 to Taquitz, left to Sunrise Way, right to Baristo Road. **Standard Game Time:** 7:05 p.m., DH 6.
Visiting Club Hotel: Palm Springs Riviera Resort and Racquet Club, 1600 North Indian Ave., Palm Springs, CA 92262. Telephone: (619) 327-8311.

RENO
SILVER SOX

Office Address: 240 West Moana Lane, Reno, NV 89509. **Mailing Address:** P.O. Box 11363, Reno, NV 89510. **Telephone:** (702) 825-0678. **FAX:** (702) 825-2296.

Affiliation (first year): Oakland A's (1992). **Years in League:** 1955-64, 1966-.
Operated by: Reno Baseball, Ltd.
President: Jerry Leider. **Vice Presidents:** Jeff Brand, Robert Cohen, Eugene Seltzer.
Executive Vice President and General Manager: Jack Patton. **Assistant General Manager:** Tom Bannon. **Director of Group Sales:** Matt Novell. **Administrative Assistant:** Jim Gregovich.
Field Manager: Gary Jones. **Coach:** Scott Budner.
Trainer: Shane Borchert.
Radio: None.
Stadium Name: Moana. **Location:** U.S. 395 to Exit 64 (Moana Lane), 5 blocks west to park. **Standard Game Times:** 7 p.m.; Sun. (April-June) 1; (July-Aug) 5.
Visiting Club Hotel: Holiday Inn Convention Center, 5851 South Virginia St., Reno, NV 89502. Telephone: (702) 825-2940.

SALINAS
SPURS

Office Address: 175 Maryal Dr., Salinas, CA 93906. **Mailing Address:** P.O. Box 4370, Salinas, CA 93912. **Telephone:** (408) 422-3812. **FAX:** (408) 422-4017.

Affiliation: Independent. **Years in League:** 1954-58, 1963-65, 1973-80, 1982-1987, 1989-.
Operated by: SACCI International.
President: Don Nomura.
General Manager: Charles Dowd. **Assistant General Manager:** Jonny Lee. **Team Coordinator:** Micheal Okumura.
Field Manager: Hide Koga.
Radio: Unavailable.
Stadium Name: Salinas Municipal. **Location:** Hwy 101 to Laurel Dr. exit,

east to Maryal Dr. **Standard Game Times:** 6:30 p.m. (April-June 6), 7 (June 6-Aug.).

Visiting Club Hotel: Ramada Inn, 808 N. Main St., Salinas, CA 93906. Telephone: (408) 424-8661.

SAN BERNARDINO
SPIRIT

Office Address: 1007 E. Highland Ave., San Bernardino, CA 92404. **Mailing Address:** P.O. Box 30160, San Bernardino, CA 92413. **Telephone:** (714) 881-1836. **FAX:** (714) 883-6279.

Affiliation (first year): Seattle Mariners (1988). **Years in League:** 1941, 1987-.

Operated by: San Bernardino Spirit Baseball Club, Inc.

Principal Owners: Hank Stickney, George DeLange, Mark Harmon.

General Manager: John LeCompte. **Assistant General Manager:** Wayne Hodes. **Director of Media:** Tom Larson. **Director of Stadium Operations:** Brian Mahoney. **Director of Ticket Sales:** Susan Bond. **Director of Food and Beverage:** Bea Shaw. **Administrative Assistant:** Mary Mendoza.

Field Manager: Ivan DeJesus. **Coaches:** Gary Wheelock, Tommy Cruz. **Trainer:** Rory Riddoch.

Radio: None.

Stadium Name: Fiscalini Field. **Location:** I-215 North to Hwy. 30 East, exit right onto Highland Ave., 3½ miles to park. **Game Times:** 7:05 p.m., Sun. (April-May) 1:05, (June-Aug) 6:05.

Visiting Club Hotel: Maruko Hotel, 295 N. "E" St., San Bernardino, CA 92401. Telephone: (714) 381-5288.

SAN JOSE
GIANTS

Office Address: 588 E. Alma Ave., San Jose, CA 95112. **Mailing Address:** P.O. Box 21727, San Jose, CA 95151. **Telephone:** (408) 297-1435. **FAX:** (408) 297-1453.

Affiliation (first year): San Francisco Giants (1988). **Years in League:** 1942, 1947-58, 1962-76, 1979-.

Operated by: Progress Sports Management.

President: Harry Stavrenos.

General Manager: Mark Wilson. **Director of Public Relations:** Buzz Hardy. **Sales Director:** Linda Pereira. **Stadium Manager:** Rick Tracy.

Field Manager: Ron Wotus. **Coaches:** Frank Reberger, Rick Miller.

Trainer: Brian Costello.

Radio Announcers: Unavailable. **No. of Games Broadcast:** Home-30, Away-30. **Flagship Station:** KSJS 90.7-FM.

Stadium Name: San Jose Municipal. **Location:** I-280 to 10th St.; U.S. 101 to Tully Road. **Game Times:** 7:15 p.m.

Visiting Club Hotel: Biltmore Hotel, 2151 Laurelwood Rd., Santa Clara, CA 95054. Telephone: (408) 988-8411.

STOCKTON
PORTS

Office Address: Billy Hebert Field, Sutter and Alpine Sts., Stockton, CA 95204. **Mailing Address:** P.O. Box 8550, Stockton, CA 95208. **Telephone:** (209) 944-5943. **FAX:** (209) 463-4937.

Affiliation (first year): Milwaukee Brewers (1979). **Years in League:** 1941, 1946-72, 1978-.

Operated by: Joy in Mudville, Inc.

Chairman: Dick Phelps. **President:** Walt Winkelman. **Chief Financial Officer:** Don Wells.

General Manager: Dan Chapman. **Director of Media Relations:** Dave Brady. **Director of Ticketing:** Alfred Spear. **Director of Merchandise:** Terry Last. **Office Manager:** Molly Rogers. **Controller:** Deborah Mikesell.

Field Manager: Tim Ireland. **Coach:** Mark Littell.
Trainer: Unavailable.
Radio Announcer: Dave Brady. **No. of Games Broadcast:** Home-68, Away-68. **Flagship Station:** KPLA 770-AM.
Stadium Name: Hebert Field. **Location:** Alpine exit east off I-5 or Wilson Way exit off Hwy. 99, west to Alpine Ave. **Standard Game Times:** 7:15 p.m.
Visiting Club Hotel: Unavailable.

VISALIA
OAKS

Office Address: 440 N. Giddings Ave., Visalia, CA 93291. **Mailing Address:** P.O. Box 48, Visalia, CA 93279. **Telephone:** (209) 625-0480. **FAX:** (209) 739-7732.
Affiliation (first year): Minnesota Twins (1977). **Years in League:** 1946-62, 1968-75, 1977-.
Operated by: JSS/USA, Inc.
Chairman of the Board: Keiichi Tsukamoto. **President:** Tatsuro Hirooka. **Secretary:** Ted Latty.
Vice President and General Manager: Bruce Bucz. **Assistant General Manager:** Acey Kohrogi.
Field Manager: Steve Liddle. **Coach:** Brian Allard.
Trainer: Joel Safly.
Radio: None.
Stadium Name: Recreation Park. **Location:** One mile north of Hwy. 198 on Giddings Avenue. **Standard Game Times:** 7:05 p.m.; Sun. (April-May) 2:05, (June-Sept.) 6:05.
Visiting Club Hotel: Holiday Inn Plaza Park, 9000 W. Airport Dr., Visalia, CA 93291. Telephone: (209) 651-5000.

CAROLINA LEAGUE

Class A

Mailing Address: P.O. Box 9503, Greensboro, NC 27429.
Telephone: (919) 273-7908. **FAX:** (919) 273-7911.
President and Treasurer: John Hopkins.
Vice President: Kelvin Bowles.
Executive Vice President: Calvin Falwell.
Secretary: Peter Kirk.
Directors: Kelvin Bowles (Salem), Robert DeLuca (Peninsula), Calvin Falwell (Lynchburg), Jim Goodman (Durham), Peter Kirk (Frederick), Larry Schmittou (Winston-Salem), Art Silber (Prince William), Tuck Tucker (Kinston).
Years League Active: 1945-1992.
1992 Opening Date: April 9. **Closing Date:** Sept. 1. **First Half Ends:** June 17.
No. of Games: 140.

John Hopkins

Divisions: Northern—Frederick, Lynchburg, Prince William, Salem. **Southern**—Durham, Kinston, Peninsula, Winston-Salem.
Playoff Format: First half division winners play second half division winners in best-of-3 series; Division winners meet in best-of-5 championship.
All-Star Game: July 22 at Salem.
Roster Limit: 25.
Statistician: Howe Sportsdata International, Boston Fish Pier, West Bldg. #2—Suite 306, Boston MA 02210.

1991 Standings (Overall)

Club (Affiliate)	W	L	Pct.	GB	'91 Manager
*†Kinston (Indians)	89	49	.645	—	Brian Graham
Winston-Salem (Cubs)	83	57	.593	7	Brad Mills
Durham (Braves)	79	58	.577	9½	Grady Little
†Prince William (Yankees)	71	68	.511	18½	Mike Hart
†Lynchbrg (Red Sox)	67	72	.482	22½	Buddy Bailey
Salem (Pirates)	63	77	.450	27	Stan Cliburn
Frederick (Orioles)	58	82	.414	32	Wally Moon
Peninsula (Mariners)	46	93	.331	43½	Steve Smith

*Won playoffs   †Won split-season pennant

Stadium Information

Club	Stadium	LF	CF	RF	Capacity	'91 Att.
Durham	Dur. Athl. Park	330	410	305	5,000	301,240
Frederick	Grove	325	400	325	5,200	318,354
Kinston	Grainger	335	390	335	4,100	100,857
Lynchburg	City	325	390	325	4,200	88,897
Peninsula	War Memorial	335	402	335	4,330	41,131
Pr. William	P.W. County	315	400	315	6,200	208,166
Salem	Municipal Field	316	420	301	5,000	131,582
Winston-Salem	Ernie Shore	370	400	335	4,280	111,333

DURHAM BULLS

Office Address: 426 Morris St., Durham, NC 27701. **Mailing Address:** P.O. Box 507, Durham, NC 27702. **Telephone:** (919) 688-8211. **FAX:** (919) 688-4593.

Affiliation (first year): Atlanta Braves (1980). **Years in League:** 1945-1971, 1980-.
Operated by: Durham Bulls Baseball Club, Inc.
President: Jim Goodman. **Vice President:** Al Mangum.
General Manager: Rob Dlugozima. **Office Manager:** Kecia Tillman. **Stadium Operations:** Bill Miller. **Operations/Souvenirs:** Stan Hughes. **Promotions:** Bobby Couch. **Receptionist:** Leisha Cowart.
Field Manager: Leon Roberts. **Coach:** Matt West.
Trainer: Dave Tomshek.
Radio Announcer: Rod Meadows. **No. of Games Broadcast:** Home-70, Away-70. **Flagship Station:** WDNC 620-AM.
Stadium Name: Durham Athletic Park. **Location:** Downtown Durham exit off I-85, right to Geer St., right ½ mile to park. **Standard Game Times:** 7:30 p.m.
Visiting Club Hotel: Red Roof Inn, I-85 at Guess Rd., Durham, NC 27705. Telephone: (919) 471-9882.

FREDERICK KEYS

Office Address: 6201 New Design Rd., Frederick, MD 21701. **Mailing Address:** P.O. Box 3169, Frederick, MD 21701. **Telephone:** (301) 662-0013. **FAX:** (301) 662-0018

Affiliation (first year): Baltimore Orioles (1989). **Years in League:** 1989-.
Operated by: Maryland Baseball Limited Partnership.
Chairman: Peter Kirk. **President** Hugh Schindel. **Vice President:** Terry Randall.
General Manager: Keith Lupton. **Assistant General Manager/Administrative Operations:** Mark Zeigler. **Assistant General Manager/Stadium Operations:** Jim Halloran. **Director of Group Sales:** Jon Danos. **Director of Special Projects:** Jay Hemond. **Director of Telemarketing:** Erick Royle. **Director of Concessions:** Pat Carter. **Director of Skybox Services:** Mark Thome. **Office Manager:** Janet Potash.
Field Manager: Bobby Miscik. **Coaches:** John O'Donoghue, Oneri Fleita.
Trainer: Mitch Bibb.
Radio Announcer: Matt Hicks. **No. of Games Broadcast:** Home-70, Away-70. **Flagship Station:** WQSI 820-AM.
Stadium Name: Harry Grove. **Location:** Junction of I-70 and Route 355 (Market Street exit). **Standard Game Times:** 7:05 p.m.; Sun. 2:05.
Visiting Club Hotel: Days Inn-Frederick, Buckeystown Pike, Frederick, MD 21701. Telephone: (301) 694-6600.

KINSTON INDIANS

Office Address: 400 East Grainger Ave., Kinston, NC 28501. **Mailing Address:** P.O. Box 3542, Kinston, NC 28502. **Telephone:** (919) 527-9111. **FAX:** (919) 527-2328.

Affiliation (first year): Cleveland Indians (1987). **Years in League:** 1956-57, 1962-74, 1978-.
Operated by: The Kinston Group, Inc.
Chairman: Tuck Tucker.
President and General Manager: North Johnson. **Vice President:** Jim Thomas. **Assistant General Manager:** Billy Johnson. **Office Manager:** Marci Smoot.
Field Manager: Dave Keller. **Coach:** Rob Swain.
Trainer: Dan DeVoe.

Radio Announcer: Jim Rosenhaus. **No. of Games Broadcast:** Home-70, Away-70. **Flagship Station:** WRNS 960-AM.

Stadium Name: Grainger. **Location:** ½ mile off Highway 11 and Route 70 Business. **Standard Game Times:** 7 p.m.; Sun. (April-June) 3, (July-Sept.) 7.

Visiting Club Hotel: Sheraton Kinston, Highway 70 by-pass, Kinston, NC 28501. Telephone: (919) 523-1300.

LYNCHBURG
RED SOX

Office Address: City Stadium, Fort Ave. & Wythe Rd., Lynchburg, VA 24501. **Mailing Address:** P.O. Box 10213, Lynchburg, VA 24506. **Telephone:** (804) 528-1144. **FAX:** (804) 846-0768.

Affiliation (first year): Boston Red Sox (1988). **Years in League:** 1966-.

Operated by: Lynchburg Baseball Corporation.

President: Calvin Falwell.

General Manager: Paul Sunwall. **Assistant General Manager/Promotions and Marketing:** Liane Lewis. **Assistant General Manager/Concessions and Sales:** Matthew Drago. **Office Manager:** Debbie Scales. **Director of Broadcasting:** Shawn Holliday. **Assistant Director of Broadcasting:** Brad Sparesus. **Administrative Assistant:** Steve Blewitt. **Field Supervisor/Sales:** Ronnie Roberts.

Field Manager: Buddy Bailey. **Coach:** Jim Bibby.

Trainer: David Duchin.

Radio Announcers: Shawn Holliday, Brad Sparesus. **No. of Games Broadcast:** Home-70, Away-70. **Flagship Station:** WLLL 930-AM.

Stadium Name: City. **Location:** U.S. 29 South to City Stadium exit; U.S. 29 North to Lynchburg College exit. **Standard Game Times:** 7 p.m.; Sun. (April-June 14) 2, (June 28-Aug.) 7.

Visiting Club Hotel: Harvey's Motel, 2018 Wards Road, Lynchburg, VA 24502. Telephone: (804) 239-2611.

PENINSULA
PILOTS

Office Address: 1889 West Pembroke Ave., Hampton, VA 23661. **Mailing Address:** 1405-H Kiln Creek Pkwy., Newport News, VA 23602. **Telephone:** (804) 872-7700. **FAX:** (804) 872-9868.

Affiliation (first year): Seattle Mariners (1990). **Years in League:** 1963-71, 1974, 1976-.

Operated by: Kiln Creek Baseball Associates, L.P.

Principal Owners: Robert and Marilyn DeLuca.

President/Chief Operating Officer: Burt Boltuch.

General Manager: Chris Kemple. **Assistant General Manager:** Troy Waller. **Office Manager:** Judy Hark.

Field Manager: Marc Hill. **Coach:** Paul Lindblad.

Trainer: Paul Harker.

Radio Announcer: Tony Mercurio. **No. of Games Broadcast:** Home-70, Away-70. **Flagship Station:** WGH 1310-AM.

Stadium Name: War Memorial. **Location:** I-64 to I-664, Powhatan exit off I-664, left to Pembroke Ave., right to park. **Game Times:** 7 p.m., 2:05.

Visiting Club Hotel: Days Inn, 1918 Coliseum Dr., Hampton, VA 23666. Telephone: (804) 826-4810.

PRINCE WILLIAM
CANNONS

Office Address: 7 County Complex Ct., Woodbridge, VA 22193. **Mailing Address:** P.O. Box 2148, Woodbridge, VA 22193. **Telephone:** (703) 590-2311. **FAX:** (703) 590-5716.

Affiliation (first year): New York Yankees (1987). **Years in League:** 1985-.

Operated by: Prince William Professional Baseball Club, Inc.

Chairman: Art Silber. **President:** Frank Boulton. **Vice President:** Bart Fisher.

General Manager: Ken Shepard. **Assistant General Manager:** George Brzezinski. **Director of Group Sales:** Mike Harris. **Director of Finance:** Pat Filippone. **Director of Telemarketing/Merchandising:** Michael Cook. **Director of Community Relations:** Stacey Brunson. **Director of Broadcasting/Media Relations:** Kevin Heilbronner. **Director of Regional Marketing:** Beth Smyth.

Field Manager: Mike Hart. **Coaches:** Dave Schuler, Ken Dominguez.

Trainer: Adam Wagner.

Radio Announcer: Kevin Heilbronner. **No. of Games Broadcast:** Away-70. **Flagship Station:** WQRA 94.3-FM.

Stadium Name: Prince William County. **Location:** I-95 to exit 53 (Lake Ridge/Occoquan), left at second light, follow Davis Ford Rd. for 7 miles, stadium on right. **Standard Game Times:** 7:30 p.m.; Sun. (April-June 14) 2, (June 28-Sept.) 6.

Visiting Club Hotel: Days Inn, 14619 Potomac Mills Rd., Woodbridge, VA 22192. Telephone: (703) 680-3800.

SALEM
BUCCANEERS

Office Address: 620 Florida St., Salem, VA 24153. **Mailing Address:** P.O. Box 842, Salem, VA 24153. **Telephone:** (703) 389-3333. **FAX:** (703) 389-9710.

Affiliation (first year): Pittsburgh Pirates (1987). **Years in League:** 1968-.

Operated by: Salem Professional Baseball Club, Inc.

President: Kelvin Bowles.

Vice President and General Manager: Sam Lazzaro. **Assistant General Manager:** Dennis Robarge. **Director of Broadcasting::** Mike Minshall. **Director of Group Sales and Community Relations:** Mike Baum. **Administrative Assistant:** Dave Shonk.

Field Manager: John Wockenfuss. **Coach:** Rick Keeton.

Trainer: Bill Zick.

Radio Announcer: Mike Minshall. **No. of Games Broadcast:** Home-70, Away-70. **Flagship Station:** WROV 1240-AM.

Stadium Name: Municipal Field. **Location:** 2 miles off I-81 near downtown Salem. **Standard Game Times:** 7 p.m.; Sun. (April-May) 3, (June-Aug.) 7.

Visiting Club Hotel: Holiday Inn South, 1927 Franklin Road SW, Roanoke, VA 24014. Telephone: (703) 343-0121.

WINSTON-SALEM
SPIRITS

Office Address: 401 W. 30th St., Winston-Salem, NC 27105. **Mailing Address:** P.O. Box 4488, Winston-Salem, NC 27115. **Telephone:** (919) 759-2233. **FAX:** (919) 759-2042.

Affiliation (first year): Chicago Cubs (1985). **Years in League:** 1945-.

Operated by: Winston-Salem Spirits Baseball, Inc.

Owner: Larry Schmittou.

Vice President/General Manager: John Roco. **Assistant General Manager/Director of Concessions:** Aaron Brandt. **Director of Promotions:** Trip Durham. **Ticket and Office Manager:** Stephanie Darr.

Field Manager: Bill Hayes. **Coach:** Lester Strode.

Trainer: Steve Melendez.

Radio: None.

Stadium Name: Ernie Shore Field. **Location:** I-40 to Cherry St. exit, north through downtown to Deacon Blvd., right to park. **Game Times:** 7 p.m., Sun. (April-May) 2:35.

Visiting Club Hotel: Holiday Inn-North, 3050 University Parkway, Winston-Salem, NC 27105. Telephone: (919) 723-2911.

FLORIDA STATE LEAGUE

Class A

Mailing Address: P.O. Box 349, Daytona Beach, FL 32115.
Telephone: (904) 252-7479. **FAX:** (904) 252-7495.
President/Treasurer: Chuck Murphy.
Vice Presidents: Ken Carson, Ronald Myers, Rob Rabenecker.
Directors: Tim Bawmann (Osceola), John Browne (Sarasota), Ken Carson (Dunedin), Frank Decker (Lakeland), Tony Flores (St. Petersburg), Steve Frick (Ft. Lauderdale), Marvin Goldklang (Miracle), Ted Guthrie (Charlotte), Bill MacKay (Winter Haven), Joe McShane (St. Lucie), Rob Rebenecker (West Palm Beach), Karl Rogozenski (Baseball City), Tom Simmons (Vero Beach), John Timberlake (Clearwater).

Chuck Murphy

Years League Active: 1919-1927, 1936-1941, 1946-1992.
1992 Opening Date: April 10. **Closing Date:** Sept. 2. **First Half Ends:** June 19.
No. of Games: 140.
Division Structure: East—Ft. Lauderdale, St. Lucie, Vero Beach, West Palm Beach. **Central**—Baseball City, Lakeland, Osceola, Winter Haven. **West**—Charlotte, Clearwater, Dunedin, Miracle, St. Petersburg, Sarasota,.
Playoff Format: Division winners and two wild-card teams meet in a postseason series, involving from four to eight teams, depending on repeat winners.
All-Star Game: June 20 at West Palm Beach.
Roster Limit: 25.
Statistician: Howe Sportsdata International, Boston Fish Pier, West Bldg. #2, Suite 306, Boston, MA 02210.

1991 Standings (Overall)

Club (Affiliate)	W	L	Pct.	GB	'91 Manager
†Clearwater (Phillies)	81	49	.623	—	Lee Elia
†Vero Beach (Dodgers)	79	52	.603	2½	Jerry Royster
Sarasota (White Sox)	75	56	.573	6½	Rick Patterson
†Lakeland (Tigers)	72	56	.563	8	John Lipon
†St. Lucie (Mets)	72	59	.550	9½	John Tamargo
*West Palm Beach (Expos)	72	59	.550	9½	Felipe Alou
Osceola (Astros)	64	63	.504	15½	Sal Butera
Miami (Independent)	63	67	.485	18	Fredi Gonzalez
Baseball City (Royals)	62	69	.473	19½	Carlos Tosca
Charlotte (Rangers)	62	70	.470	20	Bobby Molinaro
Ft. Lauderdale (Yankees)	59	69	.461	21	Glenn Sherlock
Dunedin (Blue Jays)	59	72	.450	22½	Dennis Holmberg
St. Petersburg (Cards)	47	84	.359	34½	Dave Bialas
Winter Haven (Red Sox)	43	85	.336	37	Mike Verdi

*Won playoffs †Won split-season pennant

Stadium Information

Club	Stadium	LF	CF	RF	Capacity	'91 Att.
Baseball City	Baseball City	340	410	340	8,000	21,174
Charlotte	Charlotte County	340	410	340	6,026	97,399
Clearwater	Jack Russell	340	400	340	7,384	82,631
Dunedin	Grant Field	335	400	315	6,239	67,040
Ft. Lauderdale	Yankee	332	401	320	8,300	51,362
Ft. Myers[1]	Lee County Sports	330	405	330	7,500	—
Lakeland	Joker Marchant	340	420	340	7,000	51,464
Osceola	Osceola County	330	410	330	5,100	48,341
St. Lucie	County Sports Complex	338	410	338	7,400	79,961
St. Petersburg	Al Lang	330	400	330	7,004	155,946
Sarasota	Ed Smith	340	410	340	7,500	84,951
Vero Beach	Holman	340	400	340	6,474	95,900
West Palm	Municipal	330	400	330	4,400	105,787
Winter Haven	Chain O'Lakes	340	420	340	5,000	20,323

[1] Ft. Myers franchise operated in Miami in 1991.

BASEBALL CITY
ROYALS

Office Address: 300 Stadium Way, Davenport, FL 33837. **Telephone:** (813) 424-7134. **FAX:** (813) 424-1526.

Affiliation (first year): Kansas City Royals (1988). **Years in League:** 1988-.
Operated by: Busch Entertainment Corporation.
President: Gene O'Neill.
General Manager: Karl Rogozenski. **Director of Marketing and Public Relations:** Dan Pearson. **Sales and Office Manager:** Kelli Hall.
Field Manager: Ron Johnson. **Coach:** Pete Filson.
Trainer: Frank Kyte.
Radio: None.
Stadium Name: Baseball City. **Stadium Location:** I-4 at U.S. 27. **Standard Game Times:** 6 p.m.; Sun. 1; DH 5.
Visiting Club Hotel: Holiday Inn, I-4 and US 27, Davenport, FL. 33837. Telephone: (813) 424-2211.

CHARLOTTE
RANGERS

Office Address: 2300 El Jobean Road, Pt. Charlotte, FL 33948. **Mailing Address:** P.O. Box 3609, Pt. Charlotte, FL 33949.
Telephone: (813) 625-9500. **FAX:** (813) 624-5168.

Affiliation (first year): Texas Rangers (1987). **Years in League:** 1987-.
Operated by: Texas Rangers Baseball Club, Ltd.
General Manager: Ted Guthrie. **Assistant General Manager:** Tim Murphy. **Director of Public Relations:** Rick Lindau. **Office Manager:** Sue Denny. **Field Superintendent:** Tom Burns. **Assistant Field Superintendent:** Tom Vida.
Field Manager: Bump Wills. **Coach:** Marvin White.
Trainer: Donna Van Duzer.
Radio: None.
Stadium Name: Charlotte County. **Location:** I-75 south, west on Toledo Blade Blvd. (exit 32), south on U.S. 41, S.R. 776 west to ballpark. **Standard Game Times:** 7 p.m.; Sun., 6.
Visiting Club Hotel: Days Inn, 1941 Tamiami Trail, Murdock, FL 33938. Telephone: (813) 627-8900.

CLEARWATER
PHILLIES

Office Address: 800 Phillies Dr., Clearwater, FL 34615. **Mailing Address:** P.O. Box 10336, Clearwater, FL 34617. **Telephone:** (813) 441-8638. **FAX:** (813) 447-3924.

Affiliation (first year): Philadelphia Phillies (1985). **Years in League:** 1985-.
Operated by: The Philadelphia Phillies.
President: Bill Gargano.
General Manager: John Timberlake. **Business Manager:** Roy Lake. **Operations Manager:** Eric Tobin. **Marketing Manager:** Jim Herlihy. **Field Supervisor:** Opie Cheek.
Field Manager: Bill Dancy. **Coach:** Darold Knowles.
Trainer: Craig Strobel.
Radio: None.
Stadium Name: Jack Russell. **Location:** U.S. Highway 19 north to Drew St. west, north on Greenwood Ave., to Seminole St., right to park. **Standard Game Times:** 7 p.m., Sun. 2.
Visiting Club Hotel: Howard Johnson, 410 U.S. 19 N., Clearwater, FL 34625. Telephone: (813) 797-5021.

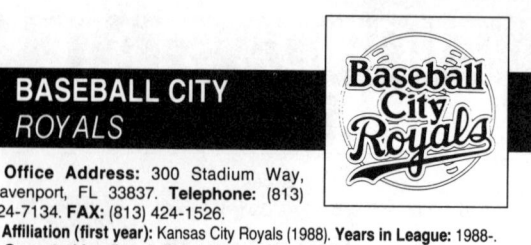

DUNEDIN
BLUE JAYS

Office Address: 311 Douglas Ave., Dunedin, FL 34698. **Mailing Address:** P.O. Box 957, Dunedin, FL 34697. **Telephone:** (813) 733-9302. **FAX:** (813) 734-7661.

Affiliation (first year): Toronto Blue Jays (1987). **Years in League:** 1978-79, 1987-.

Operated by: Toronto Blue Jays.

Director of Minor League Business: Ken Carson. **General Manager:** Gary Rigley. **Assistant General Manager:** Benjie Meleras. **Administrative Assistant:** Vicki Kiessling. **Concessions Manager:** Pat Smith.

Field Manager: Dennis Holmberg. **Coaches:** Bill Monbouquette, Hector Torres.

Trainer: Jon Woodworth.

Radio: None.

Stadium Name: Grant Field. **Location:** Douglas Ave., one block east of Alt. US 19 North. **Standard Game Times:** 7 p.m.; Sun., 2.

Visiting Club Hotels: Knights Inn, 34106 US 19 N, Palm Harbor, FL 34684. Telephone: (813) 789-2022. Countryside Hotel, 27988 US 19 N, Clearwater, FL 34623. Telephone: (813) 796-0135.

FT. LAUDERDALE
YANKEES

Office Address: 5301 NW 12th Ave., Ft. Lauderdale, FL 33309. **Telephone:** (305) 776-1921. **FAX:** (305) 776-1958.

Affiliation (first year): New York Yankees (1962). **Years in League:** 1962-.

Operated by: New York Yankees.

Chairman: Jim Ogle.

President: Mark Zettelmeyer. **General Manager:** Steve Frick. **Director of Marketing:** Mike Stanfield. **Business Manager:** Mike Plehal. **Office Manager:** Doris Zettelmeyer.

Field Manager: Brian Butterfield. **Coaches:** Mark Shiflett, Bob Mariano.

Trainer: Darren London.

Radio: None.

Stadium Name: Yankee. **Location:** I-95 and Commercial Blvd., ¼ mile west to NW 12th Ave., follow to stadium. **Standard Game Times:** 7:05 p.m.; Sun., 6:05.

Visiting Club Hotels: Marriott-Cypress Creek, 6650 N. Andrews Ave., Ft. Lauderdale, FL 33309. Telephone: (305) 771-0440; Days Inn, 3355 N. Federal Hwy., Ft. Lauderdale, FL 33306. Telephone: (305) 566-4301.

FT. MYERS
MIRACLE

Office Address: Lee County Sports Complex, 14100 Six Mile Cypress Pkwy., Ft. Myers, FL 33912. **Telephone:** (813) 768-4210. **FAX:** (813) 768-4211.

Affiliation: Independent. **Years in League:** 1978-87, 1992-.

Operated by: Greater Miami Baseball Club, L.P.

President: Michael Veeck.

General Manager: Roger Wexelberg. **Director of Operations:** Lee Smith. **Director of Sales:** Ben Creed.

Field Manager: Unavailable.

Radio Announcers: Jim Lucas, Don Wardlow. **No. of Games Broadcast:** Unavailable. **Flagship Station:** Unavailable.

Stadium Name: Lee County Sports Complex. **Location:** Daniels exit off I-75 W, left on Six Mile Cypress Pkwy. **Standard Game Times:** 7:05 p.m.; Sun. 2.

Visiting Club Hotel: Wellesley Inn, 4400 Ford St., Ft. Myers, FL 33916. Telephone: (813) 278-3949.

LAKELAND
TIGERS

Office Address: 1818 Harden Blvd., Lakeland, FL 33803. **Mailing Address:** P.O. Box 2785, Lakeland, FL 33806. **Telephone:** (813) 686-1133. **FAX:** (813) 688-1637.

Affiliation (first year): Detroit Tigers (1960). **Years in League:** 1919-26, 1953-55, 1960, 1962-64, 1967-.

Operated by: Lakeland Sports, Inc.
President: Frank Decker.
Vice President/General Manager: Ronald Myers. **Assistant General Manager:** Woody Hicks.
Field Manager: John Lipon. **Coaches:** Dan Raley, Rich Bombard.
Trainer: Steve Carter.
Radio: None.
Stadium Name: Joker Marchant. **Location:** Exit 19 on I-4, to Lakeland Hills Blvd., left for 1½ miles. **Standard Game Times:** 7 p.m.; Sun., 1. DH, 6.
Visiting Club Hotel: Unavailable.

OSCEOLA
ASTROS

Office Address: 1000 Osceola Blvd., Kissimmee, FL 34744. **Mailing Address:** P.O. Box 422229, Kissimmee, FL 34742.
Telephone: (407) 933-5500. **FAX:** (407) 847-6237.

Affiliation (first year): Houston Astros (1985). **Years in League:** 1985-.
Operated by: Houston Sports Association.
General Manager: Tim Bawmann. **Administrative Assistant:** Matt Ban. **Office Manager:** Kathy Rogacki.
Field Manager: Sal Butera. **Coaches:** Jack Billingham, Frank Cacciatore.
Trainer: Mike Freer.
Radio: Unavailable.
Stadium Name: Osceola County. **Location:** Florida Turnpike exit 244; U.S. 192 to Osceola Blvd. **Standard Game Times:** 7 p.m.; Sun., 2.
Visiting Club Hotels: Howard Johnson's, 2323 Hwy. 192, Kissimmee, FL 34743. Telephone: (407) 846-4900. Park Inn International, 2039 E. Irlo Bronson Hwy., Kissimmee, FL 34743. Telephone (407) 846-7814. Save Inn, 2225 E. Bronson Hwy., Kissimmee, FL 34743. Telephone: (407) 846-0777.

ST. LUCIE
METS

Office Address: 525 NW Peacock Blvd., Port St. Lucie, FL 34986. **Telephone:** (407) 871-2100. **FAX:** (407) 878-9802.

Affiliation (first year): New York Mets (1988). **Years in League:** 1988-.
Operated by: New York Mets.
Vice President-Operations: Joe McShane. **General Manager:** Ross Vecchio. **Ticket Manager:** Grace Benway. **Media Relations:** George McClelland. **Office Manager:** Pat Kalenowski.
Field Manager: John Tamargo. **Coaches:** Bill Latham, Bill Gardner.
Trainer: Bob Burton.
Radio Announcer: Bill Keogh. **No. of Games Broadcast:** Home-36, Away-34. **Flagship Station:** WPSL 1590-AM.
Stadium Name: Thomas J. White. **Location:** Exit 63C (St. Lucie West Blvd.) on I-95, left on NW Peacock. **Standard Game Times:** 7 p.m., DH 6, Sun. 2.
Visiting Club Hotel: Holiday Inn, 7151 Okeechobee Rd., Ft. Pierce, FL 34945. Telephone: (407) 464-5000. Radisson, 10120 S. Federal Hwy., Pt. St. Lucie, FL 34985. Telephone: (407) 337-2200.

ST. PETERSBURG
CARDINALS

Office Address: 180 2nd Ave. SE, St. Petersburg, FL 33701. **Mailing Address:** P.O. Box 12557, St. Petersburg, FL 33733. **Telephone:** (813) 822-3384. **FAX:** (813) 895-1556.

Affiliation (first year): St. Louis Cardinals (1966). **Years in League:** 1920-27, 1955-.

Operated by: Suncoast Baseball Club, Inc.

General Manager: Tony Flores. **Director of Public Relations:** Brian Borchardt. **Business Manager:** Steve Cohen. **Director of Marketing/Group Sales:** Tom Donahue.

Field Manager: Dave Bialas. **Coach:** John Stuper.

Trainer: Dan Doyel.

Stadium Name: Al Lang. **Location:** I-275 to exit 9, to 1st St. South, left 2 blocks. **Standard Game Times:** 7:05 p.m.; Sun. 5, DH 6.

Visiting Club Hotel: Unavailable.

SARASOTA
WHITE SOX

Office Address: 1090 N. Euclid Ave., Sarasota, FL 34237. **Telephone:** (813) 954-7699. **FAX:** (813) 954-5753.

Affiliation (first year): Chicago White Sox (1989). **Years in League:** 1926-27, 1961-65, 1989-.

Operated by: Sarasota White Sox, Inc.

General Manager: John Browne. **Assistant General Manager:** Michael Marek. **Director of Sales and Marketing:** Tom Van Schaack. **Director of Operations:** David Martin. **Administrative Assistant:** Jane Reifert.

Field Manager: Rick Patterson. **Coaches:** Kirk Champion, Mike Barnett.

Trainer: Scott Johnson.

Radio Announcer: Unavailable. **No. of Games Broadcast:** Away-68. **Flagship Station:** WQSA 1220-AM.

Stadium Name: Ed Smith. **Location:** I-75 to exit 40 (University Parkway), 3 miles to Tuttle Avenue, south on Tuttle to 12th Street. **Standard Game Times:** 7:00 p.m., DH and Sun., 6.

Visiting Club Hotel: Wellesley Inn, 1803 N. Tamiami Trail, Sarasota, FL 34234. Telephone: (813) 366-5128.

VERO BEACH
DODGERS

Office Address: 4001 26th St., Vero Beach, FL 32960. **Mailing Address:** P.O. Box 2887, Vero Beach, FL 32961. **Telephone:** (407) 569-4900. **FAX:** (407) 567-0819.

Affiliation (first year): Los Angeles Dodgers (1980). **Years in League:** 1980-.

Operated by: Vero Beach Dodgers.

General Manager: Tom Simmons. **Assistant General Manager:** Heath Brown.

Field Manager: Glenn Hoffman. **Coaches:** Jon Debus, Dennis Lewallyn.

Trainer: Rob Giesecke.

Radio Announcer: Andy Young. **No. of Games Broadcast:** Home-68, Away-68. **Flagship Station:** WAXE 1370-AM.

Stadium Name: Holman. **Location:** 5 miles east of I-95, 3 miles west of U.S. 1; two blocks north of Route 60. **Standard Game Times:** 7 p.m.; DH 6.

Visiting Club Hotel: Days Inn-Vero Beach Resort, 3244 Ocean Dr., Vero Beach, FL 32963. Telephone: (407) 231-2800.

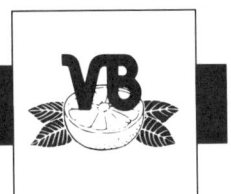

WEST PALM BEACH
EXPOS

Office Address: 715 Hank Aaron Dr., West Palm Beach, FL 33401. **Mailing Address:** P.O. Box 3566, West Palm Beach, FL 33402. **Telephone:** (407) 684-6801. **FAX:** (407) 686-0221.

Affiliation (first year): Montreal Expos (1969). **Years in League:** 1955-56, 1965-.

Operated by: West Palm Beach Expos, Inc.

General Manager: Rob Rabenecker. **Assistant General Manager:** Jay Darnell. **Business Manager:** Kevin Cummings. **Director of Media Relations/Sales:** Ron Colangelo. **Marketing Representatives:** Estelle Krieger, Brent Moore.

Field Manager: Dave Jauss. **Coach:** Chuck Kniffin.

Trainer: Sean Cunningham.

Radio Announcer: Ron Colangelo. **No. of Games Broadcast:** Home-select, Away-68. **Flagship Station:** WPBG 1290-AM.

Stadium Name: Municipal. **Location:** I-95 to Exit 53, east for ½ mile on Palm Beach Lakes Blvd. **Standard Game Times:** 7:05 p.m; Sun. 6:05.

Visiting Club Hotels: Wellesley Inn, 1910 Palm Beach Lakes Blvd., West Palm Beach, FL 33409. Telephone: (407) 689-8540.

WINTER HAVEN
RED SOX

Office Address: Chain O'Lakes Park, Cypress Garden Blvd., Winter Haven, FL 33880. **Telephone:** (813) 293-3900. **FAX:** (813) 299-4491.

Affiliation (first year): Boston Red Sox (1969). **Years in League:** 1966-67, 1969-.

Operated by: Winter Haven Red Sox, Inc.

General Manager: Bill MacKay. **Assistant General Manager:** Tom Albano.

Field Manager: Felix Maldonado. **Coach:** Unavailable.

Trainer: Jim Stricek.

Stadium Name: Chain O'Lakes Park. **Location:** ½ block east off Rt. 17 on Cypress Gardens Blvd. **Game Times:** 7 p.m.; Sun. (1st half), 1; Sun. (2nd half), 7.

Visiting Club Hotel: Holiday Inn, 1150 3rd Street SW, Winter Haven, FL 33880. Telephone: (813) 294-4451.

MIDWEST LEAGUE

Class A

Mailing Address P.O. Box 936, Beloit, WI 53512.
Telephone: (608) 364-1188. **FAX:** (608) 364-1913.
President, Treasurer: George Spelius.
Vice Presidents: Jim Cutler, Ed Larson.
Recording Secretary: Doris Krucker.
Office Secretary: Nancy Spelius.
Directors: Charles Barnhill (Madison), John Baxter (South Bend), Howard Erickson (Beloit), Doug Hahn (Appleton), Richard Holtzman (Quad City), Ed Kross (Clinton), Wally Krouse (Cedar Rapids), Clarence Krusinski (Peoria), Lee Landers (Springfield), Eric Margenau (Kenosha), William McKee (Rockford), David Walker (Burlington), Mike Woleben (Kane County), Dan Yates (Waterloo).

George Spelius

Years League Active: 1947-1992.
1992 Opening Date: April 9. **Closing Date:** Sept. 3.
No. of Games: 140.
Division Structure: Northern—Appleton, Beloit, Kane County, Kenosha, Madison, Rockford, South Bend. **Southern**—Burlington, Cedar Rapids, Clinton, Peoria, Quad City, Springfield, Waterloo.
Playoff Format: Split-season division champions (plus wild card if necessary) play best-of-3 semifinals; winners play best-of-5 final.
All-Star Game: June 22 at Peoria, Ill.
Roster Limit 25.
Statistician: Howe Sportsdata International, Boston Fish Pier, West Bldg. #2—Suite 306, Boston MA 02210.

1991 Standings (Overall)

Club (Affiliate)	W	L	Pct.	GB	'91 Manager
†*Clinton (Giants)	81	58	.583	—	Jack Mull
†Madison (Athletics)	77	61	.558	3½	Gary Jones
Rockford (Expos)	76	61	.555	4	Pat Kelly, Rob Leary
Waterloo (Padres)	75	63	.543	5½	Bryan Little
Quad City (Angels)	74	63	.540	6	Mitch Seoane
Beloit (Brewers)	70	67	.511	10	Rob Derksen
†Kane County (Orioles)	68	67	.504	11	Bob Miscik
South Bend (White Sox)	69	70	.496	12	Tommy Thompson
†Burlington (Astros)	67	70	.489	13	Tim Tolman
Cedar Rapids (Reds)	66	74	.471	15½	Frank Funk
Kenosha (Twins)	63	74	.460	18	Joel Lepel
Peoria (Cubs)	62	76	.449	18½	Bill Hayes
Springfield (Cardinals)	58	79	.423	22	Mike Ramsey
Appleton	58	81	.417	23	Joe Breeden

*Won playoffs   †Won split-season pennant

Stadium Information

		Dimensions				
Club	Stadium	LF	CF	RF	Capacity	'91 Att.
Appleton	Goodland Field	330	400	330	4,300	72,601
Beloit	Pohlman Field	325	380	325	3,800	77,487
Burlington	Community Field	330	372	325	3,500	81,811
Cedar Rapids	Veterans Mem.	325	385	325	6,000	132,820
Clinton	Riverview	335	390	325	3,000	83,943
Kane County	Kane Cty Events Ctr.	335	400	335	3,800	240,290
Kenosha	Simmons Field	330	400	330	3,000	59,331
Madison	Warner Park	350	385	350	4,000	92,663
Peoria	Meinen Field	335	383	335	5,750	212,159
Quad City	John O'Donnell	340	400	340	5,600	242,322
Rockford	Marinelli Field	330	400	330	4,300	66,524
South Bend	Coveleski Reg.	336	405	336	5,000	221,071
Springfield	Lanphier Park	320	415	320	5,000	175,017
Waterloo	Municipal	335	375	335	5,400	58,859

APPLETON
FOXES

Office Address: 1522 W. 4th St., Appleton, WI 54914. **Mailing Address:** P.O. Box 464, Appleton, WI 54912. **Telephone:** (414) 733-4152. **FAX:** (414) 733-8032.

Affiliation (first year): Kansas City Royals (1987). **Years in League:** 1962-.
Operated by: Appleton Baseball Club, Inc.
President: Doug Hahn. **Vice President:** Jim Cutler.
General Manager: Kevin Scotellaro. **Assistant General Manager:** Joe Ornstein. **Office Manager:** Cindy Ferguson. **Director of Stadium Grounds and Maintenance:** Natalie Olson.
Field Manager: Tom Poquette. **Coach:** Mike Mason.
Trainer: Brad Shores.
Radio: None.
Stadium Name: Goodland Field. **Location:** Highway 41 to College Ave. exit east, second right after viaduct. **Standard Game Times:** Mon.-Fri. (April-May 8) 6 p.m., (May 13-Sept.) 7, Sat. 5, Sun. 1:30.
Visiting Club Hotels: Exel Inn, 210 N. Westhill, Appleton, WI 54914. Telephone: (414) 733-5551.

BELOIT
BREWERS

Office Address: 2301 Skyline Dr., Beloit, WI 53511. **Mailing Address:** P.O. Box 855, Beloit, WI 53512. **Telephone:** (608) 362-2272. **FAX:** (608) 362-0418.

Affiliation (first year): Milwaukee Brewers (1982). **Years in League:** 1982-.
Operated by: Beloit Professional Baseball Association, Inc.
President: Howard Erickson.
General Manager: Steve Kretz. **Assistant General Manager:** Jim Jarecki. **Director of Public/Media Relations:** Herman Sorcher.
Field Manager: Wayne Krenchicki. **Coach:** Steve Foucault.
Trainer: Bryan Jaquette.
Radio Announcers: Rick West, Al Fagerli. **No. of Games Broadcast:** Home-15, Away-5. **Flagship Stations:** WBEL 1380-AM, WCLO 1490-AM.
Stadium Name: Pohlman Field. **Location:** I-90 to exit-81 west, right onto Cranston Rd. **Standard Game Times:** 7 p.m.
Visiting Club Hotels: Plantation Motor Inn, 2956 Milwaukee Rd., Beloit, WI 53511. Telephone: (608) 365-2501; Holiday Inn Express, 2790 Milwaukee Rd., Beloit, WI 53511. Telephone: (608) 365-6000.

BURLINGTON
ASTROS

Office Address: 2712 Mt. Pleasant St., Burlington, IA 52601. **Mailing Address:** P.O. Box 824, Burlington, IA 52601. **Telephone:** (319) 754-5705. **FAX:** (319) 754-5882.

Affiliation (first year): Houston Astros (1991). **Years in League:** 1962-.
Operated by: Burlington Baseball Club, Inc.
President: David Walker.
General Manager: Paul Marshall.
Field Manager: Steve Curry. **Coaches:** Rick Aponte, Rick Peters.
Trainer: Chris Correnti.
Radio: None.
Stadium Name: Community Field. **Location:** 1 block east of Hwy. 61 North. **Standard Game Times:** 7 p.m.; Sat.-Sun. (April-May), 2:30.
Visiting Club Hotel: Pzazz Motor Inn, 3001 Winegard Dr., Burlington, IA 52601. **Telephone:** (319) 753-2223.

CEDAR RAPIDS
REDS

Office Address: 950 Rockford Rd. SW, Cedar Rapids, IA 52404. **Mailing Address:** P.O. Box 2001, Cedar Rapids, IA 52406.
Telephone: (319) 363-3887. **FAX:** (319) 363-5631.
 Affiliation (first year): Cincinnati Reds (1980). **Years in League:** 1962-.
 Operated by: Cedar Rapids Baseball Club, Inc.
 President: Wally Krouse.
 General Manager: Jack Roeder. **Administrative Assistant:** Andy Graykowski. **Office Manager:** Nancy Cram.
 Field Manager: Mark Berry. **Coach:** Mack Jenkins.
 Trainer: Tom Iversen.
 Radio: None.
 Stadium Name: Veterans Memorial. **Location:** I-380 to Wilson Ave. west, to Rockford Road, north to stadium. **Standard Game Times:** 7 p.m.; Sun. 2 or 5.
 Visiting Club Hotel: Ramada Inn, 4747 1st Ave. SE, Cedar Rapids, IA 52403. Telephone: (319) 393-8800; Five Seasons, 350 1st. Ave. NE, Cedar Rapids, IA 52402. Telephone: (319) 363-8161.

CLINTON
GIANTS

 Mailing Address: Riverview Stadium, 6th Ave. North and 1st St., Clinton, IA 52732.
Mailing Address: P.O. Box 1295, Clinton, IA 52733. **Telephone:** (319) 242-0727. **FAX:** (319) 243-1433.
 Affiliation (first year): San Francisco Giants (1980). **Years in League:** 1956-.
 Operated by: Clinton Baseball Club, Inc.
 President: Ed Kross.
 General Manager: Kevin Temperly. **Assistant General Manager:** Gary Mayse. **Office Manager:** Jean Mehrer.
 Field Manager: Bill Stein. **Coaches:** Gary Lucas, Nelson Rood.
 Trainer: Bill Carpine.
 Radio Announcer: Gary Determan. **No. of Games Broadcast:** Home-70. **Flagship Station:** KROS 1340-AM.
 Stadium Name: Riverview. **Location:** 1½ miles north of U.S. 30 at Mississippi River bridge. **Standard Game Times:** 7:05 p.m.; Sun. (April-May) 2, (June-Aug.) 5.
 Visiting Club Hotels: Travelodge, 302 Sixth Ave. South, Clinton, IA 52732. Telephone: (319) 243-4730; Frontier Best Western, 2300 Lincolnway, Clinton, IA 52732. Telephone: (319) 242-7112.

KANE COUNTY
COUGARS

 Office Address: 34W002 Cherry Lane Rd., Geneva, IL 60134. **Telephone:** (708) 232-8811. **FAX:** (708) 232-8815.
 Affiliation (first year): Baltimore Orioles (1991). **Years in League:** 1991-.
 Operated by: Wisconsin Baseball Partnership.
 Owners, Operators: Dennis Baxter, Lew Chamberlin, Al Gordon, Pete Heitman, Mike Murtaugh, Mike Woleben.
 General Manager: Bill Larsen. **Assistant General Manager:** Scott Lane. **Group Sales Director:** Jack Mielke. **Communications Director:** David Wills.
 Field Manager: Joel Youngblood. **Coaches:** Rich Dauer, Larry McCall.
 Trainer: Peter Howell.
 Radio Announcer: David Wills. **No. of Games Broadcast:** Home-70, Away-70. **Flagship Station:** WKKD 1580-AM/95.9 FM.
 Stadium Name: Kane County Events Center. **Location:** 5 miles north of I-88 on Farnsworth Road exit. **Standard Game Times:** Mon-Fri. 7 p.m.; Sun. 4; Sat. (April-May) 2, (June-Aug.) 7.
 Visiting Club Hotel: Dunham Inn, 1600 E. Main St., St. Charles, IL. Telephone: (708) 584-5300.

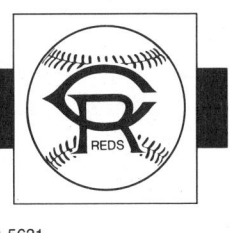

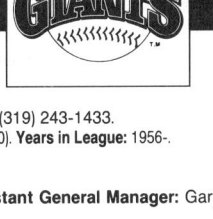

KENOSHA
TWINS

Office Address: 7817 Sheridan Rd., Kenosha, WI 53143. **Mailing Address:** P.O. Box 661, Kenosha, WI 53141. **Telephone:** (414) 657-7997. **FAX:** (414) 657-3972.

Affiliation (first year): Minnesota Twins (1984). **Years in League:** 1985-.
Operated by: Let's Play Too, Inc.
President: Eric Margenau.
General Manager: Dave Austin. **Administration:** Bill Kuehn. **Director of Concessions:** Norma Kuehn. **Office Manager:** Sue Frantal.
Field Manager: Jim Dwyer. **Coach:** Rick Anderson.
Trainer: Dan Fox.
Radio: None.
Stadium Name: Simmons Field. **Location:** I-94 to exit 50, east to Sheridan Rd., right to ballpark. **Standard Game Times:** Mon.-Fri. (April-May), 6 p.m., Sat.-Sun. 2; Mon.-Sat (June-Sept.) 7, Sun., 2 or 5.
Visiting Club Hotel: Howard Johnson Lodge, 12121 75th St., Kenosha, WI 53142. Telephone: (414) 857-2311.

MADISON
MUSKIES

Office Address: 1617 Northport Dr., Madison, WI 53704. **Mailing Address:** P.O. Box 882, Madison, WI 53701. **Telephone:** (608) 241-0010. **FAX:** (608) 241-5133.

Affiliation (first year): Oakland Athletics (1982). **Years in League:** 1982-.
Operated by: Madison Professional Baseball, Inc.
President: Charles Barnhill.
General Manager: Jay Brazeau. **Director of Operations:** John Finke. **Director of Public Relations:** Todd Budnick. **Director of Sales:** John Powell. **Office Manager:** Jan Rippl.
Field Manager: Dickie Scott. **Coach:** Gil Patterson.
Trainer: Brian Thorson.
Radio: None.
Stadium Name: Warner Park. **Location:** I-90 to Wisconsin 30 West, 5 miles to Sherman Ave, right 1 mile to Northport Dr. **Standard Game Times:** Mon.-Fri. (April-May 21) 6 p.m., Sat.-Sun, 2; Mon.-Sat. (May 22-Sept.) 7, Sun. 6.
Visiting Club Hotel: Howard Johnson Hotel and Conference Center, 4822 E. Washington Ave., Madison, WI 53704. Telephone: (608) 244-6265.

PEORIA
CHIEFS

Office Address: 1524 W. Nebraska Ave., Peoria, IL 61604. **Telephone:** (309) 688-1622. **FAX:** (309) 686-4516.

Affiliation (first year): Chicago Cubs (1985). **Years in League:** 1983-.
Operated by: Peoria Professional Baseball Limited Partnership.
President: Clar Krusinski.
General Manager: Mike Nelson. **Director of Marketing:** Ted Cox. **Director of Operations:** Chad Bailey. **Senior Account Executive:** Ralph Rashid. **Account Executive:** Greg Ayers. **Office Manager:** Barbara Lindberg.
Field Manager: Steve Roadcap. **Coach:** Ray Sadecki.
Trainer: Jim O'Reilly.
Radio Announcer: Tom Nichols. **No. of Games Broadcast:** Unavailable. **Flagship Station:** Unavailablae.
Stadium Name: Pete Vonachen. **Location:** Exit 91B (University Street North) on I-74, left on Nebraska Ave. **Standard Game Times:** 7:05 p.m.; Sun. (April-May) 2:05.
Visiting Club Hotels: Fairfield Inn by Marriott, 4203 N. War Memorial Dr., Peoria, IL 61614. Telephone: (309) 686-7600; Continental Regency Hotel, 500 Hamilton Blvd., Peoria, IL 61602. Telephone: (309) 674-2500.

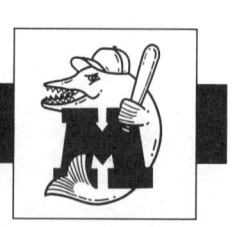

QUAD CITY
RIVER BANDITS

Office Address: 209 S. Gaines St., Davenport, IA 52802. **Mailing Address:** P.O. Box 3496, Davenport, IA 52808.
Telephone: (319) 324-2032. **FAX:** (319) 324-3109.
Affiliation (first year): California Angels (1985). **Years in League:** 1960-.
Operated by: Quad City Professional Baseball Club, Inc.
President: Richard Holtzman.
General Manager: Mike Tatoian. **Assistant General Manager:** Kerry Bubolz. **Director of Concessions:** Greg Pries. **Director of Operations:** Bill Marcus. **Director of Broadcasting and Media Relations:** David Fisher. **Director of Group Sales:** Lesley Kellison. **Office Manager:** Pam Verre.
Field Manager: Mitch Seoane. **Coaches:** Joe Georger, Matt Hyde.
Trainer: Dan Pieratt.
Radio Announcer: David Fisher. **No. of Games Broadcast:** Home-70, Away-70. **Flagship Station:** KSTT 1170-AM.
Stadium Name: John O'Donnell. **Location:** U.S. 61 at Mississippi River, next to Centennial Bridge. **Standard Game Times:** Mon.-Thur., 7 p.m.; Fri.-Sat., 7:30; Sun. (April-May) 2, (June-Aug.) 6.
Visiting Club Hotel: Unavailable.

ROCKFORD
EXPOS

Office Address: 101 15th Ave., Rockford, IL 61104. **Mailing Address:** P.O. Box 6748, Rockford, IL 61125. **Telephone:** (815) 964-5400. **FAX:** (815) 961-2002.
Affiliation (first year): Montreal Expos (1988). **Years in League:** 1988-.
Operated By: Rockford Professional Baseball Club, Inc.
President: William McKee.
General Manager: Patrick Daly. **Assistant General Manager:** Greg Schild. **Director of Stadium Operations:** Chris Gargani. **Director of Media and Public Relations:** Susan Otolski. **Office Manager:** Tona Eisele.
Field Manager: Rob Leary. **Coach:** Herm Starrette.
Trainer: Jim Young.
Radio: None.
Stadium Name: Marinelli Field. **Location:** U.S. 20 West to Highway 2, north to 15th Ave., right across Rock River, to stadium. **Standard Game Times:** 7 p.m.; Sun. 5.
Visiting Club Hotels: Howard Johnson's Motor Lodge, 3909 11th St., Rockford, IL 61109. Telephone: (815) 397-9000.; Fairfield Inn, 7712 Potawatomi Trail, Rockford, IL 61107. Telephone: (815) 397-8000; Excel Inn, 220 S. Lyford Rd., Cherry Valley, IL 61108. Telephone: (815) 332-4915.

SOUTH BEND
WHITE SOX

Office Address: 501 W. South St., South Bend, IN 46601. **Mailing Address:** P.O. Box 4218, South Bend, IN 46634. **Telephone:** (219) 284-9988. **FAX:** (219) 284-9950.
Affiliation (first year): Chicago White Sox (1988). **Years in League:** 1988-.
Operated by: Palisades Baseball, Ltd.
President: John Baxter. **Vice President, Sales and Promotions:** Rita Baxter.
General Manager: John Tull. **Assistant General Manager:** Erik Haag. **Stadium Operations Manager:** Matt Kopsea. **Ticket Manager:** Patrick Martinez. **Public Relations:** Sharon McGovern. **Concessions Manager:** Dicky Collins. **Administrative Assistant:** Sean Willis.
Field Manager: Terry Francona. **Coaches:** Mark Haley, Jaime Garcia, Jim Reinebold.

Trainer: Scott Takao.
Radio: None.
Stadium Name: Stanley Coveleski Regional. **Location:** I-80/90 toll road to South Bend exit 77. Enter U.S. 31-33 south to South Bend, to downtown (Main St.). Follow to Western Ave., right onto Western, left onto Taylor. **Standard Game Times:** 7 p.m.
Visiting Club Hotels: Howard Johnson's, 52939 US Route 31, South Bend, IN 46637. Telephone: (219) 272-1500.

SPRINGFIELD
CARDINALS

Mailing Address: 1351 N. Grand Ave. East, Springfield, IL 62702. **Mailing Address:** P.O. Box 3004, Springfield, IL 62708.
Telephone: (217) 525-6570. **FAX:** (217) 525-9340.
Affiliation (first year): St. Louis Cardinals (1982). **Years in League:** 1982-.
Operated by: Springfield Cardinals Baseball Club, Inc.
Vice President and General Manager: Lee Landers. **Assistant General Manager:** Ken Mallory. **Business Manager:** Virgil Thilker. **Director of Public Relations:** Bill Sakalares. **Director of Sales:** Gary Saunders. **Office Manager:** Bobbi Landers..
Field Manager: Rick Colbert. **Coach:** Roy Silver.
Trainer: Mike Evans.
Radio Announcer: Pete Michaud. **No. of Games Broadcast:** Home-70, Away-70. **Flagship Station:** WRVI 96.7 FM.
Stadium Name: Lanphier Park. **Location:** I-55 to Clearlake exit, right on to 11th St., right onto North Grand. **Standard Game Times:** 7 p.m.
Visiting Club Hotels: Unavailable.

WATERLOO
DIAMONDS

Office Address: 850 Park Rd., Waterloo, IA 50703. **Mailing Address:** P.O. Box 611, Waterloo, IA 50704. **Telephone:** (319) 233-8146. **FAX:** (319) 232-1006.
Affiliation (first year): San Diego Padres (1989). **Years in League:** 1958-.
Operated by: Waterloo Professional Baseball, Inc.
President: Dan Yates.
General Manager: David Simpson. **Assistant General Manager:** Brian Pfaltzgraff.
Field Manager: Keith Champion. **Coach:** Sonny Siebert.
Trainer: Unavailable.
Radio: None.
Stadium Name: Waterloo Municipal. **Location:** Park Road exit off Hwy. 57 (Broadway). **Standard Game Times:** 7 p.m.; Sun., 3; Sat. (April-May) 3, (June-Aug.) 7.
Visiting Club Hotels: Heartland Inn, 1809 LaPorte Rd., Waterloo, IA 50702. Telephone: (319) 235-4461; Holiday Inn, 5826 University, Cedar Falls, IA 50613. Telephone: (319) 277-2230.

SOUTH ATLANTIC LEAGUE

Class A

Office Address: 504 Crescent Hill, Kings Mountain, NC 28086. **Mailing Address:** P.O. Box 38, Kings Mountain, NC 28086.
Telephone: (704) 739-3466 or 487-7264. **FAX:** (704) 739-1974.
Chairman of the Board, President, Secretary-Treasurer: John Moss. **Vice Presidents:** Winston Blenckstone, Ron McKee.
Directors: Dennis Bastien (Charleston, WV), Winston Blenckstone (Myrtle Beach), Steve Bryant (Greensboro), Henry Gilbertie (Columbus), Marvin Goldklang (Charleston, SC), Harold Green (Gastonia), Richard Holtzman (Albany), Eric Margenau (Columbia), Ron McKee (Asheville), Charles Padgett (Fayetteville), Jim Pickles (Spartanburg), Charles Sanders (Macon), Bill Scripps (Augusta), Kenneth Silver (Savannah).

John Moss

Years League Active: 1948-1952, 1960-1992.
1992 Opening Date: April 9. **Closing Date:** Sept. 5. **First Half Ends:** June 20.
No. of Games: 144.
Division Structure: Northern—Asheville, Charleston W.Va., Columbia, Fayetteville, Gastonia, Greensboro, Spartanburg. **Southern**—Albany, Augusta, Charleston S.C, Columbus, Macon, Myrtle Beach, Savannah.
Playoff Format: First-half division winners play second-half division winners in best-of-3 division series. Division playoff winners meet in best-of-5 league championship series.
All-Star Game: June 22 at Columbia.
Roster Limit: Per National Association agreement (two veterans, 12 limited-service players, remainder rookies).
Statistician: Howe Sportsdata International, Boston Fish Pier, West Bldg. #2—Suite 306, Boston MA 02210.

1991 Standings (Overall)

Club (Affiliate)	W	L	Pct.	GB	'91 Manager
†Charleston, WV (Reds)	92	50	.648	—	Dave Miley
†*Columbia (Mets)	86	54	.614	5	Tim Blackwell
†Macon (Braves)	83	58	.589	8½	Roy Majtyka
Greensboro (Yankees)	73	68	.518	18½	Trey Hillman
Columbus (Indians)	73	69	.514	19	Mike Brown
Spartanburg (Phillies)	70	70	.500	21	Mel Roberts
Charleston, SC (Padres)	69	72	.489	22½	Dave Trembley
Gastonia (Rangers)	69	73	.486	23	Bump Wills
Augusta (Pirates)	68	74	.479	24	Don Werner
Sumter (Expos)	64	75	.460	26½	Lorenzo Bundy
Savannah (Cardinals)	61	77	.442	29	Larry Milbourne
Myrtle Beach (Blue Jays)	60	79	.432	30½	Garth Iorg
Fayetteville (Tigers)	58	79	.423	31½	Gerry Groninger
Asheville (Astros)	55	83	.399	35	Frank Cacciatore

*Won playoffs †Won split-season pennant

Stadium Information

Club	Stadium	Dimensions LF	CF	RF	Capacity	'91 Att.
Albany[1]	Eames Sports	335	400	335	4,000	—
Asheville	McCormick Field	326	402	300	3,500	117,625
Augusta	Heaton	330	400	330	3,600	100,141
Charleston, SC	College Park	315	436	290	6,000	119,080
Charleston, WV	Watt Powell Park	340	406	330	6,500	185,389
Columbia	Capital City	330	395	320	6,000	79,564
Columbus	Golden Park	315	415	315	6,000	96,736
Fayetteville	J.P. Riddle	330	400	330	3,200	88,380
Gastonia	Sims Legion Park	335	380	335	3,200	44,060
Greensboro	War Memorial	327	401	327	7,500	191,048
Macon	Luther Williams Field	338	400	338	3,000	107,059
Myrtle Beach	Coastal Carolina	315	400	315	3,500	62,885
Savannah	Grayson	290	400	310	8,000	99,399
Spartanburg	Duncan Park	319	376	319	3,900	54,489

[1]Albany franchise operated in Sumter in 1991.

ALBANY
POLECATS

Office Address: 608 N. Slappey Blvd., Albany, GA 31701. **Telephone:** (912) 435-6444. **FAX:** (912) 435-6618.

Affiliation (first year): Montreal Expos (1991). **Years in League:** 1992-.
Operated by: Albany Polecats Professional Baseball Club, Inc.
Owner: Richard Holtzman.
General Manager: Scott Skadan. **Assistant General Manager:** Mike Kardamis. **Director of Ticket Sales:** Dan Froehlich. **Director of Broadcasting:** Steve Selby. **Director of Group Sales:** Nick Formisano. **Office Manager:** Susan Skadan.
Field Manager: Lorenzo Bundy. **Coaches:** Gary Lance, Keith Snider.
Trainer: Unavailable.
Radio Announcer: Steve Selby. **No. of Games Broadcast:** Home-72, Away-72. **Flagship Station:** WALG 1590-AM.
Stadium Name: Paul Eames Sports Complex. **Location:** Blaylock St. exit off Rt. 82 by-pass. **Standard Game Times:** 7:05 p.m.; Sun. 2:05.
Visiting Club Hotel: Unavailable.

ASHEVILLE
TOURISTS

Office Address: 30 Buchanan Pl., Asheville, NC 28801. **Mailing Address:** P.O. Box 1556, Asheville, NC 28802. **Telephone:** (704) 258-0428. **FAX:** (704) 258-0320.

Affiliation (first year): Houston Astros (1982). **Years in League:** 1976-.
Operated by: Tourists Baseball, Inc.
President: Peter Kern.
General Manager: Ron McKee. **Assistant General Manager:** Lee McDaniel. **Concessions Manager:** Jane Lentz. **Office Manager:** Carolyn McKee.
Field Manager: Tim Tolman. **Coaches:** Jim Hickey, Bob Robertson.
Trainer: Ron Hanisch.
Radio: None
Stadium Name: McCormick Field. **Location:** I-240 to Charlotte St. exit South, left onto McCormick Place. **Standard Game Times:** 7 p.m.; Sun. 2.
Visiting Club Hotel: Cricket Inn, 1329 Tunnel Rd., Asheville, NC 28805. Telephone: (704) 298-7952.

AUGUSTA
PIRATES

Office Address: 78 Milledge Road, Augusta, GA 30904. **Mailing Address:** P.O. Box 3746, Hill Station, Augusta, GA 30904. **Telephone:** (404) 736-7889. **FAX:** (404) 736-1122.

Affiliation (first year): Pittsburgh Pirates (1988). **Years in League:** 1988-.
Operated by: Scripps Baseball Group, Inc.
President: Bill Scripps.
General Manager: Chris Scheuer. **Assistant General Manager:** Kyle Fisher. **Director of Public Relations/Concessions Manager:** T.J. Midla. **Director of Sales and Promotions:** Dave True. **Office Manager:** Nancy Crowe. **Grounds Supervisor:** Sam Clay.
Field Manager: Scott Little. **Coaches:** Julio Garcia, Dave Rajsich.
Trainer: Rodney Lich.
Radio Announcer: Mike Saeger. **No. of Games Broadcast:** Home-72, Away-72. **Flagship Station:** WGUS 1380-AM.
Stadium Name: Heaton. **Location:** I-20 to Washington Rd., to Broad St., to Milledge Rd. **Standard Game Times:** 7:30 p.m.; Sun. 6.
Visiting Club Hotel: LaQuinta Inn, 3020 Washington Rd., Augusta, GA 30907. Telephone: (404) 733-2660.

CHARLESTON
RAINBOWS

Office Address: 701 Rutledge Ave., Charleston, SC 29403. **Mailing Address:** P.O. Box 20849, Charleston, SC 29413.
Telephone: (803) 723-7241. **FAX:** (803) 723-2641.
Affiliation (first year): San Diego Padres (1985). **Years in League:** 1973-78, 1980-.
Operated by: South Carolina Baseball Club, L.P.
Principal Owner: Marvin Goldklang.
General Manager: Kevin Carpenter. **Assistant General Manager:** Steve Gliner. **Director of Marketing:** Doug Brei.
Field Manager: Dave Trembley. **Coaches:** Jaime Moreno, Fred Cambria.
Trainer: Keith Dugger.
Radio Announcer: Rich Jablonski. **No. of Games Broadcast:** Home-72, Away-24. **Flagship Station:** WOKE 1340-AM.
Stadium Name: College Park. **Location:** I-26 East to exit 219-A (Rutledge Ave.). **Standard Game Times:** 7 p.m.; DH 6.
Visiting Club Hotel: Travelodge-Airport, 4620 Dorchester Rd., Charleston, SC 29405. **Telephone:** (803) 747-7500.

CHARLESTON
WHEELERS

Office Address: 3403 MacCorkle Ave., Charleston, WV 25304. **Mailing Address:** P.O. Box 4669, Charleston, WV 25304.
Telephone: (304) 925-8222. **FAX:** (304) 344-0083.
Affiliation (first year): Cincinnati Reds (1990). **Years in League:** 1987-.
Operated by: DRB Baseball Management II, Inc.
President/General Manager: Dennis Bastien. **Vice President, Business Manager:** Lisa Bastien. **Sales and Public Relations:** Ron Plunkett. **Promotions/Marketing:** Scott Boggs. **Office and Ticket Manager:** Beth Smith.
Field Manager: P.J. Carey. **Coach:** Derek Botelho.
Trainer: Tom Spencer.
Radio Announcer: Don Cook. **No. of Games Broadcast:** Home-72, Away-72. **Flagship Station:** WVNS 96.1 FM.
Stadium Name: Watt Powell Park. **Location:** MacCorkle Avenue exit off I-77, take 35th Street Bridge exit. **Standard Game Times:** 7:30 p.m., Sun. 2.
Visiting Club Hotel: Holiday Inn-Civic Center, 100 Civic Center Drive, Charleston, WV 25301. **Telephone:** (304) 345-0600.

COLUMBIA
METS

Office Address: 301 South Assembly St., Columbia, SC 29201. **Mailing Address:** P.O. Box 7845, Columbia, SC 29202.
Telephone: (803) 256-4110. **FAX:** (803) 256-4338.
Affiliation (first year): New York Mets (1983). **Years in League:** 1960-61, 1983-.
Operated by: Columbia Professional Baseball, Inc.
President: Eric Margenau.
Vice President and General Manager: Bill Shanahan. **Assistant General Manager:** Matt Gowarty. **Assistant General Manager-Sales:** Matt Roy. **Assistant General Manager-Tickets:** Flynn Bowie. **Director of Public Relations:** Shar Player. **Director of Stadium Operations:** Bob Hook.
Field Manager: Tim Blackwell. **Coach:** Jerry Koosman, Marlin McPhail.
Trainer: David Fricke.
Radio Announcers: Brooks Melchior, Jim Powell. **No. of Games Broadcast:** Unavailable. **Flagship Station:** WVOC 560-AM.
Stadium Name: Capital City. **Location:** I-26 to city, right on South

Assembly Street, 3 miles to stadium. Near Univ. of S.C. football stadium.
Standard Game Times: 7:05 p.m.; Sun. 2:05.

Visiting Club Hotel: Travelodge, 2210 Bush River Rd., Columbia, SC 29210. Telephone: (803) 798-9665.

COLUMBUS
REDSTIXX

Office Address: 100 4th St., Columbus, GA 31901. **Mailing Address:** P.O. Box 1886, Columbus, GA 31902. **Telephone:** (404) 571-8866. **FAX:** (404) 571-9107.

Affiliation (first year): Cleveland Indians (1991). **Years in League:** 1991-.
Operated by: Columbus Professional Baseball Club of Georgia, Inc.
President: Henry Gilbertie.

Vice President and General Manager: John Dittrich. **Assistant General Manager:** Jim Walker. **Directory of Community Relations:** Carol Dean. **Director of Media Relations:** David Wilson. **Administrative Assistants:** Paul Cummings, Kristen Turner. **Business Manager:** Lois Dittrich. **Office Manager:** Rosemary Johnson.

Field Manager: Mike Brown. **Coaches:** Dan Norman, Fred Gladding.
Trainer: Teddy Blackwell.

Radio Announcers: Dave Wilson, Paul Cummings. **No. of Games Broadcast:** Home-72, Away-72. **Flagship Station:** WSTH 540-AM.

Stadium Name: Golden Park. **Location:** I-185 to exit 1 (Victory Drive), 8 miles to 4th St., stadium on left. **Standard Game Times:** 7:05; Sun. (April-May) 2:05, (June-Aug.) 6:05.

Visiting Club Hotel: Holiday Inn Airport, I-185 at Manchester Expy., Columbus, GA. 31904. Telephone: (404) 324-0231.

FAYETTEVILLE
GENERALS

Office Address: 2823 Legion Rd., Fayetteville, NC 28306. **Mailing Address:** P.O Box 64939, Fayetteville, NC 28306. **Telephone:** (919) 424-6500. **FAX:** (919) 424-4325.

Affiliation (first year): Detroit Tigers (1987). **Years in League:** 1987-.
Operated by: Fayetteville Baseball Club, Inc.

Chairman of the Board: Charles Padgett. **President:** Matt Perry. **Vice President:** Don Koonce.

General Manager: Dan McDonough. **Director of Operations:** Erick Goodnough. **Director of Public Relations/Marketing:** Jeff Taylor.

Field Manager: Gerry Groninger. **Coaches:** Dwight Lowry, Sid Monge.
Trainer: Unavailable.
Radio: Unavailable.

Stadium Name: J.P. Riddle. **Location:** I-95 to exit 40 to 301 N., left onto Owen Dr., right onto Legion Rd. **Standard Game Times:** 7:15 p.m.; Sun. 5.

Visiting Club Hotel: Econo Lodge I-95, 1952 Cedar Creek Rd., Fayetteville, NC 28306. Telephone: (919) 433-2100.

GASTONIA
RANGERS

Office Address: 1001 No. Marietta St., Gastonia, NC 28054. **Mailing Address:** P.O. Box 309, Gastonia, NC 28053. **Telephone:** (704) 867-3721. **FAX:** (704) 853-8108.

Affiliation (first year): Texas Rangers (1987). **Years in League:** 1960, 1963-70, 1972-74, 1977-.
Operated by: George Shinn Sports, Inc.
Chairman of the Board: George Shinn.

General Manager: Harold Green. **Director of Marketing:** Brian Laing. **Director of Operations:** David Haas. **Director of Broadcasting:** Matt Swierad.

Field Manager: Walt Williams. **Coaches:** Stan Cliburn, Gary Mielke. **Trainer:** Erick Kozlowski.

Radio Announcer: Matt Sweirad. **No. of Games Broadcast:** Home-72, Away-72. **Flagship Station:** WGNC 1450-AM.

Stadium Name: Sims Park. **Location:** I-85 to Hwy. 321 North exit, first right. **Standard Game Times:** 7 p.m.; Sun. 3.

Visiting Club Hotel: Innkeeper, 360 McNeil St. (I-85), Gastonia, NC 28054. Telephone: (704) 868-2000.

GREENSBORO
HORNETS

Office Address: 510 Yanceyville St., Greensboro, NC 27405. **Mailing Address:** P.O. Box 22093, Greensboro, NC 27420. **Telephone:** (919) 275-1641. **FAX:** (919) 273-7350.

Affiliation (first year): New York Yankees (1990). **Years in League:** 1979-.

Operated by: Greensboro Hornets Professional Baseball Club, Inc.
President: Steve Bryant.

General Manager: Marty Steele. **Assistant General Manger:** John Frey. **Director of Stadium Operations:** Craig Koch. **Sales Manager:** Rick Jacobson. **Director of Broadcasting:** Mike Sammond. **Director of Group Sales:** Jerry Smith. **Office Manager:** Beth Rhodes.

Field Manager: Trey Hillman. **Coaches:** Brian Milner, Mark Rose.
Trainer: Greg Spratt.

Radio Announcers: Mike Sammond, Bill Wardle. **No. of Games Broadcast:** Home-72, Away-72. **Flagship Stations:** WTHP 98.3 FM.

Stadium Name: War Memorial. **Location:** I-40/I-85 to Elm-Eugene exit, to Market St. W., to corner of Lindsay and Yanceyville Sts. **Standard Game Times:** 7:30 p.m.; Sun. 2.

Visiting Club Hotel: Travelodge, 2112 W. Meadowview Road, Greensboro, NC 27403. Telephone (919) 292-2020.

MACON
BRAVES

Office Address: Luther Williams Field, Central City Park, 7th Street, Macon, GA 31201. **Mailing Address:** P.O. Box 4525, Macon, GA 31208. **Telephone:** (912) 745-8943. **FAX:** (912) 743-5559.

Affiliation (first year): Atlanta Braves (1991). **Years in League:** 1962-63, 1980-87, 1991-.

Operated by: Atlanta National League Baseball Club, Inc.

President: Stan Kasten. **Vice President and League Director:** Charles Sanders.

General Manager: Ed Holtz. **Office Manager:** Mary Holtz. **Sales and Promotions:** Jim Tessmer.

Field Manager: Brian Snitker. **Coaches:** Glenn Hubbard, Larry Jaster.
Trainer: Willy Johnson.
Radio: None.

Stadium Name: Luther Williams Field. **Location:** Coliseum exit off Hwy. 16. One mile from junction of I-75 and I-16. **Standard Game Times:** 7 p.m.; Sun. 2.

Visiting Club Hotel: Comfort Inn, 2690 Riverside Drive, Macon, GA 31204. Telephone: (912) 746-8855.

MYRTLE BEACH
HURRICANES

Office Address: 809 Main St., Myrtle Beach, SC 29577. **Mailing Address:** P.O. Box 1110, Myrtle Beach, SC 29578. **Telephone:** (803) 626-1987. **FAX:** (803) 626-8335.

Affiliation (first year): Toronto Blue Jays (1987). **Years in League:** 1987-.

Operated by: Norwin Corporation.
President and General Manager: Winston Blenckstone. **Director of Stadium Operations:** David Blenckstone. **Sales and Promotions Director:** Stephen McCormick.
Field Manager: Doug Ault. **Coaches:** Darren Balsley, Leroy Stanton.
Trainer: Dennis Brogna.
Radio: Unavailable.
Stadium Name: Coastal Carolina. **Location:** Highway 501 to the Coastal Carolina College campus. **Standard Game Times:** 7:30 p.m.; Sun 5:30.
Visiting Club Hotel: Holiday Inn West, 101 Outlet Blvd., Myrtle Beach, SC 29577. Telephone: (803) 236-1000.

SAVANNAH
CARDINALS

Office Address: 1401 E. Victory Drive, Savannah, GA 31404. **Mailing Address:** P.O. Box 3783, Savannah, GA 31414.
Telephone: (912) 351-9150. **FAX:** (912) 352-9722.
Affiliation (first year): St. Louis Cardinals (1984). **Years in League:** 1962, 1984-.
Operated by: Savannah Professional Baseball Club, Inc.
President: Ken Silver.
General Manager: Richard Sisler. **Office Manager:** Reba Rogers. **Director of Operations:** Joe Welker. **Director of Marketing:** Robert Blumenthal.
Field Manager: Mike Ramsey. **Coach:** Ramon Ortiz.
Trainer: Peter Fagan.
Radio: None.
Stadium Name: Grayson. **Location:** I-16 to 37th St., exit left, right onto Abercorn St., left onto Victory Dr. **Standard Game Times:** 7:15 p.m; Sun. 2, DH 6:15.
Visiting Club Hotel: LaQuinta Inn, 6805 Abercorn St., Savannah, GA. Telephone: (912) 355-3004.

SPARTANBURG
PHILLIES

Office Address: 1000 Duncan Park Dr., Spartanburg, SC 29304. **Mailing Address:** P.O. Box 1721, Spartanburg, SC 29304.
Telephone: (803) 585-6279. **FAX:** (803) 582-0877.
Affiliation (first year): Philadelphia Phillies (1963). **Years in League:** 1963-.
Operated by: Harrisburg Baseball Club, Inc.
Owner: Brad Shover. **President:** Jim Pickles.
General Manager: Rosie Putnam.
Field Manager: Roy Majtyka. **Coaches:** Buzz Capra, Tony Scott.
Trainer: Gary Beatty.
Radio: None.
Stadium Name: Duncan Park. **Location:** I-85 to Pine Street exit, right on Henry Street, left on Union Street to Duncan. **Standard Game Times:** 7 p.m.; Sun. 2.
Visiting Club Hotel: Radisson Inn and Conference Center, 7136 Asheville Hwy., Spartanburg, SC 29303. Telephone: (803) 578-5530.

NEW YORK-PENN LEAGUE

Class A

Mailing Address: P.O. Box 1313, Auburn, NY 13021.
Telephone: (315) 253-2957. **FAX:** (315) 252-8705.
President, Secretary, Treasurer: Leo Pinckney.
First Vice President: Sam Nader.
Directors: Mike Billoni (Niagara Falls), Bob Burgess (Welland), Bob Fowler (Utica), Ellen Harrigan-Charles (St. Catharines), Richard Murphy (Pittsfield), Sam Nader (Oneonta), Tom O'Reilly (Jamestown), Brad Rogers (Batavia), Charles Savage (Auburn), Michael Schell (Watertown), Clyde Smoll (Elmira), Jack Tracz (Hamilton), Paul Velte (Geneva), Skip Weisman (Erie).
Years League Active: 1939-1992.
1992 Opening Date: June 15. **Closing Date:** Sept. 4.
No. of Games: 78.
Division Structure: McNamara—Oneonta, Pittsfield, Utica, Watertown. **Pinckney**—Auburn, Batavia, Elmira, Geneva. **Stedler**—Jamestown, Erie, St. Catharines, Hamilton, Niagara Falls, Welland.
Playoff Format: Three division winners and a wild card will meet in one-game semifinals. Winners meet in best-of-3 series for league championship.
All-Star Game: None.
Roster Limit: 25.
Statistician: Howe Sportsdata International, Boston Fish Pier, West Bldg. #2—Suite 306, Boston MA 02210.

1991 Standings (Overall)

Club (Affiliate)	W	L	Pct.	GB	'91 Manager
†Pittsfield (Mets)	51	26	.662	—	Jim Thrift
†*Jamestown (Expos)	51	27	.654	½	Ed Creech
†Elmira (Red Sox)	47	30	.610	4	Dave Holt
Oneonta (Yankees)	42	35	.545	9	Jack Gillis
Utica (White Sox)	39	37	.513	11½	Mike Gellinger
Auburn (Astros)	38	39	.494	13	Steve Dillard
Batavia (Phillies)	38	40	.487	13½	Ramon Aviles
Erie (Independent)	37	41	.474	14½	Barry Moss
Niagara Falls (Tigers)	36	42	.462	15½	Gary Calhoun
St. Catharines (Blue Jays)	35	42	.455	16	Doug Ault
Hamilton (Cardinals)	35	42	.455	16	Rick Colbert
Geneva (Cubs)	35	43	.449	16½	Greg Mahlberg
Welland (Pirates)	30	47	.390	21	Lee Driggers
Watertown (Indians)	27	50	.351	24	Gary Tuck

*Won playoffs †Won division title

Stadium Information

Club	Stadium	LF	CF	RF	Capacity	'91 Att.
Auburn	Falcon Park	330	409	335	3,575	58,233
Batavia	Dwyer	326	385	326	3,000	43,247
Elmira	Dunn Field	325	384	325	5,000	79,414
Erie	Ainsworth Field	320	390	295	3,500	70,546
Geneva	McDonough Park	325	370	315	2,200	35,676
Hamilton	Bernie Arbour	303	410	340	3,500	69,872
Jamestown	College	335	417	353	3,324	40,276
Niagara Falls	Sal Maglie	334	380	334	1,800	62,157
Oneonta	Damaschke Field	360	406	350	3,500	52,657
Pittsfield	Wahconah Park	330	374	340	5,200	62,525
St. Catharines	Community Park	310	400	310	3,000	35,562
Utica	Donovan	340	400	340	4,500	70,150
Watertown	Duffy Frgrnds	325	402	325	3,500	58,394
Welland	Welland Spts. Cmp.	335	400	335	4,000	37,476

AUBURN
ASTROS

Office Address: 108 N. Division St., Auburn, NY 13021. **Mailing Address:** P.O. Box 651, Auburn, NY 13021. **Telephone:** (315) 255-2489. **FAX:** (315) 255-2675.

Affiliation (first year): Houston Astros (1982). **Years in League:** 1958-80, 1982-.

Operated By: Auburn Community Baseball, Inc.
President: Charles Savage.
General Manager: Derek Duin.
Field Manager: Steve Dillard. **Coach:** Clark Crist.
Trainer: Unavailable.

Radio Announcer: Mike Dwello. **No. of Games Broadcast:** Home-30, Away-5. **Flagship Station:** WMBO 1340-AM.

Stadium Name: Falcon Park. **Location:** Approx. 1 mile north of arterial highway (Rts. 5 and 20) on North Division St. **Standard Game Times:** 7:30 p.m., DH 6; Sun., 6.

Visiting Club Hotels: Auburn Days Inn, 37 William St., Auburn, NY 13021. Telephone: (315) 252-7567.

BATAVIA
CLIPPERS

Office Address: Denio & Banks Sts., Batavia, NY 14020. **Mailing Address:** P.O. Box 802, Batavia, NY 14021. **Telephone:** (716) 343-7531. **FAX:** (716) 343-9372.

Affiliation (first year): Philadelphia Phillies (1988). **Years in League:** 1939-53, 1957-59, 1961-.

Operated by: Genesee County Professional Baseball, Inc.
President: Edward Dwyer. **Vice Presidents:** Lawrence Roth, Jerry Maley.
Treasurer: Eldoune Thornton. **Secretary:** Ronald Starkweather.

General Manager: Brad Rogers. **Assistant General Manager:** Julia Rogers. **Groundskeeper:** Dick Rogers.

Field Manager: Ramon Aviles. **Coaches:** John Martin, Floyd Radford.

Radio Announcer: Bob Brown. **No. of Games Broadcast:** Home-20, Away-10. **Flagship Station:** WBTA 1490-AM.

Stadium Name: Dwyer. **Location:** I-90 to exit 48, left onto Rt. 98 S., left onto Richmond Ave., left onto Banks St. **Standard Game Times:** 7:05 p.m.

Visiting Club Hotel: Sheraton, 8250 Park Rd., Batavia, NY 14020. Telephone: (716) 344-2100

ELMIRA
PIONEERS

Office Address: Dunn Field, Luce St., Elmira, NY 14904. **Mailing Address:** P.O. Box 238, Elmira, NY 14902. **Telephone:** (607) 734-1811. **FAX:** (607) 734-4975.

Affiliation (first year): Boston Red Sox (1973). **Years in League:** 1957-60, 1973-.

Operated by: Diamond Action, Inc.
President and General Manager: Clyde Smoll. **Assistant General Manager:** Brian Lindsay. **Administrative Assistant:** Charlene Small. **Secretary:** Jean Hoffman.

Field Manager: Dave Holt. **Coach:** Gary Roggenburk.
Trainer: Unavailable.
Radio: Unavailable.

Stadium Name: Dunn Field. **Location:** Rt. 17 to Water St. exit, over Madison Ave. bridge, left onto Maple Ave., left onto Luce St. **Standard Game Times:** 7 p.m.

Visiting Club Hotels: Guthrie Inn, 555 Spring St., Sayre, PA 18840. Telephone: (717) 888-7711; Holiday Inn Downtown, E. Water St., Elmira, NY 14901. Telephone: (607) 734-4211; Journey's End, Rt. 17, Horseheads, NY 14845. Telephone: (607) 739-2525.

ERIE
SAILORS

Office Address: 2300 Washington Place, Erie, PA 16502. **Mailing Address:** P.O. Box 488, Erie, PA 16512. **Telephone:** (814) 459-7245. **FAX:** (814) 454-1764.

Affiliation (first year): Florida Marlins (1992). **Years in League:** 1944-45, 1954-63, 1967, 1981-.

Operated by: Keystone Professional Baseball Club, Inc.

President/General Manager: Skip Weisman. **Assistant General Manager:** Kathy Lumbard-Cobb. **Director of Stadium Operations:** David Post.

Field Manager: Fredi Gonzalez. **Coach:** Marty DeMerritt.

Trainer: Todd Sorenson.

Radio: Unavailable.

Stadium Name: Ainsworth Field. **Location:** Pa. 79 N to 26th St. exit, to Browns Ave., left to 24th St. **Standard Game Times:** 7:05 p.m.; Sun., 5:05.

Visiting Club Hotel: Unavailable.

GENEVA
CUBS

Office Address: 423 Exchange St., Geneva, NY 14456. **Mailing Address:** P.O. Box 402, Geneva, NY 14456. **Telephone:** (315) 789-2827. **FAX:** (315) 781-2959.

Affiliation (first year): Chicago Cubs (1977). **Years in League:** 1958-73, 1977-.

Operated by: Geneva Cubs Baseball, Inc.

President: Paul Velte.

General Manager: Dave Oster. **Director of Operations:** Doug Estes. **Telemarketing Director:** Lynn Roberti. **Sales:** Ed Hickey.

Field Manager: Greg Mahlberg. **Coach:** Stan Kyles.

Trainer: Dick Cummings.

Radio Announcer: Unavailable. **No. of Games Broadcast:** Unavailable. **Flagship Station:** WEOS 89.7 FM.

Stadium Name: McDonough Park. **Location:** I-90 to exit 42 (Geneva), to routes 5 and 20, to Copeland Ave., turn north, right onto Washington, left onto Nursery. **Standard Game Times:** 7:30 p.m.

Visiting Club Hotel: Chanticleer Motor Lodge, 473 Hamilton St., Geneva, NY 14456. Telephone: (315) 789-7600.

HAMILTON
REDBIRDS

Office Address: 131 John St. South, Suite 203, Hamilton, Ontario, L8N 2C3. **Telephone:** (416) 527-3000. **FAX:** (416) 527-2227.

Affiliation (first year): St. Louis Cardinals (1988). **Years in League:** 1939-42, 1946-56, 1988-.

Operated by: Hamilton Baseball Associates, Inc.

Chairman and Managing General Partner: Barry Gordon. **Executive Vice President, Baseball Operations:** Jack Tracz.

Vice President and General Manager: Ben Liotta. **Vice President, Marketing and Operations:** Tony Torre.

Field Manager: Chris Maloney. **Coach:** Scott Melvin.

Trainer: Tom Nash.

Radio Announcers: Clive Boutilier, Chris Stull, Sammy Mattina. **No. of Games Broadcast:** Home-20, Away-5. **Flagship Station:** CFMU 93.3 FM.

Stadium Name: Bernie Arbour. **Location:** Queen Elizabeth Expressway to Centennial Parkway exit, right on Mud St. to Mohawk Rd. east. **Standard Game Times:** 7 p.m.; Sun., 6.

Visiting Club Hotels: Royal Connaught Hotel, 112 King St., E. Hamilton, Ontario L8N 1A8. Telephone: (416) 527-5071; Sheraton Hamilton, 116 King

St., E. Hamilton, Ontario L8P 4V3. Telephone: (416) 529-5515; Holiday Inn, 150 King St., E. Hamilton, Ontario L8N 1B2. Telephone: (416) 528-3451; Journey's End, 75 Catharine St., Hamilton, Ontario L8N 4E8. Telephone: 416-546-1800.

JAMESTOWN
EXPOS

Office Address: 485 Falconer St., Jamestown, NY 14701. **Mailing Address:** P.O. Box 338, Jamestown, NY 14702. **Telephone:** (716) 665-4092. **FAX:** (716) 665-4438.
Affiliation (first year): Montreal Expos (1977). **Years in League:** 1939-57, 1961-73, 1977-.
Operated by: Montreal Baseball Club, Ltd.
General Manager: Tom O'Reilly.
Field Manager: Q.V. Lowe. **Coach:** Jim Fleming.
Trainer: Lee Slagle.
Radio Announcers: Pete Hubbell, Skip Pierce. **No. of Games Broadcast:** Home-16, Away-4. **Flagship Station:** WJTN 1240-AM.
Stadium Name: College. **Location:** Route 17 South to exit 12, right onto route 60, left onto Buffalo St., left onto Falconer St. **Standard Game Times:** 7 p.m.; DH 6; Sun., 6.
Visiting Club Hotels: Holiday Inn, 150 W. 4th St., Jamestown, NY 14701. Telephone: (716) 664-3400; Comfort Inn, 2800 N. Main St. Jamestown, NY 14701. Telephone: (716) 664-5920; Journey's End, East Main St., Falconer, NY 14733. Telephone: (716) 665-3670.

NIAGARA FALLS
RAPIDS

Office Address: 1201 Hyde Park Blvd., Niagara Falls, NY 14305. **Telephone:** (716) 298-5400. **FAX:** (716) 297-2303.
Affiliation (first year): Detroit Tigers (1989). **Years in League:** 1939-40, 1970-79, 1982-85, 1989-.
Operated by: Niagara Falls Baseball, Inc. of Rich Baseball Operations.
President: Bob Rich Jr. **Director:** Mike Billoni.
Director of Stadium Operations: Tom Sciarrino. **Director of Sales and Marketing:** Shawn Reilly. **Business Manager:** Shannon Richards.
Field Manager: Larry Parrish. **Coaches:** Ray Korn, Stan Luketich.
Trainer: Unavailable.
Radio Announcer: Howard Simon. **No. of Games Broadcast:** Home-10, Away-20. **Flagship Station:** WJJL 1440-AM.
Stadium Name: Sal Maglie. **Location:** I-190 to exit 22 (Route 62), north to 62A, right on Hyde Park Blvd.. **Standard Game Times:** 7:05 p.m.; Sun. 6:05.
Visiting Club Hotel: Holiday Inn, Buffalo Ave. and 1st St., Niagara Falls, NY 14303. Telephone: (716) 285-2521.

ONEONTA
YANKEES

Office Address: 95 River St., Oneonta, NY 13820. **Telephone:** (607) 432-6326. **FAX:** (607) 432-1965.
Affiliation (first year): New York Yankees (1967). **Years in League:** 1966-.
Operated by: Oneonta Athletic Corp., Inc.
President and General Manager: Sam Nader. **Business and Concessions Manager:** John Nader. **Ticket Manager:** Bob Zeh.
Field Manager: Jack Gillis. **Coaches:** Fernando Arango, Joel Grampietro, Bill Schmidt.
Trainer: Mark Littlefield.
Radio: None.
Stadium Name: Damaschke Field. **Location:** Exit 15 off I-88. **Standard Game Times:** 7:15 p.m.; Sun. and DH 6.
Visiting Club Hotel: Unavailable.

PITTSFIELD
METS

Office Address: 105 Wahconah St., Pittsfield, MA 01201. **Mailing Address:** P.O. Box 328, Pittsfield, MA 01202. **Telephone:** (413) 499-6387. **FAX:** (413) 448-6031.

Affiliation (first year): New York Mets (1989). **Years in League:** 1989-.
Operated by: CD&M Associates, Inc..
President and General Manager: Richard Murphy. **Assistant General Manager:** Richard Lenfest.
Field Manager: Jim Thrift. **Coaches:** Jeff Morris, Howard Freiling.
Trainer: Larry Bennese.
Radio Announcer: Don Orsillo. **No. of Games Broadcast:** Home-5, Away-39. **Flagship Station:** WBEC 1420-AM.
Stadium Name: Wahconah Park. **Location:** Wahconah St exit off Rt. 7 north. **Standard Game Times:** 7 p.m.
Visiting Club Hotels: Berkshire Hilton Inn, Berkshire Common, Pittsfield, MA 01201. Telephone: (413) 499-2000; Super 8 Motel, Housatonic St., Lee, MA (413) 243-0143.

ST. CATHARINES
BLUE JAYS

Office Address: 426 Merritt St., St. Catharines, Ontario L2P 1P3. **Mailing Address:** P.O. Box 1088, St. Catharines, Ontario L2R 3B0. **Telephone:** (416) 641-5297. **FAX:** (416) 641-3007.

Affiliation (first year): Toronto Blue Jays (1986). **Years in League:** 1986-.
Operated by: St. Catharines Blue Jays Baseball Club.
President: Paul Beeston.
General Manager: Ellen Harrigan-Charles. **Assistant General Manager:** Marilyn Finn.
Field Manager: J.J. Cannon. **Coaches:** Reggie Cleveland, Rolando Pino.
Trainer: Scott Shannon.
Radio: None.
Stadium Name: Community Park. **Location:** Merritt Street at Seymour Ave. **Standard Game Times:** 7 p.m.
Visiting Club Hotel: Parkway Inn, 325 Ontario St., St. Catharines, Ontario L2R 5L3. Telephone: (416) 688-2324.

UTICA
BLUE SOX

Office Address: 1700 Sunset Ave., Utica, NY 13502. **Mailing Address:** P.O. Box 751, Utica, NY 13503. **Telephone:** (315) 738-0999. **FAX:** (315) 738-0992.

Operated by: Utica Baseball Club, Ltd.
Affiliation (first year): Chicago White Sox (1988). **Years in League:** 1977-.
President: Bob Fowler.
General Manager: Dan O'Hara. **Public Relations/Director of Stadium Operations:** Rob Fowler.
Field Manager: Fred Kendall. **Coaches:** Bill Ballou, Charlie Culberson.
Trainer: Rick Ray.
Radio: None.
Stadium Name: Donovan. **Location:** New York State Thruway to exit 31, Genesee St. to Burrstone Rd., right to park. **Standard Game Times:** 7 p.m.
Visiting Club Hotel: Howard Johnson, 302 N. Genesee St., Utica, NY 13502. Telephone: (315) 724-4141.

WATERTOWN
INDIANS

Office Address: 120 Washington, Watertown, NY 13601. **Mailing Address:** P.O. Box 802, Watertown, NY 13601. **Telephone:** (315) 788-8747. **FAX:** (315) 788-8841.

Affiliation (first year): Cleveland Indians (1989). **Years in League:** 1983-.
Operated by: Jefferson County Community Baseball, Inc.
President: Bob Wehrle.
General Manager: Dan Moushon. **Assistant General Manager:** Steve Lindemann. **Controller:** Theresa Chapman.
Field Manager: Shawn Pender. **Coaches:** Greg Ferlenda, Dan Williams.
Trainer: Rick Jameyson.
Radio: None.
Stadium Name: Duffy Fairgrounds. **Location:** Exit 46 on I-81, to Coffeen Street. **Standard Game Times:** 7:15 p.m; Sun., 5.
Visiting Club Hotel: Ramada Inn, Arsenal St., Watertown, NY 13601. Telephone: (315) 788-0700.

WELLAND
PIRATES

Office Address: 90 Quaker Rd., Welland, Ontario L3C 3G3. **Mailing Address:** P.O. Box 594, Welland Ontario L3B 5R3. **Telephone:** (416) 735-7634. **FAX:** (416) 735-7114.

Affiliation (first year): Pittsburgh Pirates (1989). **Years in League:** 1989-.
Operated by: Palisades Baseball, Ltd.
Managing General Partner: Alan Levin.
General Manager: Bob Burgess. **Assistant General Manager:** Tom Glick. **Director of Stadium Operations:** Brian Sloan.
Field Manager: Trent Jewett. **Coaches:** Julio Garcia, Tom Barnard.
Trainer: Ken Crenshaw.
Radio: None.
Stadium Name: Welland Sports Complex. **Location:** Highway 406 South to Welland, left on Niagara St., left on Quaker Rd. **Standard Game Times:** 7:05 p.m.
Visiting Club Hotel: Best Western Rose City Suites, 300 Prince Charles Dr., Welland, Ontario L3C 7B3. Telephone: (416) 732-0922.

NORTHWEST LEAGUE

Class A

Mailing Address: P.O. Box 4941, Scottsdale, AZ 85261.
Telephone: (602) 483-8224. **FAX:** (602) 991-5766.
President/Treasurer: Bob Richmond.
Vice President/Secretary: Tom Leip.
Directors: Robert Bavasi (Everett), Bob Beban (Eugene), Bobby Brett (Spokane), Mary Cain (Bend), Dave Elmore (Yakima), Fred Herrmann (Southern Oregon), Bill Pereira (Boise), Jerry Walker (Bellingham).
Public Relations Director: Janice Leip.
Years League Active: 1901-1922, 1937-1942, 1946-1992.
1992 Opening Date: June 17. **Closing Date:** Sept. 4.
No. of Games: 76.
Division Structure: North—Bellingham, Everett, Spokane, Yakima. **South**—Bend, Eugene, Boise, Southern Oregon.
Playoff Format: Two division winners play best-of-3 series for league championship.
All-Star Game: None.
Statistician: Howe Sportsdata International, Boston Fish Pier, West Bldg. #2—Suite 306, Boston MA 02210.

1991 Standings (Overall)

Club (Affiliate)	W	L	Pct.	GB	'91 Manager
*†Boise (Angels)	50	26	.618	—	Tom Kotchman
†Yakima (Dodgers)	44	32	.579	6	Joe Vavra
Eugene (Royals)	42	34	.553	8	Tom Poquette
Southern Oregon (A's)	40	36	.526	10	Grady Fuson
Everett (Giants)	37	38	.493	12½	Rob Ellis, Mike Bubalo
Bellingham (Mariners)	36	39	.480	13½	Dave Myers
Bend (Independent)	30	46	.395	20	Bill Stein
Spokane (Padres)	24	52	.316	26	Gene Glynn

*Won playoffs †Won division title

Stadium Information

Club	Stadium	LF	CF	RF	Capacity	'91 Att.
Bellingham	Joe Martin	325	381	320	2,200	60,484
Bend	Vince Genna	330	390	330	2,850	47,018
Boise	Memorial	335	405	335	4,500	132,611
Eugene	Civic	335	400	328	7,200	130,039
Everett	Everett Memorial	330	395	335	2,400	89,906
So. Oregon	Miles Field	332	384	344	2,900	70,164
Spokane	Interstate Fairgrounds	335	403	335	8,314	130,111
Yakima	Parker Field	330	400	312	3,148	81,835

BELLINGHAM
MARINERS

Office Address: 1316 King St., Bellingham, WA 98226. **Telephone:** (206) 671-6347. **FAX:** (206) 647-2254.

Affiliation (first year): Seattle Mariners (1977). **Years in League:** 1973-.
Operated by: Sports Enterprises, Inc.
President and General Manager: Jerry Walker. **Vice President:** William Tucker. **Assistant General Manager:** Larry Goldfarb. **Director of Ticketing:** Gary Lee.
Field Manager: Dave Myers. **Coach:** Bryan Price.
Trainer: Spyder Webb.
Radio Announcer: Unavailable. **No. of Games Broadcast:** Home-38, Away-38. **Flagship Station:** KGMI 790-AM.
Stadium Name: Joe Martin. **Location:** Two blocks east of I-5 exit #253 (Lakeway Drive). **Standard Game Times:** 7 p.m.; Sun. and holidays, 6.
Visiting Club Hotel: Unavailable.

BEND
ROCKIES

Office Address: 401 S.E. Roosevelt, Bend, OR 97702. **Mailing Address:** P.O. Box 6603, Bend, OR 97708. **Telephone:** (503) 382-8011. **FAX:** (503) 382-8875.

Affiliation (first year): Colorado Rockies (1992). **Years in League:** 1970-71, 1978-.
Operated by: Bend Baseball, Inc.
President: Mary Cain. **Vice President and General Manager:** Jack Cain. **Media Relations:** Bill Lewis. **Sales Representatives:** Lefty Dennis, Vince Genna. **Administrative Assistant:** David Haworth.
Field Manager: Gene Glynn. **Coaches:** Joe Niekro, Johnny Zizzo.
Trainer: Tom Probst.
Radio Announcers: Unavailable. **No. of Games Broadcast:** Home-38, Away-38. **Flagship Station:** KGRL 940-AM.
Stadium Name: Vince Genna. **Location:** 1 block east of Hwy. 97 in the south of Bend. **Standard Game Times:** 7 p.m.; Sun. 6.
Visiting Club Hotel: Sportsman Hotel, 3705 Highway 97, Bend, OR 97701. Telephone: (503) 382-2211.

BOISE
HAWKS

Office Address: 5600 N. Glenwood, Boise, ID 83714. **Telephone:** (208) 322-5000. **FAX:** (208) 322-7432.

Affiliation (first year): California Angels (1990). **Years in League:** 1975-76, 1978, 1985-.
Operated by: Diamond Sports, Inc.
President and General Manager: Ken Wilson. **Vice President, Assistant General Manager:** Cord Pereira. **Director of Marketing:** Bill Walter. **Director of Stadium Operations:** Michael Burton. **Director of Season Tickets:** J.J. McLeod. **Director of Broadcast Sales:** Eric Trapp. **Administrative Assistant:** John Cunningham.
Field Manager: Tom Kotchman. **Coaches:** Orv Franchuk, Howie Gershberg.
Trainer: Alan Russell.
Radio Announcer: Unavailable. **No. of Games Broadcast:** Home-38, Away-38. **Flagship Station:** KFXO 580-AM.
Stadium Name: Memorial. **Location:** Hwy. 84 to Cole Rd., south to Fairgrounds. **Game Times:** 7 p.m.
Visiting Club Hotel: Ramada Inn, 1025 S. Capitol Blvd, Boise, ID 83702. Telephone: (208) 344-7971.

EUGENE
EMERALDS

Office Address: 2077 Willamette St., Eugene, OR 97405. **Mailing Address:** P.O. Box 5566, Eugene, OR 97405. **Telephone:** (503) 342-5367. **FAX:** (503) 342-6089.

Affiliation (first year): Kansas City Royals (1984). **Years in League:** 1955-68, 1974-.

Operated by: Eugene Baseball, Inc.

President/General Manager: Bob Beban. **Director of Operations:** Kathy Schwingel. **Grounds Superintendant:** Brian Cool.

Field Manager: Bobby Meacham. **Coaches:** Tom Burgmeier, John Mizerock.

Trainer: Unavailable.

Radio Announcer: Lee Chabre. **No. of Games Broadcast:** Home-38, Away-38. **Flagship Station:** KPNW 1120-AM.

Stadium Name: Civic. **Location:** From I-5, Hwy. 126 to Downtown, west to Pearl Street, south to 20th. **Standard Game Times:** 7 p.m.; Sun. 2 and 6.

Visiting Club Hotel: Unavailable

EVERETT
GIANTS

Office Address: 2118 Broadway, Everett, WA 98201. **Mailing Address:** P.O. Box 7893, Everett, WA 98201. **Telephone:** (206) 258-3673. **FAX:** (206) 258-3675.

Affiliation (first year): San Francisco Giants (1984). **Years in League:** 1984-.

Operated by: Everett Giants, Inc.

Directors: Robert Bavasi, Margaret Bavasi.

General Manager: Melody Tucker. **Assistant General Manager, Business Operations:** Don Anderson. **Assistant General Manager, Stadium Operations:** Marv Grossman. **Assistant General Manager:** Charlie Poier. **Administrative Assistant:** Jim Averill.

Field Manager: Norm Sherry. **Coaches:** Kevin Higgins, Mike Bubalo.

Trainer: Unavailable.

Radio Announcer: Unavailable. **No. of Games Broadcast:** Home-38, Away-38. **Flagship Station:** KRKO 1380-AM.

Stadium Name: Everett Memorial. **Location:** I-5 to exit 192, corner of 39th and Broadway. **Game Times:** 7 p.m.; Sun. 6.

Visiting Club Hotel: Everett Pacific Hotel, 3105 Pine, Everett, WA 98201. Telephone: (206) 339-3333.

SOUTHERN OREGON
ATHLETICS

Office Address: 1801 South Pacific Hwy., Medford, OR 97501. **Mailing Address:** P.O. Box 1457, Medford, OR 97501. **Telephone:** (503) 770-5364. **FAX:** (503) 772-4466.

Affiliation (first year): Oakland Athletics (1979). **Years in League:** 1967-71, 1979-.

Operated by: National Sports Organization, Inc.

President: Fred Herrmann.

General Manager: William Courtney. **Groundskeeper:** Bill Morris.

Field Manager: Grady Fuson. **Coach:** Jim Slaton.

Trainer: Ric Moreno.

Radio Announcers: Nico Pemantle, Vlad Belo. **No. of Games Broadcast:** Home-38, Away-38. **Flagship Station:** KMFR 880-AM.

Stadium Name: Miles Field. **Location:** ½ mile south of Barnett Rd. on South Pacific Highway 99. **Standard Game Times:** 7 p.m.; Sun. 6.

Visiting Club Hotels: Horizon Inn, 1150 E. Barnett Rd., Medford, OR 97504. Telephone: (503) 779-5085; Motel 6, 950 Alba Dr., Medford, OR 97504. Telephone: (503) 773-4290.

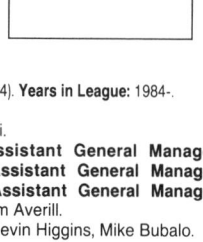

SPOKANE
INDIANS

Office Address: N. 602 Havana, Spokane, WA 99202. **Mailing Address:** P.O. Box 4758, Spokane, WA 99202. **Telephone:** (509) 535-2922. **FAX:** (509) 534-5368.

Affiliation (first year): San Diego Padres (1983). **Years in League:** 1972, 1983-.

Operated by: Longball, Inc.
President: Bobby Brett.
General Manager: Tom Leip. **Director of Sales:** Brian Viselli. **Public Relations Director:** Craig West. **Administrative Assistant:** Barbara Klante. **Marketing Director:** Dave Pier. **Marketing Assistant:** Mike Mishell. **Publications:** Janice Leip.
Field Manager: Ed Romero. **Coach:** Unavailable.
Trainer: Unavailable.
Radio Announcer: Craig West. **No. of Games Broadcast:** Home-38, Away-38. **Flagship Station:** KGA 1510-AM.
Stadium Name: Interstate Fairgrounds. **Location:** I-90 to Havana exit. **Standard Game Times:** 7 p.m.; Sun. 6.
Visiting Club Hotel: Value Inns by Cavanaugh, W. 1203 5th Ave., Spokane, WA 99204. Telephone: (509) 624-4142.

YAKIMA
BEARS

Office Address: 730 Summitview, Yakima, WA 98902. **Mailing Address:** P.O. Box 483, Yakima, WA 98907. **Telephone:** (509) 457-5151. **FAX:** (509) 457-9909.

Affiliation (first year): Los Angeles Dodgers (1988). **Years in League:** 1955-65, 1990-.

Operated by: Tradition Sports, Inc.
President: Dave Elmore.
General Manager: Steve Ford.
Field Manager: Joe Vavra. **Coach:** Tony Arnold.
Trainer: Barclay Dugger.
Radio Announcer: Bob Romero. **No. of Games Broadcast:** Home-38, Away-38. **Flagship Station:** KUTI 980-AM
Stadium Name: Parker Field. **Location:** Nob Hill exit on Highway 82, west to 16th Ave. **Standard Game Times:** 7:05 p.m.
Visiting Club Hotel: Unavailable.

APPALACHIAN LEAGUE

Rookie Classification

Mailing Address: 157 Carson Lane, Bristol, VA 24201.

Telephone: (703) 669-3644. **FAX:** 703-669-2618.

President, Secretary-Treasurer: Bill Halstead.

Administrative Assistant: Mary Halstead.

Directors: Jim Bowden (Princeton), Bill Harford (Huntington), Steve Phillips (Kingsport), Chuck LaMar (Pulaski), Doug Melvin (Bluefield), Dave Miller (Bristol), Dan O'Dowd (Burlington), Jim Rantz (Elizabethton), Mike Jorgensen (Johnson City), Del Unser (Martinsville).

Years League Active: 1921-1925, 1937-1955, 1957-1992.

1992 Opening Date: June 19. **Closing Date:** Aug. 28.

No. of Games: 68.

Division Structure: South—Bristol, Elizabethton, Johnson City, Kingsport, Pulaski. **North**—Bluefield, Burlington, Huntington, Martinsville, Princeton.

Playoff Format: Division winners play best-of 3 series.

All-Star Game: None.

Roster Limit: 30.

Statistician: Howe Sportsdata International, Boston Fish Pier, West Bldg. #2—Suite 306, Boston MA 02210.

1991 Standings (Overall)

Club (Affiliate)	W	L	Pct.	GB	'91 Manager
†Pulaski (Braves)	45	23	.662	—	Randy Ingle
Johnson City (Cardinals)	40	26	.606	4	Chris Maloney
Burlington (Indians)	40	27	.597	4½	Dave Keller
Elizabethton (Twins)	39	29	.574	6	Ray Smith
Bluefield (Orioles)	36	31	.537	8½	Gus Gil
Kingsport (Mets)	36	31	.537	8½	Andre David
Martinsville (Phillies)	27	41	.397	17½	Roly DeArmas
Princeton (Reds)	24	40	.375	19	Sam Mejias
Huntington (Cubs)	25	42	.373	19½	Steve Roadcap
Bristol (Tigers)	22	44	.333	22	Juan Lopez

†Won league title

Stadium Information

		Dimensions				
Club	Stadium	LF	CF	RF	Capacity	'91 Att.
Bluefield	Bowen Field	335	365	335	3,000	55,373
Bristol	DeVault Memorial	325	400	310	2,000	26,901
Burlington	Burlington Athletic	335	405	335	3,500	57,613
Elizabethton	O'Brien Field	330	404	325	1,500	18,115
Huntington	St. Cloud Commons	329	385	328	3,100	59,860
Johnson City	Howard Johnson	320	410	320	3,800	31,442
Kingsport	J. Fred Johnson	335	380	310	8,000	31,721
Martinsville	English Field	330	375	330	3,200	72,703
Princeton	Hunnicutt Field	340	400	340	1,500	25,203
Pulaski	Calfee Park	338	405	301	2,000	24,656

BLUEFIELD
ORIOLES

Office Address: P.O. Box 356, Bluefield, WV 24701. **Telephone:** (703) 326-1326. **FAX:** (703) 326-1318.

Affiliation (first year): Baltimore Orioles (1958). **Years in League:** 1946-55, 1957-.

Operated by: Bluefield Baseball Club, Inc.
President: George McGonagle. **General Manager:** George Fanning.
Field Manager: Mike O'Berry. **Coach:** Unavailable.
Trainer: Unavailable.
Radio: None.
Stadium Name: Bowen Field. **Location:** Rt. 460 to Westgate Shopping Center. **Standard Game Times:** 7:30 p.m.; Sun. 6:30.

Visiting Club Hotel: Ramada Inn, Cumberland Rd., Bluefield, WV 24701. Telephone: (304) 325-5420.

BRISTOL
TIGERS

Office Address: 1501 Euclid Ave., Bristol, VA 24201. **Mailing Address:** P.O. Box 1434, Bristol, VA 24203. **Telephone:** (703) 466-8310. **FAX:** (703) 466-2247.

Affiliation (first year): Detroit Tigers (1969). **Years in League:** 1921-25, 1940-55, 1969-.

Operated by: Bristol Baseball, Inc.
President: Boyce Cox.
General Manager: Bob Childress.
Field Manager: Mark Wagner. **Coaches:** Juan Lopez, Jim Van Scoyoc.
Radio Announcer: Bill Burton. **No. of Games Broadcast:** Home-34, Away-34. **Flagship Station:** WBBI 1230-AM.
Stadium Name: DeVault Memorial. **Location:** I-81 to Exit 2 onto 381, right at second stoplight. **Standard Game Times:** 7 p.m.

Visiting Club Hotel: Econo Lodge, 912 Commonwealth Ave., Bristol, VA 24201. Telephone: (703) 466-4112.

BURLINGTON
INDIANS

Office Address: 1450 Graham St., Burlington, NC 27216. **Telephone:** (919) 222-0223. **FAX:** (919) 226-2498.

Affiliation (first year): Cleveland Indians (1986). **Years in League:** 1986-.
Operated by: Burlington Baseball Club, Inc.
President: Miles Wolff.
General Manager: Mark Schuster. **Assistant General Manager:** Kevin Estrella. **Director of Stadium Operations:** David Burke.
Field Manager: Minnie Mendoza. **Coaches:** Billy Williams, Greg Booker.
Trainer: David Lassiter.
Radio Announcer: Lee Bowen. **No. of Games Broadcast:** Home-34, Away-34. **Flagship Station:** WBBB 920-AM.
Stadium Name: Burlington Athletic. **Location:** I-85 to exit 145, take 49 N., right on Mebane, right on Beaumont. **Standard Game Times:** 7:15 p.m.

Visiting Club Hotel: Ramada Inn, Ramada Rd., Burlington, NC. **Telephone:** (919) 227-5541.

ELIZABETHTON
TWINS

Office Address: 136 S. Sycamore, Elizabethton, TN 37643. **Telephone:** (615) 543-4395 or 543-7747.

Affiliation (first year): Minnesota Twins (1974). **Years in League:** 1937-42, 1945-51, 1974-.
Operated by: City of Elizabethton.
President and General Manager: Carmon Dugger. **Vice President:** Willie Church. **Secretary:** Jane Crow. **Assistant General Manager:** Bill Crow.
Field Manager: Jim Lemon. **Coaches:** Ray Smith, Rick Tomlin.
Trainers: Mike Collins, Dave McQueen.
Radio Announcers: Mike Johnson, Frank Santore. **No. of Games Broadcast:** Unavailable. **Flagship Station:** WBEJ 1240-AM.
Stadium Name: Joe O'Brien Field. **Location:** Highway 321 to Holly Lane. **Standard Game Times:** 7 p.m.
Visiting Club Hotel: Betsytowne Inn, 505 W. Elk Ave., Elizabethton, TN 37643. Telephone: (615) 543-3511; Comfort Inn, 1515 19-E Bypass, Elizabethton, TN 37643. Telephone: (615) 543-4466.

HUNTINGTON
CUBS

Office Address: 1901 Jackson Ave., Huntington, WV 25704. **Mailing Address:** P.O. Box 7005, Huntington, WV 25775. **Telephone:** (304) 429-1700. **FAX:** (304) 429-1706.
Affiliation (first year): Chicago Cubs (1990). **Years in League:** 1990-.
Operated by: Huntington Cubs Baseball, Inc.
President: Ed Poppiti.
General Manager: Bud Bickel. **Marketing Director:** Lisa Piepenbrink. **Director of Stadium Operations:** Dave Wagg. **Office Manager:** Sandy Hand. **Head Groundskeeper:** Claude Miller.
Field Manager: Phil Hannon. **Coaches:** Jim Housey, Gil Kubski.
Trainer: Greg Keuter.
Radio: Unavailable.
Stadium Name: St. Cloud Commons. **Location:** I-64 to West Huntington Exit (#5), left on Madison St., left on 19th St. West. **Standard Game Times:** 7:15 p.m.; Sun. 2.
Visiting Club Hotel: Ramada Inn, 5600 Rt. 60, Huntington, WV 25705. Telephone: (304) 736-3451.

JOHNSON CITY
CARDINALS

Office Address: 111 Legion St., Johnson City, TN 37605. **Mailing Address:** P.O. Box 568, Johnson City, TN 37605. **Telephone:** (615) 461-4850. **FAX:** (615) 461-4864.
Affiliation (first year): St. Louis Cardinals (1975). **Years in League:** 1921-24, 1937-55, 1957-61, 1964-.
President: Lonnie Lowe.
General Manager: Steven Robinson. **Assistant General Manager:** Herb Ledford. **Park Manager:** James Ellis.
Field Manager: Steve Turco. **Coach:** Orlando Thomas.
Trainer: Mike Gaddie.
Radio Announcers: Chip Kessler, Bill Mead, Paul Overbay. **No. of Games Broadcast:** Unavailable. **Flagship Station:** WJCW 910-AM.
Stadium Name: Howard Johnson Field. **Location:** I-181 to exit 32. **Standard Game Times:** 7:00 p.m., DH 6:30.
Visiting Club Hotel: Super 8, 108 Wesley St., Johnson City, TN 37601. Telephone: (615) 282-8818.

KINGSPORT
METS

Office Address: 2908 Ashley St., Kingsport, TN 37664. **Telephone:** (615) 246-6464. **FAX:** (615) 245-4761.
Affiliation (first year): New York Mets (1980). **Years in League:** 1921-25, 1938-52, 1957, 1960-63, 1969-82, 1984-.
Operated by: Greater Kingsport Baseball Association.
President: Gale Starnes. **Executive Director:** Janice Archer.

Field Manager: Andre David. **Coach:** Jesus Hernaiz, Geary Jones.
Radio Announcer: Tom Taylor. **No. of Games Broadcast:** Home-34. **Flagship Station:** WKPT 1400-AM.
Stadium Name: J. Fred Johnson. **Location:** Fort Henry Drive at Dobyns Bennett High School. **Game Times:** 7 p.m.; DH 6; Sun. 7:30.
Visiting Club Hotel: Holiday Inn, 700 Lynn Garden Dr., Kingsport, TN 37660. Telephone: (615) 247-3133.

MARTINSVILLE
PHILLIES

Office Address: Hooker Field, Commonwealth Blvd. and Chatham Hts., Martinsville, VA 24112. **Mailing Address:** P.O. Box 3614, Martinsville, VA 24115. **Telephone:** (703) 666-2000. **FAX:** (703) 666-2139.
Affiliation (first year): Philadelphia Phillies (1988). **Years in League:** 1988-.
Operated by: Martinsville Phillies Professional Baseball, Inc.
President and General Manager: Tim Cahill. **Assistant General Manager:** Troy Potthoff. **Director of Administration:** Mary Haskins.
Field Manager: Roly DeArmas. **Coaches:** Ramon Henderson, Ray Rippelmeyer.
Trainer: Unavailable..
Radio: None.
Stadium Name: Hooker Field. **Location:** Hwy. 220 to Commonwealth Blvd., east for 3 miles; Hwy. 58 to Chatham Hts., north 2 blocks. **Standard Game Times:** 7:30 p.m., DH 6.
Visiting Club Hotel: Dutch Inn, 633 Virginia Ave., Collinsville, VA 24078. Telephone: (703) 647-3721.

PRINCETON
REDS

Office Address: One Valley Bank, Courthouse Square, Princeton, WV 24740. **Mailing Address:** P.O. Box 5646, Princeton, WV 24740. **Telephone:** (304) 487-2000. **FAX:** (304) 425-6999.
Affiliation (first year): Cincinnati Reds (1991). **Years in League:** 1988-.
Operated by: Princeton Baseball Association, Inc.
President: James Thompson. **General Manager:** Jim Holland.
Field Manager: Sam Mejias. **Coach:** Darrell Rodgers.
Trainer: Billy Maxwell.
Stadium Name: Hunnicutt Field. **Location:** Exit #9 off I-77, then take US 460 West to Downtown exit. Stadium located behind Princeton High School. **Standard Game Times:** 7 p.m., DH 6.
Visiting Club Hotel: Econo Lodge, Oakvale Rd., Princeton, WV 24740. Telephone (304) 425-8711.

PULASKI
BRAVES

Office Address: Calfee Park, 5th and Pierce, Pulaski, VA 24031. **Mailing Address:** P.O. Box 814, Pulaski, VA 24031. **Telephone:** (703) 980-8200. **FAX:** Same.
Affiliation (first year): Atlanta Braves (1982). **Years in League:** 1946-50, 1952-55, 1957-58, 1969-77, 1982-.
Operated by: Pulaski Baseball Club, Inc.
President: Hiawatha Nicely.
General Manager: Frank Gahl. **Assistant General Manager:** Suzi Gahl. **Media and Public Relations Director:** Mike Shank. **Operations Director:** Gene Crowder.
Field Manager: Randy Ingle. **Coaches:** Cloyd Boyer, Fred Koenig.
Trainer: Unavailable.
Radio: None.
Stadium Name: Calfee Park. **Location:** I-81 to Pulaski exit (Rt. 11 north), 5 miles, right at Calfee Park St. **Standard Game Times:** 7 p.m.
Visiting Club Hotel: Unavailable.

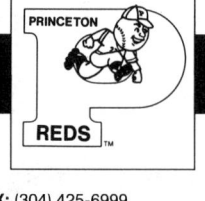

PIONEER LEAGUE

Rookie Classification

Mailing Address: P.O. Box 1144, Billings, MT 59103.
Telephone: (406) 248-3401. **FAX:** (406) 245-4143.
President, Secretary-Treasurer: Ralph Nelles.
Directors: Rene Boisvert (Helena), Howard Gaare (Great Falls), Jack Donovan (Salt Lake City), Dave Elmore (Idaho Falls), David White (Lethbridge), Bob Wilson (Billings), Miles Wolff (Butte), Bill Yuill (Medicine Hat).
Years League Active: 1939-1942, 1946-1992.
1992 Opening Date: June 17. **Closing Date:** Sept. 5.
No. of Games: 76.
Division Structure: Northern—Billings, Great Falls, Lethbridge, Medicine Hat. **Southern**—Butte, Helena, Idaho Falls, Salt Lake City.
Playoff Format: Two division winners meet in best-of-3 series for league championship.
All-Star Game: None.
Roster Limit: 30.
Statistician: Howe Sportsdata International, Boston Fish Pier, West Bldg. #2—Suite 306, Boston MA 02210.

1991 Standings (Overall)

Club (Affiliate)	W	L	Pct.	GB	'91 Manager
*†Salt Lake (Independent)	49	21	.700	—	Nick Belmonte
†Great Falls (Dodgers)	46	24	.657	3	Glenn Hoffman
Helena (Brewers)	44	26	.629	5	Harry Dunlop
Idaho Falls (Braves)	39	30	.565	9½	Steve Curry
Butte (Rangers)	29	41	.414	20	Dick Egan
Billings (Reds)	25	44	.362	23½	P.J. Carey
Medicine Hat (Blue Jays)	24	45	.348	24½	J.J. Cannon
Pocatello (Independent)	21	46	.313	26½	Rich Morales

*Won playoffs †Won division title

Stadium Information

Club	Stadium	LF	CF	RF	Capacity	'91 Att.
Billings	Cobb Field	335	410	335	4,500	80,242
Butte	Alumni Coliseum	350	410	360	5,000	29,684
Great Falls	Legion Park	335	410	335	3,834	79,176
Helena	Kindrick Lgn Fld	324	375	314	2,700	31,187
Idaho Falls	McDermott Field	350	400	340	3,800	71,292
Lethbridge[1]	Henderson	338	400	338	3,500	—
Medicine Hat	Athletic Park	350	380	350	2,600	14,722
Salt Lake	Derks Field	355	405	355	10,184	200,599

[1]Lethbridge franchise operated in Pocatello in 1991.

BILLINGS
MUSTANGS

Office Address: 3108 Reimers, Billings, MT 59102. **Mailing Address:** P.O. Box 1553, Billings, MT 59103. **Telephone:** (406) 252-1241. **FAX:** (406) 252-2968.

Affiliation (first year): Cincinnati Reds (1974). **Years in League:** 1948-63, 1969-.

Operated by: Billings Pioneer Baseball Club.
President and General Manager: Bob Wilson.
Field Manager: Donnie Scott. **Coach:** Terry Abbott.
Trainer: Mark Mann.
Radio Announcer: Glen Hebert. **No. of Games Broadcast:** Home-38, Away-38. **Station:** KCTR 970-AM.
Stadium Name: Cobb Field. **Location:** I-90 to 27th Street exit, north to 9th Avenue. **Standard Game Times:** 7 p.m.
Visiting Club Hotel: Rimrock Inn, 1203 N. 27th St., Billings, MT. Telephone: (406) 252-7107.

BUTTE
COPPER KINGS

Office Address: Montana Tech College, HPER Bldg. West Park St., Butte MT 59701. **Mailing Address:** P.O. Box 186, Butte, MT 59703. **Telephone:** (406) 723-8206. **FAX:** (406) 723-3376.

Affiliation (first year): Texas Rangers (1988). **Years in League:** 1978-85, 1987-.

Operated by: Silverbow Baseball Inc.
President: Miles Wolff. **Chief Executive Officer:** Jim McCurdy. **Vice President:** Rich Taylor.
General Manager: Mark Ruckwardt.
Field Manager: Victor Ramirez. **Coaches:** Travis Walden, Doug Sisson.
Trainer: Chuck Marquardt.
Radio Announcer: Frasier MacDonald. **Number of Games Broadcast:** Home-38. **Station:** KBOW 550-AM.
Stadium Name: Alumni Coliseum. **Location:** I-90 to Montana St. exit, north to Park Street, west to stadium (Montana Tech campus). **Standard Game Times:** 7 p.m.
Visiting Club Hotel: Unavailable.

GREAT FALLS
DODGERS

Office Address: 2600 River Dr. North, Great Falls, MT 59401. **Mailing Address:** P.O. Box 1621, Great Falls, MT 59403. **Telephone:** (406) 452-5311.

Affiliation (first year): Los Angeles Dodgers (1984). **Years in League:** 1948-63, 1969-.

Operated by: Great Falls Baseball Club, Inc.
President: Howard Gaare.
General Manager: Ray Klesh. **Office Manager:** Pam Parsons. **Head Groundskeeper:** Bill Chafin.
Field Manager: Unavailable. **Coaches:** Guy Conti, Helms Bohringer.
Trainer: Unavailable.
Radio Announcer: Gene Black. **No. of Games Broadcast:** Home-38, Away-38. **Flagship Station:** KQDI 1450-AM.
Stadium Name: Legion Park. **Location:** 11 blocks east of Havre Highway on River Drive North. **Standard Game Times:** 7 p.m.
Visiting Club Hotel: Midtown Motel, 526 2nd Ave. N, Great Falls, MT 59401. Telephone: (406) 453-2411.

HELENA
BREWERS

Office Address: Memorial and Warren Streets, Helena, MT 59604. **Mailing Address:** P.O. Box 4606, Helena, MT 59604.
Telephone: (406) 449-7616. **FAX:** (406) 449-6979.
Affiliation (first year): Milwaukee Brewers (1985). **Years in League:** 1978-.
  Operated by: Say Hey, Inc.
  President: Rene Boisvert.
  General Manager: Joe Easton. **Assistant General Manager:** Gordy Higgins. **Administrative Assistant:** Ellen Seymour.
  Field Manager: Harry Dunlop. **Coach:** Mike Caldwell.
  Trainer: Unavailable.
  Radio Announcer: Dennis Higgins. **No. of Games Broadcast:** Home-38, Away-38. **Flagship Station:** KMTX 950-AM.
  Stadium Name: Kindrick Field. **Location:** Cedar Street exit off I-15 West to Main, left on City Park. **Standard Game Times:** 7:05 p.m.; Sun. 6:05.
  Visiting Club Hotel: Kings Carriage Inn, North Last Chance, Helena, MT 59604. Telephone: (406) 442-6080.

IDAHO FALLS
GEMS

Office Address: 560 W. Elva, Idaho Falls, ID 83402. **Mailing Address:** P.O. Box 2183, Idaho Falls, ID 83403. **Telephone:** (208) 522-8363. **FAX:** (208) 522-9858.
Affiliation (first year): Atlanta Braves (1986). **Years in League:** 1940-42, 1946-.
  Operated by: Idaho Falls Gems Baseball Club, Inc.
  Vice President and General Manager: Eric Becklund.
  Field Manager: Dave Hilton. **Coaches:** Jerry Nyman, Phil Dale.
  Trainer: Unavailable.
  Radio Announcer: Dave Schultz. **No. of Games Broadcast:** Home-38, Away-38. **Flagship Station:** KID 590-AM.
  Stadium Name: McDermott Field. **Location:** I-15 to W. Broadway exit, left onto Memorial Drive to Mound Avenue, right ¼ mile to stadium. **Standard Game Times:** 7 p.m., Sun. 6.
  Visiting Club Hotel: Motel West, 1540 W. Broadway, Idaho Falls, ID 83402. Telephone: (208) 522-1112.

LETHBRIDGE
MOUNTIES

Office Address: 2601 Parkside Dr., Lethbridge, Alta. T1J 3Y2. **Telephone:** (403) 327-7975. **FAX:** (403) 327-8085.
Affiliation (first year): Independent. **Years in League:** 1975-83, 1992-.
  Operated by: Lethbridge Mounties Baseball.
  General Manager: David White. **Assistant General Manager, Sales and Marketing:** Gary Farwell.
  Field Manager: Unavailable.
  Trainer: Unavailable.
  Radio Announcer: Unavailable. **No. of Games Broadcast:** Home-38, Away-38. **Flagship Station:** Unavailable.
  Stadium Name: Henderson. **Location:** Parkside Drive off Mayor Magrath Blvd. **Standard Game Times:** 7 p.m.
  Visiting Club Hotel: Country Lodge, 7th Ave., Lethbridge, Alta. T1J 1M7.

MEDICINE HAT
BLUE JAYS

Office Address: 361 First St. SE, Medicine Hat, Alberta T1A 0A5. **Mailing Address:** P.O. Box 465, Medicine Hat, Alberta T1A 7G2. **Telephone:** (403) 526-0404. **FAX:** (403) 526-4000.
Affiliation (first year): Toronto Blue Jays (1978). **Years in League:** 1977-.
Operated by: Consolidated Sports Holdings, Ltd.
President: Bill Yuill.
General Manager: Kevin Friesen. **Administrative Assistant:** Carmen Schmidt. **Accounting:** Raymonde Christenson.
Field Manager: Jim Nettles. **Coach:** Gilbert Rondon
Trainer: Geoff Horne.
Radio: None.
Stadium Name: Athletic Park. **Location:** First Street or Dunmore Road exit off Trans Canada Highway. **Standard Game Times:** 7 p.m.; Sun., 6.
Visiting Club Hotel: Quality Inn, 951 7th St. SW, Medicine Hat, Alberta T1A 7R7. Telephone: (403) 527-8844.

SALT LAKE
TRAPPERS

Office Address: 1301 SW Temple, Salt Lake City, UT 84115. **Mailing Address:** 1325 S. Main #229, Salt Lake City, UT 84115. **Telephone:** (801) 484-9900. **FAX:** (801) 484-9910.
Affiliation: Independent. **Years in League:** 1939-42, 1946-57, 1967-69, 1985-.
Operated by: Salt Lake Trappers, Inc.
President: Jack Donovan.
General Manager: Dave Baggott. **Assistant General Manger/Business:** Holly Preston. **Assistant General Manager/Marketing:** John Stein.
Field Manager: Nick Belmonte. **Coach:** Dan Shwam.
Trainer: Kelly O'Brien.
Radio Announcers: Pete Diamond, Kurt Wilson. **No. of Games Broadcast:** Home-38, Away-38. **Flagship Station:** KALL 910-AM.
Stadium Name: Derks Field. **Location:** I-15 to 13th South exit, 4 blocks east to Derks Field. **Game Times:** 7 p.m., Sun. 1:30.
Visiting Club Hotel: Olympus Best Western, 161 W. 600 South, Salt Lake City, UT 84101. **Telephone:** (801) 521-7373.

ARIZONA LEAGUE

Rookie Classification

Mailing Address: P.O. Box 4941, Scottsdale, AZ 85261.
Telephone: (602) 483-8224. **FAX:** (602) 991-5766.
President: Bob Richmond.
Years League Active: 1988-92.
1992 Opening Date: June 21. **Closing Date:** August 31.
No. of Games: 56.
Playoff Format: None.
Member Clubs (Managers): Angels (Bill Lachemann), Athletics (Dickie Scott), Brewers (Wayne Krenchicki), Giants (Nelson Rood), Cardinals (Keith Champion), Mariners (Unavailable), Rockies/Cubs (Paul Zuvella), Padres (Ken Berry).
Playing Sites: Diablo Stadium, Tempe (Mariners); Scottsdale Community College (Athletics, Padres); Indian School Park, Scottsdale (Giants); Greenway Sports Complex, Peoria (Brewers, Cardinals); Autry Stadium Complex, Mesa (Angels).
Statistician: Howe Sportsdata International, Boston Fish Pier, West Bldg. #2—Suite 306, Boston MA 02210.

GULF COAST LEAGUE

Rookie Classification

Mailing Address: 1503 Clower Creek Dr. #H-262, Sarasota, FL 34231.
Telephone: (813) 966-6407. **FAX:** (813) 966-6872.
President: Tom Saffell.
Years League Active: 1964-92.
1992 Opening Date: June 18. **Closing Date:** August 26.
No. of Games: 60.
Playoff Format: Club with best winning percentage draws bye. Two other division winners play sudden death playoff game to determine who plays division winner with best winning percentage in best-of-3 series for league championship.
Member Clubs (Managers): Central Division—Astros (Julio Linares), Marlins (Carlos Tosca), Red Sox (Frank White), Royals (Mike Jirschele). **Eastern Division**—Braves (Jim Saul), Dodgers (John Shoemaker), Expos (Nelson Norman), Mets (Junior Roman). **Western Division**—Blue Jays (Omar Malave), Orioles (Phil Wellman), Pirates (Woody Huyke), Rangers (Chino Cadahia), Twins (Dan Rohn), White Sox (Mike Rojas), Yankees (Gary Denbo).
Roster Limit: 30.
Playing Sites: Baseball City complex (Royals); Ft. Myers complex (Twins); Osceola complex (Astros, Marlins); Pirate City complex; Bradenton (Pirates); Rangers complex, Port Charlotte (Rangers); Ed Smith complex, Sarasota (White Sox); Twin Lakes Park, Sarasota (Orioles); Yankees complex, Tampa (Yankees); Chain O'Lakes Park, Winter Haven (Red Sox); Englebert complex, Dunedin (Blue Jays); St. Lucie County complex (Mets, Dodgers); West Palm Beach Municipal Stadium and complex (Expos, Braves).
Game Times: All day games at noon.
Statistician: Howe Sportsdata International, Boston Fish Pier, West Bldg. #2—Suite 306, Boston MA 02210.

DOMINICAN SUMMER LEAGUE

Rookie Classification

Mailing Address: c/o Banco del Progresso, Av. John F. Kennedy, Santo Domingo, Dom. Rep.
Telephone: (809) 565-0714.
President: Freddy Jana.
Member Clubs, 1992: Unavailable. **Member Clubs, 1991: Eastern Division:** Braves, Astros, Dodgers, Giants, Orioles/White Sox, Rangers. **Santo Domingo Division:** Athletics, Blue Jays I, Blue Jays II, Expos, Mariners, Pirates, Tigers/Cardinals, Yankees/Mets. **Cibao Division:** Brewers, Dodgers/Padres/Angels, Indians, Royals/Cubs.

1992 DIRECTORY • **145**

MINOR LEAGUE SCHEDULES

CLASS AAA
American Association

Buffalo
APRIL
16-17-18 ..Oklahoma City
19-20-21 ....Denver
28-29-30 ....Louisville
MAY
1-2-3..........Indianapolis
10-11-12......Indianapolis
13-14-15 ..Oklahoma City
16-17-18 ....Denver
28-29-30-31 ....Nashville
JUNE
1-2-3-4........Louisville
11-12-13 ....Iowa
14-15-16 ....Omaha
25-26-27 ....Omaha
28-29-30 ....Iowa
JULY
1...................Iowa
4-5-6 ....Indianapolis
16-17 ....Louisville
24-25-26 ..Oklahoma City
27-28-29 ....Denver
AUGUST
3-4-5-6 ....Nashville
7-8-9 ....Indianapolis
19-20-21 ....Omaha
22-23 ....Iowa
24-25-26 ....Louisville
SEPTEMBER
4-5-6-7 ....Nashville

Denver
APRIL
9-10-11..........Nashville
12-13-14 ....Buffalo
22-23...............Omaha
24-25-26-27 ....Iowa
MAY
7-8 ....Omaha
9-10-11-12..........Iowa
19-20-21 ..Oklahoma City
22-23-24 ....Nashville
25-26-27 ....Buffalo
JUNE
1-2-3-4...........Omaha
11-12-13 .....Indianapolis
14-15-16 ....Louisville
25-26-27 ....Louisville
28-29-30 ....Louisville
JULY
1................Louisville
2-3 ....Omaha
18-19-20 ....Nashville
21-22-23 ....Buffalo
30-31 .....Oklahoma City
AUGUST
1-2-3-4............Iowa
5-6 ....Omaha
7-8-9 ....Oklahoma City
19-20-21 .....Indianapolis
22-23 ....Louisville
29-30-31 ..Oklahoma City
SEPTEMBER
1...........Oklahoma City

Indianapolis
APRIL
9-10-11 ....Omaha
12-13-14 ....Iowa
23-24............Nashville
25-26............Buffalo
MAY
5-6 ....Louisville
7-8-9 ....Nashville
22-23 ....Omaha
25-26-27-28 ....Louisville

JUNE
5-6-7.............Denver
8-9-10....Oklahoma City
20-21-22 ....Buffalo
23-24............Nashville
JULY
2-3 ....Nashville
7-8-9 ....Denver
10-11-12 ..Oklahoma City
18-19-20 ....Omaha
21-22-23 ....Iowa
30-31............Buffalo
AUGUST
1-2................Buffalo
3-4-5-6 ....Louisville
10-11-12 ....Denver
13-14-15 ..Oklahoma City
24-25-26 ....Nashville
28-29-30 ....Buffalo
SEPTEMBER
4-5 ....Louisville

Iowa
APRIL
16-17-18 ....Louisville
19-20-21 .....Indianapolis
28-29-30 ..Oklahoma City
MAY
1-2-3..............Denver
13-14-15 ....Louisville
16-17-18 .....Indianapolis
19-20-21 ....Omaha
JUNE
2-3-4 .....Oklahoma City
5-6-7 ....Omaha
8-9-10 ....Nashville
17-18-19 ....Buffalo
20-21-22 ..Oklahoma City
23-24 ....Denver
JULY
4-5-6 ....Denver
8-9-10 ....Nashville
11-12-13 ....Buffalo
24-25-26 ....Louisville
27-28-29 .....Indianapolis
AUGUST
7-8-9 ....Omaha
10-11-12 ....Buffalo
13-14-15 ....Nashville
24-25-26 ..Oklahoma City
27-28 ....Denver
29-30-31 ....Omaha
SEPTEMBER
5-6 ....Denver

Louisville
APRIL
9-10-11............Iowa
12-13-14 ....Omaha
22-23-24 ....Buffalo
25-26............Nashville
MAY
7-8-9 ....Buffalo
10-11-12 ....Nashville
20-21 ....Indianapolis
22-23-24 ....Iowa
29-30-31 ....Omaha
JUNE
5-6-7.....Oklahoma City
8-9-10 ....Denver
17-18-19 .....Indianapolis
20-21-22 ....Nashville
23-24............Buffalo
JULY
2-3 ....Buffalo
7-8-9 ....Oklahoma City
10-11-12 ....Denver

18-19-20 ....Iowa
21-22-23 ....Omaha
30-31 ....Nashville
AUGUST
1-2 ....Nashville
10-11-12 ..Oklahoma City
13-14-15 ....Denver
16-17-17 .....Indianapolis
31 ....Indianapolis
SEPTEMBER
1 ....Indianapolis
2-3 ....Buffalo
6-7 ....Indianapolis

Nashville
APRIL
16-17-18 ....Denver
19-20-21 ..Oklahoma City
27-28-29-30 ..Indianapolis
MAY
1-2-3............Louisville
5-6 ....Buffalo
13-14-15 ....Denver
16-17-18 ..Oklahoma City
20-21 ....Buffalo
JUNE
1-2-3-4......Indianapolis
5-6-7.............Buffalo
14-15-16 ....Iowa
17-18-19 ....Omaha
25-26-27 ....Iowa
28-29-30 ....Omaha
JULY
1................Omaha
4-5-6 ....Louisville
16-17 ....Indianapolis
24-25-26 ....Denver
27-28-29 ..Oklahoma City
AUGUST
7-8-9 ....Louisville
16-17-18 ....Buffalo
19-20-21 ....Iowa
22-23 ....Omaha
28-29-30 ....Louisville
31 ....Buffalo
SEPTEMBER
1 ....Buffalo
2-3 ....Indianapolis

Oklahoma City
APRIL
9-10-11..........Buffalo
12-13-14 ....Nashville
22-23...............Iowa
24-25-26-27 .....Omaha
MAY
4-5 ....Denver
6-7-8 ....Iowa
9-10-11-12 ....Omaha
22-23-24 ....Buffalo
25-26-27 ....Nashville
29-30-31 ....Denver
JUNE
11-12-13 ....Louisville
14-15-16 .....Indianapolis
17-18-19 ....Denver
25-26-27 ....Louisville
28-29-30 .....Indianapolis
JULY
1 ....Indianapolis
2-3 ....Iowa
16-17 ....Denver
18-19-20 ....Buffalo
21-22-23 ....Nashville
AUGUST
1-2-3-4............Omaha
5-6 ....Iowa
16-17 ....Denver

HOME GAMES ONLY

1992 DIRECTORY • 147

HOME GAMES ONLY

19-20-21 ...... Louisville
22-23 .... Indianapolis
SEPTEMBER
2-3-4 .... Iowa

OMAHA
APRIL
16-17-18 .... Indianapolis
19-20-21 ...... Louisville
28-29-30 .... Denver
MAY
1-2-3 ... Oklahoma City

4-5 .... Iowa
13-14-15 .... Indianapolis
16-17-18 .... Louisville
25-26-27 .... Iowa
JUNE
8-9-10 .... Buffalo
11-12-13 .... Nashville
20-21-22 .... Denver
23-24 .... Oklahoma City
JULY
4-5-6 ...... Oklahoma City
8-9-10 .... Buffalo
11-12-13 .... Nashville

16-17 .... Iowa
24-25-26 .... Indianapolis
27-28-29 ...... Louisville
30-31 .... Iowa
AUGUST
10-11-12 .... Nashville
13-14-15 .... Buffalo
16-17-18 .... Iowa
24-25-26 .... Denver
27-28 .... Oklahoma City
SEPTEMBER
2-3-4 .... Denver
5-6 .... Oklahoma City

International League

Columbus
APRIL
16-17 .... Richmond
18-18-20 ...... Tidewater
21-22 .... Toledo
MAY
1-2-3 .... Scranton
4-5 .... Pawtucket
7-8 .... Syracuse
9-10 .... Rochester
16-17 .... Toledo
19-20-21 ...... Tidewater
22-23-24 ...... Richmond
JUNE
6-7-8 .... Rochester
9-10-11 .... Syracuse
26-27-28 .... Scranton
29-30 .... Pawtucket
JULY
1-2 .... Pawtucket
3-4-4 .... Toledo
16-17-18-19-20 Richmond
21-22-23-24 ... Tidewater
25-26-27 .... Toledo
AUGUST
9-10 .... Toledo
12-13-14-15-16 Rochester
17-18-19-20-21 . Syracuse
31 .... Pawtucket
SEPTEMBER
1-2-3 .... Pawtucket
4-5-6-7 .... Scranton

Pawtucket
APRIL
9-10-11 .... Rochester
12-13 .... Syracuse
23-24 .... Toledo
25-26-27 .... Columbus
28-29 .... Richmond
MAY
6-7-8 .... Tidewater
16-17-18-19-20 . Scranton
21-22-23-24 ... Syracuse
25-26-27 ...... Rochester
JUNE
6-7 .... Tidewater
8-9-10-11 ..... Richmond
12-13-14 .... Toledo
22-23-24-25 .. Columbus
JULY
3-4-5-6 .... Rochester
7-8-9-10 ...... Syracuse
11-12-13 .... Scranton
29-30-31 .... Toledo
AUGUST
1-2 .... Toledo
3-4-5 .... Columbus
6-7-8-9 .... Scranton
22-23-24-25-26 . Tidewater
27-28-29-30 ... Richmond

Richmond
APRIL
9-10-11 .... Columbus
12-13-14 .... Toledo
21-22-23 ...... Rochester

24-25-26 ...... Syracuse
27 .... Tidewater
MAY
9-10-11 .... Pawtucket
12-13-14-15 ... Scranton
17 .... Tidewater
25-26-27-28 ..... Toledo
29-30-31 ...... Columbus
JUNE
1 .... Columbus
2 .... Tidewater
5 .... Tidewater
12 .... Tidewater
16-17-18 .... Scranton
19-20-21 ...... Pawtucket
23-24-24 ...... Rochester
25-26 .... Syracuse
JULY
4 .... Tidewater
5-6-7 .... Toledo
8-9-10 .... Columbus
25-26-27-28-29 . Syracuse
30-31 .... Rochester
AUGUST
1-2 .... Rochester
13-14 .... Tidewater
15-16-17 .... Scranton
18-19-20-21 ... Pawtucket
31 .... Tidewater
SEPTEMBER
2-3 .... Tidewater
5 .... Tidewater

Rochester
APRIL
15-16 .... Pawtucket
17-18-19 .... Scranton
27-28-29 ...... Syracuse
30 .... Richmond
MAY
1-2-3 .... Richmond
4-5 .... Tidewater
12-13 .... Toledo
14-15 .... Columbus
17-18-19 ...... Syracuse
29-30-31 .... Scranton
JUNE
1-2-3 .... Pawtucket
5 .... Syracuse
15-16-17 .... Toledo
18-19-20-21 ... Columbus
27-28 .... Richmond
29-30 .... Tidewater
JULY
1-2 .... Tidewater
13 .... Syracuse
16-17-18-19 ... Scranton
20-21-22-23-24 Pawtucket
AUGUST
3-4-5-6 .... Tidewater
7-8-9-10 .... Richmond
22-23-24-25 ... Columbus
26-27-28-29-30 ... Toledo
31 .... Syracuse
SEPTEMBER
1 .... Syracuse
4-5 .... Syracuse

Scranton/W-B
APRIL
9-10-11 .... Syracuse
12-13 .... Rochester
20-21 .... Pawtucket
23-24 .... Columbus
25-26-27 .... Toledo
28-29 .... Tidewater
MAY
6-7-8 .... Richmond
21-22-23-24 ... Rochester
25-26-27 ...... Syracuse
JUNE
4-5 .... Pawtucket
6-7 .... Richmond
8-9-10-11 ..... Tidewater
12-13-14 ...... Columbus
22-23-24-25 ..... Toledo
JULY
3-4-5-6 .... Syracuse
7-8-9-10 ...... Rochester
25-26-27-28 ... Pawtucket
29-30-31 ...... Columbus
AUGUST
1-2 .... Columbus
3-4-5 .... Toledo
11-12-13-14 ... Pawtucket
22-23-24-25-26 Richmond
27-28-29-30 ... Tidewater

Syracuse
APRIL
15-16 .... Scranton
17-18-19 ...... Pawtucket
30 .... Tidewater
MAY
1-2-3 .... Tidewater
4-5 .... Richmond
11-12-13 .... Columbus
14-15 .... Toledo
16 .... Rochester
20 .... Rochester
28 .... Rochester
29-30-31 ...... Pawtucket
JUNE
1-2-3 .... Scranton
12-13-14 ...... Rochester
16-17 .... Columbus
18-19-20-21 ..... Toledo
27-28 .... Tidewater
29-30 .... Richmond
JULY
1-2 .... Richmond
11-12 .... Rochester
16-17-18-19 ... Pawtucket
20-21-22-23-24 . Scranton
AUGUST
3-4-5-6 .... Richmond
7-8-9-10 ...... Tidewater
22-23-24-25 ..... Toledo
26-27-28-29-30 Columbus
SEPTEMBER
2-3 .... Rochester
6-7 .... Rochester

148 • 1992 DIRECTORY

PACIFIC COAST LEAGUE / 1992 SCHEDULE

Tidewater

APRIL
9-10-11 .... Toledo
12-13-14 ...... Columbus
21-22-23 ...... Syracuse
24-25-26 ...... Rochester

MAY
9-10-11 ...... Scranton
12-13-14-15 ... Pawtucket
16 .... Richmond
25-25-26-27 .. Columbus
29-30-31 .... Toledo

JUNE
1 .... Toledo
13-14 .... Richmond
16-17-18 ...... Pawtucket
19-20-21 .... Scranton
22-23-24 ...... Syracuse
25-26 .... Rochester

JULY
3 .... Richmond
5-6-7 .... Columbus

8-9-10 .... Toledo
11-12-13 ...... Richmond
25-26-27-28-29 Rochester
30-31 .... Syracuse

AUGUST
1-2 .... Syracuse
12 .... Richmond
15-16-17 ...... Pawtucket
18-19-20-21 ... Scranton

SEPTEMBER
1 .... Richmond
4 .... Richmond
6-7 .... Richmond

Toledo

APRIL
16-17 .... Tidewater
18-19-20 ...... Richmond
28-29 .... Columbus

MAY
1-2-3 .... Pawtucket
4-5 .... Scranton
6-7-8 .... Rochester

9-10 .... Syracuse
18 .... Columbus
19-20-21 ...... Richmond
22-23-24 ...... Tidewater

JUNE
3-4-5 .... Columbus
6-7-8 .... Syracuse
9-10-11 .... Rochester
26-27-28 ..... Pawtucket
29-30 .... Scranton

JULY
1-2 .... Scranton
11-12-13 ...... Columbus
16-17-18-19-20 . Tidewater
21-22-23-24 ... Richmond

AUGUST
6-7-8 .... Columbus
12-13-14-15-16 . Syracuse
17-18-19-21 ... Rochester
31 .... Scranton

SEPTEMBER
1-2-3 .... Scranton
4-5-6-7 .... Pawtucket

Pacific Coast League

Albuquerque

APRIL
9-10-11-12 .... Las Vegas
14-15-16-17 ...... Tacoma
23-24-25-26 ...... Phoenix
28-29-30 .... Calgary

MAY
1 .... Calgary
16-17-18-19-20 ...... L.V.
21-21-22-23-24 ...... C.S.

JUNE
4-5-6-7-8 .... Tucson
18-19-20-21 ...... Tucson
22-23-24-25 Colo. Springs

JULY
4-5-6-7-8 .... Phoenix
9-10-11-12 ...... Edmonton
25-26-27-28 ..... Phoenix

AUGUST
7-8-9-10 ...... Vancouver
11-12-13-14 Colo. Springs
27-28-29-30 ...... Tucson
31 .... Las Vegas

SEPTEMBER
1-2-3 .... Las Vegas
4-5-6-7 .... Portland

Calgary

APRIL
9-10-11-12 .. Colo. Springs
13-14-15-16-17 .. Portland

MAY
2-3-4-5 .... Tacoma
6-7-8-9-10 ..... Edmonton
16-17-18-19-20 .. Tacoma
21-22-23-24 ... Edmonton

JUNE
8-9-10-11-12 ... Vancouver
22-23-24-25 ..... Phoenix
26-27-28-29 . Albuquerque
30 .... Tucson

JULY
1-2-3 .... Tucson
16-17-18-19 ... Vancouver
21-22-23-24 ...... Tacoma
30-31 .... Portland

AUGUST
1-2 .... Portland
3-4-5-6 .... Las Vegas
15-16-17-18 .... Edmonton
19-20-21-22 ... Edmonton

SEPTEMBER
4-5-6-7 .... Vancouver

Colo. Springs

APRIL
18-19-20-21-22 . Albuquerque
28-29-30 .... Tucson

MAY
1 .... Tucson
2-3-4-5-6 ...... Las Vegas
16-17-18-19 ...... Tucson
30-31 .... Albuquerque

JUNE
1-2 .... Albuquerque
4-5-6-7 .... Las Vegas
9-10-11-12 ...... Phoenix
18-19-20-21 ...... Tacoma
26-27-28-29 ..... Portland

JULY
4-5-6-7 .... Edmonton
9-10-11-12 .... Las Vegas
29-30-31 .... Phoenix

AUGUST
1-2 .... Phoenix
3-4-5-6 .... Vancouver
15-16-17-18 ..... Phoenix
19-20-21-22 . Albuquerque
23-24-25-26 ...... Calgary

SEPTEMBER
4-5-6-7 .... Tucson

Edmonton

APRIL
11-12-12 .... Portland
14-15-17-17 .... C.S.
28-29-30 .... Tacoma

MAY
1 .... Tacoma
11-12-13-14-15 .. Port.
16-17-18-19-20 ... Van.
25-26-27-28-29 . Calgary

JUNE
13-14-15-16 ... Vancouver
18-19-20-21 ..... Phoenix
26-27-28-29 ..... Tucson
30 .... Albuquerque

JULY
1-2-3 .... Albuquerque
16-17-18-19-20 .. Tacoma
30-31 .... Tacoma

AUGUST
1-2 .... Tacoma
7-8-9-10 ...... Las Vegas
11-12-13-14 ..... Calgary
23-24-25-26 .... Portland
27-28-29-30 ... Vancouver
31 .... Calgary

SEPTEMBER
1-2-3 .... Calgary

Las Vegas

APRIL
14-15-16-17 ...... Tucson
18-19-20-21-22 . Phoenix
23-24-25-26 ..... Calgary

MAY
7-8-9-10-11 ...... Tucson
12-13-14-15 .. Colo. Springs
25-26-27-28-29 .... C.S.
30-31 .... Edmonton

JUNE
1-2 .... Edmonton
9-10-11-12 .. Albuquerque
26-27-28-29 ..... Phoenix
30 .... Portland

JULY
1-2-3 .... Portland
16-17-18-19 ...... Tucson
20-21-22-23-24 Albuquerque
30-31 .... Vancouver

AUGUST
1-2 .... Vancouver
15-16-17-18 ..... Tacoma
23-24-25-26 . Albuquerque
27-28-29-30 Colo. Springs

SEPTEMBER
4-5-6-7 .... Phoenix

Phoenix

APRIL
9-10-11-12 .... Tacoma
14-15-16-17 ... Vancouver
27-28-29-30 ... Las Vegas

MAY
1 .... Las Vegas
7-8-9-10-11 ... Colo. Springs
12-13-14-15 ...... Tucson
30-31 .... Tucson

JUNE
1-2-3 .... Tucson
4-5-6-7 .... Edmonton
13-14-15-16-17 Albuquerque
30 .... Colorado Springs

JULY
1-2-3 ..... Colorado Springs
16-17-18-19 . Albuquerque
21-22-23-24 ..... Tucson

AUGUST
3-4-5-6 ..... Albuquerque
7-8-9-10 .... Colo. Springs
11-12-13-14 ... Las Vegas
19-20-21-22 ... Las Vegas
27-28-29-30 ..... Calgary
31 .... Portland

HOME GAMES ONLY

1992 DIRECTORY • 149

HOME GAMES ONLY

Portland

APRIL
23-24-25-26-27 ... Edmonton
28-29-30 .... Vancouver

MAY
1 .... Vancouver
2-3-4-5 ..... Albuquerque
16-17-18-19 ..... Phoenix
25-26-27-28-29 . Vancouver
30-31 .... Calgary

JUNE
1-2 .... Calgary
8-9-10-11-12 ..... Tacoma
13-14-15-16 ..... Calgary
18-19-20-21 ... Las Vegas

JULY
4-5-6-7 .... Tacoma
16-17-18-19 Colo. Springs
21-22-23-24 .... Edmonton
25-26-27-28-29 .. Calgary

AUGUST
3-4-5-6 .... Edmonton
7-8-9-10 .... Tucson
13-14 .... Tacoma
19-20-21-22 ... Vancouver
29-30 .... Tacoma

Tacoma

APRIL
18-19-20-21-22 .. Edmonton
23-24-25-26-27 . Vancouver

MAY
6-7-8-9-10 .... Portland
12-13-14-15 ... Albuquerque
21-22-23-24 ..... Portland
26-27-28-29 ..... Phoenix

JUNE
4-5-6-7 .... Calgary
13-14-15-16 ... Las Vegas
22-23-24-25 .... Edmonton
30 .... Vancouver

JULY
1-2-3 .... Vancouver
8-9-10-11-12 ..... Calgary
25-26-27-28 Colo. Springs

AUGUST
3-4-5-6 .... Tucson
7-8-9-10 .... Calgary
11-12-13-14 ..... Portland
23-24-25-26 ... Vancouver

SEPTEMBER
4-5-6-7 .... Edmonton

Tucson

APRIL
9-10-11-12 .... Vancouver
18-19-20-21 ..... Calgary
23-24-25-26 .. Colo. Springs

MAY
2-3-4-5-6 .... Phoenix
21-22-23-24 ... Las Vegas
25-26-27-28-29 Albuquerque

JUNE
9-10-11-12 ..... Edmonton
13-14-15-16-17 ...... C.S.
22-23-24-25 ..... Portland

JULY
4-5-6-7-8 ..... Las Vegas
9-10-11-12 ...... Phoenix

25-26-27-28 ... Las Vegas
30-31 .... Albuquerque

AUGUST
1-2 .... Albuquerque
15-16-17-18 . Albuquerque
19-20-21-22 ..... Tacoma
23-24-25-26 ..... Phoenix
31 .... Colo. Springs

SEPTEMBER
1-2-3 .... Colo. Springs

Vancouver

APRIL
18-19-20-21 ..... Portland

MAY
2-3-4-5 .... Edmonton
7-8-9-10 .... Albuquerque
12-13-14-15 ..... Calgary
21-22-23-24 ..... Phoenix
30-31 .... Tacoma

JUNE
1-2-3 .... Tacoma
4-5-6-7 .... Portland
17-18-19-20-21 .. Calgary
22-23-24-25 ... Las Vegas
26-27-28-29 ..... Tacoma

JULY
4-5-6-7 .... Calgary
8-9-10-11-12 .... Portland
21-22-23-24 . Colo. Springs
25-26-27-28-29 . Edmonton

AUGUST
11-12-13-14 ...... Tucson
15-16-17-18 .... Edmonton
31 .... Tacoma

SEPTEMBER
1-2-3 .... Tacoma

CLASS AA
Eastern League

Albany

APRIL
13-14-15-16 .. New Britain
17-18-19 .... Reading
24-25-26 .... London

MAY
1-2-3 .... Canton
4-5-6 .... Harrisburg
13-14-15 ..... Binghamton
16-17-18 ..... Hagerstown
29-30-31 .... New Britain

JUNE
1-2-3-4 .... Reading
8-9-10 .... London
15-16-17 .... Canton
18-19-20-21 .. Harrisburg

JULY
3-4-5 .... Hagerstown
6-7-8 .... Binghamton
15-16-17 .... Reading
18-19-20 .... New Britain
27-28-29-30 ..... London

AUGUST
3-4-5-6 .... Canton
7-8-9 .... Harrisburg
18-19-20-21 .. Hagerstown
22-23-24-25 .. Binghamton

Binghamton

APRIL
16-17-18-19 .. Harrisburg
24-25-26 ..... Hagerstown
27-28-29-30 ..... Canton

MAY
7-8 .... Reading
9-10-11-12 .. New Britain
20-21 .... Albany
22-23-24 .... London
25-26-27-28 .. Harrisburg
29-30-31 .... Hagerstown

JUNE
12-13-14 .... Canton
22-23-24-25 .... Reading
26-27-28 .... New Britain
29-30 .... Albany

JULY
1-2 .... Albany
9-10-11-12 ...... London
15-16 .... Harrisburg
17-18-19-20 .. Hagerstown
31 .... Canton

AUGUST
1-2 .... Canton
11-12-13-14 .... Reading
15-16-17 .... New Britain
26-27-28 .... London
29-30-31 .... Albany

SEPTEMBER
1 .... Albany

Canton

APRIL
17-18-19 ..... Hagerstown
20-21-22-23 .. Binghamton
24-25-26 ..... Harrisburg

MAY
7-8 .... Albany
9-10-11-12 ...... London
13-14 .... New Britain
22-23-24-25 .... Reading

JUNE
1-2-3-4 ...... Hagerstown
5-6-7 .... Binghamton
8-9-10 .... Harrisburg
22-23-24-25 ..... Albany
26-27-28 .... London
29-30 .... New Britain

JULY
1-2-3 .... New Britain
4-5-6 .... Reading
15-16-16 ..... Hagerstown

24-25-26 ..... Binghamton
27-28-29-30 .. Harrisburg

AUGUST
11-12-13-14 ..... Albany
15-16-17 .... London
18-19-20 .... New Britain
30-31 .... Reading

SEPTEMBER
1 .... Reading

Hagerstown

APRIL
9-10-11-12 ...... Canton
13-14-15 ..... Binghamton
20-21-22-23 ... Harrisburg

MAY
1-2-3 .... New Britain
9-10-11-12 ..... Reading
19-20-21 .... London
22-23-24-25 ..... Albany
26-27-28 .... Canton

JUNE
5-6-7 .... Harrisburg
8-9-10 .... Binghamton
15-16-17 .... New Britain
26-27-28 .... Reading

JULY
6-7-8 .... London
10-11-12 .... Albany
21-22-23 .... Canton
24-25-26 ..... Harrisburg
27-28-29-30 .. Binghamton

AUGUST
3-4-5-6 ..... New Britain
15-16-17 .... Reading
26-27-28 .... Albany
29-30-31 .... London

SEPTEMBER
1 .... London

SOUTHERN LEAGUE/1992 SCHEDULE

Harrisburg
APRIL
9-10-11-12 ... Binghamton
13-14-15 .... Canton
27-28-29-30 .. Hagerstown
MAY
7-8 .... London
9-10-11-12 .... Albany
15-16-17 ..... New Britain
18-19 .... Reading
29-30-31 .... Canton
JUNE
2-3-4 .... Binghamton
12-13-14 ..... Hagerstown
22-23-24-25 ..... London
26-27-28 .... Albany
JULY
4-5-6 .... New Britain
7-8-9 .... Reading
17-18-19-20 ..... Canton
21-22-23 ..... Binghamton
31 .... Hagerstown
AUGUST
1-2 .... Hagerstown
11-12-13-14 ..... London
15-16-17 .... Albany
21-22-23-24 .. New Britain
25-26-27-28-29 .. Reading

London
APRIL
10-11-12 ..... New Britain
13-14-15-16 ..... Reading
28-29-30 .... Albany
MAY
1-2-3 .... Harrisburg
4-5-6 .... Canton
14-15 .... Hagerstown
16-17-18 .... Binghamton
25-26-27-28 .. New Britain

29-30-31 .... Reading
JUNE
11-12-13-14 ...... Albany
15-16-17 ...... Harrisburg
18-19-20-21 ..... Canton
29-30 .... Hagerstown
JULY
1-2 .... Hagerstown
3-4-5 .... Binghamton
15-16-17 ..... New Britain
18-19-20 .... Reading
31 .... Albany
AUGUST
1-2 .... Albany
3-4-5-6 .... Harrisburg
7-8-9 .... Canton
18-19-20-21 .. Binghamton
22-23-24-25 .. Hagerstown

New Britain
APRIL
17-18-19 .... London
20-21-22-23 ...... Albany
24-25-26 .... Reading
MAY
4-5-6 .... Binghamton
7-8 .... Hagerstown
18-19-20 .... Canton
21-22-23-24 ... Harrisburg
JUNE
1-2-3-4 .... London
5-6-7 .... Albany
8-9-10 .... Reading
18-19-20-21 .. Binghamton
22-23-24-25 .. Hagerstown
JULY
8-9 .... Canton
10-11-12 ...... Harrisburg
21-22-23 .... London
24-25-26 .... Albany

27-28-29-30 ..... Reading
AUGUST
7-8-9 .... Binghamton
11-12-13-14 .. Hagerstown
25-26-27-28-29 ... Canton
30-31 .... Harrisburg
SEPTEMBER
1 .... Harrisburg

Reading
APRIL
9-10-11-12 .... Albany
20-21-22-23 ..... London
28-29-30 ..... New Britain
MAY
1-2-3 .... Binghamton
4-5-6 .... Hagerstown
13 .... Harrisburg
15-16-17 .... Canton
20 . Harrisburg (at Scranton)
26-27-28 .... Albany
JUNE
5-6-7 .... London
11-12-13-14 .. New Britain
15-16-17 ..... Binghamton
18-19-20-21 .. Hagerstown
29-30 .... Harrisburg
JULY
1-2-3 .... Harrisburg
10-11-12 .... Canton
21-22-23 .... Albany
24-25-26 .... London
31 .... New Britain
AUGUST
1-2 .... New Britain
3-4-5-6 ...... Binghamton
7-8-9 .... Hagerstown
18-19-20 ..... Harrisburg
21-22-23-24 ..... Canton

Southern League

Birmingham
APRIL
9-10-11-12 ...... Carolina
13-14-15-16 .... Knoxville
22-23-24 .... Charlotte
MAY
2-3 .... Huntsville
6-7-8 .... Greenville
13-14-15-16 ..... Memphis
17-18 .... Huntsville
28-29-30-31 . Jacksonville
JUNE
9-10-11 ...... Chattanooga
15-16-17 .... Orlando
18-19-20 .... Chattanooga
23-24-25 .... Carolina
26-27-28-29 .... Knoxville
JULY
4-5-6-7 .... Charlotte
8-9 .... Chattanooga
22-23-24-25 ... Greenville
26 .... Chattanooga
30-31 .... Memphis
AUGUST
1-2 .... Memphis
3-3-4-5 .... Huntsville
14-15-16 ..... Jacksonville
25-26-27-28 . Chattanooga
SEPTEMBER
2-3-4-5 .... Orlando

Carolina
APRIL
17-18-19-20 .. Jacksonville
21-22-23-24 ..... Orlando
MAY
5 .... Charlotte
6-7-8 .... Chattanooga
9-9-10 .... Charlotte

13-14-15-16 ... Greenville
17-18-19-20 .... Knoxville
JUNE
2-2-3 .... Charlotte
4-5-6 .... Memphis
12-13-14 ..... Birmingham
15-16-17-18 ... Huntsville
30 .... Jacksonville
JULY
1-2-3 .... Jacksonville
4-5-5-6 .... Orlando
11-12 .... Charlotte
22-23-24-25 . Chattanooga
30-31 .... Greenville
AUGUST
1-2 .... Greenville
3-4-5 .... Knoxville
17-18-19-20 .... Charlotte
21-22-23-24 ..... Memphis
29-30-31 ..... Birmingham
SEPTEMBER
1 .... Birmingham
3-4-5 .... Huntsville

Charlotte
APRIL
17-18-19-20 ..... Orlando
25-26 .... Carolina
28-29-30 .... Huntsville
MAY
1 .... Huntsville
2-3-4 .... Memphis
12 .... Carolina
21-22-23-24 ... Greenville
25-25-26-27 .. Birmingham
29-30-31 .... Chattanooga
JUNE
1 .... Carolina
4-5-6 .... Knoxville
15-16-17-18 . Jacksonville
19-20 .... Carolina

22-23 .... Greenville
26-27-28-29 . Chattanooga
30 .... Orlando
JULY
1-2-3 .... Orlando
8-9-10 .... Carolina
15-16-17 ...... Huntsville
18-19-20-21 ..... Memphis
26-27-28-29 ..... Carolina
AUGUST
8-9 .... Greenville
10-11-12 ..... Birmingham
21-22-23-24 .... Knoxville
SEPTEMBER
2-3-4-5 ..... Jacksonville

Chattanooga
APRIL
9-10-11-12 ..... Knoxville
13-14-15-16 .... Charlotte
25-26-27 ..... Birmingham
28-29-20 .... Memphis
MAY
1 .... Memphis
9-10-11-12 ... Birmingham
14-15-16 .... Orlando
21-22-22-23 ..... Carolina
JUNE
5-6-7-8 .... Huntsville
12-13-14 ..... Jacksonville
15-15-16-17 ... Greenville
22-23-24-25 .... Knoxville
JULY
2-3 .... Huntsville
10-11-12 ..... Birmingham
15-15-16-17 ..... Memphis
18-19-20-21 ... Greenville
27-28-29 ..... Birmingham
AUGUST
7-8-9 .... Carolina
10-11-12-13 ..... Orlando

1992 DIRECTORY • 151

HOME GAMES ONLY

Greenville

APRIL
9-10-11-12 ..... Charlotte
13-14-15-16 ..... Carolina
19-20 .... Knoxville
25-26 .... Knoxville
28-29-30 ..... Birmingham

MAY
1 .... Birmingham
2-3-4-5 ..... Chattanooga
18-19-20 ...... Memphis
25-25-26-27 . Jacksonville
28-29-30-31 ..... Orlando

JUNE
9-10-11 .... Huntsville
19-20 .... Knoxville
24-25 .... Charlotte
26-27-28-29 ..... Carolina

JULY
10-11-12 ...... Knoxville
15-16-17 ..... Birmingham
27-28-29 ...... Knoxville

AUGUST
3-4-5 .... Memphis
6-7 .... Charlotte
10-11-12-13 . Jacksonville
14-14-15-16 ..... Orlando
25-26-27-28 ... Huntsville

SEPTEMBER
3-4-5 .... Chattanooga

Huntsville

APRIL
17-18-19-20 . Chattanooga
21-22-23-24 ... Greenville
27 .... Memphis

MAY
4-5 .... Birmingham
6-7-8 .... Orlando
9-10-11-12 .. Jacksonville
19-20 .... Birmingham
25-26-27-28 ... Knoxville
29-30-31 .... Carolina

JUNE
1-1-2-3 .... Memphis
12-13-14 .... Charlotte
19-20 .... Memphis
30 .... Chattanooga

JULY
1 .... Chattanooga
4-5-6 .... Greenville
10-11-12 .... Memphis
18-19-20-21 .. Birmingham
23-24-25-26 ..... Orlando
27-28-29 .... Jacksonville

AUGUST
9-10-11-12 ..... Knoxville
13-14-15-16 ..... Carolina

Jacksonville

APRIL
9-10-11-12 ...... Memphis
13-14-15 ...... Huntsville
25-25-26 .... Orlando
27-28-29 ...... Knoxville

MAY
1-2-3-4 .... Carolina
13-14-15-16 .... Charlotte
17-18-19-20 . Chattanooga

JUNE
1-2-3-4 .... Greenville
5-6-7 .... Birmingham
9-10-11 .... Orlando
22-23-24-25 ... Huntsville
26-27-28 .... Memphis

JULY
10-11-12 .... Orlando
15-16-17-18 ... Knoxville
19-19-20-21 .... Carolina
30-31 .... Charlotte

AUGUST
1-2 .... Charlotte
3-4-5 .... Chattanooga
8-9 .... Orlando
17-18-19-20 ... Greenville
21-22-23-24 . Birmingham
27-28 .... Orlando

Knoxville

APRIL
17-18 .... Greenville
21-22-23-24 . Jacksonville

MAY
6-6-7-8 .... Charlotte
9-10-11-12 .... Greenville
13-14-15-16 ... Huntsville
21-22-23-24 .. Birmingham

JUNE
1-1-2-3 ..... Chattanooga
8-9-10 .... Carolina
12-13-14 .... Orlando
15-16-17-18 .... Memphis

JULY
1-2-3 .... Greenville
4-5-6 .... Jacksonville
7-8-9 .... Greenville
23-24-25 ...... Charlotte
30-31 .... Huntsville

AUGUST
1-2 .... Huntsville
6-6-7-8 ...... Birmingham
17-18-19-20 . Chattanooga
25-26-27-28 .... Carolina
29-30-31 .... Orlando

SEPTEMBER
1 .... Orlando

Memphis

APRIL
17-18-19-20 .. Birmingham
21-22-23-24 . Chattanooga
25-26 .... Huntsville

MAY
6-7-8 .... Jacksonville
9-10-11-12 ..... Orlando
21-22-23-24 ... Huntsville
25-26-27-28 .... Carolina
29-29-30-31 ... Knoxville

JUNE
8-9-10-11 ..... Charlotte
12-13-14 ...... Greenville
30 .... Birmingham

JULY
1-2-3 .... Birmingham
4-5-5-6 ..... Chattanooga
7-8-9 .... Huntsville
23-24-25-26 . Jacksonville
27-28-29 .... Orlando

AUGUST
6-7-8 .... Huntsville
10-11-12 ...... Carolina
13-14-15-16 ... Knoxville
17 .... Huntsville
26-27-28 ...... Charlotte
29-30-31 ...... Greenville

SEPTEMBER
1 .... Greenville

Orlando

APRIL
9-10-11-12 .... Huntsville
13-14-15 ...... Memphis
27-28-29-30 .... Carolina

MAY
1-2-3-4 .... Knoxville
17-18-19-20 ... Charlotte
21-21-22-23 . Jacksonville
25-25-26-27 . Chattanooga

JUNE
1-2-3-4 ...... Birmingham
5-6-7-8 .... Greenville
19-20-21 .... Jacksonville
22-23-24-25 .... Memphis
26-27-28 ...... Huntsville

JULY
8-9 .... Jacksonville
15-16-17-18 .... Carolina
19-20-21 ...... Knoxville
31 .... Chattanooga

AUGUST
1-2 .... Chattanooga
3-3-4-5 .... Charlotte
6-7 .... Jacksonville
18-19-20 .... Birmingham
21-22-23-24 ... Greenville
25-26 .... Jacksonville

Texas League

Arkansas

APRIL
10-11-11-13-14 ... Shreveport
25-25-27-28-29 .... Tulsa
30 .... Jackson

MAY
1-2-2-4 .... Jackson
11-12-13-14-15 ..... Midland
16-16-18-19-20 ..... El Paso

JUNE
2-3-4-5-6-6 ...... Shreveport
15-16-17-18-19-19 .... Jack.

JULY
2-3-4-4-6-7 .... Tulsa
22-23-24-25-25 .... S.A.
27-28-29-30-31 .... Wichita

AUGUST
7-8-8-10-11 .... Tulsa
12-13-14-15-15 ... Jackson
27-28-29-29-31 . Shreveport

El Paso

APRIL
15-16-17-18-19 .. Midland
20-21-22-23-24 ... Wichita

MAY
5-6-7-8-9 .... San Antonio
22-23-24-25-26 ... Jackson
27-28-29-30-31 . Arkansas

JUNE
8-9-10-11-12-13 .. Midland
14-15-16-17-18-19 .. Wichita

JULY
2-3-4-5-6-7 .. San Antonio
22-23-24-25-26 . Shreveport
27-28-29-30-31 ...... Tulsa

AUGUST
12-13-14-15-16 ... Wichita
17-18-19-20-21 .. Midland
27-27-28-29-30 ...... S.A

Jackson

APRIL
10-11-12-13-14 ..... Tulsa
20-21-22-23-24 .. Arkansas
25-26-27-28-29 ... Shreve.

MAY
11-12-13-14-15 ... El Paso
16-17-18-19-20 .. Midland

152 • 1992 DIRECTORY

CALIFORNIA LEAGUE/1992 SCHEDULE

JUNE
2-3-4-5-6-7 ....Tulsa
20-21-22-23-24-25 .Arkansas
JULY
2-3-4-5-6-7 ...Shreveport
22-23-24-25-26 ...Wichita
27-28-29-30-31 .....S.A.
AUGUST
7-8-9-10-11 ...Shreveport
22-23-24-25-26 .Arkansas
27-28-29-30-31 .....Tulsa

Midland
APRIL
20-21-22-23-24 ......S.A.
30 ....El Paso
MAY
1-2-3-4 ....El Paso
6-7-8-9-10 ....Wichita
22-23-24-25-26 .Arkansas
27-28-29-30-31 ..Jackson
JUNE
14-15-16-17-18-19 ...S.A.
20-21-22-23-24-25 .El Paso
JULY
2-3-4-5-6-7 ....Wichita
22-23-24-25-26 .....Tulsa
27-28-29-30-31 ...Shreve.
AUGUST
6-7-8-9-10 ....El Paso
12-13-14-15-16 ......S.A.
27-28-29-30-31 ...Wichita

San Antonio
APRIL
10-11-12-13-14 ..Midland
26-27-28-29.....El Paso
30 ....Wichita
MAY
1-2-3-4..........Wichita

11-12-13-14-15.....Tulsa
16-17-18-19-20 ..Shreveport
JUNE
2-3-4-5-6-7 ......Midland
20-21-22-23-24-25 .Wich.
26-27-28-29-30..El Paso
JULY
1 ....El Paso
8-9-10-11-12 .....Arkansas
14-15-16-17-18 ..Jackson
AUGUST
1-2-3-4-5 ....El Paso
7-8-9-10-11 ......Wichita
22-23-24-25-26 ..Midland

Shreveport
APRIL
15-16-17-18-18 ..Jackson
30 ....Tulsa
MAY
1-2-3-4 ....Tulsa
5-6-7-8-9 ....Arkansas
22-23-24-25-26 ...Wichita
27-28-29-30-31 .....S.A.
JUNE
8-9-10-12-13-13 .Jackson
14-15-16-17-18-19 .Tulsa
26-27-28-29-30 .Arkansas
JULY
1 ....Arkansas
8-9-10-11-12 ....El Paso
14-15-16-17-18 ..Midland
AUGUST
1-2-3-4-5 ....Arkansas
17-18-19-20-21 ..Jackson
22-23-24-25-26 .....Tulsa

Tulsa
APRIL
15-16-17-18-19 .Arkansas

20-21-22-23...Shreveport
MAY
5-6-7-8-9........Jackson
22-23-24-25-26 .....S.A.
27-28-29-30-31 ...Wichita
JUNE
8-9-10-11-12-13 Arkansas
20-21-22-23-24-25 Shreveport
26-27-28-29-30 ..Jackson
JULY
1 ....Jackson
8-9-10-11-12.....Midland
15-16-17-18-18...El Paso
AUGUST
1-2-3-4-5........Jackson
12-13-14-15-15-16 ...Shr.
17-18-19-20-21 .Arkansas

Wichita
APRIL
10-11-12-13-14...El Paso
15-16-17-18-19 .....S.A.
25-26-27-28-29 ..Midland
MAY
11-12-13-14-15...Shreve.
16-17-18-19-20 .....Tulsa
JUNE
2-3-4-5-6-7 ......El Paso
8-9-10-11-12-13 .....S.A.
26-27-28-29-30 ..Midland
JULY
1 ....Midland
8-9-10-11-12 ...Jackson
14-15-16-17-18 .Arkansas
AUGUST
1-2-3-4-5 ....Midland
17-18-19-20-21 ......S.A.
22-23-24-25-26...El Paso

CLASS A
California League

Bakersfield
APRIL
9-10 ....High Desert
11-12-13....Palm Springs
17-18-19 .San Bernardino
21-22-23 ......San Jose
MAY
1-2-3-3 ....Visalia
5-6-7 ....High Desert
14-15-16-17 .........S.B.
18 ....Visalia
27-28-29 ....Reno
30-31 ....Stockton
JUNE
1 ....Stockton
9-10-11 ....Salinas
12-13-14 ....Modesto
19 ....Reno
30 ....Stockton
JULY
1-2 ....Stockton
7-8-9 ....Visalia
10-11-12-12 ..High Desert
16-17........Palm Springs
18-19-20 ....Salinas
27-28-29-30 Palm Springs
AUGUST
7-8 ....Reno
11-12-13 ....San Jose
14-15-16 .San Bernardino
19-20 ....Visalia
21-22-23 ....Modesto

High Desert
APRIL
14-15-16......Bakersfield

17-18-19 ....Salinas
20-21-22 ....Modesto
30 ....Bakersfield
MAY
2-3-4 ....San Jose
8-9-10-10 ....Visalia
12-13-14 ....Reno
18-18-19-20..Palm Springs
27-28-29 ....Stockton
30-31 .....San Bernardino
JUNE
1 ....San Bernardino
12-13-14....Palm Springs
15-16 ....Bakersfield
20-21-22 ....Reno
23 ....Palm Springs
29-30 .....San Bernardino
JULY
1-2 ....San Bernardino
3-4-5 ....Visalia
7-8-9 ....San Jose
16-17......San Bernardino
18-19-20....Palm Springs
24-25-26 ......Bakersfield
28-29-30 ....Stockton
AUGUST
10-11-12 ....Modesto
14-15-16 ....Salinas
21-22-23 ....Visalia

Modesto
APRIL
9-10 ....Stockton
11-12-13 ....Reno
24-25-26 .San Bernardino
27-28-29 .....High Desert
30 ....Stockton

MAY
1-2-3 ....Stockton
14-15-16-17 .....Salinas
18 ....Stockton
19-20-21-22.......Visalia
27-28-29 ....San Jose
30-31 ....Palm Springs
JUNE
1 ....Palm Springs
2-3-4 ....Bakersfield
7-8 ....Salinas
19-20-21 ....Stockton
23-24-25 ......Bakersfield
JULY
1-2 ....San Jose
6-7-8 ....Palm Springs
16-17............Visalia
18-19-20 ....Reno
21-22-23 .San Bernardino
26 ....San Jose
31 ....High Desert
AUGUST
1-2 ....High Desert
14-15-16 ....San Jose
17-18-19-20 ....Reno
25-26-27 ....Salinas

Palm Springs
APRIL
14-15-16 ....Salinas
17-18-19 ....Modesto
MAY
1-2 ......San Bernardino
4-5-6 ....Visalia
8-9-10 ....San Jose
11 ....High Desert
15-16-17 ....Reno

1992 DIRECTORY • 153

HOME GAMES ONLY

CAROLINA LEAGUE/1992 SCHEDULE

22-23-24	Stockton
25-25-26	High Desert
27-28-29	San Bernardino
JUNE	
6-7-8	Bakersfield
9-10-11	Visalia
15-16	San Bernardino
19	San Bernardino
24-25	High Desert
26-27-28	Reno
JULY	
10-11-12	San Jose
13	High Desert
15	High Desert
20	High Desert
21-22-23	Bakersfield
24-25-26	Visalia
31	Stockton
AUGUST	
1-2	Stockton
4-5-6	Modesto
17-18-19	Salinas
21-22	San Bernardino
28-29-30	Bakersfield

Reno
APRIL
14-15-16	San Jose
17-18-19	Visalia
24-25-26	Palm Springs

MAY
4-5-6-7	Modesto
8-9-10	Bakersfield
22-23-24	Salinas
25-26	Modesto

JUNE
5-6-7	High Desert
8-9-10	San Bernardino
12-13-14-14	San Jose
15-16	Stockton
30	Salinas

JULY
1-2	Salinas
7-8-9	Stockton
10-11-12	San Bernardino
13-14-15-15	Modesto
24-25-26	Salinas
28-29-30	San Jose
31	Bakersfield

AUGUST
1-2	Bakersfield
11-12-13	Visalia
14-15-16	Palm Springs
24-25-26-27	Stockton
28-29-30	High Desert

Salinas
APRIL
9-10	Reno
21-22-23	Palm Springs
24-25-26	Stockton

MAY
1-2-3-3	Reno
4-5	Stockton
8-9-10	San Bernardino
11-12-13	Bakersfield
18-19-20-21	San Jose
27-28-29	Visalia
30-31	San Jose

JUNE
| 3-4 | High Desert |

5-6	Modesto
15-16	Modesto
20-21-22	Bakersfield
26-27-28	Modesto

JULY
3-4-5	Palm Springs
7-8-9	San Bernardino
14-15	Stockton
21-22-23	Reno
28-29-30	Modesto

AUGUST
3-4-5-6	High Desert
7-8-9	Visalia
21-22-23	Stockton
28-29-30	San Jose

San Bernardino
APRIL
9-10	Palm Springs
11-12-13	Salinas
14-15-16	Modesto
27-28-29	Bakersfield
30	Palm Springs

MAY
3-3	Palm Springs
5-6-7	San Jose
18-19-20	Reno
21-22-23-24	High Desert
25-26	Stockton

JUNE
2-3-4	Visalia
12-13-14	Visalia
20-21-22	Palm Springs
23-24-25	Reno
26-27-28	High Desert

JULY
3-4-5-6	Bakersfield
13-14-15	San Jose
27-28-29	Visalia

AUGUST
3-4-5-6	Stockton
7-8-9	Modesto
11-12-13	Salinas
18-19	High Desert
23-24	Palm Springs
25-26-27	Bakersfield

San Jose
APRIL
17-18-19	Stockton
24-25-26	High Desert
27-28-29-30	Reno

MAY
11-12-13	Modesto
15-16-17	Stockton
22-23-24	Bakersfield
25-25-26	Salinas

JUNE
1	Salinas
2-3-4	Palm Springs
5-6-7	San Bernardino
9-10-11	Modesto
15-16	Visalia
26-27-28-29	Visalia
30	Modesto

JULY
3-4-5	Reno
16-17	Salinas
18-19-20	San Bernardino
24-25	Modesto
27	Salinas

| 31 | Salinas |

AUGUST
1-2	Salinas
3-4-5	Bakersfield
8-9-10	Palm Springs
18-19-20	Stockton
21-22-23	Reno
25-26-27	High Desert

Stockton
APRIL
11-12-12-13	San Jose
14-15-16	Visalia
20-21-22-23	Reno
27-28-29	Palm Springs

MAY
6-7	Salinas
8-9-10	Modesto
11-12-13	San Bernardino
19-20-21	Bakersfield

JUNE
2-3-4	Reno
8-9-10	High Desert
12-13-14	Salinas
23-24-25	San Jose
26-27-28	Bakersfield

JULY
3-4-5	Modesto
10-11-12-12-13	Salinas
16-17	Reno
21-22-23	San Jose
24-25-26	San Bernardino

AUGUST
7-8-9	High Desert
11-12-13	Palm Springs
14-15-16	Visalia
28-29-30	Modesto

Visalia
APRIL
9-10	San Jose
11-12-13	High Desert
20-21-22-23	S.B.
24-25-26-26	Bakersfield
28-29-30	Salinas

MAY
12-13-14	Palm Springs
15-16-17	High Desert
23-24	Modesto
25-26	Bakersfield
30-31	Reno

JUNE
1	Reno
5-6-7	Stockton
19-20-21-22	San Jose
23-24-25	Salinas
30	Palm Springs

JULY
1-2	Palm Springs
10-11-12-12	Modesto
14-15	Bakersfield
18-19-20	Stockton
21-22-23	High Desert
31	San Bernardino

AUGUST
1	San Bernardino
4-5-6	Reno
17-18	Bakersfield
24	High Deseet
25-26-27	Palm Springs
28-29-30	San Bernardino

Carolina League

Durham
APRIL
9-10-11-12	Kinston
13-14-15	Peninsula
23-24-25-26	Frederick
27-28-29	Lynchburg

MAY
| 7-8-9-10 | Winston-Salem |
| 14-15-16-17 | P.W. |

| 18-19-20 | Salem |
| 29-30-31 | Kinston |

JUNE
1-2-3-4	Peninsula
12-13-14	Frederick
15-16-17	Kinston
26-27-28	Winston-Salem

JULY
| 5-6-7 | Salem |

8-9-10	Prince William
15-16-17	Lynchburg
18-19-20	Peninsula
29-30-31	Frederick

AUGUST
1-2-3-4	Lynchburg
11-12-13	Winston-Salem
22-23-24-25	Salem
26-27-28	Prince William

154 • 1992 DIRECTORY

FLORIDA STATE LEAGUE/1992 SCHEDULE

Frederick
APRIL
13-14-15 .. Winston-Salem
16-17-18-19 ... Lynchburg
27-28-29 .... Salem
30 .... Peninsula
MAY
1-2-3 .... Peninsula
11-12-13 .... Durham
14-15-16-17 ..... Kinston
26-27-28 ... Prince William
JUNE
1-2-3-4 ... Winston-Salem
5-6-7 .... Lynchburg
15-16-17 .... Salem
19-20-21 .... Peninsula
29-30 .... Durham
JULY
1 .... Durham
2-3-4 .... Kinston
11-12-13 .. Prince William
15-16-17 ...... Lynchburg
18-19-20 .. Winston-Salem
AUGUST
1-2-3-4 .... Salem
5-6-7 .... Peninsula
14-15-16-17 ..... Durham
19-20-21 .... Kinston
29-30-31 ... Prince William
SEPTEMBER
1 .... Prince William

Kinston
APRIL
13-14-15 .... Salem
16-17-18-19 .... P.W.
27-28-29 .. Winston-Salem
30 .... Durham
MAY
1-2-3 .... Durham
7-8-9-10 .... Peninsula
11-12-13 ...... Lynchburg
21-22-23-24 .... Frederick
25-26-27-28 .... Peninsula
JUNE
1-2-3-4 .... Salem
5-6-7 ...... Prince William
15-16-17 .. Winston-Salem
19-20-21 .... Durham
29-30 .... Lynchburg
JULY
1 .... Lynchburg
8-9-10 .... Frederick
18-19-20 .... Salem
23-24-25 .. Prince William
AUGUST
1-2-3-4 ... Winston-Salem
5-6-7 .... Durham
14-15-16-17 ... Lynchburg
26-27-28 .... Frederick
29-30 .... Peninsula

Lynchburg
APRIL
9-10-11-12 ..... Frederick
20-21-22 .... Durham
23-24-25-26 ..... Kinston
MAY
4-5-6 ...... Prince William
7-8-9-10 .... Salem
14-15-16-17 .... Peninsula
18-19-20 .. Winston-Salem
29-30-31 .... Frederick
JUNE
8-9-10-11 .... Durham
12-13-14 .... Kinston
22-23-24-25 .... P.W.
26-27-28 .... Salem
JULY
2-3-4 .... Peninsula
5-6-7 ..... Winston-Salem
23-24-25 .... Frederick
26-27-28 .... Durham
29-30-31 .... Kinston
AUGUST
8-9-10 .... Prince William
11-12-13 .... Salem
19-20-21 ...... Peninsula
22-23-24-25 ...... W-S

Peninsula
APRIL
9-10-11-12 .... Salem
20-21-22 ... Prince William
23-24-25-26 .... W-S
MAY
4-5-6 .... Durham
18-19-20 .... Frederick
21-22-23-24 ... Lynchburg
29-30-31 .... Salem
JUNE
8-9-10-11 .. Prince William
12-13-14 .. Winston-Salem
22-23-24-25 ..... Durham
26-27-28 .... Kinston
JULY
5-6-7 .... Frederick
8-9-10 .... Lynchburg
11-12-13 .... Kinston
15-16-17 .... Salem
26-27-28 .. Prince William
29-30-31 .. Winston-Salem
AUGUST
8-9-10 .... Durham
11-12-13 .... Kinston
22-23-24-25 .... Frederick
26-27-28 ...... Lynchburg

Prince William
APRIL
9-10-11-12 .... W-S
13-14-15 ...... Lynchburg
23-24-25-26 ...... Salem
27-28-29 ...... Peninsula
MAY
7-8-9-10 .... Frederick
18-19-20 .... Kinston
21-22-23-24 ..... Durham
29-30-31 .. Winston-Salem
JUNE
1-2-3-4 .... Lynchburg
12-13-14 .... Salem
15-16-17 ...... Peninsula
26-27-28 .... Frederick
JULY
2-3-4 .... Durham
5-6-7 .... Kinston
15-16-17 .. Winston-Salem
18-19-20 ...... Lynchburg
29-30-31 .... Salem

AUGUST
1-2-3-4 .... Peninsula
11-12-13 .... Frederick
19-20-21 .... Durham
22-23-24-25 ..... Kinston

Salem
APRIL
16-17-18-19 ..... Durham
20-21-22 .... Kinston
30 .... Prince William
MAY
1-2-3 ..... Prince William
4-5-6 .... Frederick
11-12-13 ...... Peninsula
14-15-16-17 .... W-S
26-27-28 ...... Lynchburg
JUNE
5-6-7 .... Durham
8-9-10-11 .... Kinston
19-20-21 .. Prince William
22-23-24-25 .... Peninsula
29-30 .... Peninsula
JULY
1 .... Peninsula
8-9-10 .... Winston-Salem
11-12-13 ...... Lynchburg
23-24-25 .... Durham
26-27-28 .... Kinston
AUGUST
5-6-7 ..... Prince William
8-9-10 .... Frederick
14-15-16-17 .... Peninsula
26-27-28 .. Winston-Salem
29-30-31 ...... Lynchburg
SEPTEMBER
1 .... Lynchburg

Winston-Salem
APRIL
16-17-18-19 .... Peninsula
20-21-22 .... Frederick
30 .... Lynchburg
MAY
1-2-3 .... Lynchburg
4-5-6 .... Kinston
11-12-13 ... Prince William
21-22-23-24 ...... Salem
26-27-28 .... Durham
JUNE
5-6-7 .... Peninsula
8-9-10-11 ...... Frederick
19-20-21 ...... Lynchburg
22-23-24-25 ..... Kinston
29-30 ...... Prince William
JULY
1 .... Prince William
2-3-4 .... Salem
11-12-13 .... Durham
23-24-25 ...... Peninsula
26-27-28 .... Frederick
AUGUST
5-6-7 .... Lynchburg
8-9-10 .... Kinston
14-15-16-17 .... P.W.
19-20-21 .... Salem
29-30-31 .... Durham
SEPTEMBER
1 .... Durham

Florida State League

Baseball City
APRIL
12-13-13-14 ..... Dunedin
18-19 .... West Palm Beach
20 .... Winter Haven
23 .... Lakeland
25 .... Osceola
28-29 ..... St. Petersburg
MAY
6 .... Lakeland
10-11-12-13 ..... Charlotte
19-20 ...... Winter Haven
21-22 .... Lakeland
23-24 .... Osceola
26 .... Lakeland
31 .... Ft. Lsuderdale
JUNE
1-2-3 ...... Ft. Lauderdale
4-5 .... Winter Haven
6 .... Lakeland
17-19-20-21 ..... Osceola
23-24 ...... St. Petersburg
30 .... West Palm Beach
JULY
1 .... West Palm Beach
6-7-8 ...... Winter Haven
12 .... Lakeland
18-19-20-21 .... St. Lucie
22 .... Lakeland
24-25 ...... Winter Haven

HOME GAMES ONLY

1992 DIRECTORY • 155

FLORIDA STATE LEAGUE / 1992 SCHEDULE

HOME GAMES ONLY

26-27-28-29...Clearwater
AUGUST
5-6-10............Osceola
11-12-13-14....Sarasota
15-16-17-18..Vero Beach
20................Lakeland
22................Lakeland
27-28-29-30...Ft. Myers

Charlotte
APRIL
10................Sarasota
14-15......St. Petersburg
17.............Clearwater
18-19..........Ft. Myers
24-25-26-27...Ft. Laud.
29-30............Ft. Myers
MAY
2-3.............Clearwater
8-9...............Dunedin
14-15...........Sarasota
19-20-21-22...Vero Beach
25-26.....St. Petersburg
27-28-29-30.....Osceola
JUNE
4-5......West Palm Beach
8-9-10-11......Lakeland
16-17.............Dunedin
18-19..........Clearwater
29...............Sarasota
JULY
2-3................Dunedin
9-10-11-12....St. Lucie
20-21............Sarasota
22-23...........Ft. Myers
26-27.....St. Petersburg
30-31.............Dunedin
AUGUST
1-2.............Clearwater
5-6......West Palm Beach
9-10......St. Petersburg
11-12-13-14.......W.H.
23-24-25-26.Baseball City
31..............Clearwater
SEPTEMBER
1-2...............Ft. Myers

Clearwater
APRIL
11................Dunedin
12-13-14-15....Osceola
16...............Charlotte
18..........St. Petersburg
23...............Ft. Myers
26-27...........Sarasota
30................Lakeland
MAY
4-5..............Charlotte
8-9........Ft. Lauderdale
14-15.....St. Petersburg
19-20-21-22.......W.P.B.
27-28-29-30.Baseball City
31.........St. Petersburg
JUNE
2-3...............Ft. Myers
8-9...............Sarasota
12-13.............Dunedin
16.........St. Petersburg
23-25-29........Lakeland
JULY
3..........St. Petersburg
4................Charlotte
7-8...............Ft. Myers
11-12.............Dunedin
14-15-16.......Ft. Myers
18-19............Osceola
21..........St. Petersburg
22-23-24-25....St. Lucie
30-31.............Sarasota
AUGUST
3-4-5-6.......Vero Beach
13-14.............Dunedin
15-16............Charlotte
19-20.......Ft. Lauderdale
23-24-25-26........W.H.

Dunedin
APRIL
10.............Clearwater
18-19...........Sarasota
24-25-26-27.......W.P.B.
28-29-30...Winter Haven
MAY
2-3........St. Petersburg
6-7...............Charlotte
10-11............Lakeland
14-15...........Ft. Myers
17..........St. Petersburg
19-20-21-22....Ft. Laud.
27-28............Ft.Myers
JUNE
2-3................Charlotte
4-5...............Sarasota
8-9-10-11.......Osceola
14-15..........Clearwater
19..........St. Petersburg
20-21............Charlotte
24...........Winter Haven
30................Charlotte
JULY
1................Charlotte
9-10..........Clearwater
13-15-16-17..Baseball City
18..........St. Petersburg
21...............Ft. Myers
22-23-24-25..Vero Beach
AUGUST
1..........St. Petersburg
2................Ft. Myers
3-4-5-6..........St. Lucie
11-12..........Clearwater
16...............Ft. Myers
17..........St. Petersburg
21-22............Sarasota
25-26............Lakeland
27-28............Sarasota
SEPTEMBER
1..........St. Petersburg

Ft. Lauderdale
APRIL
11......West Palm Beach
12-13...........St. Lucie
14-15....West Palm Beach
16-17............Osceola
20-21-22-23...Sarasota
MAY
6-7.............Clearwater
14-15-16-17......W.H.
23-24-25-26....Ft. Myers
29-30........Vero Beach
JUNE
4-5-6-7....St. Petersburg
8-9.....West Palm Beach
10...............St. Lucie
11...........Vero Beach
15-16-17.......St. Lucie
20-21...West Palm Beach
23-24........Vero Beach
25-29..West Palm Beach
30................Osceola
JULY
1................Osceola
4................St. Lucie
5-6-7-8.........Charlotte
16-17.........Vero Beach
18-19-20-21....Lakeland
29...............St. Lucie
30-31......Baseball City
AUGUST
1-2..........Baseball City
7-8-9-10.........Dunedin
13-14............St. Lucie
21-22..........Clearwater
23-24-29.....Vero Beach
SEPTEMBER
1......West Palm Beach

Ft. Myers
APRIL
10........St. Petersburg
12-13-14-15......W.H.
16-17...........Sarasota
20-21-22......Clearwater
24-25-26-27....St. Lucie
28...............Charlotte
MAY
1................Charlotte
4-5...............Dunedin
6-7-8-9..........W.P.B.
16-17............Sarasota
21-22.....St. Petersburg
29-30.............Dunedin
31................Charlotte
JUNE
1................Charlotte
8-9-10-11...Baseball City
16-17............Sarasota
23-24-25........Osceola
29.................Osceola
30................Sarasota
JULY
1................Sarasota
4................Sarasota
5-6............Clearwater
9-10-11-12..Vero Beach
17.............Clearwater
19...............Sarasota
20................Dunedin
24-25............Charlotte
30-31......St. Petersburg
AUGUST
3-4-5-6.....Ft. Lauderdale
11-12-13-14....Lakeland
15................Dunedin
17-18............Charlotte
25-26......St. Petersburg
31................Dunedin

Lakeland
APRIL
11...........Winter Haven
16-17-18-18..Vero Beach
21-22............Osceola
24.........Baseball City
25-26......Winter Haven
29-30.........Clearwater
MAY
1..............Clearwater
2-3-4-5...Ft. Lauderdale
7............Baseball City
9............Winter Haven
12-13............Dunedin
25..........Baseball City
27........St. Petersburg
31................St. Lucie
JUNE
1-2-3............St. Lucie
4................Osceola
7............Baseball City
12-13-14-15...Ft. Myers
16-18............Osceola
19-20-21...Winter Haven
24.............Clearwater
JULY
4...........Winter Haven
6-8..............Osceola
9-10-11-11..Baseball City
13-15-17...St. Petersburg
23.........Baseball City
24-25............Osceola
26-27-28-29....Sarasota
AUGUST
5-6..........Winter Haven
15-16-17-18......W.P.B.
19..........Baseball City
21................Osceola
23-24............Dunedin
27-28-29-30....Charlotte

Osceola
APRIL
10-11.......Baseball City

156 • 1992 DIRECTORY

FLORIDA STATE LEAGUE / 1992 SCHEDULE

HOME GAMES ONLY

18-19 ...... Ft. Lauderdale
20 .... Lakeland
23-24 ..... Winter Haven
26 .... Baseball City
27 .... Lakeland
28-29-30 .... Sarasota
MAY
1 .... Sarasota
8-9 .... Baseball City
10-11-12-13 .... Ft. Myers
14-17 .... St. Lucie
19-20 .... Lakeland
25-26 ...... Winter Haven
31 .... Vero Beach
JUNE
1-2-3 .... Vero Beach
5 .... Lakeland
7 .... Winter Haven
12-13 ...... St. Petersburg
JULY
2-3 .... Ft. Lauderdale
4 .... Baseball City
5-7 .... Lakeland
11-12 ..... Winter Haven
13-15-16-17 .... Charlotte
18-19-20-21 ..... W.P.B.
22-23 ..... Winter Haven
26-27-28-29 ..... Dunedin
AUGUST
3-4 .... Baseball City
7-8 .... Lakeland
9 .... Winter Haven
11-12 ...... St. Petersburg
15-16 .... St. Lucie
27-28-29-30 ... Clearwater
31 .... Baseball City
SEPTEMBER
1 .... Baseball City
2 .... Lakeland

St. Lucie
APRIL
11-14 .... Vero Beach
20-21-22-23 .... Charlotte
30 .... Ft. Lauderdale
MAY
1 .... Ft. Lauderdale
2-3-4-5 .... Baseball City
12-13 ..... Ft. Lauderdale
15-16 .... Osceola
23-24-25-26 .... Dunedin
28 .... Vero Beach
29-30 .. West Palm Beach
JUNE
4-5-6-7 .... Clearwater
8-9 .... Vero Beach
14-18-19-23-24 ... W.P.B.
25-29 .... Vero Beach
30 .... Winter Haven
JULY
1-2-3 ...... Winter Haven
5-6-7-8 .... Sarasota
13-14 ..... Ft. Lauderdale
26-27 .. West Palm Beach
28 .... Ft. Lauderdale
30-31 .... Lakeland
AUGUST
1-2 .... Lakeland
7-8-9-10 .... Ft. Myers
11-12 ..... Ft. Lauderdale
17-18 .... Osceola
19-20-21-22 .... St. Pete.
25-27 .... Vero Beach
29 ..... West Palm Beach
31 .... Vero Beach
SEPTEMBER
2 .... Ft. Lauderdale

Sarasota
APRIL
11 .... Charlotte
12-13-14-15 .... Lakeland
24-25 .... Clearwater
MAY
2-3 .... Ft. Myers
6-7 .... Vero Beach

10-13 ..... St. Petersburg
16-17 .... Charlotte
19-20-21-22 ..... St. Lucie
27-28-29-30 .... W.H.
31 .... Dunedin
JUNE
1 .... Dunedin
2-3 .... St. Petersburg
6-7 .... Dunedin
10-11 .... Clearwater
12-13-14-15 . Baseball City
18-19 .... Ft. Myers
20-21 .... Clearwater
23-24-25 .... Charlotte
JULY
2-3 .... Ft. Myers
9-10-11-12 ...... W.P.B.
18 .... Ft. Myers
22-23-24-25 .... Ft. L.
AUGUST
1 .... Ft. Myers
2-5-6 ...... St. Petersburg
7-8 .... Vero Beach
17-18 .... Clearwater
19-20 .... Dunedin
23-24-25-26 ..... Osceola
29-30 .... Dunedin
31 .... St. Petersburg

St. Petersburg
APRIL
11 .... Ft. Myers
12-13 .... Charlotte
16-17 .... Dunedin
19 .... Clearwater
24-25-26-27 .. Vero Beach
30 .... Baseball City
MAY
1 .... Baseball City
4-5 .... Sarasota
6-7-8-9 .... St. Lucie
11-12 .... Sarasota
16 .... Dunedin
19-20 .... Ft. Myers
23-24 .... Charlotte
28-29-30 .... Lakeland
JUNE
1 .... Clearwater
9-11 .... Winter Haven
14-15 .... Osceola
17 .... Clearwater
18 .... Dunedin
20-21 .... Ft. Myers
25-29 .... Baseball City
30 .... Clearwater
JULY
1-2 .... Clearwater
4 .... Dunedin
9-10-11-12 . Ft. Lauderdale
16 .... Lakeland
19 .... Dunedin
20 .... Clearwater
22-23-24-25 ..... W.P.B.
28-29 .... Charlotte
AUGUST
3-4 .... Sarasota
7-8 .... Charlotte
13-14 .... Osceola
15-16 .... Sarasota
18 .... Dunedin
23-24 .... Ft. Myers
28-30 ...... Winter Haven
SEPTEMBER
2 .... Dunedin

Vero Beach
APRIL
10 .... St. Lucie
12-13 .. West Palm Beach
15 .... St. Lucie
20-21-22-23 ..... Dunedin
28-29 ..... Ft. Lauderdale
30 ...... West Palm Beach
MAY
1 .... West Palm Beach
2-3-4-5 ..... Winter Haven

8-9 .... Sarasota
10-11 .... St. Lucie
14-15-16-17 . Baseball City
23-24-25-26 ... Clearwater
27 .... St. Lucie
JUNE
4-5-6-7 .... Ft. Myers
12-13-13 .. Ft. Lauderdale
15 ...... West Palm Beach
18-19 ..... Ft. Lauderdale
20-21 .... St. Lucie
30 .... Lakeland
JULY
1-2-3 .... Lakeland
5-6-7-8 .... St. Petersburg
13-15 .. West Palm Beach
26-27 ..... Ft. Lauderdale
30-31 .... Osceola
AUGUST
1-1 .... Osceola
9-10 .... Sarasota
11-12 .. West Palm Beach
19-20-21-22 .... St. Lucie
26-28 .... St. Lucie
30 .... Ft. Lauderdale
SEPTEMBER
1 .... St. Lucie
2 .... West Palm Beach

West Palm Beach
APRIL
10 .... Ft. Lauderdale
16-17 .... Baseball City
20-21-22-23 ..... St. Pete.
28-29 .... St. Lucie
MAY
2-3-4-5 .... Osceola
10-11 ..... Ft. Lauderdale
12-13 .... Vero Beach
14-15-16-17 .... Lakeland
23-24-25-26 .... Sarasota
27-28 ..... Ft. Lauderdale
JUNE
6-7 .... Charlotte
10 .... Vero Beach
11-12-13 .... St. Lucie
16-17 .... Vero Beach
JULY
2-3 .... Baseball City
4 .... Vero Beach
5-6-7-8 .... Dunedin
16-17 .... St. Lucie
28-29 .... Vero Beach
30-31 ...... Winter Haven
AUGUST
1-2 .... Winter Haven
3-4 .... Charlotte
7-8-9-10 .... Clearwater
13-14 .... Vero Beach
19-20-21-22 .... Ft. Myers
23-24 .... St. Lucie
25-26-27-28 .... Ft. L.
30 .... St. Lucie
31 .... Ft. Lauderdale

Winter Haven
APRIL
10 .... Lakeland
16-17-17-18 ..... St. Lucie
21-22-27 .... Baseball City
MAY
1 .... Dunedin
6-7 .... Osceola
8 .... Lakeland
10-11-12-13 ... Clearwater
21-22 .... Osceola
23-24 .... Lakeland
31 ...... West Palm Beach
JUNE
1-2-3 ... West Palm Beach
6 .... Osceola
8-10 ...... St. Petersburg
12-13-14-15 .... Charlotte
16 .... Baseball City
17 .... Lakeland

1992 DIRECTORY • **157**

HOME GAMES ONLY

18 ....Baseball City
23-25-29 ....Dunedin
JULY
5 ....Baseball City
9-10 ....Osceola
13-15-16-17 ...Sarasota
18-19-20-21 ..Vero Beach

26-27-28-29 ...Ft. Myers
AUGUST
3-3 ....Lakeland
7-8 ....Baseball City
10 ....Lakeland
15-16-17-18 .....Ft. L.
19-20 ....Osceola

21 ....Baseball City
22 ....Osceola
27-29 ...St. Petersburg
31 ....Lakeland
SEPTEMBER
1 ....Lakeland
2 ....Baseball City

Midwest League

Appleton

APRIL
11-12 ....Kenosha
14-15 ....Peoria
16-17 ....South Bend
26-27-28-29 ....Waterloo
30 ....South Bend
MAY
1 ....South Bend
2-3 ....Kane County
7-8 ....Kenosha
13-14-15-16 ...Quad City
17-18-19-20 .......C.R.
29-30 ....Beloit
JUNE
2-3 ....Madison
4-5 ....Rockford
14 ....Madison
17-18 ....Beloit
19-20 ....Kane County
24-25 ....South Bend
JULY
4-5-6-7 ....Springfield
12-13 ....Beloit
17-18 ....Peoria
19-20-21-22 .....Clinton
29-30 ......Kane County
AUGUST
8-9 ....Rockford
11 ....Madison
13-14 ....Rockford
15-16 ....Kane County
17-18 ....Kenosha
21-22-23-24 ...Burlington
29-30 ....Kenosha
31 ....Madison
SEPTEMBER
1 ....Madison
2-3 ....South Bend

Beloit

APRIL
9-10 ....Appleton
15 ....Kane County
16-17 ....Kenosha
18-19 ....Rockford
26-27 ....Kane County
28-29 ....South Bend
30 ....Waterloo
MAY
1 ....Waterloo
9-10-11-12 ......Clinton
15-16 ....Rockford
23-24 ....Kane County
25-26-27-28 ..Springfield
31 ....Burlington
JUNE
1-2-3 ....Burlington
9-10 ....Kenosha
11-12 ....Appleton
15-16 ....Madison
26-27 ....South Bend
28-29-30 ...Cedar Rapids
JULY
1 ....Cedar Rapids
4-5 ....Rockford
6-7-8-9 ....Quad City
10-11 ....Waterloo
21-22 ....South Bend
23-24-25-26 ....Appleton
28 ....Rockford

AUGUST
6-7 ....Kenosha
11-12 ....Kane County
13-14 ....Madison
17-18 ....Madison
20 ....Rockford
21 ....Kane County
29-30-31 ....Peoria
SEPTEMBER
1 ....Peoria

Burlington

APRIL
11-12 ....Springfield
14-15 ....Waterloo
18-19-20-21 ....Appleton
28-29 ......Cedar Rapids
30 ....Clinton
MAY
1 ....Clinton
2-3 ....Springfield
7-8 ....Kane County
9 ....Quad City
11-12-13-14 ..South Bend
17-18-19-20 ....Kenosha
23-24 ....Waterloo
25-26 ....Waterloo
29-30 ......Cedar Rapids
JUNE
9-10 ....Clinton
11-12 ....Quad City
14-15-16-17 ....Rockford
30 ....Waterloo
JULY
1 ....Waterloo
4-5-6-7 ....Madison
8-9 ....Clinton
15-16 ....Kane County
23-24 ....Waterloo
25-26 ....Quad City
29-30-31 ....Beloit
AUGUST
1 ....Beloit
6-7 ....Peoria
11-12 ......Cedar Rapids
13-14 ....Springfield
15-16 ....Peoria
18 ....Quad City
29-30 ....Springfield
31 ....Cedar Rapids
SEPTEMBER
1 ....Cedar Rapids

Cedar Rapids

APRIL
9-10 ....Peoria
14-15 ....Madison
18-19 ....Clinton
20-21-22-23 .....Beloit
26-27 ....Springfield
MAY
2-3 ....Quad City
13-14 ....Waterloo
15-16 ....Burlington
23-24-25-26 ....Rockford
JUNE
4-5-6-7 ......Kane County
9-10 ....Peoria
11-12 ....Clinton
13-14 ....Quad City
17-18 ....Burlington
20 ....Waterloo
24-25 ....Springfield

26-27 ....Peoria
6-7-8-9 ....South Bend
10-11 ....Clinton
12-13 ....Burlington
19-20-21-22 ....Kenosha
23-24 ....Clinton
25-26 ....Madison
31 ....Appleton
AUGUST
1-2-3 ....Appleton
13-14 ....Quad City
15 ....Waterloo
17-18 ....Peoria
19-20 ....Springfield
29-30 ....Waterloo
SEPTEMBER
2-3 ....Quad City

Clinton

APRIL
9-10 ....Burlington
16-17 ......Cedar Rapids
20-21 ....Waterloo
22-23-24-25 ....Kenosha
28-29 ....Peoria
MAY
2-3 ....Rockford
13-14 ....Peoria
15-16-17-18 ..South Bend
19-20 ....Springfield
23-24-25-26 ....Appleton
31 ....Quad City
JUNE
1-2-3 ....Quad City
13-14 ....Springfield
15-16 ....Burlington
19 ....Rockford
26-27 ....Quad City
28-29 ....Burlington
30 ....Madison
JULY
1-2-3 ....Madison
6-7 ....Peoria
15-16-17-18 .....Beloit
25-26 ....Waterloo
27-28 ......Cedar Rapids
31 ....Springfield
AUGUST
1 ....Springfield
2-3 ....Waterloo
4-5 ....Cedar Rapids
7 ....Rockford
8-9 ....Kane County
19-20 ....Burlington
25-26 ....Quad City
27-28 ....Springfield
SEPTEMBER
2-3 ....Kane County

Kane County

APRIL
9-10 ....Rockford
14 ....Beloit
16-17-18-19 ...Quad City
22-23 ....Burlington
24-25 ....Madison
28-29 ....Rockford
MAY
5-6 ....Springfield
15-16 ....Kenosha
17-18 ....Beloit
21-22 ....Clinton

158 • 1992 DIRECTORY

MIDWEST LEAGUE/1992 SCHEDULE

HOME GAMES ONLY

27-28 ....Clinton
29-30 ....Springfield
31 ....Kenosha
JUNE
1 ....Kenosha
9-10 ....South Bend
13-14 ....South Bend
15-16 ....Appleton
17-18 ....Madison
24-25 ....Beloit
26-27 ....Appleton
28-29 ....Kenosha
JULY
2-3-4-5 ....Cedar Rapids
8-9 ....Peoria
10-11 ....Rockford
21-22 ....Burlington
23-24 ....Madison
27-28 ....Peoria
AUGUST
2-3 ....Rockford
13-14 ....South Bend
19-20 ....Appleton
22 ....Beloit
23-24-25-26 ......Waterloo
27-28 ....Madison
31 ....Kenosha
SEPTEMBER
1 ....Kenosha

Kenosha
APRIL
9-10 ....Madison
14-15 ....Quad City
18-19 ....South Bend
26-27 ....Peoria
28-29 ....Madison
MAY
2 ....South Bend
5-6 ....Appleton
9-10-11-12 . Cedar Rapids
13-14 ....Kane County
25-26 ....Kane County
27-28 ....Appleton
29-30 ....Peoria
JUNE
4-5 ....South Bend
11-12-13-14 ....Waterloo
15-16 ....Rockford
19-20 ....Beloit
26-27 ....Madison
JULY
6-7 ....Kane County
8-9-10-11 ....Appleton
12-13 ....Rockford
23-24 ....Quad City
25-26-27-28 ...Springfield
AUGUST
2-3 ....Madison
8-9-10 ....South Bend
11-12-13-14 ......Clinton
15-16 ....Beloit
23-24 ....Beloit
25-26-27-28 ...Burlington
SEPTEMBER
2-3 ....Rockford

Madison
APRIL
11-12 ....Beloit
20-21 ....Kane County
22-23 ....Rockford
26-27 ....South Bend
30 ....Kenosha
MAY
1 ....Kenosha
2-3 ....Beloit
5-6-7-8 ....Clinton
17-18-19-20 ....Quad City
21-22 ....Cedar Rapids
31 ....Appleton
JUNE
1 ....Appleton
4-5-6-7 ....Burlington
9-10 ....Appleton
11-12 ....Rockford

13 ....Appleton
19-20 ....South Bend
24-25 ....Kenosha
28-29 ....South Bend
JULY
8-9-10-11 ....Springfield
12-13 ....Kane County
15-16 ....Appleton
19-20-21-22 ......Peoria
31 ....Kenosha
AUGUST
1 ....Kenosha
8-9 ....Beloit
12 ....Appleton
15-16 ....Rockford
19-20-21-22 ....Waterloo
23-24 ....South Bend
25-26 ....Cedar Rapids
29-30 ....Kane County
SEPTEMBER
2-3 ....Beloit

Quad City
APRIL
9-10 ....Waterloo
11-12 ....Peoria
20-21 ....Kenosha
24-25 ....Cedar Rapids
26-27 ....Clinton
28-29 ....Springfield
MAY
5-6 ....Rockford
7-8 ....Waterloo
10 ....Burlington
11-12 ....Springfield
21-22 ....Burlington
25 ....Peoria
27-28-29-30 ..South Bend
JUNE
4-5-6-7 ....Beloit
9-10 ....Rockford
16 ....Peoria
19-20 ....Burlington
24-25 ....Clinton
28-29 ....Waterloo
30 ....Appleton
JULY
1-2-3 ....Appleton
4-5 ....Kenosha
15-16 ....Springfield
17-18 ....Cedar Rapids
27-28-29-30 ......Madison
AUGUST
2-3 ....Burlington
4-5-6-7 ....Kane County
8 ....Peoria
15-16 ....Springfield
17 ....Burlington
19-20-21 ....Peoria
27-28 ....Cedar Rapids
29-30 ....Clinton

Peoria
APRIL
18-19-20 ....Springfield
30 ....Cedar Rapids
MAY
1 ....Cedar Rapids
5-6-7-8 ....Beloit
9-10-11-12 ......Madison
15-16 ....Waterloo
19-20 ....Kane County
21-22 ....Appleton
26 ....Quad City
27-28 ....Burlington
31 ....Waterloo
JUNE
1 ....Waterloo
2-3 ....Cedar Rapids
6-7 ....Clinton
11-12 ....Kane County
13-14 ....Burlington
15 ....Quad City
17-18 ....Clinton
28-29 ....Appleton
30 ....Kenosha

JULY
1-2-3 ....Kenosha
4-5 ....Clinton
10-11 ....Burlington
15-16 ....Cedar Rapids
23-24-25-26 ....Rockford
29-30 ....Clinton
31 ....South Bend
AUGUST
1-2-3 ....South Bend
4-5 ....Burlington
9 ....Quad City
10-11 ....Springfield
13-14 ....Waterloo
22-23-24 ....Quad City
26 ....Springfield
SEPTEMBER
2-3 ....Waterloo

Rockford
APRIL
11-12 ....Clinton
14-15 ....South Bend
16-17 ....Peoria
24-25-26-27 ...Burlington
30 ....Kane County
MAY
1 ....Kane County
7-8-9-10 ....Springfield
11-12 ....Appleton
13-14 ....Beloit
17-18 ....Peoria
27-28-29-30 .....Madison
JUNE
2-3 ....Kane County
6-7 ....Kenosha
13-14 ....Beloit
17-18 ....Kenosha
20 ....Clinton
JULY
2-3 ....Beloit
6-7-8-9 ....Waterloo
15-16 ....South Bend
17-18 ....Madison
19-20-21-22 ....Quad City
27 ....Beloit
29-30 ....Kenosha
31 ....Kane County
AUGUST
1 ....Kane County
4-5 ....Kenosha
6 ....Clinton
11-12 ....South Bend
17-18 ....Kane County
19 ....Beloit
21-22-23-24 ...........C.R.
25-26-27-28 ......Appleton

South Bend
APRIL
11-12 ....Kane County
20-21 ....Rockford
22-23-24-25 ....Peoria
MAY
3 ....Kenosha
5-6-7-8 .....Cedar Rapids
9-10 ....Appleton
19-20-21-22 ....Beloit
23-24-25-26 .....Madison
31 ....Rockford
JUNE
1 ....Rockford
2-3 ....Kenosha
6-7 ....Appleton
11-12 ....Springfield
15-16-17-18 ....Waterloo
30 ....Kane County
JULY
1 ....Kane County
10-11-12-13 ...Quad City
17-18-19-20 ...Burlington
23-24 ....Springfield
25-26 ....Kane County
27-28 ....Appleton
AUGUST
4-5-6-7 ....Madison

1992 DIRECTORY • **159**

HOME GAMES ONLY

15-16-17-18 ...... Clinton
20-21-22 .... Kenosha
25-26-27-28 ...... Beloit
29-30-31 .... Rockford
SEPTEMBER
1 .... Rockford

Springfield
APRIL
9-10 .... South Bend
14-15 .... Clinton
16-17 .... Burlington
21 .... Peoria
22-23-24-25 ..... Appleton
30 .... Quad City
MAY
1 .... Quad City
13-14-15-16 ..... Madison
17-17 .... Waterloo
21-22-23-24 ..... Kenosha
31 .... Cedar Rapids
JUNE
1 .... Cedar Rapids
2-3 .... Waterloo
4-5 .... Peoria
15-16 .... Cedar Rapids
17-18 .... Quad City
19-20 .... Peoria

26-27 .... Waterloo
28-29-30 .... Rockford
JULY
1 .... Rockford
2-3 .... Burlington
12-13 .... Peoria
17-18-19-20 .. Kane County
21-22 .... Waterloo
29-30 .... South Bend
AUGUST
2-3-4-5 .... Beloit
6-7-8-9 ..... Cedar Rapids
21-22-23-24 ...... Clinton
25 .... Peoria
31 .... Quad City
SEPTEMBER
1 .... Quad City
2-3 .... Burlington

Waterloo
APRIL
11-12 .... Cedar Rapids
16-17-18-19 ..... Madison
22-23 .... Quad City
24-25 .... Beloit
MAY
2-3 .... Peoria
5-6 .... Burlington

9-10-11-12 .. Kane County
19-20-21-22 .... Rockford
23-24 .... Quad City
27-28 .... Cedar Rapids
29-30 .... Clinton
JUNE
4-5 .... Clinton
6-7-8-9 .... Springfield
19 .... Cedar Rapids
24-25 .... Peoria
JULY
2-3-4-5 .... South Bend
12-13 .... Clinton
15-16-17-18 .... Kenosha
19-20 .... Beloit
27-28 .... Burlington
29-30 .... Cedar Rapids
31 .... Quad City
AUGUST
1 .... Quad City
4-5-6-7 .... Appleton
8-9 .... Burlington
11-12 .... Quad City
16 .... Cedar Rapids
17-18 .... Springfield
27-28 .... Peoria
31 .... Clinton
SEPTEMBER
1 .... Clinton

South Atlantic League

Albany
APRIL
17-18-19-20 ... Columbus
21-22-23-24 ... Columbia
MAY
4-5-6-7 .... Savannah
8-9 .... Macon
14-15-16-17 . Myrtle Beach
18-19-20-21 . Spartanburg
26-27 .... Gastonia
28-29 .... Augusta
JUNE
3-4 .... Charleston, SC
5-6 .... Macon
11-12 .... Columbus
13-14-15-16 . Fayetteville
30 .... Gastonia
JULY
1 .... Gastonia
10-11 .... Macon
15-16 .... Columbus
23-24-25-26 . Myrtle Beach
27-28-29-30 .... Char WV
AUGUST
4-5-6-7 .... Greensboro
8-9 .... Columbus
10-11-12-13 ..... Augusta
17-18 ..... Charleston, SC
25-26 .... Savannah
27-28 ..... Charleston, SC
31 .... Savannah
SEPTEMBER
1 .... Savannah
2-3-4-5 .... Asheville

Asheville
APRIL
17-18-19 .... Spartanburg
21-22 .... Gastonia
25-26 .... Albany
29-30 .... Gastonia
MAY
1-2 .... Albany
8-9-10-11 ..... Columbia
12-13-14-15 .... Savannah
22-23-24-25 ..... Augusta
JUNE
1-2 .... Fayetteville
6 .... Spartanburg
7-8 .... Greensboro
9-10-11-12 ..... Char WV

15-16 .... Columbus
17-18 .... Greensboro
24-25 .... Columbus
26-27-28-29 . Myrtle Beach
30 .... Columbia
JULY
1 .... Columbia
4-5 ...... Charleston, WV
8-9 .... Gastonia
15-16 .... Greensboro
17-18 .... Columbia
21-22 .... Fayetteville
23-24-25-26 .... Char SC
27-28-29-30 ..... Macon
AUGUST
8-9 .... Spartanburg
12-13 .... Greensboro
17-18 .... Charleston, WV
19-20 .... Spartanburg
29-30 .... Fayetteville

Augusta
APRIL
17-18-19-20 .... Gastonia
21-22-23-24 .... Char WV
25-26 ..... Charleston, SC
29-30 .... Myrtle Beach
MAY
1-2 .... Columbia
6-7 .... Charleston, SC
14-15 .... Columbus
16-17 .... Spartanburg
18-19-20-21 .... Savannah
26-27 .... Macon
30-31 .... Albany
JUNE
1-2 .... Spartanburg
7-8 .... Columbia
9-10 .... Albany
19-20 .... Myrtle Beach
26-27-28-29 ..... Albany
JULY
10-11-12-13 . Fayetteville
15-16 ..... Charleston, SC
25-26 .... Columbus
27-28 ..... Charleston, SC
31 .... Asheville
AUGUST
1-2-3 .... Asheville
8-9 .... Savannah
17-18-19-20 .. Greensboro
23-24-25-26 . Myrtle Beach

27-28 .... Columbus
29-30-31 .... Macon
SEPTEMBER
1 .... Macon
4-5 .... Columbia

Charleston, SC
APRIL
17-18-19-20 ...... Macon
29-30 .... Spartanburg
MAY
1-2 .... Spartanburg
4-5 .... Augusta
8-9-10-11 . Charleston, WV
18-19-20-21 ... Columbus
24-25 .... Greensboro
26-27 .... Myrtle Beach
28-29-30-31 .... Asheville
JUNE
7-8 .... Albany
9-10 .... Myrtle Beach
11-12 .... Savannah
13-14 .... Augusta
19-20 .... Albany
JULY
4-5 .... Greensboro
8-9 .... Augusta
10-11 .... Myrtle Beach
17-18-19-20 .... Savannah
29-30 .... Myrtle Beach
31 .... Albany
AUGUST
1-2-3 .... Albany
4-5-6-7 .... Gastonia
10-11-12-13 ...... Macon
14-15 .... Columbia
23-24-25-26 . Fayetteville
31 .... Columbia
SEPTEMBER
1 .... Columbia
2-3-4-5 .... Columbus

Charleston, WV
APRIL
17-18-19-20 .... Savannah
27-28-29-30 ...... Albany
MAY
1-2 .... Myrtle Beach
4-5-6-7 .... Asheville
14-15-16-17 .... Gastonia
18-19-20-21 ...... Macon
28-29-30-31 . Fayetteville

160 • 1992 DIRECTORY

SOUTH ATLANTIC LEAGUE / 1992 SCHEDULE — HOME GAMES ONLY

Asheville

JUNE
1-2 .... Columbia
13-14 .... Greensboro
15-16-17-18 ...... Spart.
19-20 .... Asheville
24-25 ...... Myrtle Beach
26-27-28-29 .. Columbus
30 .... Charleston, SC

JULY
1-2-3 .... Charleston, SC
15-16 .... Fayetteville
17-18-19-20 ..... Augusta
21-22-23-24 .. Greensboro

AUGUST
4-5-6-7 ...... Spartanburg
12-13-14-15 .... Gastonia
21-22-23-24 .... Columbia
25-26-27-28 ... Asheville

Columbia

APRIL
9-10 .... Asheville
15-16 ...... Myrtle Beach
17-18-19-20 .. Fayetteville
29-30 .... Greensboro

MAY
4-5 .... Spartanburg
12-13 .... Gastonia
14-15-16 .... Char SC
22-23-24-25 ... Char WV
26-27-28-29 ... Columbus

JUNE
3-4 .... Augusta
5-6 .... Myrtle Beach
9-10 .... Greensboro
13-14 .... Asheville
15-16 .... Augusta
24-25 .... Spartanburg
26-27-28-29 .. Fayetteville

JULY
2-3 .... Asheville
4-4 .... Spartanburg
6-7-8-9 ...... Greensboro
15-16 .... Gastonia
19-20-21-22 ...... Albany
25-26 .... Savannah
31 .... Charleston, WV

AUGUST
1-2-3 .... Charleston, WV
8-9 .... Macon
12-13 .... Savannah
27-28 .... Macon
29-30 .... Gastonia

SEPTEMBER
2-3 .... Augusta

Columbus

APRIL
11-12-13-14 .... Char WV
15-16 .... Asheville
21-22-23-24 ...... M.B.

MAY
4-5-6-7 ...... Greensboro
8-9-10-11 ...... Augusta
12-13 .... Albany
22-23-24-25 .... Gastonia

JUNE
5-6 .... Charleston, SC
7-8-9-10 ...... Savannah
13-14 .... Macon
17-18 .... Albany
19-20 .... Macon

JULY
4-5 .... Macon
6-7-8-9 ...... Fayetteville
10-11-12-13 .... Columbia
17-18-19-20 ...... Spart.
21-22 ...... Myrtle Beach
31 .... Savannah

AUGUST
1-2-3 .... Savannah
4-5-6-7 .... Augusta
17-18 .... Macon
19-20-21-22 .... Char SC
23-24 .... Albany

Fayetteville

APRIL
9-10-11-12 ...... Augusta
13-14-15-16 .... Char SC
21-22 .... Greensboro
25-26 .... Charleston, WV
29-30 .... Columbus

MAY
1-2 .... Columbus
10-11 .... Savannah
14-15 .... Spartanburg
16-17 .... Asheville
18-19 .... Greensboro
22-23 .... Greensboro
24-25 .... Spartanburg
26-27 .... Asheville

JUNE
5-6 .... Gastonia
7-8 ...... Charleston, WV
17-18 .... Columbia
24-25 .... Gastonia
30 .... Savannah

JULY
1 .... Savannah
2-3-4-5 .... Albany
17-18 .... Greensboro
19-20 .... Asheville
23-24 .... Columbia
29-30 .... Columbia

AUGUST
2-3 .... Spartanburg
4-5-6-7 .... Macon
10-11 ...... Myrtle Beach
14-15 .... Augusta
19-20 .... Charleston, WV
21-22 ...... Myrtle Beach
31 .... Greensboro

SEPTEMBER
1 .... Greensboro
2-3 ...... Charleston, WV
4-5 .... Gastonia

Gastonia

APRIL
9-10-11-12 ...... Char SC
13-14 .... Albany
23-24 .... Asheville
25-26 .... Charleston, WV
27-28 .... Fayetteville

MAY
1-2 .... Greensboro
4-5-6-7 .... Macon
8-9-10-11 ... Myrtle Beach
18-19 .... Columbia
20-21 .... Fayetteville

JUNE
3-4 .... Asheville
7-8 .... Spartanburg
11-12 .... Columbia
13-14 .... Spartanburg
15-16 .... Greensboro

JULY
2-3-4-5 .... Savannah
6-7 .... Asheville
10-11 .... Spartanburg
17-18 .... Albany
21-22-23-24 ..... Augusta
25-26 .... Charleston, WV
27-28-29-30 ... Columbus

AUGUST
8-9 .... Fayetteville
10-11 .... Columbia
17-18 .... Fayetteville
19-20 .... Columbia
21-22 .... Asheville
23-24 .... Greensboro
27-28 .... Spartanburg
31 .... Charleston, WV

SEPTEMBER
1 .... Charleston, WV
29-30 .... Albany
31 .... Asheville

SEPTEMBER
1 .... Asheville

Greensboro

APRIL
9-10-11-12 .... Albany
13-14-15-16 ..... Augusta
23-24 .... Fayetteville
25-26 .... Gastonia
27-28 .... Asheville

MAY
10-11 .... Spartanburg
12-13 .... Charleston, SC
14-15-16-17 ...... Macon
20-21 .... Columbia
30-31 .... Columbia

JUNE
1-2 .... Gastonia
3-4-5-6 .. Charleston, WV
19-20 .... Fayetteville
24-25 .... Charleston, SC
26-27-28-29 ... Savannah
30 .... Columbus

JULY
1-2-3 .... Columbus
10-11-12-13 .... Asheville
19-20 .... Gastonia
25-26-27-28 .. Fayetteville
29-30 .... Spartanburg

AUGUST
8-9-10-11 ...... Char WV
14-15 .... Spartanburg
25-26 .... Columbia
27-28-29-30 ...... M.B.

SEPTEMBER
2-3 .... Gastonia
4-5 .... Spartanburg

Macon

APRIL
9-10 .... Columbus
11-12-13-14 .... Asheville
15-16 .... Spartanburg
21-22-23-24 .... Char SC
25-26-27-28 .... Columbia

MAY
1-2 .... Savannah
10-11 .... Albany
12-13 .... Augusta
24-25 .... Savannah

JUNE
1-2 .... Albany
3-4 .... Savannah
7-8 .... Myrtle Beach
9-10-11-12 .. Fayetteville
17-18 .... Augusta
24-25 .... Albany
26-27-28-29 .... Gastonia

JULY
6-7-8-9 .... Charleston, WV
12-13 .... Albany
15-16 .... Spartanburg
17-18-19-20 ...... M.B.
21-22 .... Charleston, SC
23-24 .... Columbus
31 .... Greensboro

AUGUST
1-2-3 .... Greensboro
14-15 .... Augusta
19-20 .... Savannah
21-22 .... Augusta
25-26 .... Columbus

SEPTEMBER
4-5 .... Savannah

Myrtle Beach

APRIL
17-18-19-20 .. Greensboro
27-28 .... Charleston, SC

MAY
4-5-6-7 ...... Fayetteville
12-13 .... Charleston, WV
18-19-20-21 ... Asheville
22-23-24-25 ..... Albany
28-29-30-31 ..... Macon

JUNE
1-2-3-4 .... Columbus
11-12 .... Augusta

HOME GAMES ONLY

13-14	Savannah
15-16-17-18	Char SC
30	Macon

JULY
1-2-3	Macon
4-5-6-7	Augusta
12-13	Charleston, SC
15-16	Savannah
27-28	Savannah
31	Gastonia

AUGUST
1-2-3	Gastonia
4-5-6-7	Columbia
8-9	Charleston, SC
12-13-14-15	Columbus
19-20	Albany
31	Spartanburg

SEPTEMBER
1-2-3	Spartanburg
4-5	Charleston, WV

Savannah
APRIL
9-10	Myrtle Beach
11-12-13-14	Columbia
15-16	Albany
25-26	Myrtle Beach
27-28	Augusta
29-30	Macon

MAY
8-9	Fayetteville
16-17	Columbus
22-23	Charleston, SC
26-27-28-29	Greensboro
30-31	Columbus

JUNE
1-2	Charleston, SC
5-6	Augusta
15-16	Macon
17-18-19-20	Gastonia
24-25	Augusta

JULY
6-7	Charleston, SC
8-9	Myrtle Beach
10-11-12-13	Char WV
21-22-23-24	Spart.
29-30	Augusta

AUGUST
4-5-6-7	Asheville
10-11	Columbus
14-15	Albany
17-18	Myrtle Beach
21-22	Albany
23-24	Macon
27-28	Fayetteville
29-30	Charleston, SC

SEPTEMBER
2-3	Macon

Spartanburg
APRIL
9-10	Charleston, WV
11-12-13-14	M.B.
20	Asheville
21-22-23-24	Savannah

25-26-27-28	Columbus

MAY
6-7	Columbia
8-9	Greensboro
12-13	Fayetteville
22-23	Macon
26-27	Charleston, WV
28-29-30-31	Gastonia

JUNE
3-4	Fayetteville
5	Asheville
9-10	Gastonia
11-12	Greensboro
19-20	Columbia
26-27-28-29	Char SC
30	Augusta

JULY
1-2-3	Augusta
6-7-8-9	Albany
12-13	Gastonia
25-26	Macon
27-28	Columbia
31	Fayetteville

AUGUST
1	Fayetteville
10-11	Asheville
12-13	Fayetteville
17-18	Columbia
21-22	Greensboro
23-24	Asheville
25-26	Gastonia
29-30	Charleston, WV

Short-Season Class A
New York-Penn League

Auburn
JUNE
16	Elmira
18	Batavia
19	Geneva
22	Batavia
24	Elmira
26	Geneva
28	Watertown
29	Utica

JULY
5	Elmira
8	Batavia
10-11	St. Catharines
12-13	Oneonta
14	Utica
16	Watertown
18-19	Hamilton
20	Elmira
25	Geneva
27-28	Jamestown
29-30	Pittsfield
31	Welland

AUGUST
1	Welland
4-5	Niagara Falls
8	Geneva
17-18	Erie
20	Batavia
21	Elmira
24	Batavia
26	Geneva
27	Elmira
29	Geneva
31	Batavia

SEPTEMBER
3	Elmira

Batavia
JUNE
15	Geneva
17	Auburn
19	Elmira
21	Auburn

23	Geneva
25	Elmira
27-28	Oneonta
29-30	Pittsfield

JULY
3-4	Utica
6	Geneva
9	Auburn
11	Niagara Falls
18-19	Erie
21	Hamilton
23	Jamestown
26	Hamilton
28	Elmira
29-30	Watertown

AUGUST
1	St. Catharines
4	Welland
6	Geneva
9	St. Catharines
11	Welland
13	Elmira
16	Niagara Falls
17	Jamestown
19	Auburn
22	Geneva
23	Auburn
25	Elmira
28	Geneva
30	Elmira

SEPTEMBER
1	Auburn
2	Geneva

Elmira
JUNE
15	Auburn
17	Geneva
20	Batavia
21-22	Geneva
26	Batavia
23	Auburn
29-30	Watertown

JULY
2	Oneonta

6	Auburn
10	Geneva
12-13	Pittsfield
16-17	Utica
18-19	Niagara Falls
21	Auburn
27	Batavia
29	Oneonta
31	Jamestown

AUGUST
1	Jamestown
2-3	St. Catharines
10	Geneva
12	Batavia
15-16	Erie
17-18	Welland
19-20	Hamilton
22	Auburn
26	Batavia
28	Auburn
29	Batavia
31	Geneva

SEPTEMBER
2	Auburn

Erie
JUNE
16	Jamestown
17-18	Welland
19-20	Niagara Falls
21-22	St. Catharines
26	Jamestown
27-28	Hamilton

JULY
5	Jamestown
8-9	Pittsfield
10-11	Oneonta
12-13	St. Catharines
15	Jamestown
25-26	Elmira
27-28	Utica
30	Jamestown
31	Geneva

AUGUST
1	Geneva

162 • 1992 DIRECTORY

NEW YORK-PENN LEAGUE / 1992 SCHEDULE

HOME GAMES ONLY

2-3 .... Batavia
10-11 .... Watertown
12-13 .... Auburn
14 .... Niagara Falls
21-22 .... Jamestown
24 .... Niagara Falls
25-26 .... Welland
31 .... Hamilton
SEPTEMBER
1 .... Hamilton

Geneva
JUNE
16 .... Batavia
18 .... Elmira
20 .... Auburn
24 .... Batavia
25 .... Auburn
27-28 .... Pittsfield
29-30 .... Oneonta
JULY
1 .... Utica
5 .... Batavia
11 .... Elmira
12-13 .... Watertown
18-19 .... Welland
24 .... Auburn
27-28 ...... Niagara Falls
29 .... Utica
AUGUST
2-3 .... Hamilton
4-5 .... Erie
7 .... Batavia
9 .... Auburn
11 .... Elmira
14-15 .... Jamestown
19-20 ...... St. Catharines
21 .... Batavia
23-24 .... Elmira
25 .... Auburn
27 .... Batavia
30 .... Auburn
SEPTEMBER
1 .... Elmira
3 .... Batavia

Hamilton
JUNE
16 .... St. Catharines
18 .... Niagara Falls
21-22 .... Welland
24 .... Niagara Falls
26 .... St. Catharines
29-30 .... Jamestown
JULY
1-2 .... Erie
3 .... Welland
7 .... St. Catharines
10-11 .. Utica (at Glens Falls)
13 .... Welland
15 .... St. Catharines
20 .... Batavia
22-23 .... Geneva
24 .... Niagara Falls
25 .... Batavia
27-28 .... Pittsfield
29 .... St. Catharines
AUGUST
6-7 .... Watertown
8-9 .... Elmira
10-11 .... Auburn
12-13 .... Oneonta
21 .... St. Catharines
23-24 .... Jamestown
25 .... Niagara Falls
27-28 .... Erie
SEPTEMBER
3 .... St. Catharines

Jamestown
JUNE
15 .... Erie
19-20 .... Hamilton
22 .... Niagara Falls
23-24 ...... St. Catharines
25 .... Erie

27 .... Welland
JULY
1 .... Welland
3 .... Niagara Falls
6 .... Erie
12-13 ...... Niagara Falls
14 .... Erie
16-17 .... Hamilton
18-19 ...... St. Catharines
24 .... Batavia
25-26 .... Pittsfield
29 .... Erie
AUGUST
2-3 .... Auburn
4-5 .... Elmira
8-9 .... Oneonta
10-11 .... Utica
12-13 .... Geneva
18 .... Batavia
19-20 .... Watertown
31 .... Welland
SEPTEMBER
1 .... Welland
2-3 .... Erie

Niagara Falls
JUNE
17 .... Hamilton
21 .... Jamestown
23 .... Hamilton
25-26 .... Welland
28 .... St. Catharines
29-30 .... Erie
JULY
2 .... St. Catharines
4 .... Jamestown
6 .... Welland
8-9 .... Elmira
10 .... Batavia
15 .... Welland
16-17 .... Erie
22-23 .... Auburn
25-26 .... Watertown
29 .... Welland
31 .... Hamilton
AUGUST
8-9 .... Utica
10-11 .... Oneonta
12-13 .... Pittsfield
15 .... Batavia
17-18 .... Geneva
21 .... Welland
26 .... Hamilton
28 .... St. Catharines
29-30 .... Jamestown
SEPTEMBER
1 .... St. Catharines
3 .... Welland

Oneonta
JUNE
17 .... Utica
19-20 .... Watertown
22 .... Utica
25-26 .... Pittsfield
JULY
1 .... Elmira
3-4 .... Auburn
8-9 .... Jamestown
14-15 .... Geneva
16-17 .... Batavia
20-21 .... Erie
22 .... Utica
30 .... Elmira
AUGUST
1 .... Utica
2-3 .... Pittsfield
4-5 .... St. Catharines
6-7 .... Niagara Falls
17-18 .... Hamilton
19-20 .... Welland
21-22 .... Watertown
24 .... Utica
27-28 .... Pittsfield
30 .... Utica
31 .... Watertown

SEPTEMBER
1 .... Watertown
3 .... Pittsfield

Pittsfield
JUNE
15-16 .... Oneonta
21-22 .... Watertown
23-24 .... Utica
JULY
1-2 .... Auburn
3-4 .... Elmira
5-6 .... Oneonta
14-15 .... Batavia
16-17 .... Geneva
21-22 .... Jamestown
31 .... Watertown
AUGUST
1 .... Watertown
4-5 .... Hamilton
6-7 .... Erie
8-9 .... Welland
15-16 .... Oneonta
17-18 ...... St. Catharines
19-20 ...... Niagara Falls
25-26 .... Utica
29-30 .... Watertown
31 .... Utica
SEPTEMBER
1 .... Utica
2 .... Oneonta

St. Catharines
JUNE
15 .... Hamilton
17-18 .... Jamestown
20 .... Welland
25 .... Hamilton
27 .... Niagara Falls
29 .... Welland
JULY
1 .... Niagara Falls
3-4 .... Erie
6 .... Hamilton
14 .... Hamilton
16 .... Welland
20-21 .... Geneva
23-24 .... Elmira
25-26 .... Oneonta
27-28 .... Watertown
30 .... Hamilton
31 .... Batavia
AUGUST
6-7 .... Auburn
8 .... Batavia
10-11 .... Pittsfield
12-13 .... Utica
22 .... Hamilton
24 .... Welland
25-26 .... Jamestown
27 .... Niagara Falls
29-30 .... Erie
31 .... Niagara Falls
SEPTEMBER
2 .... Hamilton

Utica
JUNE
15 .... Watertown
18 .... Oneonta
19-20 .... Pittsfield
21 .... Oneonta
25 .... Watertown
27-28 .... Elmira
30 .... Auburn
JULY
2 .... Geneva
5 .... Watertown
8-9 .... Hamilton
12-13 .... Batavia
15 .... Auburn
18-19 .... Pittsfield
20-21 .... Welland
23 .... Oneonta
30 .... Geneva
31 .... Oneonta

1992 DIRECTORY • 163

HOME GAMES ONLY

AUGUST
- 2-3 .... Niagara Falls
- 5 .... Watertown
- 6-7 .... Jamestown
- 15-16 ...... St. Catharines
- 18 .... Watertown
- 19-20 .... Erie
- 21-22 .... Pittsfield
- 23 .... Oneonta
- 27 .... Watertown
- 29 .... Oneonta

SEPTEMBER
- 2 .... Watertown

Watertown
JUNE
- 16 .... Utica
- 17-18 .... Pittsfield
- 23-24 .... Oneonta
- 26 .... Utica
- 27 .... Auburn

JULY
- 1-2 .... Batavia
- 3-4 .... Geneva
- 6 .... Utica

- 8-9 .... St. Catharines
- 10-11 .... Jamestown
- 14-15 .... Elmira
- 17 .... Auburn
- 18-19 .... Oneonta
- 20-21 .... Niagara Falls
- 23-24 .... Pittsfield

AUGUST
- 2-3 .... Welland
- 4 .... Utica
- 8-9 .... Erie
- 14-15 .... Hamilton
- 17 .... Utica
- 23-24 .... Pittsfield
- 25-26 .... Oneonta
- 28 .... Utica

SEPTEMBER
- 3 .... Utica

Welland
JUNE
- 15-16 .... Niagara Falls
- 19 .... St. Catharines
- 23-24 .... Erie
- 28 .... Jamestown

- 30 .... St. Catharines

JULY
- 2 .... Jamestown
- 4 .... Hamilton
- 5 .... Niagara Falls
- 8-9 .... Geneva
- 10-11 .... Pittsfield
- 12 .... Hamilton
- 14 .... Niagara Falls
- 17 .... St. Catharines
- 23-24 .... Erie
- 25-26 .... Utica
- 27-28 .... Oneonta
- 30 .... Niagara Falls

AUGUST
- 5 .... Batavia
- 6-7 .... Elmira
- 10 .... Batavia
- 12-13 .... Watertown
- 14-15 .... Auburn
- 22 .... Niagara Falls
- 23 .... St. Catharines
- 27-28 .... Jamestown
- 29-30 .... Hamilton

SEPTEMBER
- 2 .... Niagara Falls

Northwest League

Bellingham
JUNE
- 17 .... Everett
- 19 .... Everett
- 22 .... Everett
- 23-24-25 .... Spokane

JULY
- 2-3-4 .... Yakima
- 12-13 .... Bend
- 14-15 .... Boise
- 21-22-23 .... Bend
- 24-25-26 .... Boise
- 27 .... Everett
- 29 .... Everett
- 31 .... So. Oregon

AUGUST
- 1-2 .... So. Oregon
- 3-4 .... Eugene
- 11-12-13 .... Bend
- 14-15 .... So. Oregon
- 22 .... Everett
- 24-25-26 .... Yakima

SEPTEMBER
- 2-3-4 .... Spokane

Bend
JUNE
- 17-18 .... Boise
- 23-24-25 ..... So. Oregon
- 29-30 .... Eugene

JULY
- 1 .... Eugene
- 6-7-8-9-10 .... Everett
- 16-17-18-19-20 ..... Bell.
- 27-28 .... Boise

AUGUST
- 5-6-7-8-9 .... Yakima
- 16-17-18-19-20 . Spokane
- 21-22 .... Boise
- 27-28-29 ..... So. Oregon
- 30-31 .... Eugene

SEPTEMBER
- 1 .... Eugene

Boise
JUNE
- 19-20-21-22 .... Bend
- 23-24-25-26-27-28 .. Eug.

JULY
- 6-7-8-9-10 .... Bellingham
- 16-17-18-19-20 ... Everett
- 29-30 .... Bend

AUGUST
- 5-6-7-8-9 .... Spokane

- 16-17-18-19-20 ... Yakima
- 30-31 .... So. Oregon

SEPTEMBER
- 1-2-3-4 .... So. Oregon

Eugene
JUNE
- 19-20-21-22 ... So.Oregon

JULY
- 2-3-4 .... Boise
- 11-12-13 .... Spokane
- 14-15 .... Yakima
- 22-23 .... Spokane
- 24-25-26 .... Yakima
- 29-30 .... So. Oregon

AUGUST
- 5-6-7-8-9 .... Everett
- 16-17-18-19-20 ..... Bell.
- 24-25-26 .... Bend
- 27-28-29 .... Boise

SEPTEMBER
- 2-3-4 .... Bend

Everett
JUNE
- 18 .... Bellingham
- 20-21 .... Bellingham
- 29-30 .... Yakima

JULY
- 1 .... Yakima
- 2-3-4 .... Spokane
- 11-12-13 .... Boise
- 14-15 .... Bend
- 22-23 .... Boise
- 24-25-26 .... Bend
- 28 .... Bellingham
- 30 .... Bellingham
- 31 .... Eugene

AUGUST
- 1-2 .... Eugene
- 3-4 .... So. Oregon
- 11-12-13 .... So. Oregon
- 14-15 .... Bend
- 21 .... Bellingham
- 24-25-26 .... Spokane

SEPTEMBER
- 2-3-4 .... Yakima

So. Oregon
JUNE
- 16-17 .... Eugene
- 26-27-28 .... Bend
- 29-30 .... Boise

JULY
- 1 .... Boise
- 2-3-4 .... Bend

- 11-12-13 .... Yakima
- 14-15 .... Spokane
- 22-23 .... Yakima
- 24-25-26 .... Spokane
- 27-28 .... Eugene

AUGUST
- 5-6-7-8-9 ..... Bellingham
- 16-17-18-19-20 ... Everett
- 21-22 .... Eugene
- 24-25-26 .... Boise

Spokane
JUNE
- 19-20-21-22 .... Yakima
- 26-27-28 .... Everett
- 29-30 .... Bellingham

JULY
- 1 .... Bellingham
- 6-7-8 .... Eugene
- 9-10 .... So. Oregon
- 16-17 .... Eugene
- 18-19-20 ... So. Oregon
- 29-30 .... Yakima
- 31 .... Boise

AUGUST
- 1 .... Boise
- 2-3-4 .... Bend
- 11-12-13 .... Boise
- 14-15 .... Bend
- 27-28-29 ...... Bellingham
- 30-31 .... Everett

SEPTEMBER
- 1 .... Everett

Yakima
JUNE
- 17-18 .... Spokane
- 23-24-25 .... Everett
- 26-27-28 ...... Bellingham

JULY
- 6-7-8 .... So. Oregon
- 9-10 .... Eugene
- 16-17 .... So. Oregon
- 18-19-20 .... Eugene
- 27-28 .... Spokane
- 31 .... Bend

AUGUST
- 1 .... Bend
- 2-3-4 .... Boise
- 11-12-13 .... Bend
- 14-15 .... Boise
- 21-22 .... Spokane
- 27-28-29 .... Everett
- 30-31 .... Bellingham

SEPTEMBER
- 1 .... Bellingham

164 • 1992 DIRECTORY

ROOKIE LEAGUES

Appalachian League

Bluefield
JUNE
25-26-27....Kingsport
28-29-30......Princeton
JULY
4-5-6............Huntington
7-8-9............Burlington
18-19-20.....Martinsville
31...............Kingsport
AUGUST
1-2..............Kingsport
9-10-11........Martinsville
12-13..........Elizabethton
14-15...........Pulaski
17-18-19......Princeton
23-24-25......Burlington
26-27-28......Huntington

Bristol
JUNE
19-20-21....Johnson City
25-26-27....Elizabethton
JULY
1-2-3............Burlington
7-8-9............Kingsport
15-16-17........Pulaski
21-22...........Martinsville
23-24............Bluefield
28-29-30.........Pulaski
AUGUST
3-4................Kingsport
6-7-8........Johnson City
9-10-11........Burlington
20-21-22.....Elizabethton
25................Kingsport

Burlington
JUNE
22-23-24.........Bluefield
28-29-30......Huntington
JULY
4-5-6............Martinsville
10-11-12.......Princeton
18-19-20..........Bristol
25-26-27..........Bristol
28-29-30......Huntington
AUGUST
3-4-5............Bluefield
12-13............Kingsport
14-15.......Johnson City
20-21-22......Princeton
26-27-28.....Martinsville

Elizabethton
JUNE
22-23-24....Johnson City
28-29-30.......Kingsport

JULY
1-2-3............Pulaski
10-11-12........Bristol
18-19-20.......Pulaski
21-22..........Burlington
23-24........Martinsville
31..................Bristol
AUGUST
1-2..................Bristol
6-7-8............Princeton
17-18-19.......Kingsport
23-24-25...Johnson City
26-27-28......Princeton

Huntington
JUNE
19-20-21.........Bluefield
22-23-24..........Pulaski
JULY
1-2-3............Princeton
10-11-12......Martinsville
15-16-17......Burlington
25-26-27.......Princeton
AUGUST
3-4-5...............Pulaski
6-7-8..............Bluefield
12-13...............Bristol
14-15...........Elizabethton
17-18-19......Burlington
20-21-22.....Martinsville

Johnson City
JUNE
25-26-27..........Pulaski
28-29-30.....Martinsville
JULY
4-5-6................Bristol
7-8-9.........Elizabethton
18-19-20.......Kingsport
21-22..............Bluefield
23-24...........Huntington
25-26-27.......Kingsport
28-29-30.....Martinsville
AUGUST
3-4-5..........Elizabethton
20-21-22.........Pulaski
26-27-28..........Bristol

Kingsport
JUNE
19-20-21..........Pulaski
22-23-24..........Bristol
JULY
1-2-3........Johnson City
10-11-12.......Bluefield
15-16-17....Elizabethton
21-22...........Huntington
23-24............Princeton
28-29-30....Elizabethton

AUGUST
4..................Bristol
9-10-11....Johnson City
20-21-22.....Bluefield
23-24..............Bristol
26-27-28........Pulaski

Martinsville
JUNE
19-20-21......Burlington
25-26-27......Huntington
JULY
1-2-3............Bluefield
7-8-9............Princeton
13-14-15..Johnson City
25-26-27........Bluefield
31................Huntington
AUGUST
1-2..............Huntington
6-7-8............Burlington
12-13............Pulaski
14-15............Kingsport
17-18-19...Johnson City
23-24-25......Princeton

Princeton
JUNE
19-20-21....Elizabethton
22-23-24....Martinsville
25-26-27......Burlington
JULY
5-5-6........Elizabethton
15-16-17......Bluefield
18-19-20....Huntington
28-29-30......Bluefield
31..............Burlington
AUGUST
1-2..............Burlington
3-4-5........Martinsville
9-10-11......Huntington
12-13.......Johnson City
14-15............Bristol

Pulaski
JUNE
28-29-30..........Bristol
JULY
4-5-6............Kingsport
7-8-9.........Huntington
10-11-12...Johnson City
21-22...........Princeton
23-24..........Burlington
25-26-27...Elizabethton
31............Johnson City
AUGUST
1-2..........Johnson City
6-7-8...........Kingsport
9-10-11....Elizabethton
17-18-19........Bristol
23-24-25......Huntington

Pioneer League

Billings
JUNE
20-21........Medicine Hat
22-23-24......Great Falls
29-30............Lethbridge
JULY
1..................Lethbridge
2-3............Medicine Hat
4-5..............Lethbridge
15-16-17-18....Salt Lake
19-20-21............Butte
27-28...........Lethbridge
29-30..........Great Falls
AUGUST
5-6-7-8..........Idaho Falls
9-10-11...........Helena
20-21-22....Medicine Hat
29-30.........Great Falls
SEPTEMBER
3-4-5..........Great Falls

Butte
JUNE
17-18-19........Salt Lake
21-22...............Helena

27.................Helena
30..............Idaho Falls
JULY
1...............Idaho Falls
3....................Helena
7-8-9..........Great Falls
10-11-12-13.....Billings
23-24..............Helena
25-26-27.....Idaho Falls
28-29..........Salt Lake
AUGUST
5-6-7-8.....Medicine Hat
9-10-11......Lethbridge

HOME GAMES ONLY — PIONEER LEAGUE/1992 SCHEDULE

21-22 ....Idaho Falls
26-27 ....Salt Lake
31 ....Helena
SEPTEMBER
1-2-3.............Helena

Great Falls
JUNE
17-18-19 ....Billings
20-21 ....Lethbridge
25-26 ....Billings
27-28 ....Lethbridge
JULY
4-5 ....Medicine Hat
15-16-17-18 ....Butte
19-20-21 ....Salt Lake
25-26 ....Billings
27-28 ......Medicine Hat
AUGUST
7-8................Helena
9-10-11 ......Idaho Falls
13-14 ....Helena
20-21-22 ......Lethbridge
23-24-25....Medicine Hat
31 ....Billings
SEPTEMBER
1-2................Billings

Helena
JUNE
17-18-19......Idaho Falls
20 ....Butte
28-29 ....Butte
30 ....Salt Lake
JULY
1 ....Salt Lake
2-4-5...............Butte
15-16-17-18.Medicine Hat
19-20-21 ......Lethbridge
25-26-27 ....Salt Lake
28-29 ....Idaho Falls
AUGUST
3-4 ....Butte
5-6 ....Great Falls
15 ....Great Falls
16-17-18-19 ......Billings

24-25 ....Salt Lake
29-30 ....Idaho Falls
SEPTEMBER
4-5 ....Butte

Idaho Falls
JUNE
23-24-25-26 ....Butte
27-28-29 ....Salt Lake
JULY
4-5 ....Salt Lake
15-16-17-18 ...Lethbridge
19-20-21....Medicine Hat
30-31 ....Helena
AUGUST
1-2 ....Helena
3-4..............Salt Lake
13-14-15 ....Billings
16-17-18-19...Great Falls
23-24-25 ....Butte
26-27-28 ....Helena
31 ....Salt Lake
SEPTEMBER
1-2..............Salt Lake

Lethbridge
JUNE
17-18-19....Medicine Hat
25-26 ....Medicine Hat
JULY
2-3 ....Great Falls
7-8-9 ....Idaho Falls
10-11-12-13 .....Helena
23-24 ....Billings
25-26 ....Medicine Hat
31 ....Billings
AUGUST
1..................Billings
2-3 ....Great Falls
13-14-15 ....Salt Lake
16-17-18-19 ....Butte
23-24-25 ....Billings
26-27-28 ......Great Falls

31 ....Medicine Hat
SEPTEMBER
1-2 ....Medicine Hat

Medicine Hat
JUNE
22-23-24 ......Lethbridge
27-28 ....Billings
29-30 ....Great Falls
JULY
1 ....Great Falls
7-8-9.............Helena
10-11-12-13...Idaho Falls
23-24 ....Great Falls
29-30 ....Lethbridge
31 ....Great Falls
AUGUST
1 ....Great Falls
2-3 ....Billings
13-14-15 ....Butte
16-17-18-19....Salt Lake
26-27-28 ....Billings
29-30 ....Lethbridge
SEPTEMBER
3-4-5..........Lethbridge

Salt Lake City
JUNE
20-21-22......Idaho Falls
23-24-25-26 ......Helena
JULY
2-3 ....Idaho Falls
7-8-9.............Billings
10-11-12-13...Great Falls
23-24 ....Idaho Falls
30-31 ....Butte
AUGUST
1-2 ....Butte
5-6-7-8........Lethbridge
9-10-11 .....Medicine Hat
21-22-23 ....Helena
28-29-30 ....Butte
SEPTEMBER
3-4-5 ....Idaho Falls

166 • 1992 DIRECTORY

INTERNATIONAL BASEBALL

MEXICAN LEAGUE

Class AAA

Mailing Address: Angel Pola #16, Col. Periodista, C.P. 11220, Mexico, D.F. **Telephone:** (905) 557-10-07 or (905) 557-14-08.
President: Pedro Treto Cisneros.
Assistant to the President/Public Relations: Nestor Alva Brito.
Years League Active: 1955-1992.
1992 Opening Date: March 18. **Closing Date:** August 19.
No. of Games, Regular Season: 134.
Division Structure: South—Campeche, Cordoba, Mexico City Red Devils, Mexico City Tigers, Minatitlan, Tabasco, Veracruz, Yucatan; **North**—Aguascalientes, Jalisco, Monclova, Monterrey Industrials, Monterrey Sultans, Saltillo, Two Laredos, Union Laguna.
Playoff Format: Three-tier playoffs involving top four teams in each division, with the winners in each division playing a best-of-7 series for league championship.
All-Star Game: June 11 in Merida.
Roster Limit: 25.
Statistician: Ana Luisa Perea, Angel Pola #16, Col. Periodista, C.P. 11220 Mexico, D.F.

Aguascalientes Railroadmen

Office Address: Av. Adolfo Lopez Mateos No. 407, Despacho 306 Ote, Aguascalientes, Aguascalientes. **Telephone:** (491) 15-80-33 or 15-24-79.
Operated by: Club Rieleros.
President: Benjamin Romo Munoz.
General Manager: Ernesto Rios Gonzalez.
Field Manager: Gregorio Luque.

Campeche Pirates

Office Address: Unidad Deportiva 20 De Nov. Local 4, Campeche, Campeche. **Telephone:** (981) 660-71 or 638-07.
Operated by: Empresa Promotora Artistica y Deportiva de Campeche.
President: Gustavo Ortiz.
General Manager: Manuel Cortes. **General Administrator:** Socorro Morales.
Field Manager: Jorge Tellaeche.

Cordoba Coffeegrowers

Office Address: Av. Adolfo Lopez Mateos, Cordoba, Veracruz. **Telephone:** (271) 417-42 or 278-08.
Operated by: Deportivo Cafeteros de Cordoba.
President: Evelio Brito Gomez.
Field Manager: Bernardo Calvo Perez.

Jalisco Cowboys

Office Address: Fray Antonio de Segovia No. 666, Colonia Universitaria, Guadalajara, Jalisco. **Telephone:** (36) 50-18-13 or 50-18-20
Operated by: Espectaculos Artisticos y Deportivos de Occidente.
President: Guillermo Cosio Gaona.
General Manager: Jose Luis Gutierrez Aguilar.
Field Manager: Roberto Castellon.

Mexico City Red Devils

Office Address: Av. Cuauhtemoc #451-101 or 102 Col. Piedad Narvarte C.P. 03020, Mexico, D.F. **Telephone:** (915) 543-10-75 and 536-31-36.
Operated by: Club Deportivo Mexico Rojos, S.A.
President: Roberto Mansur Galan. **Vice President:** Chara Mansur.
General Manager: Pedro Mayorquin.
Field Manager: Ramon Montoya.

Mexico City Tigers

Office Address: Tuxpan No. 45-A 5th Floor, Col. Roma, C.P. 06760 Mexico D.F. **Telephone:** (905) 584-02-16 or 584-02-49.
Operated by: Club de Beisbol Tigres.
General Manager: Jose Luis Huerta.
Field Manager: Oswaldo Alvarez.

Minatitlan
Office Address: Merida y Justo Sierra, Minatitlan, Veracruz. **Telephone:** (922) 402-08.
  Operated by: Club de Beisbol Petroleros de Minatitlan.
  President: Santiago Burelo Toledo.
  General Manager: Simeon Dominguez Pitalua.
  Field Manager: Francisco Estrada.

Monclova Steelers
Office Address: Venustiano Carranza No. 221, Altos Monclava, Coahuila. **Telephone:** (863) 374-33.
  Operated by: Espectaculos y Deportes de Monclova.
  President: Jorge Williamson Bosques.
  General Manager: Miguel Sotelo.
  Field Manager: Jose Soto Acuna.

Monterrey Industrials
Office Address: Rio Panuco No. 452 Oriente, Col. del Valle, Monterrey, Nuevo Leon. **Telephone:** (83) 78-62-32 or 78-59-65.
  Operated by: Club de Beisbol Industriales de Monterrey.
  President: Jose Canales Cantu.
  General Manager: Rogelio Treto Cisneros.
  Field Manager: Marcelo Juarez.

Monterrey Sultans
Office Address: Av. Manuel L. Barragan S/N A.P. 870, V.P. 64820, Estadio Monterrey, Monterrey, Nuevo Leon. **Telephone:** (83) 51-91-86 or 51-39-61.
  Operated by: Club de Beisbol Monterrey.
  President: Jose Maiz Carcia.
  General Manager: Roberto Magdeleno Ramirez.
  Field Manager: Aurelio Rodriguez.

Saltillo Sarape Makers
Office Address: Hidalgo Norte No. 337 C.P. 25000, Saltillo, Coahuila. **Telephone:** (841) 208-72.
  Operated by: Club de Beisbol Saltillo.
  President: Armando Guadiana Tijerina.
  General Manager: Victor Favela.
  Field Manager: Juan Navarrete.

Tabasco Olmecas
Office Address: Venustiano Carranza #148, Villahermosa, Tabasco. **Telephone:** (831) 446-92 or 446-93.
  Operated by: Deportes y Espectaculos de Tabasco.
  President: Diego Rosique Palavicini. **Vice President:** Manuel Manrique Cortinas.
  General Manager: Jorge Luis Vergara.
  Field Manager: Rodolfo Sandoval.

Owls of the Two Laredos
Office Address: Ave. Obregon No. 1035, Nuevo Laredo, Tamaulipas. **Telephone:** (871) 271-92 or 271-93.
  Operated by: Empresa Deportiva de Nuevo Laredo.
  President: Victor Lozano Rendon.
  General Manager: Jorge Luis Lozano Guajardo.
  Field Manager: Jose Guerrero Cano.

Union Laguna Cotton Pickers
Office Address: Calle Gutemberg, Estadio de la Revolucion C.P. 27000, Torreon, Coahuila. **Telephone:** (17) 17-43-35.
  Operated by: Concesiones, S.A.
  President: Jorge Duenes Zurita. **Vice President:** Antonio Duenes Zurita.
  General Manager: Guillermo Garibay.
  Field Manager: Marco Antonio Vazquez.

Veracruz Eagles
Office Address: Domicilio Conocido, Veracruz, Veracruz. **Telephone:** (573) 56-57 or (655) 90-32.
  Operated by: Club Deportivo Aguila.
  President: Vicente Perez Avella. **Vice President:** Alfonso Pasquel.
  General Manager: Andres Gutierrez de la Fuente.
  Field Manager: Jack Pierce.

Yucatan Lions
Office Address: Calle 14 No. 70, Col. Chuminopolis, C.P. 97158, Merida, Yucatan. **Telephone:** (99) 27-09-45 or 27-19-00 ext. 317.
  Operated by: Desarrollo Inmobiliario Siglo XXI.
  President: Arturo Millet Molina. **Vice President:** Jorge Menendez Torre.
  Field Manager: Fernando Villaescusa.

JAPANESE BASEBALL

Mailing Address: Imperial Tower, 7F, 1-1-1 Uchisaiwai-cho, Chiyoda-Ku, Tokyo 100, Japan. **Telephone:** 03-3502-0022. **FAX:** 03-3502-0140.
Commissioner: Ichiro Yoshikuni.
Secretary General: Kiyoshi Honami.

PACIFIC LEAGUE

Mailing Address: Asahi Bldg. 9F, 6-6-7 Ginza, Chuo-ku, Tokyo 104. **Telephone:** 03-3573-1551. **FAX:** 03-3572-5843.
President: Kazuo Harano. **Secretary General:** Shigeru Murata.

1991 Standings, 1992 Stadiums

Club	W	L	T	Pct.	GB	Stadium	Cap.
Seibu Lions	81	43	6	.653	—	Seibu Lions	37,008
Kintetsu Buffaloes	77	48	5	.616	4½	Fujiidera	32,000
Orix Blue Wave	64	63	3	.504	18½	Kobe Green	35,000
Nippon Ham Fighters	53	72	5	.424	28½	Tokyo Dome	56,000
Fukuoka Daiei Hawks	53	73	4	.445	29	Heiwadai	33,890
Lotte Orions	48	77	5	.384	33½	Chiba Marine	30,000

Chiba Lotte Orions

Mailing Address: WBG Marivewest 25F, 2-6 Nakase, Chibashi, Chiba-ken 261-71. **Telephone:** Unavailable. **FAX:** Unavailable.
Chairman of the Board: Takeo Shigemitsu.
General Manager: Toshio Abe.
Field Manager: Soroku Yagicawa.
1992 Foreign Players: Mike Diaz, Max Venable.

Fukuoka Daiei Hawks

Mailing Address: Otemon Pine Bldg. 6F, 1-1-12 Otemon, Chuo-ku, Fukuoka 810. **Telephone:** 092-711-1189. **FAX:** 092-731-5504.
Chairman of the Board: Isao Nakauchi.
President: Hisashi Tanabe.
General Manager: Yasuyuki Sakai.
Field Manager: Koichi Tabuchi.
1992 Foreign Players: Mike Laga, Lee Tunnell, Boomer Wells.

Kintetsu Buffaloes

Mailing Address: Kintetsu Namba Bldg. 7F, 4-1-15 Namba, Chuo-ku, Osaka 542. **Telephone:** 06-644-5557. **FAX:** 06-641-7422.
Chairman of the Board: Yoshinori Ueyama.
President and General Manager: Yasuo Maeda.
Field Manager: Akira Ogi.
1992 Foreign Players: Billy Bean, Ralph Bryant, Jessie Reid.

Nippon Ham Fighters

Mailing Address: Roppongi Denki Bldg. 6F, 6-1-20 Roppongi, Minato-ku, Tokyo 106. **Telephone:** 03-3403-9131. **FAX:** 03-3403-9143.
Chairman of the Board: Yoshinori Okoso.
President: Saburo Mochida.
General Manager: Masayuki Dobashi.
Field Manager: Masayuki Dobashi.
1992 Foreign Players: Bill Bathe, Mike Marshall, Matt Winters.

Orix Blue Wave

Mailing Address: Kanri Center, 2F, Midoridai, Suma-ku, Kobe 654-01. **Telephone:** 078-795-1001. **FAX:** 078-795-1005.
Chairman of the Board: Yoshihiko Miyauchi.
President: Toshio Saruwatari.
General Manager: Shigeyoshi Ino.
Field Manager: Shozo Doi.
1992 Foreign Players: Don Schulze, Kelvin Torve. **Coach:** Jim Colborn.

Seibu Lions

Mailing Address: Seibu Lions Stadium, 2135 Kami-Yamaguchi, Tokorozawa-shi, Saitama-ken 359. **Telephone:** 0429-24-1155. **FAX:** 0429-28-1919.
Chairman of the Board: Yoshiaki Tsutsumi.

General Manager: Nobuhito Shimizu.
Field Manager: Masaaki Mori.
1992 Foreign Players: Orestes Destrade, Taigen Kaku (Taiwan), Ray Young.

CENTRAL LEAGUE

Mailing Address: Asahi Bldg. 3F, 6-6-7 Ginza, Chuo-ku, Tokyo 104. **Telephone:** 03-3572-1673. **FAX:** 03-3571-4545.
President: Hiromori Kawashima.
Secretary General: Ryoichi Shibusawa.
Planning Department: Masaaki Nagino.

1991 Standings, 1992 Stadiums

Club	W	L	T	Pct.	GB	Stadium	Cap.
Hiroshima Carp	74	56	2	.569	—	Hiroshima	32,920
Chunichi Dragons	71	59	1	.546	3	Nagoya	35,000
Yakult Swallows	67	63	2	.515	7	Meiji Jingu	48,785
Yomiuri Giants	66	64	0	.508	8	Tokyo Dome	56,000
Taiyo Whales	64	66	1	.492	10	Yokohama	30,000
Hanshin Tigers	48	82	0	.369	26	Koshien	58,000

Chunichi Dragons

Mailing Address: Chunichi Bldg. 9F, 4-1-11 Sakae, Naka-ku, Nagoya 460. **Telephone:** 052-252-5226. **FAX:** 052-251-8649.
Chairman of the Board: Miichiro Kato.
President: Satoru Nakayama.
General Manager: Hiroo Ito.
Field Manager: Morimichi Takagi.
1992 Foreign Players: Scott Anderson, Mark Ryal.

Hanshin Tigers

Mailing Address: 1-47 Koshien-cho, Nishinomiya-shi, Hyogo-ken 663. **Telephone:** 0798-46-1515. **FAX:** 0798-40-0934.
Chairman of the Board: Shunjiro Kuma.
President: Kazuhiko Miyoshi.
General Manager: Kuniaki Sawada.
Field Manager: Katsuhiro Nakamura.
1992 Foreign Players: Tom O'Malley, Jim Paciorek.

Hiroshima Toyo Carp

Mailing Address: 5-25 Motomachi, Naka-ku, Hiroshima 730. **Telephone:** 082-221-2040. **FAX:** 082-228-5013.
Chairman of the Board: Kohei Matsuda.
General Manager: Chitomi Takahashi.
Field Manager: Koji Yamamoto.
1992 Foreign Players: Marty Brown.

Yakult Swallows

Mailing Address: Yakult Bldg. 7F, 1-1-19 Higashi-Shimbashi, Minato-ku, Tokyo 105. **Telephone:** 03-3574-0671. **FAX:** 03-3574-6764.
Chairman of the Board: Hisami Matsuzono.
President: Kazuo Soma.
General Manager: Itaru Taguchi.
Field Manager: Katsuya Nomura.
1992 Foreign Players: Jack Howell, Johnny Ray.

Yokohama Taiyo Whales

Mailing Address: Kinoshita Shoji Bldg. 7F, 4-43 Masago-cho, Naka-ku, Yokohama 231. **Telephone:** 045-681-0811. **FAX:** 045-661-2500.
Chairman of the Board: Keijiro Nakabe.
President: Hiroshi Okazaki.
General Manager: Kaoru Sakurai.
Field Manager: Yutaka Sudo.
1992 Foreign Players: R.J. Reynolds, Larry Sheets.

Yomiuri Giants

Mailing Address: 1-3-7 Uchikanda, Chiyoda-ku, Tokyo 101. **Telephone:** 03-3295-7711. **FAX:** 03-3295-7731.
Chairman of the Board: Toru Shoriki.
General Manager: Takeshi Yuasa.
Field Manager: Motoshi Fujita.
1992 Foreign Players: Chuck Cary, Denny Gonzalez, Yorkis Perez.

WINTER BASEBALL

Arizona Fall Baseball League
Address: Unavailable. **Telephone:** Unavailable.
President: Mike Port.
Team Locations: Chandler, Phoenix (2), Scottsdale, Sun City, Tucson.

Hawaiian Winter League
Address: 733 Bishop St., PRI Tower, Suite 1465, Honolulu, HI 96813.
Telephone: (808) 536-7874. **FAX:** (808) 536-7946.
Chairman: Robert Berg. **President:** Bob Richmond.
Team Locations: Honolulu (Oahu), Lahaina (Maui), Wailuku (Maui), Hilo (Hawaii).

Caribbean Baseball Confederation
Mailing Address: 171-A, C.P. 83190, Hermosillo, Sonora, Mexico.
Telephone: (011-52-621) 4-35-62 and 4-86-20. **FAX:** (011-52-621) 4-95-17.
Commissioner: Horacio Lopez Diaz (Mexico).
Administrator: Israel Gonzalez.

Dominican League
Mailing Address: Ave. 27 de Febrero No. 218, Edificio Standard Quimica, 4 ta. Planta, Apartado, Santo Domingo, Dom. Rep. **Telephone:** (809) 567-6371. **FAX:** (809) 567-5720.
President: Dr. Leonardo Matos Berrido.

AGUILAS
Apartado Postal #111
Estadio Cibao
Santiago, Dom. Rep.
President: **Ricardo Hernandez.**
ph: (809) 575-4310
1991-92 Manager: **Brian Graham.**

AZUCAREROS
Apartado Postal #145
Zona Franca La Romana,
Dom. Rep.
President: **Arturo Gil.**
ph: (809) 556-4955.
1991-92 Manager: **Luis Silverio.**

ESCOGIDO
Estadio Quisqueya
Santo Domingo, Dom. Rep.
President: **Daniel Aquino.**
ph: (809) 565-1910.
1990-91 Manager: **Felipe Alou.**

ESTRELLAS
Avenida Independicia No. 33
San Pedro de Macoris, Dom. Rep.
Vice President: **Manuel Antun**
ph: (809) 529-3340.
1991-92 Manager: **Nelson Norman.**

LICEY
Estadio Quisqueya
Santo Domingo, Dom. Rep.
President: **Domingo Pichardo.**
ph: (809) 567-3090,
1991-92 Manager: **Leo Posada.**

Mexican Pacific League
Mailing Address: Pesqueria No. 401-R Altos, Edificio Borques, Navojoa, Sonora, Mexico. **Telephone:** (011-52-642) 2-31-00. **FAX:** (011-52-642) 2-72-50
President: Arturo Leon Lerma.

CULIACAN
Carret. Intern. al Norte y Calle Deportiva
Culiacan, Sinaloa, Mexico
President: **Juan Manuel Ley.**
ph: (671) 6-18-99.
1991-92 Manager: **Jorge Tellaeche.**

GUASAVE
Ave. Obregon #43
Guasave, Sinaloa, Mexico
President: **Reynaldo Valencia Amador.**
ph: (687) 2-14-31.
1991-92 Manager: **Carlos Paz.**

HERMOSILLO
Nayarti 130, Local 4
Hermosillo, Sonora, Mexico
President: **Enrique Mazon.**
ph: (621) 4-07-80.
1991-92 Manager: **Maximino Leon.**

LOS MOCHIS
Angel Flores #473.
Los Mochis, Sinaloa, Mexico
President: **Mario Lopez Valdez.**
ph: (681) 8-25-05.
1991-92 Manager: **Aurelio Rodriguez.**

MAZATLAN
Estadio Teodoro Mariscal
Apartado Postal 488
Mazatlan, Sinaloa, Mexico
President: **Hermilo Diaz Bringas.**
ph: (698) 3-30-12.
1991-92 Manager: **Leobardo Figueroa.**

MEXICALI
Calzada Ex-Avacion.
Mexicali, Baja California.
President: **Mario Hernandez.**
ph: (656) 67-00-40.
1991-92 Manager: **Francisco Estrada.**

NAVOJOA
Pesqueira y Matamoros Desp. #8
Novojoa, Sonora, Mexico
President: **Victor Cuevas Garibay.**
ph: (642) 2-14-33.
1991-92 Manager: **Lorenzo Bundy.**

OBREGON
Yucatan y Nayarit #294
Edifico C, Dpto. #11
Ciudad Obregon, Sonora, Mexico
President: **Luis Felipe Garcia de Leon.**
ph: (641) 4-11-56.
1991-92 Manager: **Mario Mendoza.**

Puerto Rican League

Mailing Address: Edificio First Federal, Ave. Munoz Rivera, Rio Piedras, PR 00925. **Telephone:** (809) 765-6285 or 765-7285. **FAX:** (809) 767-3028.
President: Peter Ortiz. **Executive Director:** Benny Agosto.

ARECIBO
Apartado 582
Arecibo, PR 00616
President: **Josue D. Vega.**
ph: (809) 878-2776.
1991-92 Manager: **Steve Swisher.**

BAYAMON
Juan Ramon Loubriel Stadium
Bayamon, Puerto Rico 00619
Co-owners: **Hector Vasquez**
Johnny Vasquez
ph: (809) 758-2565.
1991-92 Manager: **Ramon Aviles.**

MAYAGUEZ
Box 3089, Marina Station
Mayaguez, PR 00709
President: **Ivan Mendez.**
ph: (809) 834-1111.
1991-92 Manager: **Pat Kelly.**

PONCE
P.O. Box 1524
Ponce, PR 00731
President: **Jose Cangiano.**
ph: (809) 842-6116.
1991-92 Manager: **Orlando Gomez.**

SAN JUAN
Apartado 4223
Bayamon, PR 00936
President: **Angel Umpierre.**
ph: (809) 754-1300.
1991-92 Manager: **Jerry Royster.**

SANTURCE
PO Box 1144
San Juan, PR 00936
President: **Reinaldo Paniagua Diez.**
ph: (809) 764-0089.
1991-92 Manager: **Max Oliveras.**

Venezuelan League

Mailing Address: Avenida Sorbona, Edif. Marta-2do. Piso, No. 25, Colinas de Bello Monte, Caracas, Venezuela. **Telephone:** (011-58-2) 751-2079 or 751-1891. **FAX:** (011-58-2) 751-0891.
President: Carlos Larrazabal Garcia.
Division Structure: Eastern—Caracas, LaGuaira, Magallanes, Puerto La Cruz. **Western**—Aragua, Cabimas, Lara, Zulia.

ARAGUA
Estadio Jose Perez Colmenares
Barrio La Demoncracia
Maracay-Edo.
Aragua, Venezuela
President: **Homero Diaz Osuna.**
ph: (011-58-43) 54-46-32.
1991-92 Manager: **Rick Down.**

CABIMAS
Avenida 11 (Veritos)
Edificio 95-5, Piso 3
Maracaibo, Edo.
Zulia, Venezuela
President: **Beto Finol.**
ph: (011-58-6) 191-0083.
1991-92 Manager: **Jose Martinez.**

CARACAS
Avenida Francisco de Miranda
Centro Seguros
Piso 4, La Paz, Oficina North 426
Caracas, Venezuela
President: **Pablo Morales Chirinos.**
ph: (011-58-2) 238-06-91.
1991-92 Manager: **Phil Regan.**

LaGUAIRA
Edif. Cada, Avda. Soublette
Piso 1, Oficina No. 8
LaGuaira, Venezuela
President: **Pedro Padron Panza.**
ph: (011-58-31) 25-5-79.
1991-92 Manager: **Ozzie Virgil**

LARA
Av. Rotaria, Estadio Barquisimeto
Barquisimeto-Edo.
Lara, Venezuela
President: **Aldolfo Alvarez.**
ph: (011-58-51) 42-45-43.
1991-92 Manager: **Domingo Carrasquel.**

MAGALLANES
Estadio Jose Bernardo Perez
Valencia-Edo Carabobo
Valencia, Venezuela
President: **Jose Ettedgui.**
ph: (011-58-41) 21-59-44.
1991-92 Manager: **Rick Sweet.**

ORIENTE
Ave. Stadium
Centro Comercial Novocentro
2do piso, local 2-4
Puerto La Cruz,
Edo. Anzoategui, Venezuela
President: **Gioconda de Marquez.**
ph: (011-58-81) 66-25-36.
1991-92 Manager: **Rick Patterson.**

ZULIA
Ave. 8 (Santa Rita)
Edificio Las Carolinas Local M-10
Maracaibo, Zulia, Venezuela
President: **Lucas Rincon.**
ph: (011-58-61) 92-03-35.
1991-92 Manager: **Ruben Amaro.**

Australian Baseball League

Mailing Address: P.O. Box 827, Potts Point, New South Wales, Australia, 2011. **Telephone:** (011-61-2) 357-3595. **FAX:** (011-61-2) 357-7068.
General Manager: George Anderson.
Member Clubs (1991-92 Managers): Adelaide Giants (Phil Alexander), Brisbane Bandits (Steve Gilmore), Daikyo Dolphins (Adrian Meagher), Melbourne Bushrangers (Dan McConnon), Perth Heat (Mike Young), Sydney Blues (xxx), Sydney Wave (Tad Powers), Waverly Reds (Phil Dale).

COLLEGE & AMATEUR

COLLEGE BASEBALL

National Collegiate Athletic Association

Mailing Address: 6201 College Blvd., Overland Park, KS 66211. **Telephone:** (913) 339-1906. **FAX:** (913) 339-0026.

Executive Director: Richard Schultz. **Director of Championships:** Dennis Poppe. **Baseball Media Contact:** Jim Wright. **Chairman, Baseball Committee:** Gene McArtor, University of Missouri.

1993 National Convention: Jan. 13-16, at Dallas, Texas.

Championship Tournaments

NCAA Division I
College World Series, May 29-June 6, 1992, Omaha, Neb.
Regionals, May 21-24 or May 22-25, 1992 on campus sites.

NCAA Division II
World Series, May 23-30, 1992, Montgomery, Ala.

NCAA Division III
World Series, May 21-26, 1992, Battle Creek, Mich.

National Association of Intercollegiate Athletics

Mailing Address: 1221 Baltimore Ave., Kansas City, MO 64105. **Telephone:** (816) 842-5050. **FAX:** (816) 421-4471.

Chief Executive Officer: James Chasteen. **Baseball Administrator:** Charlie Eppler.

Championship Tournament

NAIA World Series, May 22-28, 1992, Des Moines, Iowa.

National Junior College Athletic Association

Mailing Address: P.O. Box 7305, Colorado Springs, CO 80933. **Telephone:** (719) 590-9788.

Executive Director: George Killian. **Baseball Tournament Director:** Sam Suplizio.

Championship Tournament

Junior College World Series, May 23-30, 1992, Grand Junction, Colo.

American Baseball Coaches Association

Office Address: 35 Montague Rd., North Amherst, MA 01059. **Mailing Address:** P.O. Box 665, North Amherst, MA 01059. **Telephone:** (413) 549-2626. **FAX:** (413) 549-4242.

Executive Director: Dick Bergquist. **Administrative Assistant:** Sarah Roys. **President:** Jim Dimick, St. Olaf (Minn.) College.

1993 National Convention: Jan. 8-11 at Atlanta, Ga.

National Federation of State High School Associations

Office Address: 11724 NW Plaza Circle, Kansas City, MO 64195. **Mailing Address:** P.O. Box 20626, Kansas City, MO 64195. **Telephone:** (816) 464-5400.

Executive Director: Brice Durbin. **Associate Director:** Fritz McGinness. **Director of Public Relations:** Bruce Howard.

National High School Baseball Coaches Association

Mailing Address: P.O. Box 12354, Omaha, NE 68112. **Telephone:** (402) 457-1962. **FAX:** Same.

Executive Director: Jerry Miles. **Administrative Assistant:** Elaine Miles. **President:** Richard Hofman, Westminster Christian High, Miami, Fla.

1992 National Convention: Nov. 27-29. Site: Unavailable.

NCAA Division I Conference Offices

ATLANTIC COAST CONFERENCE
Mailing Address: P.O. Drawer ACC, Greensboro, NC 27419.
Telephone: (919) 854-8787. **FAX:** (919) 854-8797.
Baseball Members: Clemson, Duke, Florida State, Georgia Tech, Maryland, North Carolina, North Carolina State, Virginia, Wake Forest.
Assistant Service Bureau Director: Brian Morrison.
1992 Tournament: May 9-13 at Greenville, S.C.

ATLANTIC-10 CONFERENCE
Mailing Address: 10 Woodbridge Center Drive, Woodbridge, NJ 07095.
Telephone: (908) 634-6900. **FAX:** (908) 634-6923.
Baseball Members: East—Massachusetts, Rhode Island, Rutgers, St. Joseph's, Temple. **West**—Duquesne, George Washington, St. Bonaventure, West Virginia.
Director of Communications: Ray Cella.
1992 Tournament: May 8-10 at Boyertown, Pa.

BIG EAST CONFERENCE
Mailing Address: 56 Exchange Terrace, Providence, RI 02903.
Telephone: (401) 272-9108. **FAX:** (401) 751-8540.
Baseball Members: Boston College, Connecticut, Georgetown, Pittsburgh, Providence, St. John's, Seton Hall, Villanova.
Sports Information Assistants: Joe Gomes, Maura Toole.
1992 Tournament: May 12-15 at Bristol, Conn.

BIG EIGHT CONFERENCE
Mailing Address: 104 W. Ninth St., Baltimore Place, Suite 408, Kansas City, MO 64105.
Telephone: (816) 471-5088. **FAX:** (816) 471-4601.
Baseball Members: Iowa State, Kansas, Kansas State, Missouri, Nebraska, Oklahoma, Oklahoma State.
Service Bureau Director: Jeff Bollig.
1992 Tournament: May 15-17 at Oklahoma City, Okla.

BIG SOUTH CONFERENCE
Mailing Address: 1551 21st Ave. N., Suite 13, Myrtle Beach, SC 29577.
Telephone: (803) 448-9998. **FAX:** (803) 626-7167.
Baseball Members: Campbell, Charleston Southern, Coastal Carolina, Davidson, Liberty, UNC Asheville, Radford, Winthrop.
Public Relations Assistant: Karen Clark.
1992 Tournament: May 15-17, at Conway, S.C.

BIG TEN CONFERENCE
Mailing Address: 1500 W. Higgins Road, Park Ridge, IL 60068.
Telephone: (708) 696-1010. **FAX:** (708) 696-1110.
Baseball Members: Illinois, Indiana, Iowa, Michigan, Michigan State, Minnesota, Northwestern, Ohio State, Penn State, Purdue.
Assistant Communications Director: Dennis LaBissoniere.
1992 Tournament: May 14-17 at regular-season champion.

BIG WEST CONFERENCE
Mailing Address: 1700 E. Dyer Road, Suite 140, Santa Ana, CA 92705.
Telephone: (714) 261-2525. **FAX:** (714) 261-2528.
Baseball Members: UC Irvine, UC Santa Barbara, Cal State Fullerton, Fresno State, Long Beach State, Nevada-Las Vegas, New Mexico State, Pacific, San Jose State.
Director of Information Services: Andy Geerken.
1992 Tournament: None.

COLONIAL ATHLETIC ASSOCIATION
Mailing Address: 2550 Professional Road, Ste. 16, Richmond, VA 23235.
Telephone: (804) 272-1616. **FAX:** (804) 272-1688.
Baseball Members: East Carolina, George Mason, James Madison, UNC Wilmington, Old Dominion, Richmond, William & Mary.
Information Director: Tripp Sheppard.
1992 Tournament: May 12-15 at Greenville, N.C.

EAST COAST CONFERENCE
Mailing Address: 946 Farnsworth Ave., Bordentown, NJ 08505.
Telephone: (609) 298-4009. **FAX:** (609) 298-6023.
Baseball Members: Brooklyn, Central Connecticut State, Hofstra, Maryland-Baltimore County, Rider, Towson State.
Information Director: Marie Wasniak.
1992 Tournament: May 8-10, at Lawrenceville, N.J.

EASTERN COLLEGE ATHLETIC CONFERENCE
Mailing Address: P.O. Box 3, Centerville, MA 02632.
Telephone: (508) 771-5060. **FAX:** (508) 771-9481.
Baseball Members: North Atlantic Section—Boston University, Delaware, Drexel, Hartford, Maine, New Hampshire, Northeastern, Vermont. **Northeast Conference**—Fairleigh Dickinson, Long Island, Marist, Monmouth, Mount St. Mary's, St. Francis, Wagner. **Metro Atlantic**

Athletic Conference **North**—Canisius, LeMoyne, Niagara, Siena. **MAAC South**—Fairfield, Iona, LaSalle, Manhattan, St. Peter's. **Patriot League**—Bucknell, Colgate, Fordham, Holy Cross, Lafayette, Lehigh.
Publicity Director: John Garner.
1992 Tournament: May 13-16 at Orono, Maine.

EASTERN INTERCOLLEGIATE BASEBALL LEAGUE
Mailing Address: 120 Alexander St., Princeton, NJ 08544.
Telephone: (609) 258-6426. **FAX:** (609) 258-1690.
Baseball Members: Army, Brown, Columbia, Cornell, Dartmouth, Harvard, Navy, Pennsylvania, Princeton, Yale.
Director of Public Information: Roger Yrigoyen.
1992 Tournament: None.

GREAT MIDWEST CONFERENCE
Mailing Address: 35 E. Wacker Drive, Chicago, IL 60601.
Telephone: (312) 553-0483. **FAX:** (312) 553-0495.
Baseball Members: Alabama-Birmingham, Cincinnati, Memphis State, Saint Louis.
Director of Media Relations: Tim Stephens.
1992 Tournament: May 13-15 at Birmingham, Ala.

METRO CONFERENCE
Mailing Address: Two Ravinia Drive, Suite 210, Atlanta, GA 30346.
Telephone: (404) 395-6444. **FAX:** (404) 395-6423.
Baseball Members: Louisville, UNC Charlotte, South Florida, Southern Mississippi, Tulane, Virginia Commonwealth, Virginia Tech.
Assistant Director of Communications: Tim Parker.
1992 Tournament: May 13-17 at New Orleans, La.

MID-AMERICAN CONFERENCE
Mailing Address: Four SeaGate, Suite 102, Toledo, OH 43604.
Telephone: (419) 249-7177. **FAX:** (419) 249-7199.
Baseball Members: Ball State, Bowling Green State, Central Michigan, Eastern Michigan, Kent State, Miami (Ohio), Ohio, Toledo, Western Michigan.
Director of Media Relations: John McNamara.
1992 Tournament: May 14-16 at regular-season champion.

MID-CONTINENT CONFERENCE
Mailing Address: 300 E. Shannon Blvd., Suite 118, Naperville, IL 60563.
Telephone: (708) 416-7560. **FAX:** (708) 416-7564.
Baseball Members: East—Akron, Cleveland State, Wright State, Youngstown State. **West**—Eastern Illinois, Illinois-Chicago, Northern Illinois, Valparaiso, Western Illinois.
Publicity Director: Tom Lessig.
1992 Tournament: May 15-18 at Chicago, Ill.

MID-EASTERN ATHLETIC CONFERENCE
Mailing Address: P.O. Box 21205, Greensboro, NC 27420.
Telephone: (919) 275-9961. **FAX:** (919) 275-9964.
Baseball Members: Bethune-Cookman, Coppin State, Delaware State, Florida A&M, Howard, Maryland-Eastern Shore, North Carolina A&T State.
Director of Service Bureau: Larry Barber.
1992 Tournament: April 16-18 at Tallahassee, Fla.

MIDWESTERN COLLEGIATE CONFERENCE
Mailing Address: Pan American Plaza, 201 S. Capitol St., Suite 500, Indianapolis, IN 46225.
Telephone: (317) 237-5622. **FAX:** (317) 237-5620.
Baseball Members: Butler, Dayton, Detroit, Evansville, Notre Dame, Xavier.
Assistant Director of Communications: Teresa Kuehn.
1992 Tournament: May 13-16 at South Bend, Ind.

MISSOURI VALLEY CONFERENCE
Mailing Address: 100 N. Broadway, Suite 1135, St. Louis, MO 63102.
Telephone: (314) 421-0339. **FAX:** (314) 421-3505.
Baseball Members: Bradley, Creighton, Illinois State, Indiana State, Northern Iowa, Southern Illinois, Southwest Missouri State, Wichita State.
Assistant Commissioner, Communications: Ron English.
1992 Tournament: May 13-16 at Wichita, Kan.

OHIO VALLEY CONFERENCE
Mailing Address: 278 Franklin Road, Suite 103, Brentwood, TN 37027.
Telephone: (615) 371-1698. **FAX:** (615) 371-1788.
Baseball Members: Austin Peay State, Eastern Kentucky, Middle Tennessee, Morehead State, Murray State, Southeast Missouri State, Tennessee State, Tennessee Tech.
Sports Information Director: Angela Hazel.
1992 Tournament: May 14-17 at Nashville, Tenn.

PACIFIC-10 CONFERENCE
Mailing Address: 800 S. Broadway, Suite 400, Walnut Creek, CA 94596.
Telephone: (510) 932-4411. **FAX:** (510) 932-4601.
Baseball Members: North—Gonzaga, Oregon State, Portland, Portland State, Washington, Washington State. **South**—Arizona, Arizona State, California, UCLA, Southern California, Stanford.
Public Relations Assistant: Dean Diltz.
1992 Tournament: North—None. **South**—None.

SOUTHEASTERN CONFERENCE
Mailing Address: 2201 Civic Center Blvd., Birmingham, AL 35203.
Telephone: (205) 458-3010. **FAX:** (205) 458-3030.
Baseball Members: East—Florida, Georgia, Kentucky, South Carolina, Tennessee, Vanderbilt. **West**—Alabama, Arkansas, Auburn, Louisiana State, Mississippi, Mississippi State.
Assistant Director of Media Relations: Graham Edwards.
1992 Tournament: May 13-17 at New Orleans, La.

SOUTHERN CONFERENCE
Mailing Address: One W. Pack Square, Suite 1508, Asheville, NC 28801.
Telephone: (704) 255-7872. **FAX:** (704) 251-5006.
Baseball Members: Appalachian State, The Citadel, East Tennessee State, Furman, Georgia Southern, Marshall, Virginia Military, Western Carolina.
Sports Information Director: Geoff Cape.
1992 Tournament: April 23-26 at Charleston, S.C.

SOUTHLAND CONFERENCE
Mailing Address: 1309 W. 15th St., Suite 303, Plano, TX 75075.
Telephone: (214) 424-4833. **FAX:** (214) 424-4099.
Baseball Members: McNeese State, Nicholls State, Northeast Louisiana, Northwestern State, Sam Houston State, Southwest Texas State, Stephen F. Austin State, Texas-Arlington.
Media Relations Intern: Bruce Ludlow.
1992 Tournament: None.

SOUTHWEST CONFERENCE
Mailing Address: P.O. Box 569420, Dallas, TX 75356.
Telephone: (214) 634-7353. **FAX:** (214) 638-5482.
Baseball Members: Baylor, Houston, Rice, Texas, Texas A&M, Texas Christian, Texas Tech.
Director of Media Relations: Bo Carter.
1992 Tournament: None.

SOUTHWESTERN ATHLETIC CONFERENCE
Mailing Address: Louisiana Superdome, 1500 Sugar Bowl Drive, New Orleans, LA 70112.
Telephone: (504) 523-7574. **FAX:** (504) 523-7513.
Baseball Members: East—Alabama State, Alcorn State, Jackson State, Mississippi Valley State. **West**—Grambling State, Prairie View A&M, Southern, Texas Southern.
Director of Publicity: Lonza Hardy.
1992 Tournament: May 1-3 at Natchez, Miss.

SUN BELT CONFERENCE
Mailing Address: One Galleria Blvd., Suite 2115, Metairie, LA 70001.
Telephone: (504) 834-6600. **FAX:** (504) 834-6806.
Baseball Members: East—Arkansas-Little Rock, Central Florida, Jacksonville, South Alabama, Western Kentucky. **West**—Arkansas State, Lamar, Louisiana Tech, New Orleans, Southwestern Louisiana, Texas-Pan American.
Associate Communications Director: John Massey.
1992 Tournament: May 13-16 at Eastern Division champion.

TRANSAMERICA ATHLETIC CONFERENCE
Mailing Address: 337 S. Milledge Ave., Suite 200, Athens, GA 30605.
Telephone: (404) 548-3369. **FAX:** (404) 548-0674.
Baseball Members: East—Charleston, Florida International, Mercer, Stetson. **West**—Centenary, Samford, Southeastern Louisiana.
Assistant Commissioner, Information: Ted Gumbart.
1992 Tournament: May 8-10 at Western Division champion.

WEST COAST CONFERENCE
Mailing Address: 400 Oyster Point Blvd., Suite 221, South San Francisco, CA 94080.
Telephone: (415) 873-8622. **FAX:** (415) 873-7846.
Baseball Members: Loyola Marymount, Pepperdine, St. Mary's, San Diego, San Francisco, Santa Clara.
Public Relations Assistant: Kyle McRae.
1992 Tournament: None.

WESTERN ATHLETIC CONFERENCE
Mailing Address: 14 West Dry Creek Circle, Littleton, CO 80120.
Telephone: (303) 795-1962. **FAX:** (303) 795-1960.
Baseball Members: Air Force, Brigham Young, Colorado State, Hawaii, New Mexico, San Diego State, Utah, Wyoming.
Assistant Director of Media Relations: Dan Willis.
1992 Tournament: May 14-16 at Honolulu, Hawaii.

NCAA Division I Teams

AIR FORCE ACADEMY
Air Force Academy, CO 80840.
Head Coach: **Paul Mainieri.**
  ph: (719) 472-2057.
Baseball SID: **Dave Toller.**
  ph: (719) 472-2313, 3950.

AKRON, The University of
Akron, OH 44325.
Head Coach: **Dave Fross.**
  ph: (216) 972-7277.
Baseball SID: **Joey Arrietta.**
  ph: (216) 972-7468.

ALABAMA, University of
P.O. Box K
Tuscaloosa, AL 35486.
Head Coach: **Barry Shollenberger.**
  ph: (205) 348-6161.
Baseball SID: **Steve Sikes.**
  ph: (205) 348-6084.

ALABAMA-BIRMINGHAM, Univ. of
University Station
Birmingham, AL 35294.
Head Coach: **Pete Rancont.**
  ph: (205) 934-5181.
Baseball SID: **Reid Adair.**
  ph: (205) 934-0722.

ALABAMA STATE UNIVERSITY
P.O. Box 271
Montgomery, AL 36101.
Head Coach: **Larry Watkins.**
  ph: (205) 293-4228.
Baseball SID: **Jack Jeffrey.**
  ph: (205) 240-6857.

ALCORN STATE UNIVERSITY
P.O. Box 510
Lorman, MS 39096.
Head Coach: **Willie McGowan.**
  ph: (601) 877-6279.
Baseball SID: **Gus Howard.**
  ph: (601) 877-6501.

APPALACHIAN STATE UNIV.
Broome-Kirk Gymnasium
Boone, NC 28608.
Head Coach: **Jim Morris.**
  ph: (704) 262-6097.
Baseball SID: **Rick Covington.**
  ph: (704) 262-3080.

ARIZONA, University of
Room 229, McKale Center
Tucson, AZ 85721.
Head Coach: **Jerry Kindall.**
  ph: (602) 621-4102.
Baseball SID: **Sean Fitzpatrick.**
  ph: (602) 621-4163.

ARIZONA STATE UNIVERSITY
IAC Building
Tempe, AZ 85287.
Head Coach: **Jim Brock.**
  ph: (602) 965-6085.
Baseball SID: **Frank Reed.**
  ph: (602) 965-6592.

ARKANSAS, University of
Broyles Athletic Complex
Fayetteville, AR 72701.
Head Coach: **Norm DeBriyn.**
  ph: (501) 575-3655.
Baseball SID: **Mark Krizmanich.**
  ph: (501) 575-2751.

ARKANSAS-LITTLE ROCK, U. of
2801 South University
Little Rock, AR 72204.
Head Coach: **Gary Hogan.**
  ph: (501) 663-8095.
Baseball SID: **Bob Beumer.**
  ph: (501) 569-3449.

ARKANSAS STATE UNIVERSITY
P.O. Box 1000
State University, AR 72467.
Head Coach: **Bill Bethea.**
  ph: (501) 972-2541.
Baseball SID: **Dixie Keller.**
  ph: (501) 972-2541.

ARMY (U.S. Military Academy)
West Point, NY 10996.
Head Coach: **Dan Roberts.**
  ph: (914) 938-3712, 3268.
Baseball SID: **Bob Beretta.**
  ph: (914) 938-3303.

AUBURN UNIVERSITY
P.O. Box 351
Auburn University, AL 36831.
Head Coach: **Hal Baird.**
  ph: (205) 844-9750.
Baseball SID: **Kent Partridge.**
  ph: (205) 844-9806.

AUSTIN PEAY STATE UNIV.
Clarksville, TN 37044.
Head Coach: **Gary McClure.**
  ph: (615) 648-7902.
Baseball SID: **Brad Kirtley.**
  ph: (615) 648-7561.

BALL STATE UNIVERSITY
2000 University Ave.
Muncie, IN 47306.
Head Coach: **Pat Quinn.**
  ph: (317) 285-8907.
Baseball SID: **Bob Moore.**
  ph: (317) 285-8242.

BAYLOR UNIVERSITY
3031 Dutton
Waco, TX 76711.
Head Coach: **Mickey Sullivan.**
  ph: (817) 755-3029.
Baseball SID: **Terry Tacker.**
  ph: (817) 755-3043.

BETHUNE-COOKMAN COLLEGE
640 Second Ave.
Daytona Beach, FL 32115.
Head Coach, Baseball SID: **Gary Francis.**
  ph: (904) 255-1401, ext. 263.

BOSTON COLLEGE
Chestnut Hill, MA 02167.
Head Coach: **Richard Maloney.**
  ph: (617) 552-3092.
Baseball SID: **Dick Kelley.**
  ph: (617) 552-3039.

BOSTON UNIVERSITY
285 Babcock St.
Boston, MA 02215.
Head Coach: **Bill Mahoney.**
  ph: (617) 353-5409.
Baseball SID: **Dan Furlong.**
  ph: (617) 353-2872.

BOWLING GREEN STATE UNIV.
Bowling Green, OH 43403.
Head Coach: **Danny Schmitz.**
  ph: (419) 372-7065.
Baseball SID: **Mark Kunstmann.**
  ph: (419) 372-7077.

BRADLEY UNIVERSITY
1501 W. Bradley Ave.
Peoria, IL 61625.
Head Coach: **Dewey Kalmer.**
  ph: (309) 677-2684.
Baseball SID: **Joe Dalfonso.**
  ph: (309) 677-2624.

BRIGHAM YOUNG UNIVERSITY
Provo, UT 84602.
Head Coach: **Gary Pullins.**
  ph: (801) 378-5049.

Baseball SID: **Mike Twitty**.
ph: (801) 378-4911.

BROOKLYN COLLEGE
Bedford Avenue and Avenue H
Brooklyn, NY 11210.
Head Coach: **Peter Alborano**.
ph: (718) 780-5366.
Baseball SID: **Lenn Margolis**.
ph: (718) 780-4222.

BROWN UNIVERSITY
Box 1932
Providence, RI 02912.
Head Coach: **Frank Castelli**.
ph: (800) 662-2266, ext. 3090.
Baseball SID: **Chris Humm**.
ph: (401) 863-2219.

BUCKNELL UNIVERSITY
Lewisburg, PA 17837.
Head Coach: **Gene Depew**.
ph: (717) 524-1134.
Baseball SID: **Bob Behler**.
ph: (717) 524-1227.

BUTLER UNIVERSITY
4600 Sunset Ave.
Indianapolis, IN 46208.
Head Coach: **Steve Farley**.
ph: (317) 283-9721.
Baseball SID: **Jim McGrath**.
ph: (317) 283-9414.

C.W. POST
Greenvale, NY 11548.
Head Coach: **Dick Vining**.
ph: (516) 299-2289.
Baseball SID: **Robert Gesslein**.
ph: (516) 299-2333.

CALIFORNIA, University of
Memorial Stadium
Berkeley, CA 94720.
Head Coach: **Bob Milano**.
ph: (510) 643-6006.
Baseball SID: **Scott Ball**.
ph: (510) 642-5363.

UC IRVINE
Campus and University Drives
Irvine, CA 92717.
Head Coach: **Mike Gerakos**.
ph: (714) 856-6745.
Baseball SID: **Tony Altobelli**.
ph: (714) 856-5814.

UCLA
405 Hilgard Ave.
Los Angeles, CA 90024.
Head Coach: **Gary Adams**.
ph: (213) 477-8702.
Baseball SID: **Jonathan Forster**.
ph: (213) 206-6831.

UC SANTA BARBARA
Ward Memorial Fwy.
Santa Barbara, CA 93106.
Head Coach: **Al Ferrer**.
ph: (805) 893-2021.
Baseball SID: **Bill Mahoney**.
ph: (805) 893-3428.

CAL STATE FULLERTON
800 North State College Blvd.
Fullerton, CA 92634.
Head Coach: **Augie Garrido**.
ph: (714) 773-3789.
Baseball SID: **Tim Murphy**.
ph: (714) 773-3970.

CAL STATE NORTHRIDGE
18111 Nordhoff St.
Northridge, CA 91330.
Head Coach: **Bill Kernen**.
ph: (818) 885-3233.
Baseball SID: **Deana Allington**.
ph: (818) 885-3243.

CAMPBELL UNIVERSITY
Box 10
Buies Creek, NC 27506.
Head Coach: **John Daurity**.
ph: (919) 893-4111 ext. 2310.
Baseball SID: **Stan Cole**.
ph: (919) 893-4111 ext. 2313.

CANISIUS COLLEGE
2001 Main St.
Buffalo, NY 14208.
Head Coach: **Don Colpoys**.
ph: (716) 858-7030.
Baseball SID: **John Maddock**.
ph: (716) 888-2977.

CENTENARY COLLEGE
Box 41188, Gold Dome
Shreveport, LA 71134.
Head Coach: **Andy Watson**.
ph: (318) 869-5275.
Baseball SID: **Cory Rogers**.
ph: (318) 869-5092.

CENTRAL CONNECTICUT STATE
1615 Stanley St.
New Britain, CT 06050.
Head Coach: **George Redman**.
ph: (203) 827-7639.
Baseball SID: **Brent Rutkowski**.
ph: (203) 827-7824.

CENTRAL FLORIDA, Univ. of
Orlando, FL 32816.
Head Coach: **Jay Bergman**.
ph: (407) 823-2261.
Baseball SID: **Bob Cefalo**.
ph: (407) 823-2464.

CENTRAL MICHIGAN UNIV.
Broomfield Road
Mt. Pleasant, MI 48859.
Head Coach: **Dean Kreiner**.
ph: (517) 774-6670.
Baseball SID: **Fred Stabley**.
ph: (517) 774-3277.

CHAPMAN COLLEGE
333 N. Glassell
Orange, CA 92666.
Head Coach: **Mike Weathers**.
ph: (714) 997-6663.
Baseball SID: **Derek Anderson**.
ph: (714) 997-6900.

CHARLESTON, College of
Charleston, SC 29424.
Head Coach: **Ralph Ciabattari**.
ph: (803) 792-5916.
Baseball SID: **Tony Ciuffo**.
ph: (803) 792-5465.

CHARLESTON SOUTHERN UNIV.
P.O. Box 10087
Charleston, SC 29411.
Head Coach: **Jamie Futrell**.
ph: (803) 863-7688.
Baseball SID: **Jack Jordan**.
ph: (803) 863-7679.

CHICAGO STATE UNIVERSITY
95th & King Dr.
Chicago, IL 60628.
Head Coach: **Kevin McCray**.
ph: (312) 995-3655.
Baseball SID: **Lisette Moore**.
ph: (312) 995-2217.

CINCINNATI, University of
Cincinnati, OH 45221.
Head Coach: **Richard Skeel**.
ph: (513) 556-7762.
Baseball SID: **Doug Tammaro**.
ph: (513) 556-5191.

THE CITADEL
P.O. Box 7, Citadel Station
Charleston, SC 29409.

Head Coach: **Fred Jordan**.
 ph: (803) 792-5070.
Baseball SID: **Mike Hoffman**.
 ph: (803) 792-5120.

CLEMSON UNIVERSITY
Box 31
Clemson, SC 29633.
Head Coach: **Bill Wilhelm**.
 ph: (803) 656-2101.
Baseball SID: **Bob Bradley**.
 ph: (803) 656-2101, 2114.

CLEVELAND STATE UNIVERSITY
2451 Euclid Ave.
Cleveland, OH 44115.
Head Coach: **Kevin Rhomberg**.
 ph: (216) 687-4822.
Baseball SID: **Kelly Portolese**.
 ph: (216) 687-2094.

COASTAL CAROLINA COLLEGE
P.O. Box 1954
Conway, SC 29526.
Head Coach: **John Vrooman**.
 ph: (803) 349-2932.
Baseball SID: **Chris Collier**.
 ph: (803) 349-2822.

COLGATE UNIVERSITY
P.O. Box 338
Hamilton, NY 13346.
Head Coach: **Mike Doherty**.
 ph: (315) 824-7574.
Baseball SID: **Brian DePasquale**.
 ph: (315) 824-7602.

COLORADO STATE UNIVERSITY
Fort Collins, CO 80523.
Head Coach: **Kirk Mason**.
 ph: (303) 491-6227.
Baseball SID: **Jim Miller**.
 ph: (303) 491-5067.

COLUMBIA UNIVERSITY
116th Street and Broadway
New York, NY 10027.
Head Coach: **Paul Fernandes**.
 ph: (212) 854-2543.
Baseball SID: **Bill Steinman**.
 ph: (212) 854-2534.

CONNECTICUT, University of
Department of Athletics, U-78
2111 Hillside Road
Storrs, CT 06269.
Head Coach: **Andy Baylock**.
 ph: (203) 486-2458.
Baseball SID: **Mike Enright**.
 ph: (203) 486-3531.

COPPIN STATE COLLEGE
2500 W. North Ave.
Baltimore, MD 21216.
Head Coach: **Jason Booker**.
 ph: (410) 383-5686.
Baseball SID: **Michael Preston**.
 ph: (410) 383-5642.

CORNELL UNIVERSITY
P.O. Box 729
Ithaca, NY 14851.
Head Coach: **Tom Ford**.
 ph: (607) 255-6604.
Baseball SID: **Dave Wohlhueter**.
 ph: (607) 255-3752.

CREIGHTON UNIVERSITY
2500 California
Omaha, NE 68178.
Head Coach: **Todd Wenberg**.
 ph: (402) 280-2720.
Baseball SID: **Kevin Sarver**.
 ph: (402) 280-2488.

DARTMOUTH COLLEGE
Alumni Gym
Hanover, NH 03755.
Head Coach: **Bob Whalen**.
 ph: (603) 646-2477.
Baseball SID: **Stephen Dravis**.
 ph: (603) 646-2468.

DAVIDSON COLLEGE
P.O. Box 1750
Davidson, NC 28036.
Head Coach: **Dick Cooke**.
 ph: (704) 892-2368.
Baseball SID: **John Maxwell**.
 ph: (704) 892-2815.

DAYTON, University of
300 College Park
Dayton, OH 45469.
Head Coach: **Mark Schlemmer**.
 ph: (513) 229-4456.
Baseball SID: **Matt Zircher**.
 ph: (513) 229-4460.

DELAWARE, University of
Newark, DE 19711.
Head Coach: **Bob Hannah**.
 ph: (302) 831-8596.
Baseball SID: **Scott Selheimer**.
 ph: (302) 831-2186.

DELAWARE STATE COLLEGE
1200 N. Dupont Highway
Dover, DE 19901.
Head Coach: **Harry Van Sant**.
 ph: (302) 739-3528.
Baseball SID: **Matt Santos**.
 ph: (302) 739-4926.

DETROIT, University of
4001 W. McNichols
Detroit, MI 48221.
Head Coach: **Bob Miller**.
 ph: (313) 993-1725.
Baseball SID: **Ken Lasky**.
 ph: (313) 993-1745.

DREXEL UNIVERSITY
32nd and Chestnut Streets
Philadelphia, PA 19104.
Head Coach: **Donald Maines**.
 ph: (215) 590-8931.
Baseball SID: **John Szefc**.
 ph: (215) 590-8946.

DUKE UNIVERSITY
Cameron Indoor Stadium
Durham, NC 27706.
Head Coach: **Steve Traylor**.
 ph: (919) 684-2358.
Baseball SID: **Warren Miller**.
 ph: (919) 684-2633.

DUQUESNE UNIVERSITY
A.J. Palumbo Center
Pittsburgh, PA 15282.
Head Coach: **Rich Spear**.
 ph: (412) 434-6569.
Baseball SID: **Sue Ryan**.
 ph: (412) 434-6560.

EAST CAROLINA UNIVERSITY
Sports Medicine Building
Greenville, NC 27858.
Head Coach: **Gary Overton**.
 ph: (919) 757-4604.
Baseball SID: **Carolyn Justice-Henson**.
 ph: (919) 757-4522.

EAST TENNESSEE STATE UNIV.
Johnson City, TN 37614.
Head Coach: **Ken Campbell**.
 ph: (615) 929-4496.
Baseball SID: **John Cathey**.
 ph: (615) 929-4220.

EASTERN ILLINOIS UNIVERSITY
Lantz Building, Grant Street
Charleston, IL 61920.
Head Coach: **Dan Callahan**.
 ph: (217) 581-2522.

Baseball SID: **Dave Kidwell.**
 ph: (217) 581-6408.

EASTERN KENTUCKY UNIV.
205 Begley Building
Richmond, KY 40475.
Head Coach: **Jim Ward.**
 ph: (606) 622-2128.
Baseball SID: **Karl Park.**
 ph: (606) 622-1230.

EASTERN MICHIGAN UNIV.
Bowen Fieldhouse
Ypsilanti, MI 48197.
Head Coach: **Roger Coryell.**
 ph: (313) 487-0315.
Baseball SID: **Mark Simpson.**
 ph: (313) 487-0317.

EVANSVILLE, University of
1800 Lincoln Ave.
Evansville, IN 47722.
Head Coach: **Jim Brownlee.**
 ph: (812) 479-2059.
Baseball SID: **Will Hancock.**
 ph: (812) 479-2350.

FAIRFIELD UNIVERSITY
N. Benson Road
Fairfield, CT 06430.
Head Coach: **John Slosar.**
 ph: (203) 254-4000, ext. 2278.
Baseball SID: **Victor D'Ascenzo.**
 ph: (203) 254-4000, ext. 2877.

FAIRLEIGH DICKINSON UNIV.
1000 River Road
Teaneck, NJ 07666.
Head Coach: **Dennis Sasso.**
 ph: (201) 692-2208.
Baseball SID: **Carmine Faccenda.**
 ph: (201) 692-2149.

FLORIDA, University of
Box 14485
Gainesville, FL 32604.
Head Coach: **Joe Arnold.**
 ph: (904) 375-4683, ext. 4400.
Baseball SID: **Steve McClain.**
 ph: (904) 375-4683, ext. 6115.

FLORIDA A&M UNIVERSITY
Martin Luther King Jr. Blvd.
Tallahassee, FL 32307.
Head Coach: **Joe Durant.**
 ph: (904) 599-3202.
Baseball SID: **Alvin Holland.**
 ph: (904) 599-3200.

FLORIDA INTERNATIONAL UNIV.
Tamiami Trail
Miami, FL 33199.
Head Coach: **Danny Price.**
 ph: (305) 348-3166.
Baseball SID: **Stuart Davidson.**
 ph: (305) 348-2084.

FLORIDA STATE UNIVERITY
P.O. Drawer 2195
Tallahassee, FL 32306.
Head Coach: **Mike Martin.**
 ph: (904) 644-1073.
Baseball SID: **Donna Turner.**
 ph: (904) 644-1403.

FORDHAM UNIVERSITY
Bronx, NY 10458.
Head Coach: **Dan Gallagher.**
 ph: (212) 579-2439.
Baseball SID: **Joe Favorito.**
 ph: (212) 579-2445.

FRESNO STATE UNIVERSITY
North Gym, Room 153
Fresno, CA 93740.
Head Coach: **Bob Bennett.**
 ph: (209) 278-2718.
Baseball SID: **David Haglund.**
 ph: (209) 278-2509.

FURMAN UNIVERSITY
Poinsett Highway
Greenville, SC 29613.
Head Coach: **Tom Wall.**
 ph: (803) 294-2146.
Baseball SID: **Clark Happonstall.**
 ph: (803) 294-3062.

GEORGE MASON UNIVERSITY
4400 University Drive
Fairfax, VA 22030.
Head Coach: **Billy Brown.**
 ph: (703) 993-3282.
Baseball SID: **Carl Sell.**
 ph: (703) 993-3261.

GEORGE WASHINGTON UNIV.
600 22nd St. NW
Washington, DC 20052.
Head Coach: **Jay Murphy.**
 ph: (202) 994-0327.
Baseball SID: **Bob Ludwig.**
 ph: (202) 994-9003.

GEORGETOWN UNIVERSITY
37th and O Streets NW
Washington, DC 2005,..
Head Coach: **Larry Geracioti.**
 ph: (202) 687-2462.
Baseball SID: **Bill Hurd.**
 ph: (202) 687-2492.

GEORGIA, University of
P.O. Box 1472
Athens, GA 30613.
Head Coach: **Steve Webber.**
 ph: (404) 542-7915.
Baseball SID: **Mike Nayman.**
 ph: (404) 542-1621.

GEORGIA SOUTHERN UNIV.
Landrum Box 8085
Statesboro, GA 30460.
Head Coach: **Jack Stallings.**
 ph: (912) 681-5187.
Baseball SID: **Matt Rogers.**
 ph: (912) 681-5239.

GEORGIA STATE UNIVERSITY
University Plaza
Atlanta, GA 30303.
Head Coach: **Kurt Seibert.**
 ph: (404) 651-1198.
Baseball SID: **Martin Harmon.**
 ph: (404) 651-2071.

GEORGIA TECH
Georgia Tech Athletic Association
Atlanta, GA 30332.
Head Coach: **Jim Morris.**
 ph: (404) 894-5471.
Baseball SID: **Mike Stamus.**
 ph: (404) 894-5445.

GONZAGA UNIVERSITY
E. 502 Boone Ave.
Spokane, WA 99258.
Head Coach: **Steve Hertz.**
 ph: (509) 328-4220 ext. 4226.
Baseball SID: **Oliver Pierce.**
 ph: (509) 328-4220 ext. 6373.

GRAMBLING STATE UNIVERSITY
Grambling, LA 71245.
Head Coach: **Wilbert Ellis.**
 ph: (318) 274-2218.
Baseball SID: **Stanley Lewis.**
 ph: (318) 274-2761.

GRAND CANYON UNIVERSITY
P.O. Box 11097
Phoenix, AZ 85061.
Head Coach: **Gil Stafford.**
 ph: (602) 589-2806.
Baseball SID: **Beth Narofsky.**
 ph: (602) 589-2795.

HARTFORD, University of
200 Bloomfield Ave.

West Hartford, CT 06117.
Head Coach: **Dan Gooley**.
 ph: (203) 243-4656.
Baseball SID: **Jim Keener**.
 ph: (203) 243-4620.

HARVARD UNIVERSITY
Department of Athletics
60 John F. Kennedy St.
Cambridge, MA 02138.
Head Coach: **Leigh Hogan**.
 ph: (617) 495-2629.
Baseball SID: **Tim Bonang**.
 ph: (617) 495-2206.

HAWAII, University of
1337 Lower Campus Road
Honolulu, HI 96822.
Head Coach: **Les Murakami**.
 ph: (808) 956-6247.
Baseball SID: **Tom Yoshida**.
 ph: (808) 956-7523.

HOFSTRA UNIVERSITY
Physical Fitness Center
Hempstead, NY 11550.
Head Coach: **Rich Martin**.
 ph: (516) 463-5065.
Baseball SID: **Kevin Hines**.
 ph: (516) 463-6764.

HOLY CROSS COLLEGE
College Street
Worcester, MA 01610.
Head Coach: **Jack Whalen**.
 ph: (508) 793-2572.
Baseball SID: **Heidi McGuigan**.
 ph: (508) 793-2780.

HOUSTON, University of
4800 Calhoun Blvd.
Houston, TX 77004.
Head Coach: **Bragg Stockton**.
 ph: (713) 749-4279.
Baseball SID: **Paul Pinkston**.
 ph: (713) 749-4382.

HOWARD UNIVERSITY
511 Gresham Place NW
Washington, DC 20059.
Head Coach: **Chuck Hinton**.
 ph: (202) 806-7162.
Baseball SID: **Jessie Batten**.
 ph: (202) 806-7182.

ILLINOIS, University of
Assembly Hall, Room 115
1800 S. First St.
Champaign, IL 61820.
Head Coach: **Itchy Jones**.
 ph: (217) 333-8605.
Baseball SID: **Dave Johnson**.
 ph: (217) 333-1391.

ILLINOIS-CHICAGO, Univ. of
Box 4348
Chicago, IL 60680.
Head Coach: **Dean Refakes**.
 ph: (312) 996-8645.
Baseball SID: **Doug Smiley**.
 ph: (312) 996-5880.

ILLINOIS STATE UNIVERSITY
Normal, IL 61761.
Head Coach: **Jeff Stewart**.
 ph: (309) 438-5151.
Baseball SID: **Chris Padgett**.
 ph: (309) 438-3825.

INDIANA UNIVERSITY
Athletic Department, Assembly Hall
Bloomington, IN 47405.
Head Coach: **Bob Morgan**.
 ph: (812) 855-1680.
Baseball SID: **Gregg Elkin**.
 ph: (812) 855-2421.

INDIANA STATE UNIVERSITY
Terre Haute, IN 47809.
Head Coach: **Bob Warn**.
 ph: (812) 237-4051.
Baseball SID: **Tom James**.
 ph: (812) 237-4160.

IONA COLLEGE
715 North Ave.
New Rochelle, NY 10801.
Head Coach: **Dave Torromeo**.
 ph: (914) 633-2334.
Baseball SID: **Gary Stanley**.
 ph: (914) 636-1385.

IOWA, University of
Iowa City, IA 52242.
Head Coach: **Duane Banks**.
 ph: (319) 335-9389.
Baseball SID: **Mike Lageschulte**.
 ph: (319) 335-9411.

IOWA STATE UNIVERSITY
Department of Athletics
Ames, IA 50011.
Head Coach: **Bobby Randall**.
 ph: (515) 294-4132.
Baseball SID: **Denise Seomin**.
 ph: (515) 294-3372.

JACKSON STATE UNIVERSITY
1325 West Lynch St.
Jackson, MS 39217.
Head Coach: **Robert Braddy**.
 ph: (601) 968-2425.
Baseball SID: **Samuel Jefferson**.
 ph: (601) 968-2273.

JACKSONVILLE UNIVERSITY
University Boulevard North
Jacksonville, FL 32211.
Head Coach: **Terry Alexander**.
 ph: (904) 744-3950, ext. 3416.
Baseball SID: **Felicia Sass**.
 ph: (904) 744-3950, ext. 3450.

JAMES MADISON UNIVERSITY
South Main
Harrisonburg, VA 22807.
Head Coach: **Ray Heatwole**.
 ph: (703) 568-3630.
Baseball SID: **Curt Dudley**.
 ph: (703) 568-6154.

KANSAS, University of
Allen Fieldhouse
Lawrence, KS 66045.
Head Coach: **Dave Bingham**.
 ph: (913) 864-4196.
Baseball SID: **Matt Finnigan**.
 ph: (913) 864-3417.

KANSAS STATE UNIVERSITY
Ahearn Field House
Manhattan, KS 66506.
Head Coach: **Mike Clark**.
 ph: (913) 532-5723.
Baseball SID: **Chris Theisen**.
 ph: (913) 532-6735.

KENT STATE UNIVERSITY
Kent, OH 44242.
Head Coach: **Danny Hall**.
 ph: (216) 672-3696.
Baseball SID: **John Wagner**.
 ph: (216) 672-2110.

KENTUCKY, University of
Memorial Coliseum
Lexington, KY 40506.
Head Coach: **Keith Madison**.
 ph: (606) 257-8829.
Baseball SID: **Brian Carter**.
 ph: (606) 257-3838.

LAFAYETTE COLLEGE
Easton, PA 18042.
Head Coach: **Greg Fogel**.
 ph: (215) 250-5476.
Baseball SID: **Steve Pulver**.
 ph: (215) 250-5122.

LAMAR UNIVERSITY
Box 10038

Beaumont, TX 77710.
Head Coach: **Jim Gilligan.**
 ph: (409) 880-8974.
Baseball SID: **Joe Lee Smith.**
 ph: (409) 880-8329.
LA SALLE UNIVERSITY
1900 W. Olney Ave., Box 805
Philadelphia, PA 19141.
Head Coach: **Gene McDonnell.**
 ph: (215) 951-1516.
Baseball SID: **Dawn Wright.**
 ph: (215) 951-1605.
LeMOYNE COLLEGE
LeMoyne Heights
Syracuse, NY 13214.
Head Coach: **Richard Rockwell.**
 ph: (315) 445-4450.
Baseball SID: **Kim Bouck.**
 ph: (315) 445-4412.
LEHIGH UNIVERSITY
436 Brodhead Ave.
Bethlehem, PA 18015.
Head Coach: **Stan Schultz.**
 ph: (215) 758-3175.
Baseball SID: **Matt Winkler.**
 ph: (215) 758-3174.
LIBERTY UNIVERSITY
Box 20000
Lynchburg, VA 24506.
Head Coach: **Johnny Hunton.**
 ph: (804) 582-2100.
Baseball SID: **Mike Montoro.**
 ph: (804) 582-2292.
LONG BEACH STATE UNIV.
1250 Bellflower Blvd.
Long Beach, CA 90840.
Head Coach: **Dave Snow.**
 ph: (213) 985-4661.
Baseball SID: **Shayne Schroeder.**
 ph: (213) 985-7978.
LONG ISLAND UNIVERSITY
University Plaza
Brooklyn, NY 11201.
Head Coach: **Frank Giannone.**
 ph: (718) 488-1538.
Baseball SID: **Bob Gesslein.**
 ph: (718) 488-1030.
LOUISIANA STATE UNIVERSITY
P.O. Box 93008
Baton Rouge, LA 70894.
Head Coach: **Skip Bertman.**
 ph: (504) 388-4148.
Baseball SID: **Bill Franques.**
 ph: (504) 388-8226.
LOUISIANA TECH UNIVERSITY
Ruston, LA 71272.
Head Coach: **Mike Kane.**
 ph: (318) 257-4111.
Baseball SID: **Hank Largin.**
 ph: (318) 257-3144.
LOUISVILLE, University of
Louisville, KY 40292.
Head Coach: **Gene Baker.**
 ph: (502) 588-0103.
Baseball SID: **Nancy Smith.**
 ph: (502) 588-6581.
LOYOLA MARYMOUNT UNIV.
Loyola Blvd. @ W. 80th
Los Angeles, CA 90045.
Head Coach: **Jody Robinson.**
 ph: (310) 338-2765.
Baseball SID: **Bruce Meyers.**
 ph: (310) 338-7643.
MAINE, University of
Orono, ME 04469.
Head Coach: **John Winkin.**
 ph: (207) 581-1096.
Baseball SID: **Joe Roberts.**
 ph: (207) 581-1086.

MANHATTAN COLLEGE
Department of Athletics
Bronx, NY 10471.
Head Coach: **Stu Schmelz.**
 ph: (212) 920-0936.
Baseball SID: **Jeff Bernstein.**
 ph: (212) 920-0228.
MARIST COLLEGE
North Road
Poughkeepsie, NY 12601.
Head Coach: **Art Smith.**
 ph: (914) 575-3000, ext. 2570.
Baseball SID: **Ben Sullivan.**
 ph: (914) 575-3000, ext. 2322.
MARSHALL UNIVERSITY
P.O. Box 1360
Huntington, WV 25715.
Head Coach: **Howard McCann.**
 ph: (304) 696-5277.
Baseball SID: **Gary Richter.**
 ph: (304) 696-5275.
MARYLAND, University of
College Park, MD 20740.
Head Coach: **Tom Bradley.**
 ph: (301) 314-7122.
Baseball SID: **Chuck Walsh.**
 ph: (301) 314-7065.
MARYLAND-BALT. COUNTY, U. of
5401 Wilkens Ave.
Baltimore, MD 21228.
Head Coach: **John Jancuska.**
 ph: (410) 455-2239.
Baseball SID: **Jerry Milani.**
 ph: (410) 455-2639.
MARYLAND-E. SHORE, U. of
Princess Anne, MD 21853.
Head Coach: **Kaye Pinhey.**
 ph: (301) 651-2200, ext. 607.
Baseball SID: **Sheila Benton.**
 ph: (301) 651-2200, ext. 591.
MASSACHUSETTS, University of
Department of Athletics
Amherst, MA 01003.
Head Coach: **Michael Stone.**
 ph: (413) 545-3120.
Baseball SID: **Howard Davis.**
 ph: (413) 545-2439.
McNEESE STATE UNIVERSITY
Athletic Department Box A-10
Lake Charles, LA 70609.
Head Coach: **Tony Robichaux.**
 ph: (318) 475-5484.
Baseball SID: **Louis Bonnette.**
 ph: (318) 475-5207.
MEMPHIS STATE UNIVERSITY
Athletic Department
Memphis, TN 38152.
Head Coach: **Bob Kilpatrick.**
 ph: (901) 678-2452.
Baseball SID: **Mark Owens.**
 ph: (901) 678-2337.
MERCER UNIVERSITY
1400 Coleman Ave.
Macon, GA 31207.
Head Coach: **Barry Myers.**
 ph: (912) 752-2738.
Baseball SID: **Bobby Pope.**
 ph: (912) 752-2994.
MIAMI, University of
Number One Hurricane Drive
Coral Gables, FL 33124.
Head Coach: **Ron Fraser.**
 ph: (305) 284-4171.
Baseball SID: **Ken Lee.**
 ph: (305) 284-3244.
MIAMI UNIVERSITY
Millett Hall
Oxford, OH 45056.
Head Coach: **Jon Pavlisko.**
 ph: (513) 529-6631.

Baseball SID: **Brian Teter.**
ph: (513) 529-4327.

MICHIGAN, University of
1000 S. State St.
Ann Arbor, MI 48109.
Head Coach: **Bill Freehan.**
ph: (313) 747-4550.
Baseball SID: **Jim Schneider.**
ph: (313) 763-1381.

MICHIGAN STATE UNIVERSITY
116 Linton Hall
East Lansing, MI 48824.
Head Coach: **Tom Smith.**
ph: (517) 355-0259.
Baseball SID: **Amy Stabley.**
ph: (517) 355-2271.

MIDDLE TENNESSEE STATE U.
Murfreesboro, TN 37132.
Head Coach: **Steve Peterson.**
ph: (615) 898-2984.
Baseball SID: **Bo Henley.**
ph: (615) 898-2450.

MINNESOTA, University of
516 15th Ave. S.E.
Bierman Building, Room 208
Minneapolis, MN 55455.
Head Coach: **John Anderson.**
ph: (612) 625-1060.
Baseball SID: **Bill Crumley.**
ph: (612) 625-4090.

MISSISSIPPI, University of
University, MS 38677.
Head Coach: **Don Kessinger.**
ph: (601) 232-7519.
Baseball SID: **Jack Duggan.**
ph: (601) 232-7522.

MISSISSIPPI STATE UNIVERSITY
P.O. Box 5327
Mississippi State, MS 39762.
Head Coach: **Ron Polk.**
ph: (601) 325-2805.
Baseball SID: **Scott Stricklin.**
ph: (601) 325-2703.

MISSISSIPPI VALLEY STATE U.
P.O. Box 743
Itta Bena, MS 38941.
Head Coach: **Cleotha Wilson.**
ph: (601) 254-9041, ext. 6309.
Baseball SID: **Charles Prophet.**
ph: (601) 254-9041, ext. 6369.

MISSOURI, University of
Columbia, MO 65211.
Head Coach: **Gene McArtor.**
ph: (314) 882-0731.
Baseball SID: **Jack Watkins.**
ph: (314) 882-3241.

MONMOUTH COLLEGE
Cedar Avenue
West Long Branch, NJ 07764.
Head Coach: **Walter Woods.**
ph: (908) 571-3415.
Baseball SID: **John Paradise.**
ph: (908) 571-3415.

MOREHEAD STATE UNIVERSITY
Morehead, KY 40351.
Head Coach: **Frank Spaniol.**
ph: (606) 783-2881.
Baseball SID: **Randy Stacy.**
ph: (606) 783-2500.

MOUNT ST. MARY'S COLLEGE
Emmitsburg, MD 21727.
Head Coach: **Bob Hampton.**
ph: (301) 447-5296.
Baseball SID: **Dave Reeder.**
ph: (301) 447-5384.

MURRAY STATE UNIVERSITY
Murray, KY 42071.
Head Coach: **Johnny Reagan.**
ph: (502) 762-4892.
Baseball SID: **Tim Tucker.**
ph: (502) 762-4270.

NAVY (U.S. Naval Academy)
Annapolis, MD 21402.
Head Coach: **Joe Duff.**
ph: (301) 267-2831.
Baseball SID: **Scott Strasemeier.**
ph: (301) 268-6226.

NEBRASKA, University of
116 South Stadium
Lincoln, NE 68588.
Head Coach: **John Sanders.**
ph: (402) 472-2269.
Baseball SID: **Chris Anderson.**
ph: (402) 472-2263.

NEVADA, University of
Reno, NV 89557.
Head Coach: **Gary Powers.**
ph: (702) 784-4180.
Baseball SID: **Paul Stuart.**
ph: (702) 784-4600.

NEVADA-LAS VEGAS, Univ. of
4505 Maryland Parkway
Las Vegas, NV 89154.
Head Coach: **Fred Dallimore.**
ph: (702) 739-3499.
Baseball SID: **Jim Gemma.**
ph: (702) 739-3207.

NEW HAMPSHIRE, University of
Durham, NH 03824.
Head Coach: **Ted Connor.**
ph: (603) 862-3902.
Baseball SID: **Jim Epstein.**
ph: (603) 862-3906.

NEW MEXICO, University of
Albuquerque, NM 87131.
Head Coach: **Rich Alday.**
ph: (505) 277-5121.
Baseball SID: **Greg Remington.**
ph: (505) 277-2026.

NEW MEXICO STATE UNIV.
Box 30001, Department 145
Las Cruces, NM 88003.
Head Coach: **Elliott Avent.**
ph: (505) 646-5813.
Baseball SID: **Steve Shutt.**
ph: (505) 646-3929.

NEW ORLEANS, University of
Lakefront
New Orleans, LA 70148.
Head Coach: **Tom Schwaner.**
ph: (504) 286-7021.
Baseball SID: **Ed Cassiere.**
ph: (504) 286-6284.

NIAGARA UNIVERSITY
Niagara University, NY 14109.
Head Coach: **Jim Mauro.**
ph: (716) 285-1212, ext. 431.
Baseball SID: **Bill Kellick.**
ph: (504) 285-1212, ext. 427.

NICHOLLS STATE UNIVERSITY
Thibodaux, LA 70310.
Head Coach: **Mike Knight.**
ph: (504) 448-4795.
Baseball SID: **Ron Mears.**
ph: (504) 448-4282.

NORTH CAROLINA, University of
P.O. Box 2126
Chapel Hill, NC 27515.
Head Coach: **Mike Roberts.**
ph: (919) 962-2351.
Baseball SID: **Steve Kirschner.**
ph: (919) 962-2123.

UNC ASHEVILLE
One University Heights
Asheville, NC 28804.
Head Coach: **Jim Bretz.**
ph: (704) 251-6459.

Baseball SID: **Mike Gore**.
　ph: (704) 251-6459.

UNC CHARLOTTE
UNCC Station
Charlotte, NC 28213.
Head Coach: **Jeff Edmonds**.
　ph: (704) 547-4937.
Baseball SID: **Tom Whitestone**.
　ph: (704) 547-4937.

UNC GREENSBORO
1000 Spring Garden
Greensboro, NC 27412.
Head Coach: **Michael Gaski**.
　ph: (919) 334-3427.
Baseball SID: **Stacey Bartimoccia**.
　ph: (919) 334-5615.

UNC WILMINGTON
Highway 132
Wilmington, NC 28403.
Head Coach: **Mark Scalf**.
　ph: (919) 395-3570.
Baseball SID: **Joe Browning**.
　ph: (919) 395-3236.

NORTH CAROLINA A&T STATE U.
Corbett Sports Center
Greensboro, NC 27411.
Head Coach: **Herb Jackson**.
　ph: (919) 334-7686.
Baseball SID: **Charles Mooney**.
　ph: (919) 334-7582.

NORTH CAROLINA STATE UNIV.
P.O. Box 5187
Raleigh, NC 27695.
Head Coach: **Ray Tanner**.
　ph: (919) 515-3613.
Baseball SID: **Jim Kelsey**.
　ph: (919) 515-2102.

NORTHEAST LOUISIANA UNIV.
Malone Stadium
Monroe, LA 71209.
Head Coach: **Lou St. Amant**.
　ph: (318) 342-5395.
Baseball SID: **Robby Edwards**.
　ph: (318) 342-5460.

NORTHEASTERN UNIVERSITY
360 Huntington Ave.
Boston, MA 02115.
Head Coach: **Neil McPhee**.
　ph: (617) 437-3657.
Baseball SID: **Chris Price**.
　ph: (617) 437-2691.

NORTHEASTERN ILLINOIS UNIV.
5500 N. St. Louis Ave.
Chicago, IL 60625.
Head Coach: **Jim Hawrysko**.
　ph: (312) 583-4050, ext. 2884.
Baseball SID: **Tom Lake**.
　ph: (312) 583-4050, ext. 6241.

NORTHERN ILLINOIS UNIV.
Dekalb, IL 60115.
Head Coach: **Spanky McFarland**.
　ph: (815) 753-0147.
Baseball SID: **Kari Brackett**.
　ph: (815) 753-1706.

NORTHERN IOWA, University of
23rd and College
Cedar Falls, IA 50614.
Head Coach: **Dave Schrage**.
　ph: (319) 273-6323.
Baseball SID: **Kevin Kane**.
　ph: (319) 273-3642.

NORTHWESTERN UNIVERSITY
1501 Central St.
Evanston, IL 60201.
Head Coach: **Paul Stevens**.
　ph: (708) 491-4652.
Baseball SID: **Barry Neumann**.
　ph: (708) 491-7503.

NORTHWESTERN STATE UNIV.
Natchitoches, LA 71497.
Head Coach: **Jim Wells**.
　ph: (318) 357-4139.
Baseball SID: **Tommy Newsom**.
　ph: (318) 357-6467.

NOTRE DAME, University of
Notre Dame, IN 46556.
Head Coach: **Pat Murphy**.
　ph: (219) 239-6366.
Baseball SID: **Kevin Malloy**.
　ph: (219) 239-7516.

OHIO UNIVERSITY
Convocation Center
Athens, OH 45701.
Head Coach: **Joe Carbone**.
　ph: (614) 593-1180.
Baseball SID: **Mike Williams**.
　ph: (614) 593-1299.

OHIO STATE UNIVERSITY
St. John Arena
Columbus, OH 43210.
Head Coach: **Bob Todd**.
　ph: (614) 292-1075.
Baseball SID: **Bob Goldring**.
　ph: (614) 292-6861.

OKLAHOMA, University of
Gallagher-Iba Arena
180 W. Brooks, Room 235
Norman, OK 73019.
Head Coach: **Larry Cochell**.
　ph: (405) 325-8355.
Baseball SID: **Mike Treps**.
　ph: (405) 325-8231.

OKLAHOMA STATE UNIVERSITY
Stillwater, OK 74078.
Head Coach: **Gary Ward**.
　ph: (405) 744-5849.
Baseball SID: **Chris Kirby**.
　ph: (405) 744-5749.

OLD DOMINION UNIVERSITY
H&PE Building
Norfolk, VA 23529.
Head Coach: **Pat McMahon**.
　ph: (804) 683-4360.
Baseball SID: **Carol Hudson**.
　ph: (804) 683-3372.

OREGON STATE UNIVERSITY
Gill Coliseum 207
Corvallis, OR 97331.
Head Coach: **Jack Riley**.
　ph: (503) 737-2825.
Baseball SID: **Steve Fenk**.
　ph: (503) 737-3720.

PACE UNIVERSITY
861 Bedford Road
New York, NY 10570.
Head Coach: **Fred Calaicone**.
　ph: (914) 773-3411.
Baseball SID: **John Balkam**.
　ph: (914) 773-3411.

PACIFIC, University of the
Stockton, CA 95211.
Head Coach: **Quincey Noble**.
　ph: (209) 946-2709.
Baseball SID: **Mike Martiniz**.
　ph: (209) 946-2479.

PENNSYLVANIA, University of
Weightman Hall-N
Philadelphia, PA 19104.
Head Coach: **Bob Seddon**.
　ph: (215) 898-6282.
Baseball SID: **Brad Schlozman**.
　ph: (215) 898-6128.

PENN STATE UNIVERSITY
University Park, PA 16802.
Head Coach: **Joe Hindelang**.
　ph: (814) 863-0239.

Baseball SID: **Jeff Brewer**.
ph: (814) 865-1757.

PEPPERDINE UNIVERSITY
24255 Pacific Coast Highway
Malibu, CA 90263.
Head Coach: **Andy Lopez**.
ph: (213) 456-4199.
Baseball SID: **Michael Zapolski**.
ph: (213) 456-4333.

PITTSBURGH, University of
P.O. Box 7436
Pittsburgh, PA 15213.
Head Coach: **Mark Jackson**.
ph: (412) 648-8208.
Baseball SID: **Ron Wahl**.
ph: (412) 648-8240.

PORTLAND, University of
5000 N. Willamette Blvd.
Portland, OR 97203.
Head Coach: **Terry Pollreisz**.
ph: (503) 283-7117.
Baseball SID: **Steve Walker**.
ph: (503) 283-7117.

PORTLAND STATE UNIVERSITY
P.O. Box 751
Portland, OR 97207.
Head Coach: **Jack Dunn**.
ph: (503) 725-3852.
Baseball SID: **Larry Sellers**.
ph: (503) 725-5600.

PRAIRIE VIEW A&M UNIV.
Prairie View, TX 77446.
Head Coach: **John Tankersley**.
ph: (409) 857-4290.
Baseball SID: **Jackie Davis**.
ph: (409) 857-2114.

PRINCETON UNIVERSITY
P.O. Box 71
Jadwin Gym
Princeton, NJ 08544.
Head Coach: **Tom O'Connell**.
ph: (609) 258-5059.
Baseball SID: **Mike Falk**.
ph: (609) 258-3568.

PROVIDENCE COLLEGE
River Avenue
Providence, RI 02918.
Head Coach: **Paul Kostacopoulos**.
ph: (401) 865-2273.
Baseball SID: **Tim Connor**.
ph: (401) 865-2272.

PURDUE UNIVERSITY
Mackey Arena
West Lafayette, IN 47907.
Head Coach: **Steve Green**.
ph: (317) 494-3998.
Baseball SID: **Jim Ross**.
ph: (317) 494-3200.

RADFORD UNIVERSITY
Box 5760
Radford, VA 24142.
Head Coach: **Scott Gines**.
ph: (703) 831-5881.
Baseball SID: **Mike Ashley**.
ph: (703) 831-5221.

RHODE ISLAND, Univ. of
Kingston, RI 02881.
Head Coach: **Dave Morris**.
ph: (401) 792-2750.
Baseball SID: **Jim Norman**.
ph: (401) 792-5356.

RICE UNIVERSITY
P.O. Box 1892
Houston, TX 77251.
Head Coach: **Wayne Graham**.
ph: (713) 527-6022.
Baseball SID: **Mark Sanders**.
ph: (713) 527-4034.

RICHMOND, University of
Robins Center
Richmond, VA 23173.
Head Coach: **Ron Atkins**.
ph: (804) 289-8320.
Baseball SID: **Phil Stanton**.
ph: (804) 289-8320.

RIDER COLLEGE
2083 Lawrenceville Road
Lawrenceville, NJ 08648.
Head Coach: **Sonny Pittaro**.
ph: (609) 896-5054.
Baseball SID: **Bud Focht**.
ph: (609) 896-5138.

RUTGERS UNIVERSITY
Louis Brown Athletic Center
P.O. Box 1149
Piscataway, NJ 08855.
Head Coach: **Fred Hill**.
ph: (908) 932-3553.
Baseball SID: **Michael Matts**.
ph: (908) 932-4200.

SACRAMENTO STATE UNIV.
6000 J St.
Sacramento, CA 95819.
Head Coach: **John Smith**.
ph: (916) 278-7225.
Baseball SID: **Donna Yates**.
ph: (916) 278-6896.

ST. BONAVENTURE UNIVERSITY
St. Bonaventure, NY 14778.
Head Coach: **Larry Sudbrook**.
ph: (716) 375-2461.
Baseball SID: **Jim Engelhardt**.
ph: (716) 375-2319.

ST. FRANCIS COLLEGE
180 Remsen St.
Brooklyn, NY 11201.
Head Coach: **Frank DelGeorge**.
ph: (718) 522-2300, ext. 365.
Baseball SID: **Patrick Horne**.
ph: (718) 522-2300, ext. 885.

ST. JOHN'S UNIVERSITY
Jamaica, NY 11439.
Head Coach: **Joe Russo**.
ph: (718) 990-6148.
Baseball SID: **Chris DeLorenzo**.
ph: (718) 990-6367.

ST. JOSEPH'S UNIVERSITY
5600 City Ave.
Philadelphia, PA 19131.
Head Coach: **Chris Loschiavo**.
ph: (215) 660-1718.
Baseball SID: **Ken Krsolovic**.
ph: (215) 660-1704.

SAINT LOUIS UNIVERSITY
3672 W. Pine
St. Louis, MO 63108.
Head Coach: **Bob Hughes**.
ph: (314) 658-3172.
Baseball SID: **Russ Brightman**.
ph: (314) 658-2524.

ST. MARY'S COLLEGE
Moraga, CA 94575.
Head Coach: **Don Jamerson**.
ph: (510) 631-4400.
Baseball SID: **Claude Hagopian**.
ph: (510) 631-4402.

ST. PETER'S COLLEGE
2641 Kennedy Blvd.
Jersey City, NJ 07306.
Head Coach: **Bruce Sabatini**.
ph: (201) 915-9115.
Baseball SID: **Tim Camp**.
ph: (201) 915-9101.

SAM HOUSTON STATE UNIV.
P.O. Box 2268
Huntsville, TX 77341.

Head Coach: **John Skeeters**.
  ph: (409) 294-1731.
Baseball SID: **Tom Waddill**.
  ph: (409) 294-1764.

SAMFORD UNIVERSITY
800 Lakeshore Drive
Birmingham, AL 35229.
Head Coach: **Tommy Walker**.
  ph: (205) 870-2134.
Baseball SID: **Riley Adair**.
  ph: (205) 870-2799.

SAN DIEGO, University of
Alcala Park
San Diego, CA 92110
Head Coach: **John Cunningham**.
  ph: (619) 260-8894.
Baseball SID: **John Rollo**.
  ph: (619) 260-4745.

SAN DIEGO STATE UNIVERSITY
San Diego, CA 92182.
Head Coach: **Jim Dietz**.
  ph: (619) 594-5547.
Baseball SID: **Dave Kuhn**.
  ph: (619) 594-5547.

SAN FRANCISCO, University of
San Francisco, CA 94117.
Head Coach: **Ken Bowman**.
  ph: (415) 666-6891.
Baseball SID: **Pete LaFleur**.
  ph: (415) 666-6161.

SAN JOSE STATE UNIVERSITY
San Jose, CA 95192.
Head Coach: **Sam Piraro**.
  ph: (408) 924-1255.
Baseball SID: **Chris Freshour**.
  ph: (408) 924-1217.

SANTA CLARA, University of
Tosa Pavillion
Santa Clara, CA 95053.
Head Coach: **John Oldham**.
  ph: (408) 554-4882.
Baseball SID: **Lee Klusky**.
  ph: (408) 554-4661.

SETON HALL UNIVERSITY
400 S. Orange Ave.
South Orange, NJ 07079.
Head Coach: **Mike Sheppard**.
  ph: (201) 761-9557.
Baseball SID: **Mark Rizzi**.
  ph: (201) 761-9493.

SIENA COLLEGE
Route 9
Loudonville, NY 12211.
Head Coach: **Tony Rossi**.
  ph: (518) 783-2528.
Baseball SID: **John D'Argenio**.
  ph: (518) 783-2411.

SOUTH ALABAMA, University of
307 University Blvd.
Mobile, AL 36688.
Head Coach: **Steve Kittrell**.
  ph: (205) 460-6876.
Baseball SID: **Fred Huff**.
  ph: (205) 460-7035.

SOUTH CAROLINA, University of
Columbia, SC 29208.
Head Coach: **June Raines**.
  ph: (803) 777-3829.
Baseball SID: **Tom Price**.
  ph: (803) 777-5204.

SOUTH FLORIDA, University of
4202 E. Fowler Ave.
Tampa, FL 33620.
Head Coach: **Eddie Cardieri**.
  ph: (813) 974-3105.
Baseball SID: **Jack Heilig**.
  ph: (813) 974-4092.

SOUTHEAST MISSOURI STATE U.
One University Plaza
Cape Girardeau, MO 63701.
Head Coach: **Palmer Muench**.
  ph: (314) 651-2645.
Baseball SID: **Ron Hines**.
  ph: (314) 651-2294.

SOUTHEASTERN LOUISIANA U.
P.O. Box 880, University Station
Hammond, LA 70402.
Head Coach: **Greg Marten**.
  ph: (504) 549-2253.
Baseball SID: **Larry Hymel**.
  ph: (504) 549-2341.

SOUTHERN UNIVERSITY
Southern Branch Post Office
Baton Rouge, LA 70813.
Head Coach: **Roger Cador**.
  ph: (504) 771-2513.
Baseball SID: **Rodney Lockett**.
  ph: (504) 771-2601.

SOUTHERN CALIFORNIA, Univ. of
Heritage Hall
Los Angeles, CA 90089.
Head Coach: **Mike Gillespie**.
  ph: (213) 740-8444.
Baseball SID: **Nancy Mazmanian**.
  ph: (213) 740-8480.

SOUTHERN ILLINOIS, Univ. of
Carbondale, IL 62901.
Head Coach: **Sam Riggleman**.
  ph: (618) 453-2802.
Baseball SID: **Gene Green**.
  ph: (618) 453-7236.

SOUTHERN MISSISSIPPI, Univ. of
Southern Station Box 5161
Hattiesburg, MS 39401.
Head Coach: **Hill Denson**.
  ph: (601) 266-5017.
Baseball SID: **Torye Hurst**.
  ph: (601) 266-4503.

SOUTHERN UTAH STATE UNIV.
Cedar City, UT 84720.
Head Coach: **Steve Rollo**.
  ph: (801) 586-7932.
Baseball SID: **Jim Robinson**.
  ph: (801) 586-7752.

SOUTHWEST MISSOURI STATE U.
901 S. National
Springfield, MO 65804.
Head Coach: **Keith Guttin**.
  ph: (417) 836-5242.
Baseball SID: **Mark Stillwell**.
  ph: (417) 836-5402.

SOUTHWEST TEXAS STATE U.
136 Jowers Center
San Marcos, TX 78666.
Head Coach: **Steve Prentice**.
  ph: (512) 245-2114.
Baseball SID: **Jeff Honeycutt**.
  ph: (512) 245-2966.

SOUTHWESTERN LOUISIANA, U. of
201 Reinhardt Drive
Lafayette, LA 70506.
Head Coach: **Mike Boulanger**.
  ph: (318) 231-6093.
Baseball SID: **Christopher Lakos**.
  ph: (318) 231-6330.

STANFORD UNIVERSITY
Department of Athletics
Stanford, CA 94305.
Head Coach: **Mark Marquess**.
  ph: (415) 723-4528.
Baseball SID: **Rob Goodman**.
  ph: (415) 723-4418.

STEPHEN F. AUSTIN STATE U.
P.O. Box 13010
Nacogdoches, TX 75962.

Head Coach: **Pete Smith.**
 ph: (409) 568-4350.
Baseball SID: **Greg Brown.**
 ph: (409) 568-2606.

STETSON UNIVERSITY
Campus Box 8317
DeLand, FL 32720.
Head Coach: **Pete Dunn.**
 ph: (904) 822-8106.
Baseball SID: **Dick Westervelt.**
 ph: (904) 822-8131.

TEMPLE UNIVERSITY
McGonigle Hall
Philadelphia, PA 19122.
Head Coach: **Skip Wilson.**
 ph: (215) 787-7477.
Baseball SID: **Mike Mahoney.**
 ph: (215) 787-7446.

TENNESSEE, University of
P.O. Box 47
Knoxville, TN 37901.
Head Coach: **Rod Delmonico.**
 ph: (615) 974-2057.
Baseball SID: **Randy O'Neill.**
 ph: (615) 974-1212.

TENNESSEE STATE UNIVERSITY
3500 John A. Merritt Blvd.
Nashville, TN 37209.
Head Coach: **Allen Robinson.**
 ph: (615) 320-3598.
Baseball SID: **Johnny Franks.**
 ph: (615) 320-3596.

TENNESSEE TECH
Department of Athletics
P.O. Box 5057
Cookeville, TN 38501.
Head Coach: **David Mays.**
 ph: (615) 372-3925.
Baseball SID: **Rob Schabert.**
 ph: (615) 372-3088.

TEXAS, University of
P.O. Box 7399
Austin, TX 78713.
Head Coach: **Cliff Gustafson.**
 ph: (512) 471-1404.
Baseball SID: **Craig Hammett.**
 ph: (512) 471-7437.

TEXAS-ARLINGTON, University of
Athletic Department
Box 19079
Arlington, TX 76019.
Head Coach: **Butch McBroom.**
 ph: (817) 273-2032.
Baseball SID: **Steve Weller.**
 ph: (817) 273-2239.

TEXAS-PAN AMERICAN, Univ. of
1201 W. University Drive
Edinburg, TX 78539.
Head Coach: **Al Ogletree.**
 ph: (512) 381-2234.
Baseball SID: **Jim McKone.**
 ph: (512) 381-2240.

TEXAS-SAN ANTONIO, Univ. of
San Antonio, TX 78249.
Head Coach: **Jimmy Shankle.**
 ph: (512) 691-4805.
Baseball SID: **Rick Nixon.**
 ph: (512) 691-4551.

TEXAS A&M UNIVERSITY
Athletic Department
College Station, TX 77843.
Head Coach: **Mark Johnson.**
 ph: (409) 845-9534.
Baseball SID: **Alan Cannon.**
 ph: (409) 845-5725.

TEXAS CHRISTIAN UNIVERSITY
Fort Worth, TX 76129.
Head Coach: **Lance Brown.**
 ph: (817) 921-7985.
Baseball SID: **Kent Johnson.**
 ph: (817) 921-7969.

TEXAS SOUTHERN UNIVERSITY
3100 Cleburne St.
Houston, TX 77004.
Head Coach: **Candy Robinson.**
 ph: (713) 527-7993.
Baseball SID: **Joe Quada.**
 ph: (713) 527-7270.

TEXAS TECH UNIVERSITY
P.O. Box 4199
Lubbock, TX 79409.
Head Coach: **Larry Hays.**
 ph: (806) 742-3355.
Baseball SID: **Kelly Robinson.**
 ph: (806) 742-2770.

TOLEDO, University of
2801 W. Bancroft St.
Toledo, OH 43606.
Head Coach: **Stan Sanders.**
 ph: (419) 537-2526.
Baseball SID: **Todd Edmond.**
 ph: (419) 537-3791.

TOWSON STATE UNIVERSITY
Towson, MD 21204.
Head Coach: **Mike Gottlieb.**
 ph: (410) 830-3775.
Baseball SID: **Dan O'Connell.**
 ph: (410) 830-2232.

TULANE UNIVERSITY
Monk Simons Building
New Orleans, LA 70118.
Head Coach: **Joe Brockhoff.**
 ph: (504) 865-1201.
Baseball SID: **Troy Mitchell.**
 ph: (504) 865-5506.

UTAH, University of
John Huntsman Center
Salt Lake City, UT 84112.
Head Coach: **Rick Sofield.**
 ph: (801) 581-3526.
Baseball SID: **Jim Olson.**
 ph: (801) 581-3511.

VALPARAISO UNIVERSITY
Valparaiso, IN 46383.
Head Coach: **Paul Twenge.**
 ph: (219) 464-5239.
Baseball SID: **Bill Rogers.**
 ph: (219) 464-5232.

VANDERBILT UNIVERSITY
Box 120158
2601 Jess Neely Drive
Nashville, TN 37212.
Head Coach: **Roy Mewbourne.**
 ph: (615) 322-4122.
Baseball SID: **Zack McMillin.**
 ph: (615) 322-4121.

VERMONT, University of
86 S. Williams St.
Burlington, VT 05401.
Head Coach: **Bill Currier.**
 ph: (802) 656-3074.
Baseball SID: **Dick Whittier.**
 ph: (802) 656-1109.

VILLANOVA UNIVERSITY
Villanova, PA 19085.
Head Coach: **George Bennett.**
 ph: (215) 645-6469.
Baseball SID: **Bill Dyer.**
 ph: (215) 645-4120.

VIRGINIA, University of
P.O. Box 3785
University Hall
Charlottesville, VA 22903.
Head Coach: **Dennis Womack.**
 ph: (804) 982-5775.
Baseball SID: **David Hardee.**
 ph: (804) 982-5500.

VIRGINIA COMMONWEALTH U.
819 W. Franklin St.
Richmond, VA 23284.
Head Coach: **Tony Guzzo.**
  ph: (804) 367-1267.
Baseball SID: **Mark Halstead.**
  ph: (804) 367-8818.

VIRGINIA MILITARY INSTITUTE
Athletic Department
Cameron Hall
Lexington, VA 24450.
Head Coach: **Chris Finwood.**
  ph: (703) 464-7609.
Baseball SID: **Wade Branner.**
  ph: (703) 464-7253.

VIRGINIA TECH
364 Jamerson Center
Blacksburg, VA 24061.
Head Coach: **Chuck Hartman.**
  ph: (703) 231-6417.
Baseball SID: **Dave Smith.**
  ph: (703) 231-6726.

WAGNER COLLEGE
Staten Island, NY 10301.
Head Coach: **Richard Vitaliano.**
  ph: (718) 390-3483.
Baseball SID: **Scott Morse.**
  ph: (718) 390-3427.

WAKE FOREST UNIVERSITY
P.O. Box 7265
Winston-Salem, NC 27109.
Head Coach: **George Greer.**
  ph: (919) 759-5570.
Baseball SID: **Dan Zacharias.**
  ph: (919) 759-5640.

WASHINGTON, University of
Graves Building
Seattle, WA 98195.
Head Coach: **Bob MacDonald.**
  ph: (206) 543-9365.
Baseball SID: **Jeff Bechthold.**
  ph: (206) 543-8333.

WASHINGTON STATE UNIV.
107 Bohler Gym
Pullman, WA 99164.
Head Coach: **Bobo Brayton.**
  ph: (509) 335-0211.
Baseball SID: **Scott Spencer.**
  ph: (509) 335-0270.

WEST CHESTER UNIVERSITY
West Chester, PA 19383.
Head Coach: **Carl Giuranna.**
  ph: (215) 436-2152.
Baseball SID: **Tom DiCamillo.**
  ph: (215) 436-3316.

WEST VIRGINIA UNIVERSITY
Box 877
Morgantown, WV 26507.
Head Coach: **Dale Ramsburg.**
  ph: (304) 293-2308.
Baseball SID: **John Antonik.**
  ph: (304) 293-2821.

WESTERN CAROLINA UNIV.
Cullowhee, NC 28723.
Head Coach: **Keith LeClair.**
  ph: (704) 227-7373.
Baseball SID: **Steve White.**
  ph: (704) 227-7171.

WESTERN ILLINOIS UNIVERSITY
Macomb, IL 61455.
Head Coach: **Dick Pawlow.**
  ph: (309) 298-1521.
Baseball SID: **Mike Stevens.**
  ph: (309) 298-1133.

WESTERN KENTUCKY UNIV.
College Heights
Bowling Green, KY 42101.
Head Coach: **Joel Murrie.**
  ph: (502) 745-6023, 6078.
Baseball SID: **Paul Just.**
  ph: (502) 745-4298.

WESTERN MICHIGAN UNIV.
Kalamazoo, MI 49008.
Head Coach: **Fred Decker.**
  ph: (616) 387-8149.
Baseball SID: **John Beatty.**
  ph: (616) 387-4104.

WICHITA STATE UNIVERSITY
Campus Box 18
Wichita, KS 67208.
Head Coach: **Gene Stephenson.**
  ph: (316) 689-8142.
Baseball SID: **Scott Schumacher.**
  ph: (316) 689-3265.

WILLIAM & MARY, College of
P.O. Box 399
Williamsburg, VA 23185.
Head Coach: **Bill Harris.**
  ph: (804) 221-3399.
Baseball SID: **Jeff Nygaard.**
  ph: (804) 221-3344.

WINTHROP COLLEGE
Rock Hill, SC 29733.
Head Coach: **Joe Hudak.**
  ph: (803) 329-2129.
Baseball SID: **Jack Frost.**
  ph: (803) 329-2129.

WISCONSIN-MILWAUKEE, Univ. of
P.O. Box 413
Athletic Building
Milwaukee, WI 53201.
Head Coach: **Scott Kugi.**
  ph: (414) 229-5670.
Baseball SID: **Paul Helgren.**
  ph: (414) 229-4593

WRIGHT STATE UNIVERSITY
P.O. Box 516
Dayton, OH 45401.
Head Coach: **Ron Nischwitz.**
  ph: (513) 873-3667.
Baseball SID: **Chris Bame.**
  ph: (513) 873-2771.

WYOMING, University of
U.W. Station
Box 3414
Laramie, WY 82071.
Head Coach: **Bill Kinneberg.**
  ph: (307) 766-2340.
Baseball SID: **Steve Weakland.**
  ph: (307) 766-2256.

XAVIER UNIVERSITY
Victory Parkway
Cincinnati, OH 45207.
Head Coach: **Larry Redwine.**
  ph: (513) 745-2890.
Baseball SID: **Tom Eiser.**
  ph: (513) 745-3416.

YALE UNIVERSITY
402-A Yale Station
New Haven, CT 06520.
Head Coach: **Don Brown.**
  ph: (203) 432-1467.
Baseball SID: **Steve Conn.**
  ph: (203) 432-1456.

YOUNGSTOWN STATE UNIV.
410 Wick Ave.
Youngstown, OH 44555.
Head Coach: **Dan Kubacki.**
  ph: (216) 742-3485.
Baseball SID: **Bill James.**
  ph: (216) 742-3192.

AMATEUR BASEBALL

U.S. Olympic Committee

Mailing Address: 1750 East Boulder St., Boulder, CO 80909. **Telephone:** (719) 632-5551. **FAX:** (719) 578-4677.

President: William Hybl. **Executive Director:** Harvey Schiller. **Director of Public Relations:** Mike Moran.

International Baseball Association

Mailing Address: International Headquarters, Suite 490, 201 S. Capitol Ave., Indianapolis, IN 46225. **Telephone:** (317) 237-5757. **FAX:** (317) 237-5758.

President: Dr. Robert Smith, United States. **Mailing Address:** Greenville College, Greenville, IL 62246. **Telephone:** (618) 664-1840.

Executive Director: David Osinski.

1992 Summer Olympiad: July 25-Aug. 9 at Barcelona, Spain

1992 AAA World Youth Championships: Aug. 20-Sept. 1 at Monterrey, Mexico.

III IBA World All-Star Game: Aug. 24. Site: Unavailable.

I IBA Merit Cup: Sept. 10-20 at Cocoa, Fla.

United States Baseball Federation

Mailing Address: 2160 Greenwood Ave., Trenton, NJ 08609. **Telephone:** (609) 586-2381. **FAX:** (609) 587-1818. **Telephone, Millington, Tenn., Training Base:** (901) 872-8326.

Chairman of the Board: Lew Hays. **President:** Mark Marquess. **Executive Vice President:** Neil Lantz. **Secretary:** Tom Hicks. **Treasurer:** Gale Montgomery.

Executive Director/Chief Executive Officer: Richard Case. **Associate Director:** Wanda Rutledge. **Director of Operations:** Barbara Case. **Executive Assistant:** Pam Case.

Program Director: Scott Bollwage. **Communications Director:** Bob Bensch. **Special Projects Manager:** Paul Seiler.

National Members: American Amateur Baseball Congress, American Legion Baseball, Dixie Baseball, National Amateur Baseball Federation, National Baseball Congress, Pony Baseball, Inc., NCAA, NAIA, NJCAA, National Federation of State High School Athletic Associations, American Baseball Coaches Association, Police Athletic League (PAL), YMCA of the USA, Little League Baseball.

XXVth Summer Olympics: July 26-Aug. 5 at Barcelona, Spain.

1992 World Junior Baseball Championship: Aug. 20-Sept. 1 at Monterrey, Mexico.

National Junior Baseball Championship: June 30-July 4. Site: Unavailable.

1992 Junior Olympic Super Series: Aug. 20-27. Site: Unavailable.

Baseball Canada

Mailing Address: 1600 James Naismith Dr., Gloucester, Ont. K1B 5N4. **Telephone:** (613) 748-5606. **FAX:** (613) 748-5767.

Executive Director: Bill Martin. **High Performance Director:** Bernie Beckman. **Technical Director:** Lorne Korol.

National Baseball Congress

National Headquarters: P.O. Box 1420, Wichita, KS 67201. **Telephone:** (316) 267-3372. **FAX:** (316) 267-3382.

President: Bob Rich Jr. **Executive Vice President:** Melinda Rich.

General Manager: Steve Shaad. **Director of Baseball Operations and Tournament Director:** Larry Davis. **Director of Administration:** Dian Overaker. **Marketing and Public Relations Coordinator:** Rick Orienza. **Stadium Manager:** Mark Schimming. **Coordinator of National Development:** Lance Deckinger.

1992 National Tournament: Aug. 5-16 at Wichita, Kan.

Year Founded: 1931.

Summer College Leagues
CAPE COD LEAGUE

Mailing Address: P.O. Box 164, South Harwich, MA 02661. **Telephone:** (508) 385-3122 and (401) 294-3341. **Commissioner:** Fred Ebbett. **President:** Judy Scarafile.

BOURNE BRAVES
42 Tan Bark Road
Marstons Mills, MA 02648
General Manager: **Ed Gendron.**
ph.: (508) 428-0525.
Head Coach: **Bob Gendron.**

BREWSTER WHITE CAPS
350 Run Hill Road
Brewster, MA 02631
General Manager: **Barry Souder.**
ph.: (508) 896-5665.
Head Coach: **Darren Mazeroski.**

CHATHAM A's
239 Northgate Rd.
North Chatham, MA 02650.
General Manager: **Jack Hammond**
ph.: (508) 945-4442.
Head Coach: **Rich Hill.**

COTUIT KETTLEERS
P.O. Box 371
Cotuit, MA 02635.
General Manager: **Arnold Mycock.**
ph.: (508) 428-2782.
Head Coach: **Roger Bidwell.**

FALMOUTH COMMODORES
33 Wintergreen Rd..
Mashpee, MA 02649
General Manager: **Chuck Sturtevent.**
ph.: (508) 477-5724.
Head Coach: **Arthur "Ace" Adams.**

HARWICH MARINERS
17 Meadow View Rd.
Topsfield, MA 01983.
General Manager: **Joe Bateman.**
ph.: (508) 887-8997.
Head Coach: **Steve Ring.**

HYANNIS METS
244 Rolling Hitch Rd.
Centreville, MA 02632.
General Manager: **David Sauro.**
ph.: (508) 778-0807.
Head Coach: **Dave Malpass.**

ORLEANS CARDINALS
P.O. Box 504
Orleans, MA 02653.
General Manager: **Dick Smith.**
ph.: (508) 255-2979.
Head Coach: **Rolando Casanova.**

WAREHAM GATEMEN
27 Mattapoisett Neck Road..
Mattapoisett, MA 02739.
General Manager: **Jim Hubbard.**
ph.: (508) 758-6579.
Head Coach: **Don Reed.**

YARMOUTH-DENNIS RED SOX
8 Hosking Ln.
South Yarmouth, MA 02664.
General Manager: **Jack Martin.**
ph.: (508) 394-9466.
Head Coach: **John Barlowe.**

ALASKA CENTRAL LEAGUE

Mailing Address: P.O. Box 1332, Kenai, AK 99611. **Telephone:** (907) 269-4122.
Executive Director: Jack Slama.
Member Clubs: Anchorage Glacier Pilots, Mat-Su Miners, Kenai Peninsula Oilers.

ALASKA LEAGUE

Mailing Address: 1625 Old Steese Hwy., Fairbanks, AK 99701. **Telephone:** (907) 452-1991.
Commissioner: Ralph Seekins.
Member Clubs: Alaska Goldpanners, Anchorage Buccaneers, Hawaii Island Movers, Mendocino County (Calif.) Blue Jays.

ATLANTIC COLLEGIATE LEAGUE

Mailing Address: 130 Colony Ave., Park Ridge, NJ 07656. **Telephone:** (201) 391-9376.
President: Bob Pertsas.
Commissioner: John Belson.
Member Clubs: Jersey Pilots, New Jersey A's, Long Island (N.Y.) Sound, New York Generals, Nassau (N.Y.) Collegians, Quakertown (Pa.) Blazers, Brooklyn Clippers, Monmouth (N.J.) Royals.

CENTRAL ILLINOIS COLLEGIATE LEAGUE

Mailing Address: R.R. 13, Box 369, Bloomington, IL 61704. **Telephone:** (309) 828-4429. **FAX:** same.
Commissioner: Mike Woods.
Director of Operations: Tom Lamonica.
Member Clubs: Champaign County Colts, Danville Dans, Decatur Blues, Fairview Heights Mets, Springfield Rifles, Twin City Stars.

GREAT LAKES LEAGUE

Mailing Address: P.O. Box 1121, Bowling Green, OH 43402. **Telephone:** (419) 354-5556.
Commissioner: Lou Laslo.
President: Ron Miller. **Secretary:** Larry Bialorucki.
Member Clubs: Bowling Green Breeze, Central Ohio-Delaware, Cincinnati Spirit, Columbus All-Americans, Grand Lake Mariners, Lima Locos, Sandusky Bay All-Stars, Toledo Glass Sox.

JAYHAWK LEAGUE

Mailing Address: 5 Adams Place, Halstead, KS 67056. **Telephone:** (316) 835-2589 or 283-4591.

Commissioner: Bob Considine.

Member Clubs: Amarillo (Texas) Texans, Clarinda (Iowa) A's, Elkhart (Kan.) Dusters, Hays (Kan.) Larks, Liberal (Kan.) Bee Jays, Nevada (Mo.) Griffons, Red Oak (Iowa) Red Sox, Wichita (Kan.) Broncos, St. Josephs (Mo.) Cardinals.

NORTHEASTERN COLLEGIATE LEAGUE

Mailing Address: 905 Ontario St., Schenectady, NY 12306. **Telephone:** (518) 372-5296.

Commissioner: Hank Caputo. **Assistant Commissioner:** Joe Antonio.

Chairman of the Board: Jim Burke. **Treasurer:** Forrest Davis. **Secretary/Public Relations:** Dick Cuykendall.

Member Clubs: Broome Rangers, Cohocton Red Wings, Cortland Apples, Horsehead Generals, Ithaca Ithacains, Little Falls Diamonds, Rome Indians, Schenectady Mohawks.

SAN DIEGO COLLEGIATE LEAGUE

Mailing Address: 948 Jasmine Ct., Carlsbad, CA 92009.

Commissioner: Jerry Clements.

Member Clubs: American—Angels, Aztecs, Royals. **National**—Cubs, Mets, Padres.

SHENANDOAH VALLEY LEAGUE

Mailing Address: P.O. Box 2246, Staunton, VA 24401. **Telephone:** (703) 885-8901 or 886-1748.

President: David Biery.

Member Clubs: Front Royal Cardinals, Harrisonburg Turks, New Market Rebels, Staunton Braves, Waynesboro Generals, Winchester Royals.

Men's Senior Baseball League

(30 and Over)

Mailing Address: 8 Sutton Terrace, Jericho, NY 11753. **Telephone:** (516) 931-2615. **FAX:** (516) 931-4310.

President and Founder: Steven Sigler. **Vice President:** Gary D'Ambrisi.

MEN'S ADULT BASEBALL LEAGUE

(18 and Over)

Mailing Address: 7159 Navajo Rd., Ste. 321, San Diego, CA 92149. **Telephone:** (619) 287-5676. **FAX:** (619) 229-0786.

President: Michael Micheli. **Vice President:** Joe Loomis. **National Directors:** Steven Sigler, Gary D'Ambrisi.

YOUTH BASEBALL

Little League Baseball, Inc.

International Headquarters: P.O. Box 3485, Williamsport, PA 17701. **Telephone:** (717) 326-1921. **FAX:** (717) 326-1074.

Chairman: Dr. Luke LaPorta. **Vice Chairman:** James Whittington.

President, Chief Executive Officer: Dr. Creighton Hale. **Vice President:** James Stopper. **Secretary:** Beverly Gray.

First Vice President: Steve Keener. **Financial Vice President:** Daniel Roupp. **Vice President, Operations:** Joseph Losch.

Eastern Region Director: Donald Soucy.
Southern Region Director: Arnold White. **Western Region Director:** Carl Magee. **Central Region Director:** Ronald Scott. **Latin American Director:** Jose Luis Purcell. **Little League Canada:** Joe Shea. **European Director:** Gary Marullo. **Far East Director:** Toshikuni Yahiro.

Director of Communications: Dennis Sullivan. **Director of Special Projects:** Scott Rosenberg.

Year Founded: 1939.

Age Classifications, World Series

Little League (6-12)		Williamsport, Pa., Aug. 24-29
Junior League (13)		Taylor, Mich., Aug. 17-22
Senior League (13-15)		Kissimmee, Fla., Aug. 17-22
Big League (16-18)		Ft. Lauderdale, Fla., Aug. 15-22.

All Amer. Amateur Baseball Assoc.

Mailing Address: 340 Walker Dr., Zanesville, OH 43701. **Telephone:** (614) 453-7349.

President: Roger Tremaine.
Vice Presidents: James McElroy, George Arcurio Jr.
Treasurer: William Fertitta.
Secretary and Executive Director: Tom Checkush.
1992 National Tournament: Aug. 10-15 at Johnstown, Pa.
Year Founded: 1945.

American Amateur Baseball Congress

National Headquarters: 118-19 Redfield Plaza, P.O. Box 467, Marshall, MI 49068. **Telephone:** (616) 781-2002. **FAX:** (616) 781-2060.

President: Joe Cooper.
Year Founded: 1935.

Age Classifications, National Tournaments

Roberto Clemente (8 and under)		Jonesboro, Ga., July 30-Aug. 2.
Willie Mays (10 and under)		Rex, Ga., Aug. 6-9.
Pee Wee Reese (12 and under)		Jonesboro, Ga., Aug. 6-9.
Sandy Koufax (14 and under)		Spring, Tex., Aug. 5-9.
Mickey Mantle (16 and under)		Waterbury, Conn., Aug. 6-11.
Connie Mack (18 and under)		Farmington, N.M., Aug. 14-21.
Stan Musial (unlimited)		Battle Creek, Mich., Aug. 21-25.

American Legion Baseball

National Headquarters: National Americanism Commission, P.O. Box 1055, Indianapolis, IN 46206. **Telephone:** (317) 635-8411.

Program Coordinator: Jim Quinlan.
Year Founded: 1926.
1992 World Series: Aug. 26-30 at Fargo, N.D.

Babe Ruth Baseball

International Headquarters: 1770 Brunswick Pike, P.O. Box 5000, Trenton, NJ 08638. **Telephone:** (609) 695-1434. **FAX:** (609) 695-2505.

President/Chief Executive Officer: Ronald Tellefsen.

Vice President/Secretary/Treasurer: Rosemary Schoellkopf.

Commissioners: Robert Faherty, Jimmy Stewart.

Director of Development: Russell Diethrick.
Year Founded: 1951.

Age Classifications, National Tournaments

Bambino (6-12)	Alachua, Fla., Aug. 15-22
13	Houma, La., Aug. 22-29
13-15	Vallejo, Calif., Aug. 22-29
16-18	Jamestown, N.Y., Aug. 22-29

Collegiate Summer Baseball Assoc.

Mailing Address: 3723 Hermes Dr., Cincinnati, OH 45247. **Telephone:** (513) 385-8831.
Commissioner: Jim Kindt.
Regional Directors: James Beavers (Roswell, GA), Ralph Ciabattari (Ladson, SC), Len Di Forte (Wheaton, IL), Bill Kline (Portsmouth, VA).

Continental Amateur Baseball Assoc.

Mailing Address: 82 University St., Westerville, OH 43081. **Telephone:** (614) 882-1361.
Executive Director: Roger Tremaine.

Dixie Baseball Association

Mailing Address: P.O. Box 222, Lookout Mountain, TN 37350. **Telephone:** (615) 821-6811.
Executive Director: Nick Senter.
Commissioner, Dixie Boys/Majors: Jimmy Brown. **President, Dixie Boys/Majors:** Ted Jones. **Deputy Commissioner, Dixie Boys/Majors:** Charles Melton.
Commissioner, Dixie Youth: Gale Montgomery. **Deputy Commissioner, Dixie Youth:** Wes Skelton. **President, Dixie Youth:** Matt Goyak. **Vice President, Dixie Youth:** Oliver Norton.

National Amateur Baseball Fed.

National Headquarters: 12406 Keynote Lane, Bowie, MD 20715. **Telephone:** (301) 262-0770. **FAX:** (301) 262-5005.
Executive Director: Charles Blackburn.
Year Founded: 1914.

Age Classifications, National Tournaments

Freshman (12 and under)	Sylvania, Ohio, July 16-19.
Sophomore (14 and under)	Northville, Mich., July 23-26.
Junior (16 and under)	Northville, Mich., July 30-Aug.2.
High School (high school students)	Apopka, Fla., July 30-Aug. 2.
Senior (18 and under)	Youngstown, Ohio, Aug. 6-9.
College (20 and under)	Hempstead, NY, Aug. 13-16.
Major (unlimited)	Louisville, Ky., Aug. 20-23.

National Association of Police Athletic Leagues

Mailing Address: 200 Castlewood Dr., North Palm Beach, FL 33408. **Telephone:** (407) 844-1823. **FAX:** (407) 863-6120.
Executive Director: Joseph Johnson. **Director of Marketing and Member Services:** Sally Cunningham. **National Program Coordinator:** Tina Lux.

Pony Baseball, Inc.

National Headquarters: P.O. Box 225, Washington, PA 15301. **Telephone:** (412) 225-1060. **FAX:** (412) 225-9852.
President: Roy Gillespie. **Administrative Director:** Abraham Key.
Year Founded: 1951.

Age Classifications, National Tournaments

Shetland (5-6)	No National Tournament
Pinto (7-8)	No National Tournament
Mustang (9-10)	No National Tournament
Bronco (11-12)	Citrus Heights, Calif., Aug. 13-18
Pony (13-14)	Washington, Pa., Aug. 14-21
Colt (15-16)	Lafayette, Ind., Aug. 11-18
Palomino (17-18)	Greensboro, N.C., Aug. 12-16.

U.S. Amateur Baseball Assoc.

Mailing Address: 7101 Lake Bellinger Way, Edmonds, WA 98020. **Telephone:** (206) 363-7130.
Director: Al Rutledge.
Year Founded: 1969.

Age Classifications, National Tournaments

14 and Under	Duncan, B.C., Aug. 15-23
15 and Under	Mount Vernon, Wash., Aug. 14-23.
16 and Under	Fresno, Calif., July 24-31.
18 and Under	Hoquiam-Aberdeen, Wash., July 31-Aug. 9

1992 DIRECTORY INDEX

MAJOR LEAGUE TEAMS

American League

Page	Club	Phone	FAX
12	Baltimore	410-685-9800	Unavailable
14	Boston	617-267-9440	617-236-6797
16	California	714-937-7200	714-634-3410
18	Chicago	312-924-1000	312-451-5116
20	Cleveland	216-861-1200	216-566-1287
22	Detroit	313-962-4000	313-962-5591
24	Kansas City	816-921-2200	816-921-5775
26	Milwaukee	414-933-4114	414-933-7323
28	Minnesota	612-375-1366	612-375-7417
30	New York	212-293-4300	212-293-8431
32	Oakland	510-638-4900	510-568-3770
34	Seattle	206-628-3555	206-628-3340
36	Texas	817-273-5222	817-273-5206
38	Toronto	416-341-1000	416-341-1250

National League

Page	Club	Phone	FAX
42	Atlanta	404-522-7630	404-614-1391
44	Chicago	312-404-2827	312-404-4000
46	Cincinnati	513-421-4510	513-421-7342
66	Colorado	303-292-0200	303-830-8977
67	Florida	305-779-7070	305-779-7130
48	Houston	713-799-9500	713-799-9562
50	Los Angeles	213-224-1500	213-224-1269
52	Montreal	514-253-3434	514-253-8282
54	New York	718-507-6387	718-565-4382
56	Philadelphia	215-463-6000	215-389-3050
58	Pittsburgh	412-323-5000	412-323-5024
60	St. Louis	314-421-3060	314-425-0640
62	San Diego	619-282-4494	619-282-2228
64	San Francisco	415-468-3700	415-467-0485

MINOR LEAGUE TEAMS

Page	Club	League	Phone	FAX
122	Albany GA	SAL	912-435-6444	912-435-6618
88	Albany NY	Eastern	518-869-9236	518-869-9237
83	Albuquerque	PCL	505-243-1791	505-842-0561
116	Appleton	Midwest	414-733-4152	414-733-8032
97	Arkansas	Texas	501-664-1555	501-664-1834
122	Asheville	SAL	704-258-0428	704-258-0320
128	Auburn	NYP	315-255-2489	315-255-2675
122	Augusta	SAL	404-736-7889	404-736-1122
101	Bakersfield	Cal	805-322-1363	805-322-6199
110	Baseball City	FSL	813-424-7134	813-424-1526
128	Batavia	NYP	716-343-7531	716-343-9372
134	Bellingham	Northwest	206-671-6347	206-647-2254
116	Beloit	Midwest	608-362-2272	608-362-0418
134	Bend	Northwest	503-382-8011	503-382-8875
142	Billings	Pioneer	406-252-1241	406-252-2968
88	Binghamton	Eastern	607-723-6387	607-723-7779
92	Birmingham	Southern	205-988-3200	205-988-9698
138	Bluefield	Appy	703-326-1326	703-326-1318
134	Boise	Northwest	208-322-5000	208-322-7432
138	Bristol	Appy	703-466-8310	706-466-2247
75	Buffalo	Am. Assoc.	716-846-2000	716-846-2258
116	Burlington IA	Midwest	319-754-5705	319-754-5882
138	Burlington NC	Appy	919-222-0223	919-226-2498
142	Butte	Pioneer	406-723-8206	406-723-3376
83	Calgary	PCL	403-284-1111	403-284-4343
88	Canton-Akron	Eastern	216-456-5100	216-456-5450
92	Carolina	Southern	919-269-2287	919-269-4910
117	Cedar Rapids	Midwest	319-363-3887	319-363-5631
123	Charleston SC	SAL	803-723-7241	803-723-2641
123	Charleston WV	SAL	304-925-8222	304-344-0083

Page	Club	League	Phone	FAX
110	Charlotte FL	FSL	813-625-9500	813-624-5168
92	Charlotte NC	Southern	803-548-8051	803-548-8055
93	Chattanooga	Southern	615-267-2208	615-267-4258
110	Clearwater	FSL	813-441-8638	813-447-3924
117	Clinton	Midwest	319-242-0727	319-243-1433
83	Colorado Spgs.	PCL	719-597-1449	719-597-2491
123	Columbia	SAL	803-256-4110	803-256-4338
124	Columbus GA	SAL	404-571-8866	404-571-9107
79	Columbus OH	IL	614-462-5250	614-462-3271
75	Denver	Am. Assoc.	303-433-2032	303-433-1428
111	Dunedin	FSL	813-733-9302	813-734-7661
106	Durham	Carolina	919-688-8211	919-688-4593
84	Edmonton	PCL	403-429-2934	403-426-5640
138	Elizabethton	Appy	615-543-4395	—
97	El Paso	Texas	915-755-2000	915-757-0671
128	Elmira	NYP	607-734-1811	607-734-4975
129	Erie	NYP	814-459-7245	814-454-1764
135	Eugene	Northwest	503-342-5367	503-342-6089
135	Everett	Northwest	206-258-3673	206-258-3675
124	Fayetteville	SAL	919-424-6500	919-424-4325
111	Ft. Lauderdale	FSL	305-776-1921	305-776-1958
111	Ft. Myers	FSL	813-768-4210	813-768-4211
106	Frederick	Carolina	301-662-0013	301-662-0018
124	Gastonia	SAL	704-867-3721	704-853-8108
129	Geneva	NYP	315-789-2827	315-781-2959
142	Great Falls	Pioneer	406-452-5311	—
125	Greensboro	SAL	919-275-1641	919-273-7350
93	Greenville	Southern	803-299-3456	803-277-7369
89	Hagerstown	Eastern	301-791-6266	301-791-6066
129	Hamilton	NYP	416-527-3000	416-527-2227
89	Harrisburg	Eastern	717-231-4444	717-231-4445
143	Helena	Pioneer	406-449-7616	406-449-6979
101	High Desert	Cal	619-246-6287	619-246-3197
139	Huntington	Appy	304-429-1700	304-429-1706
93	Huntsville	Southern	205-882-2562	205-880-0801
143	Idaho Falls	Pioneer	208-522-8363	208-522-9858
75	Indianapolis	Am. Assoc.	317-269-3545	317-269-3541
76	Iowa	Am. Assoc.	515-243-6111	515-243-5152
97	Jackson	Texas	601-981-4664	601-981-4669
94	Jacksonville	Southern	904-358-2846	904-358-2845
130	Jamestown	NYP	716-665-4092	716-665-4438
139	Johnson City	Appy	615-461-4850	615-461-4864
117	Kane County	Midwest	708-232-8811	708-232-8815
118	Kenosha	Midwest	414-657-7997	414-657-3972
139	Kingsport	Appy	615-246-6464	615-245-4761
106	Kinston	Carolina	919-527-9111	919-527-2328
94	Knoxville	Southern	615-637-9494	615-523-9913
112	Lakeland	FSL	813-686-1133	813-688-1637
84	Las Vegas	PCL	702-386-7200	702-386-7214
143	Lethbridge	Pioneer	403-327-7975	403-327-8085
89	London	Eastern	519-645-2255	519-673-1837
76	Louisville	Am. Assoc.	502-367-9121	502-368-5120
107	Lynchburg	Carolina	804-528-1144	804-846-0768
125	Macon	SAL	912-745-8943	912-743-5559
118	Madison	Midwest	608-241-0010	608-241-5133
140	Martinsville	Appy	703-666-2000	703-666-2139
144	Medicine Hat	Pioneer	403-526-0404	403-526-4000
95	Memphis	Southern	901-272-1687	901-278-3354
98	Midland	Texas	915-683-4251	915-683-0994
101	Modesto	Cal	209-529-7368	209-529-7213
125	Myrtle Beach	SAL	803-626-1987	803-626-8335
73	Nashville	Am. Assoc.	615-242-4371	615-256-5684
90	New Britain	Eastern	203-224-8383	203-225-6267
130	Niagara Falls	NYP	716-298-5400	716-297-2303
73	Oklahoma City	Am. Assoc.	405-946-8989	405-942-4198
74	Omaha	Am. Assoc.	402-734-2550	402-734-7166
130	Oneonta	NYP	607-432-6326	607-432-1965
95	Orlando	Southern	407-872-7593	407-649-1637
112	Osceola	FSL	407-933-5500	407-847-6237
102	Palm Springs	Cal	619-325-4487	619-325-9467
79	Pawtucket	IL	401-724-7300	401-724-2140
107	Peninsula	Carolina	804-872-7700	804-872-9868
118	Peoria	Midwest	309-688-1622	309-686-4516

1992 DIRECTORY • 197

Page	Club	League	Phone	FAX
84	Phoenix	PCL	602-275-0500	602-220-9425
131	Pittsfield	NYP	413-499-6387	413-448-6031
85	Portland	PCL	503-223-2837	503-274-0316
107	Prince William	Carolina	703-590-2311	703-590-5716
140	Princeton	Appy	304-487-2000	304-425-6999
140	Pulaski	Appy	703-980-8200	703-980-8200
119	Quad City	Midwest	319-324-2032	319-324-3109
90	Reading	Eastern	215-375-8469	215-373-5868
102	Reno	Cal	702-825-0678	702-825-2296
79	Richmond	IL	804-359-4444	804-359-0731
80	Rochester	IL	716-467-3000	716-467-6732
119	Rockford	Midwest	815-964-5400	815-961-2002
131	St. Catharines	NYP	416-641-5297	416-641-3007
112	St. Lucie	FSL	407-871-2100	407-878-9802
113	St. Petersburg	FSL	813-822-3384	813-895-1556
108	Salem	Carolina	703-389-3333	703-389-9710
102	Salinas	Cal	408-422-3812	408-422-4017
144	Salt Lake	Pioneer	801-484-9900	801-484-9910
98	San Antonio	Texas	512-434-9311	512-434-9431
103	San Bernardino	Cal	714-881-1836	714-881-6279
103	San Jose	Cal	408-297-1435	408-297-1453
113	Sarasota	FSL	813-954-7699	813-954-5753
126	Savannah	SAL	912-351-9150	912-352-9722
80	Scranton	IL	717-963-6556	717-963-6564
98	Shreveport	Texas	318-636-5555	318-636-5670
119	South Bend	Midwest	219-284-9988	219-284-9950
135	So. Oregon	Northwest	503-770-5364	503-772-4466
126	Spartanburg	SAL	803-585-6279	803-582-0877
136	Spokane	Northwest	509-535-2922	509-534-5368
120	Springfield	Midwest	217-525-6570	217-525-9340
103	Stockton	Cal	209-944-5943	209-463-4937
81	Syracuse	IL	315-474-7833	315-474-2658
85	Tacoma	PCL	206-752-7707	206-752-7135
81	Tidewater	IL	804-461-5600	804-461-0405
81	Toledo	IL	419-893-9483	419-893-5847
86	Tucson	PCL	602-325-2621	602-327-2371
99	Tulsa	Texas	918-744-5901	918-747-3267
131	Utica	NYP	315-738-0999	315-738-0992
86	Vancouver	PCL	604-872-5232	604-872-1714
113	Vero Beach	FSL	407-569-4900	407-567-0819
104	Visalia	Cal	209-625-0480	209-739-7732
120	Waterloo	Midwest	319-233-8146	319-232-1006
132	Watertown	NYP	315-788-8747	315-788-8841
132	Welland	NYP	416-735-7634	416-735-7114
114	West Palm Bch	FSL	407-684-6801	407-686-0221
99	Wichita	Texas	316-267-3372	316-267-3382
108	Winston-Salem	Carolina	919-759-2233	919-759-2042
114	Winter Haven	FSL	813-293-3900	813-299-4491
136	Yakima	Northwest	509-457-5151	509-457-9909

Phone and FAX numbers for minor league offices can be found on page 73.

OTHER ORGANIZATIONS

Page	Organization	Phone	FAX
194	AAABA	614-453-7349	—
194	AABC	616-781-2002	616-781-2060
175	ABCA	413-549-2626	413-549-4242
192	Alaska League	907-452-1991	—
192	Alaska Central League	907-269-4122	—
11	American League	212-339-7600	212-593-7138
194	American Legion Baseball	317-635-8411	—
69	Assoc. of Prof. BB Players of America	714-892-9900	714-897-0233
192	Atlantic Collegiate League	201-391-9376	—
173	Australian League	62-2-357-3595	61-2-357-7068
194	Babe Ruth Baseball	609-695-1434	609-695-2505
69	Baseball Assistance Team	212-339-7884	212-355-0007
191	Baseball Canada	613-748-5606	613-748-5767
69	Baseball Chapel	201-838-8111	201-838-7070
70	BB Writers Assoc. of America	516-757-6562	516-757-6817
71	Beckett Publications	214-991-2630	214-991-8930
192	Cape Cod League	508-385-3122	—
70	CBS Radio	212-975-8117	212-975-3515
70	CBS TV	212-975-4321	—

198 • 1992 DIRECTORY

Page	Organization	Phone	FAX
192	Central Illinois Collegiate League	309-828-4429	309-828-4429
195	Collegiate Summer BB Assoc.	513-385-8831	—
195	Continental Amateur BB Assoc.	614-882-1361	—
195	Dixie Baseball Association	615-821-6811	—
172	Dominican League	809-567-6371	809-567-5720
70	Elias Sports Bureau	212-869-1530	—
70	ESPN Radio	203-585-2661	203-585-2213
70	ESPN TV	203-585-2000	203-585-2422
192	Great Lakes League	419-354-5556	—
70	Howe Sportsdata International	617-951-0070	617-737-9960
191	International Baseball Assoc.	317-237-5757	317-237-5758
170	Japanese Baseball	03-3502-0022	03-3502-0140
193	Jayhawk League	316-835-2589	—
71	Krause Publications	715-445-2214	715-445-4087
194	Little League Baseball, Inc	717-326-1921	717-326-1074
69	MLB Alumni Association	813-822-3399	813-822-6300
9	MLB International Partners	212-841-1414	212-841-1439
9	MLB Player Relations Comm.	212-339-7400	212-371-2242
68	MLB Productions	201-807-0888	201-807-0272
9	MLB Properties	212-339-7900	212-339-7628
69	MLB Umpire Dev. Program	813-823-1286	813-821-5819
68	Major Leage Players Assoc.	212-826-6808	212-752-3649
68	Major League Scouting Bureau	714-458-7600	714-458-9454
68	Major League Umpires Assoc.	215-979-3200	—
71	Bill Mazeroski's Baseball	206-282-2322	206-284-2083
193	Men's Adult Baseball League	619-287-5676	619-229-0786
193	Men's Senior Baseball League	516-931-2615	516-931-4310
168	Mexican League	905-557-10-07	—
172	Mexican Pacific League	52-642-2-31-00	52-642-2-72-50
195	National Amateur Basebal Fed.	301-262-0770	301-262-5005
71	National Assoc. of Baseball Writers and Broadcasters	813-823-4050	813-821-5819
175	NAIA	816-842-5050	816-421-4471
191	National Baseball Congress	316-267-3372	316-267-3382
69	Nat'l Baseball Hall of Fame	607-547-9988	607-547-5980
175	NCAA	913-339-1906	913-339-0026
175	National Fed. of State High School Associations	816-464-5400	—
175	National High School Baseball Coaches Assoc.	402-457-1962	402-457-1962
175	NJCAA	719-590-9788	—
41	National League	212-339-7700	—
193	Northeastern Collegiate League	518-372-5296	—
9	Office of the Commissioner	212-339-7800	212-355-0007
173	Puerto Rican League	809-765-6285	809-767-3028
195	Police Athletic Leagues	407-844-1823	407-863-6120
195	Pony Baseball, Inc.	412-225-1060	412-225-9852
71	SABR	216-575-0500	216-575-0502
193	Shenandoah Valley League	703-885-8901	—
71	The Sporting News	314-997-7111	314-993-7723
71	Sports Illustrated	212-522-1212	212-522-0610
71	SportsTicker	201-309-1200	201-860-9742
195	US Amateur Baseball Assoc.	206-363-7130	—
191	US Baseball Federation	609-586-2381	609-587-1818
191	US Olympic Committee	719-632-5551	719-578-4677
71	USA Today	703-276-3400	703-558-3905
71	USA Today Baseball Weekly	703-276-3400	703-558-4678
173	Venezuelan League	58-2-751-2079	58-2-751-0891

TOLL FREE PHONE NUMBERS

Airlines

Air Canada	800-776-3000
Alaska Airlines	800-426-0333
Aloha Airlines	800-227-4900
American Airlines	800-433-7300
Continental Airlines	800-525-0280
Delta Airlines	800-221-1212
Northwest Airlines	800-225-2525
Olympic Airways	800-223-1226
Trans World Airlines	800-221-2000
United Airlines	800-631-1500
U.S. Air	800-428-4322

Car Rentals

Alamo (except Florida)	800-327-9633
American International	800-527-0202
Avis	800-331-1212 (USA)
	800-331-2112 (International)
Budget	800-527-0700
Dollar	800-421-6868
General	800-327-7607
Hertz	800-654-3131 (USA)
	800-654-3001 (Canada)
National	800-328-4567

Hotels/Motels

Best Western	800-528-1234
Choice Hotels	800-424-6423
Courtyard by Marriott	800-321-2211
Days Inn	800-325-2525
Hilton Hotels	800-445-8667
Holiday Inns	800-465-4329
Howard Johnsons Motor Lodges	800-654-2000
Hyatt Hotels	800-228-9000
Marriott Hotels	800-228-9290
Omni Hotels	800-843-6664
Radisson Hotels	800-333-3333
Ramada Inns	800-228-2828
Sheraton Hotels	800-325-3535
TraveLodge	800-225-3050
Westin Hotels	800-228-3000

NOTES

SERVICE DIRECTORY

APPAREL

A.J. Advertising, Inc.
201-265-2600
Fax: 201-265-4841

American Promotions, Inc.
609-694-4333
Fax: 609-694-4338

DeLong
515-236-3106
Fax: 515-236-4891

Fantastic Sports Promotions
619-569-4101
Fax: 569-0603

HA-LO Advertising Specialties
708-676-5377
Fax: 708-674-8819

Inkwell Promotions
908-536-2822
Fax: 908-972-2547

Insta Graphic Systems
(310) 404-3000
Fax: (310) 404-3010

Liebe Co.
314-532-1614/800-325-4141
Fax: 314-536-1438

Majestic Athletic Wear
215-863-6161/800-955-8555
Fax: 215-863-7006

Merchandising Milestones
516-676-7600
Fax: 516-759-2508

Midwest Sporting Goods
414-228-1813
Fax: 414-228-1808

Mizuno Sports
415-342-4100/800-736-8326
Fax: 415-342-4178

Native Sun Sportswear
813-323-2828/800-777-5800
Fax: 813-327-3938

Opti Sportswear, Inc.
415-826-4455/800-678-6784
Fax: 415-826-2019

Pittsburgh Souvenir & Novelty
412-366-3456/800-321-8797
Fax: 412-366-7421

Rawlings Sporting Goods
314-349-3500/800-729-5464
Fax: 314-349-3588

Roman Company
508-583-5515/800-288-5515
Fax: 508-588-7350

Russell Athletic
205-329-5034
Fax: 205-329-4640

Seven Sons and Company, Inc.
803-574-7660/800-722-5794
Fax: 803-574-7611

Starter Sportswear, Inc.
203-781-4000/800-331-STAR
Fax: 203-776-3689

Swingster Athletic
816-943-5002/800-848-8028
Fax: 816-943-5190

Trench Manufacturing Co.
1298 Main Street
Buffalo, NY 14209
800-828-7350
Fax: 716-885-0369

W.A. Goodman & Sons/DeBeer
213-582-4390
Fax: 213-582-1377

ATHLETIC TRAINING/SPORTS MEDICINE

ATEC Grand Slam USA
115 Post Street
Santa Cruz, CA 95060
408-439-9048/800-547-6273
Fax: 408-439-7832

Cripps First Aid & Med. Supply
314-567-9908
Fax: 314-567-6706

Health Evaluation Programs, Inc.
708-696-1824/800-323-2178

JUGS, Inc.
503-692-1635/800-547-6843
Fax: 503-691-1100

Micro Bio-Medics, Inc.
914-699-1700/800-431-2743
Fax: 914-699-1759

Speed Pitch Indicator Company
415-465-8090
Fax: 415-451-6137

Sportsmaster
1-800-522-0151

W.A. Goodman & Sons/DeBeer
213-582-4390
Fax: 213-582-1377

BAGS & LUGGAGE

Buck's Bags, Inc.
Box 7884
Boise, ID 83707
208-344-4400/800-284-2247
Fax: 208-344-6244

Ed's West, Inc.
212-244-5610/800-325-7229
Fax: 212-564-2176

Gainmore International, Inc.
713-499-2777
Fax: 713-261-1117

Midwest Sporting Goods
414-228-1813
Fax: 414-228-1808

Mitre Sports
615-367-7154/800-626-8390
Fax: 615-367-7320

Paul Pryor Travel Bags, Inc.
813-531-8400

BASEBALLS

ATEC Grand Slam USA
115 Post Street
Santa Cruz, CA 95060
408-439-9048/800-547-6273
Fax: 408-439-7832

Baden Sports, Inc.
206-235-1830/800-544-8731
Fax: 206-235-1892

Diamond Sports
213-598-9717

Hollywood Bases, Inc.
916-741-9433/800-421-2243
Fax: 800-468-6640

JUGS, Inc.
503-692-1635/800-547-6843
Fax: 503-691-1100

Quality Network Enterprises
213-469-5336

Rawlings Sporting Goods
314-349-3500/800-729-5464
Fax: 314-349-3588

Tru-Pitch
813-573-9701
Fax: 813-572-4487

> **Wilson Sporting Goods Co.**
> 2233 West St.
> River Grove, IL 60171
> 708-456-6100/800-628-1188
> Fax: 708-452-3132

Worth Sports Company
615-455-0691
Fax: 615-454-9164

BATS

Cooper Sports by Irwin
416-533-3521
Fax: 416-533-0715

Easton Sports, Inc.
415-347-3900/800-347-3901
Fax: 415-347-1035

> **Hillerich & Bradsby Co.**
> P.O. Box 35700
> Louisville, KY 40232
> 502-585-5226/800-282-2287
> Fax: 502-585-1179

Mizuno Sports
415-342-4100/800-736-8326
Fax: 415-342-4178

Pro Insignia
715-386-1535/800-533-0726
Fax: 715-386-1554

Rawlings Sporting Goods
314-349-3500/800-729-5464
Fax: 314-349-3588

Tru-Pitch
813-573-9701
Fax: 813-572-4487

Worth Sports Company
615-455-0691
Fax: 615-454-9164

BATTING CAGES

> **ATEC Grand Slam USA**
> P.O. Box 1573
> Santa Cruz, CA 95060
> 408-425-1484/800-547-6237
> Fax: 408-425-7832

JUGS, Inc.
503-692-1635/800-547-6843
Fax: 503-691-1100

National Batting Cages, Inc.
503-357-7039/800-547-8800
Fax: 503-357-5067

Tru-Pitch
813-573-9701
Fax: 813-572-4487

BATTING GLOVES

Champion Glove
515-265-2551
Fax: 515-265-7210

Easton Sports, Inc.
415-347-3900/800-347-3901
Fax: 415-347-1035

> **Hillerich & Bradsby Co.**
> P.O. Box 35700
> Louisville, KY 40232
> 502-585-5226/800-282-2287
> Fax: 502-585-1179

Midwest Sporting Goods
414-228-1813
Fax: 414-228-1808

Rawlings Sporting Goods
314-349-3500/800-729-5464
Fax: 314-349-3588

> **Wilson Sporting Goods Co.**
> 2233 West St.
> River Grove, IL 60171
> 708-456-6100/800-628-1188
> Fax: 708-452-3132

CAMPS

> **Florida Baseball Schools**
> 1207 Mellonville Ave.
> Sanford, FL 32771
> 800-346-1677

Jim Evans Academy of Pro Umpiring
512-346-9555
Fax: 512-335-5411

> **Playball Baseball Academy**
> P.O. Box 4855
> Fort Lauderdale, FL 33338
> 305-776-6217
> Fax: 305-772-4510

CAPS/HEADWEAR

American Promotions, Inc.
609-694-4333/800-426-8054
Fax: 609-694-4338

Associated Premium Corporation
513-542-5300
Fax: 513-542-4415

DeLong
515-236-3106
Fax: 515-236-4891

E & M Sales Company
609-428-5562/800-999-5173
Fax: 609-428-9728

Ed's West, Inc.
212-244-5610/800-325-7229
Fax: 212-564-2176

Fantastic Sports Promotions
619-569-4101
Fax: 569-0603

Inkwell Promotions
908-536-2822
Fax: 908-972-2547

Midwest Sporting Goods
414-228-1813
Fax: 414-228-1808

> **New Era Cap Co., Inc.**
> 8061 Erie Road
> Derby, NY 14047
> 716-549-0445/800-289-7227
> Fax: 716-549-5424

Pittsburgh Souvenir & Novelty
412-366-3456/800-321-8797
Fax: 412-366-7421

Promotions
813-884-1116
Fax: 813-882-0366

Roman Company
508-583-5515/800-288-5515
Fax: 508-588-7350

Sports Souvenirs Corporation
309-787-1600/800-447-4829
Fax: 309-787-0886

Starter Sportswear, Inc.
203-781-4000/800-331-STAR
Fax: 203-776-3689

Twins Enterprise
617-437-1384/800-446-6046
Fax: 617-437-7581

CATCHING EQUIPMENT

Diamond Sports
213-598-9717

Easton Sports, Inc.
415-347-3900/800-347-3901
Fax: 415-347-1035

Rawlings Sporting Goods
314-349-3500/800-729-5464
Fax: 314-349-3588

> **Wilson Sporting Goods Co.**
> 2233 West St.
> River Grove, IL 60171
> 708-456-6100/800-628-1188
> Fax: 708-452-3132

COMPUTER SERVICES

DI/AN Controls, Inc.
508-559-8000
Fax: 508-559-8658

Mercury Tickets
306-244-8117
Fax: 306-244-7345

Schlumberger Technologies
804-523-2160
Fax: 804-523-2173

DRINK CUPS

A.J. Advertising, Inc.
201-265-2600
Fax: 201-265-4841

American Promotions, Inc.
609-694-4333/800-426-8054
Fax: 609-694-4338

Associated Premium Corp.
513-542-5300
Fax: 513-542-4415

Eagle Affiliates
718-649-8007/800-221-0434
Fax: 718-649-1717

Hunter Manufacturing Group
606-254-7573/800-237-1869
Fax: 606-254-7614

Merchandising Milestones
516-676-7600
Fax: 516-759-2508

National Design Corporation
619-448-6824/800-544-1462
Fax: 619-448-2255

Whirley Industries, Inc.
814-723-7600/800-825-5575
Fax: 814-723-3245

ENTERTAINMENT

Allison Bly The Dynamite Lady!
813-886-2697

> **Bleacher Preacher Promotions**
> 7847 W. Church St.
> Morton Grove, IL 60053
> 708-965-8138
> Jerry Pritikin

Captain Dynamite
(713) 928-6035

Entertainment Concepts
614-457-9563

Famous Chicken
619-278-1987

Hollywood Starlets Entertainment
818-892-0506

> **Jericho The Miracle Dog**
> 2317 NE 2nd St.
> Pompano Beach, FL 33062
> 305-943-0551

Max Patkin
(215) 783-5933

> **Morganna "The Kissing Bandit"**
> P.O. Box 20281
> Columbus, OH 43220
> 614-457-9563

Southern Int'l. Fireworks
404-924-1777/800-327-1771
Fax: 404-591-0800

Steele's Silver Bullets
216-926-2530/800-321-3885
Fax: 216-926-2530

FENCING—PORTABLE

> **All Sports Fencing**
> 2058 N. Millo Ave. Suite 205
> Claremont, CA 91711
> 800-925-4472
> Fax: 800-627-4472

FOOD/BEVERAGE SVC./SUPPLY

ARA Leisure Services, Inc.
215-238-3445/800-999-8989
Fax: 215-238-4099

> **Caddy Cupholder/**
> **Bergin International, Inc.**
> Suite #810
> 800 West Pender St.
> Vancouver, B.C. Canada V6C 2V6
> 604-327-2374/800-688-8490
> Fax: 604-327-4530

> **Carolina Fine Snacks/Peanuts**
> 3718 Alliance Drive
> Greensboro, NC 27407
> 919-852-1900

Coca-Cola USA
404-676-6140
Fax: 404-676-5925

Dug-out Sunflower Seeds
614-792-0777
Fax: 614-792-2029

Legend Food Products
415-472-4280
Fax: 415-472-6123

> **Slush Puppie Corporation**
> 1950 Radcliff Drive
> Cincinnati, OH 45204
> 513-244-2400/800-543-0860
> Fax: 513-251-3458

Sportservice Corporation
716-858-5000/800-828-7240
Fax: 716-858-5424

Volume Services
803-597-8331/800-733-6110
Fax: 803-597-8218

FOOTWEAR

> **Eastbay**
> 427 Third Street
> Wausau, WI 54401
> 800-826-2205
> Fax: 800-628-6302

Mitre Sports
615-367-7154/800-626-8390
Fax: 615-367-7320

Mizuno Sports
415-342-4100/800-736-8326
Fax: 415-342-4178

Rawlings Sporting Goods
314-349-3500/800-729-5464
Fax: 314-349-3588

GIFT ITEMS

Ace Novelty Co, Inc.
206-644-1820
Fax: 206-641-5035

American Promotions, Inc.
609-694-4333/800-426-8054
Fax: 609-694-4338

Associated Premium Corporation
513-542-5300
Fax: 513-542-4415

Ball Qube
800-543-1470

Clarin Corporation
708-295-2200/800-323-9062
Fax: 234-9001

Dan Brechner & Co.
516-437-8400/800-645-8142

Eagle Affiliates
718-649-8007/800-221-0434
Fax: 718-649-1717

Geographics by Bevis
205-435-4306/800-292-3847

Hunter Manufacturing Group, Inc.
606-254-7573/800-237-1869
Fax: 606-254-7614

Intern'l Quality Packaging
213-426-4077
Fax: 213-424-9059

Market Identity
800-927-8070
Fax: 818-341-8904

National Design Corporation
619-448-6824/800-544-1462
Fax: 619-448-2255

O'Neill Importing
708-893-6070/800-248-6468
Fax: 708-893-6384

P & K Products Co.
708-695-7070/800-624-5353
Fax: 708-695-3493

Peter David, Inc.
2222 Verus Street
San Diego, CA 92154
619-429-0901
Fax: 619-575-0405

Promotions
813-884-1116
Fax: 813-882-0366

Seven Sons and Company, Inc.
803-574-7660/800-722-5794
Fax: 803-574-7611

Sports Products Corp.
216-267-6540/800-645-2376
Fax: 216-267-0532

Sports Souvenirs Corporation
309-787-1600/800-447-4829
Fax: 309-787-0886

Under The Sun
714-946-6217

GLOVES

Cooper Sports by Irwin
416-533-3521
Fax: 416-533-0715

Diamond Sports
213-598-9717

Easton Sports, Inc.
415-347-3900/800-347-3901
Fax: 415-347-1035

Hillerich & Bradsby Co.
P.O. Box 35700
Louisville, KY 40232
502-585-5226/800-282-2287
Fax: 502-585-1179

Mizuno Sports
415-342-4100/800-736-8326
Fax: 415-342-4178

Rawlings Sporting Goods
314-349-3500/800-729-5464
Fax: 314-349-3588

Worth Sports Company
615-455-0691
Fax: 615-454-9164

LIGHTING

General Electric Sports Lighting
217-732-3200
Fax: 217-735-4442

NETTING/POSTS

ATEC Grand Slam USA
115 Post Street
Santa Cruz, CA 95060
408-439-9048/800-547-6273
Fax: 408-439-7832

Burbank Sport Nets
904-261-3671
Fax: 904-261-3980

C & H Welding And Metal
813-748-0011/800-248-5192
Fax: 813-748-0012

JUGS, Inc.
503-692-1635/800-547-6843
Fax: 503-691-1100

National Batting Cages, Inc.
503-357-7039/800-547-8800
Fax: 503-357-5067

Nylon Net Company
901-774-1500
Fax: 901-774-8130

Tru-Pitch
813-573-9701
Fax: 813-572-4487

PITCHING MACHINES

ATEC Grand Slam USA
P.O. Box 1573
Santa Cruz, CA 95060
408-425-1484/800-547-6237
Fax: 408-425-7832

JTI
818-718-1058
Fax: 818-718-1062

JUGS, Inc.
503-692-1635/800-547-6843
Fax: 503-691-1100

Tru-Pitch
813-573-9701
Fax: 813-572-4487

W.A. Goodman & Sons/DeBeer
213-582-4390
Fax: 213-582-1377

PLAYING FIELD PRODUCTS/SERVICES

Astroturf Industries, Inc.
314-997-8200/800-358-8553
Fax: 314-997-6071

ATEC Grand Slam USA
P.O. Box 1573
Santa Cruz, CA 95060
408-425-1484/800-547-6237
Fax: 408-425-7832

Balsam Corporation/Astroturf
314-997-8200/800-358-8553
Fax: 314-997-6071

C & H Welding And Metal
813-748-0011/800-248-5192
Fax: 813-748-0012

Diamond-Dry
217-732-3200
Fax: 217-735-4442

DJ Industries, Inc.
P.O. Box 105
Sandy, UT 84092
801-972-0110
Fax: 801-972-0280

Hollywood Bases, Inc.
916-741-9433/800-421-2243
Fax: 800-468-6640

Kromer Co.
800-373-0337
Fax: 612-472-3458

National Batting Cages, Inc.
503-357-7039/800-547-8800
Fax: 503-357-5067

P & K Products Co.
708-695-7070/800-624-5353
Fax: 708-695-3493

Partac Peat Corporation
Kelsey Park
Great Meadows, NJ 07838
908-637-4191/800-247-BEAM
Fax: 908-637-8421

Promats, Inc.
800-678-6287
Fax: 303-482-7740

Rogers Sports Corp.
717-653-6543
Fax: 717-653-2600

Southern Turf Nurseries/STN Sports
P.O. Box 667
Norcross, GA 30091
800-522-7333
Fax: 404-242-8332

Sportsfields, Inc.
708-371-0917

Stabilizer, Inc.
602-952-8009/800-336-2468
Fax: 602-852-0718

Whirley Industries, Inc.
814-723-7600/800-825-5575
Fax: 814-723-3245

PREMIUM/GIVE-AWAY ITEMS

American Promotions, Inc.
609-694-4333/800-426-8054
Fax: 609-694-4338

Associated Premium Corp.
513-542-5300
Fax: 513-542-4415

Baden Sports
206-235-1830/800-544-8731
Fax: 206-235-1892

Clarin Corporation
708-295-2200/800-323-9062
Fax: 708-234-9001

Custom Pin & Design
518-523-2810
Fax: 518-523-3758

Fanatics
P.O. Box 4201
Rocky Mount, NC
919-985-3534

Fantastic Sports Merchandise
619-569-4101
Fax: 619-569-0603

HA-LO Advertising Specialties
708-676-5377
Fax: 708-674-8819

Hillerich & Bradsby Co.
P.O. Box 35700
Louisville, KY 40232
502-585-5226/800-282-2287
Fax: 502-585-1179

Hunter Manufacturing Group, Inc.
606-254-7573/800-237-1869
Fax: 606-254-7614

Inkwell Promotions
908-536-2822
Fax: 908-972-2547

International Quality Packaging
1308 E. 29th Street
Long Beach, CA 90806-1842
800-PIC-BAGS
Fax: 213-424-9059

KR Industries
200 N. Artesian
Chicago, IL 60612
800-621-6097/312-666-1100
Fax: 312-738-0170

Market Identity
800-927-8070
Fax: 818-341-8904

Merchandising Milestones, Ltd.
516-676-7600
Fax: 516-759-2508

National Design Corporation
619-448-6824/800-544-1462
Fax: 619-448-2255

O' Neill Importing
708-893-6070/800-248-6468
Fax: 708-893-6384

Peter David, Inc.
2222 Verus Street
San Diego, CA 92154
619-429-0901
Fax: 619-575-0405

Promotions
813-884-1116
Fax: 813-882-0366

R. A. Briggs & Company
708-438-2345/800-366-2346
Fax: 708-438-2386

Sports Products Corp.
216-267-6540
Fax: 216-267-0532

Sports Souvenirs Corporation
309-787-1600/800-447-4829
Fax: 309-787-0886

Steiner Manufacturing & Sales, Inc.
617 Sackett Street
Brooklyn, NY 11217
800-445-4321
Fax: 718-858-3897

Whirley Industries
814-723-7600/800-825-5575
Fax: 814-723-3245

PRINTING

Eagle Affiliates
718-649-8007/800-221-0434
Fax: 718-649-1717

Globe Ticket And Label Co.
404-762-9711

Inkwell Promotions
908-536-2822
Fax: 908-972-2547

Insta Graphic Systems
310-404-3000
Fax: 310-404-3010

International Quality Packaging
213-426-4077
Fax: 213-424-9059

Mercury Tickets
306-244-8117
Fax: 306-244-7345

Multi-Ad Services, Inc.
800-447-1950 ext. 415
Fax: 309-692-5444

Ticket Craft, Inc.
516-826-1500/800-645-4944
Fax: 516-826-0163

Weldon, Williams & Lick, Inc.
501-783-4113
Fax: 501-783-7050

PROFESSIONAL SERVICES

American Specialty Underwriters Insurance
617-938-6300
Fax: 617-938-0996

Baseball Opportunities
P.O. Box 4941
Scottsdale, AZ 85261-4941
602-483-8224

Global Sports Productions, Ltd.
800-350-9481
Fax: 310-395-6533

Thomas E. Wood, Inc./K & K
513-852-6381
Fax: 513-852-6428

Ulis J. Temos Associates
3224 Sterner Road
Nazareth, PA 18064
215-837-1393
Fax: 215-837-9264

PUBLIC RELATIONS

Wirz & Associates
16 Knight Street
Norwalk, CT 06851
203-866-9245
Fax: 203-866-9628

PUBLICATIONS

Baseball Underground
617-277-0208

Low And Inside
P.O. Box 290228
Minneapolis, MN 55429

RADAR EQUIPMENT

ATEC Grand Slam USA
P.O. Box 1573
Santa Cruz, CA 95060
408-425-1484/800-547-6237
Fax: 408-425-7832

JUGS, Inc.
503-692-1635/800-547-6843
Fax: 503-691-1100

Radar Sales
612-557-6654

Speed Pitch Indicator Company
415-465-8090
Fax: 415-451-6137

Sport Electronics
312 E. 55th St.
P.O. Box 696
Hinsdale, IL 60521
800-248-4142/708-920-1808
Fax: 708-920-1819

Tru-Pitch
813-573-9701
Fax: 813-572-4487

SCOREBOARDS

Daktronics Inc.
605-692-6145/800-843-9879
Fax: 605-697-5171

Fairtron Corporation
515-265-5305/800-247-0265
Fax: 515-265-3364

SCREEN PRINTERS

Gainmore International, Inc.
713-499-2777
Fax: 713-261-1117

HA-LO Advertising Specialties
708-676-5377
Fax: 708-674-8819

Inkwell Promotions
908-536-2822
Fax: 908-972-2547

Merchandising Milestones, Ltd.
516-676-7600
Fax: 516-759-2508

Promotions
813-884-1116
Fax: 813-882-0366

Ralph Lentz Co., Inc.
704-782-0319

Trench Manufacturing Co.
716-885-0017/800-828-7350
Fax: 716-885-0369

W. A. Goodman & Sons/DeBeer
213-582-4390
Fax: 213-582-1377

STADIUM ARCHITECTS/CONSTRUCTION

Ellerbe Becket, Inc.
605 West 47th
Kansas City, MO 64112
816-561-4443
Fax: 816-561-2863

HNTB Sports Architecture
1201 Walnut, Suite 700
Kansas City, MO 64106
816-472-1201
Fax: 816-472-4060

HOK Sports Facilities Group
323 W. 8th St., Suite 700
Kansas City, MO 64105
816-221-1576
Fax: 816-221-5816

Lehrer McGovern Bovis
387 Park Avenue South
New York, NY 10016
212-576-8717
Fax: 212-532-1763

Lescher & Mahoney, Inc.
813-254-9811
Fax: 813-254-4230

Thursday Architects
1807 W. Sunnyside Ave.
Chicago, IL 60640
312-271-7781
Fax: 312-275-1858

STADIUM SEATING

American Desk Mfg. Co.
817-773-1776/800-433-3142
Fax: 817-773-7370

American Seating Company
901 Broadway Ave., N.W.
Grand Rapids, MI 49504-4499
616-732-6895
Fax: 616-732-6446

Caddy Cupholder/Bergin International
604-327-2374/800-688-8490
Fax: 604-327-4530

Clarin Corporation
708-295-2200
Fax: 708-234-9001

Contour Seats, Inc.
P.O. Box 509
Allentown, PA 18105
215-395-5144/800-247-4509
Fax: 215-398-7099

KR Industries
200 N. Artesian
Chicago, IL 60612
800-621-6097/312-666-1100
Fax: 312-738-0170

Southern Bleacher Co.
Post Office Box One
Graham, TX 76046
817-549-0733
Fax: 817-549-1365

Sturdisteel Company
P.O. Box 2655
Waco, TX 76702
800-433-3116
Fax: 817-857-3244

TELEMARKETING

I.D.S. Unlimited Inc.
6717 Odana Road Suite 2
Madison, WI 53719
608-833-1845
Fax: 608-833-1939

TICKETS

Celebrity Ticket
Box 83
Metuchen, NJ 08840
908-220-0330
Fax: 908-754-5726

Globe Ticket and Label Co.
404-762-9711

Mercury Tickets
306-244-8117
Fax: 306-244-7345

National Ticket Co.
717-648-6803
Fax: 800-326-9320

Select Ticketing Systems
315-479-6663/800-333-8448
Fax: 315-471-2715

Sport Productions, Inc.
216-591-2400
Fax: 216-591-2424

Ticket Craft, Inc.
516-826-1500/800-645-4944
Fax: 516-826-0163

Weldon, Williams & Lick, Inc.
501-783-4113
Fax: 501-783-7050

TOWELS

American Promotions, Inc.
609-694-4333/800-426-8054
Fax: 609-694-4338

McArthur Towels, Inc.
608-356-8922
Fax: 608-356-7587

Ralph Lentz Co., Inc.
704-782-0319

Sports Souvenirs Corp.
309-787-1600/800-447-4829
Fax: 309-787-0886

TRADING CARDS

Barry Colla Photography
408-247-7196/800-822-0028

Classic
404-942-1429

Donruss
901-775-5525

Fleer
215-455-2000

Impel Marketing Inc.
919-361-8249

Multi-Ad Services, Inc.
309-692-1530/800-447-1950
Fax: 309-692-5444

Procards, Inc.
215-970-5933
Fax: 215-970-5935

Score
203-227-8882

Sportsprint
404-525-6845/800-966-6845
Fax: 404-525-7733

Topps
718-768-8900

Upper Deck
5909 Sea Otter Place
Carlsbad, CA 92008-1989
714-692-1013

TRAVEL

Baseball Odyssey, Inc.
202-966-6422
Fax: 202-966-6423

Jay Buckley Tours
P.O. Box 213
La Crosse, WI 54602-0213
608-788-9200

TROPHIES/AWARDS/JEWELRY

Balfour Company
508-222-3600/800-LGB-UNIV
Fax: 508-222-2698

E & M Sales Company
609-428-5562/800-999-5173
Fax: 609-428-9728

Henri Studio—Stone Statuary
803-763-1360
Fax: 803-769-0855

O'Neill Importing
708-893-6070/800-248-6468
Fax: 708-893-6384

Schneidereit Glass
510-635-8575
Fax: 510-562-9408

UNIFORMS

DeLong
515-236-3106
Fax: 515-236-4891

Opti Sportswear, Inc.
415-826-4455/800-678-6784
Fax: 415-826-2019

Ralph Lentz Co., Inc.
704-782-0319

Rawlings Sporting Goods
314-349-3500/800-729-5464
Fax: 314-349-3588

Russell Athletic
205-329-5034
Fax: 205-329-4640

W.A. Goodman & Sons/DeBeer
213-582-4390
Fax: 213-582-1377

Wilson Sporting Goods Co.
2233 West St.
River Grove, IL 60171
708-456-6100/800-628-1188
Fax: 708-452-3132

Worth Sports Company
615-455-0691
Fax: 615-454-9164

VIDEO/AUDIO/MUSIC CASSETTES

Crawford Communications
404-876-7149
Fax: 404-892-2355

L & R Productions, Inc.
203-528-5177
203-291-9341

RS Productions
800-777-2709

Sony Corporation
201-930-7215
Fax: 201-930-7937

Sound Creations
21 Royal Oak Rd.
Lawrenceville, NJ 08648
609-882-5222
Fax: 609-396-4442

New Era Cap Company, Inc. manufactures the current:
- Batting
- ERA
- Home Run
- MVP
- World Champion cap

The record shows that **100%** of all Professional Baseball teams use New Era Caps. We are proud of our record and thank Professional Baseball for placing us in such a prominent position.

Since 1920
New Era Cap Co., Inc.
Box 208, Derby, NY 14047
716 549-0445

ATEC Grand Slam U.S.A.
CASEY
PITCHING MACHINE

Throws any type of pitch, any speed, any spin, for hitting and infield, outfield and catchers drills.

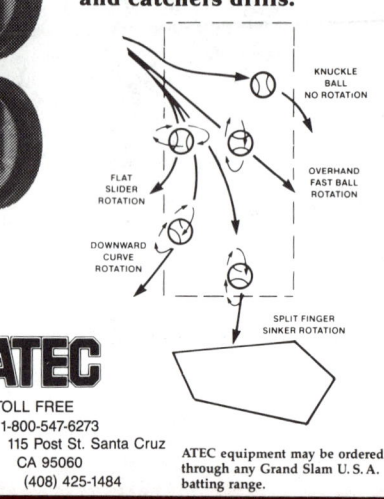

KNUCKLE BALL NO ROTATION
FLAT SLIDER ROTATION
OVERHAND FAST BALL ROTATION
DOWNWARD CURVE ROTATION
SPLIT FINGER SINKER ROTATION

ATEC
TOLL FREE
1-800-547-6273
115 Post St. Santa Cruz
CA 95060
(408) 425-1484

ATEC equipment may be ordered through any Grand Slam U.S.A. batting range.

STURDISTEEL
A TRADITION OF QUALITY

"For all Your Stadium Needs" For more than 50 years, the tradition of quality at Sturdisteel has been based on our commitment to our customers to research, design, engineer, fabricate and install the finest seating available at fair and competitive prices. Sturdisteel's expert craftsmanship of permanent grandstands, portable bleachers and aluminum stadium seats sets the standard in outdoor seating.

RECENT INSTALLATIONS:

Reading Phillies	Reading, PA
Minnesota Twins Spring Training Complex	Fort Myers, FL
El Paso Diablos	El Paso, TX
Tacoma Athletics	Tacoma, WA
Midland Angels	Midland, TX

Sturdisteel®

A Division of Schultz Industries, Inc.
P.O. Box 2655 • Waco, Texas 76702-2655
1-800-433-3116 (USA) • 1-817-857-3744 • FAX 1-817-857-3244

Unparalleled baseball grandstands.

The trademark of Southern Bleacher. Baseball grandstands from Southern Bleacher will assure you of the highest quality and best value in design, engineering, manufacturing and installation. Custom mitered grandstand designs can be enhanced with integral roof and skybox systems that distinguish Southern's engineering integrity. Plus, reserved section spectators will be comfortable for all nine innings in the contoured SOBCO Aluminum Stadium Chair. Southern offers design/build services in the expansion of your existing steel or concrete stadium. Base line additions can be designed to provide a continuous crosswalk from the original structure. Wood seating sections can be renovated with aluminum bench seating. Since 1946 the name Southern Bleacher has stood for unparalleled achievements in permanent grandstands, stadium seating and portable bleachers.

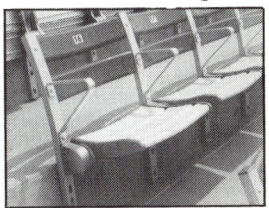

Southern® BLEACHER COMPANY

P.O. Box One, Graham, Texas 76046
Toll Free: 1-800/433-0912　In Texas: 817/549-0733　FAX: 817/549-1365

ALL THE FACTS AT YOUR FINGERTIPS

There's no better way to prepare for the upcoming baseball season than with Baseball America's 1992 Almanac.

For each major league organization, you can easily reference any player at any level—either a major leaguer, a ripe-and-ready pitcher on the verge of making the bigs or last year's first-round draft pick.

Also included are articles on each minor league, profiling the best teams and their top prospects. The same is done for the Mexican League, the Japanese Leagues and the Dominican Summer League.

Also included are a complete list of the amateur draft with analysis, stats and stories from college baseball and full coverage of Team USA at the Pan American Games.

BASEBALL AMERICA'S 1992 ALMANAC

BASEBALL AMERICA • P.O. BOX 2089 • DURHAM, NC 27702

Please send me _____ copy(s) of the 1992 Almanac at $9.95 each.

☐ My check or money order is enclosed.

Please bill my   ☐ MasterCard   ☐ VISA   ☐ American Express

Card No. _____ Exp. Date _____

Name _____

Address _____

Phone (_____) _____

City _____

State _____ Zip _____

For Faster Service On Credit Card Orders, Call

1-800-845-2726

M-F, 9:00-5:00 EST

DIR92

'Big League Profits!'

Who else but the Steiner Boys could have created the perfect profit center for all baseball concessionaires?

So meet the SPORTS CARD CENTER, our internationally-famous baseball card vending machine that stimulates fan support and adds revenue *without* increasing overhead!

The SPORTS CARD CENTER allows your people to concentrate on selling other items while this pro goes to work selling *your* Team Sets, baseball cards and our collectible (and profitable!) FunStickers.

The SPORTS CARD CENTER, features price-adjustable coin mechanisms and comes guaranteed from Steiner for a full year, parts AND labor!

Interested? The call is Free!

- ***ALSO AVAILABLE NOW***—Capsule machine sells Official Major League mini-batting helmets!
- Bat'n Ball keychains–customized with/without team name
- Official Licensed Major League Stickers for all teams!

STEINER
THE STEINER BOYS
"WE VEND OVER BACKWARDS!"

Steiner
MANUFACTURING & SALES
617 Sackett Street, Brooklyn, NY 11217

MADE IN U.S.A!

800 445 4321 • 718 875 0835 • FAX: 718 858 3897

IT'S HOW YOU THROW THE GAME!

BY WES RINKER
FORMER PROFESSIONAL PLAYER
SCOUT AND INSTRUCTOR

THE BASEBALL BOOK FOR EVERYONE

LEARN HOW TO THROW A ROUND-BALL-SQUARE

"Don't Let Winter Go To Waste"

NOW, A BOOK ON THROWING FOR ALL POSITIONS!

As the late Harry Moore, scout for the Montreal Expos explained it . . . "Wes Rinker has the best baseball throwing instruction I've ever seen!"

"There are hundreds of baseball books on the market, but only a select few that are really worth reading. This is one of them. Now one has studied the art of throwing like Wes Rinker. If you read and follow what he says, you will throw better, no matter what level of baseball you may be playing or coaching."

—TIM POVTAK, sportswriter, Orlando Sentinel

Call Now:

1-800-346-1677

or, to save C.O.D. charges, send check or money order for $9.95 plus $1.75 for postage and handling to:

It's How You Throw The Game!
Box 2112 • Sanford, FL 32772

Don't Be A Draftbook Dodger, It Could Cost You 25 Years

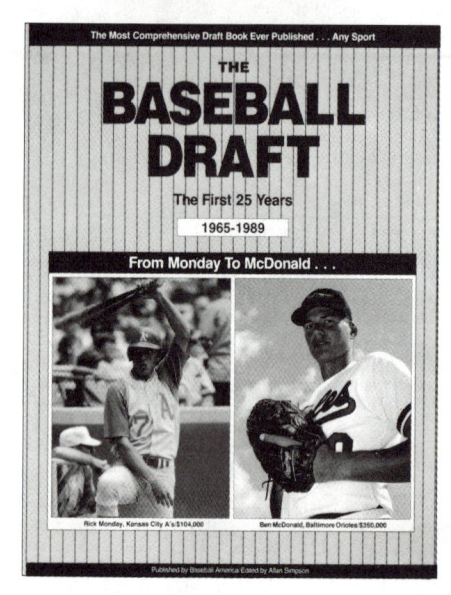

The Most Comprehensive Draft Book Ever Published... Any Sport

THE BASEBALL DRAFT

The First 25 Years
1965-1989

From Monday To McDonald...

Rick Monday, Kansas City A's/$104,000   Ben McDonald, Baltimore Orioles/$350,000

Published by Baseball America Edited by Allan Simpson

Make Baseball America's *THE BASEBALL DRAFT: The First 25 Years* your first-round selection. **It is the most comprehensive draft book ever published... any sport**, for only **$19.95**.

- 312 pages featuring more than 200 stories and 400 photos on the most intriguing names of the draft era
- A complete listing of every player ever drafted, 1965-1989... more than 31,000 names
- Club-by-club, year-by-year selections highlighting which players reached the big leagues
- Draft Trivia: The best and worst drafts, father-son acts, bonus information, the biggest flops, most selections by state
- Players who went straight to the big leagues; players who were overlooked in the draft
- Comprehensive charts on the first-round picks
- Reggie Jackson, Mike Ivie, David Clyde, Steve Chilcott, Kirk Gibson, Jim Abbott — all the fascinating names of the draft era... in one book!

....

Baseball America • Dept. D1 • P.O.Box 2089 • Durham, NC 27702

☐ Please send me ____ copies of **THE BASEBALL DRAFT** @ $19.95 each
☐ My check or money order is enclosed.
☐ Please bill my: ☐ Visa ☐ MC ☐ American Express

Card No._____ Exp. Date_____
Name_____
Address_____
City_____ State_____ Zip_____

For faster service on credit card orders call:
1-800-845-2726 M-F, 9:00-5:00, ET